# Pierre de Thomas
# Scholar, Diplomat, and Crusader

# Pierre de Thomas

## Scholar, Diplomat, and Crusader

### Frederick J. Boehlke, Jr.

Philadelphia
University of Pennsylvania Press

Published in Great Britain, India, and Pakistan
by the Oxford University Press
London, Bombay, and Karachi

Library of Congress Catalogue Card Number: 65–23579

7501
Printed in the United States of America

# Preface

FOR MY FIRST INTRODUCTION TO PIERRE DE THOMAS, I AM indebted to the discussion of his life and work in A. S. Atiya's book *The Crusade in the Later Middle Ages,* published in 1938. A statement in this work (page 129, note 2) that Pierre's life would be a suitable subject for a monograph encouraged me to delve deeper into the subject. An examination of the sources cited by Atiya, especially Mézières' biography in the *Acta Sanctorum,* convinced me that this man's life was not only worthy of study but also of great interest.

I wish to express my thanks to Dr. Kenneth M. Setton of the University of Pennsylvania for his interest, encouragement, and assistance throughout the period of this study. He supervised it as a doctoral dissertation and has given valuable advice in subsequent revisions. He was always ready to give aid and counsel when needed. He was especially helpful in arranging for microfilm copies of the records of the Venetian Collegio to be secured for the Henry Charles Lea Library of the University of Pennsylvania, thus making it possible for me to consult these important records, some pertinent parts of which had not been published. I am also thankful to Dr. Norman P. Zacour, now of Franklin and Marshall College, Lancaster, Pennsylvania, for his many valuable suggestions and other assistance.

My thanks are also due to Rev. Roland Murphy, prior of Whitefriars Hall, the Carmelite house of the Old Observance in Washington, D.C., and to other members of his order for an invitation to use their valuable Carmelitana Collection and for many courtesies which were extended to me while I was working there. Rev. Claver Smith and Rev. Keith Egan, who served as librarians at Whitefriars Hall during the time when I did my major research, were especially helpful.

The person who was most helpful to me in the course of this study was Rev. Dr. Joachim Smet, O. Carm., of the International College of St. Albert in Rome. I met him shortly after he had completed his critical edition of the biography of Pierre de Thomas by Philippe de Mézières. He presented me with a copy of it at a time when it would have been impossible to secure one without considerable delay. This work has proved to be of inestimable value. Not only did it furnish a more accurate edition of the chief source for Pierre's life and thus overcome some difficulties that would have arisen had I been forced to rely on the *Acta Sanctorum* edition, but it also provided a helpful introduction to the archival materials and a valuable bibliographical guide. Although I had already discovered most of the bibliography and eventually would have discovered most of the remainder, Father Smet's book saved me much time and greatly facilitated this study.

Father Smet also gave me encouragement and valuable advice in our conversation and in subsequent correspondence. He also rendered a great service in making the greater part of the papal records concerning Pierre de Thomas available on microfilm, as noted in my bibliography. To do so, he took time out of a busy schedule to draw up a list of letters which he had found and to send them to the Vatican Library so that the microfilm could be prepared. This microfilm is the property of the Carmelite Order and was lent to me for the period of my research. It is now in the Carmelitana Collection at White-friars Hall in Washington, D.C. A positive copy, by permission of the Carmelites, is in the Lea Library at the University of Pennsylvania. Although an effort has been made in the foot-notes to indicate the extent of my debt to Joachim Smet, it has been so great that the effort may not always have succeeded.

I wish to acknowledge the assistance which I received from Mrs. Delphine Richardson of the University of Pennsylvania Library, who cooperated cheerfully in securing needed books by interlibrary loan. Similar services were performed by Miss Carolyn Wray and Mrs. Sarah Bowling Holland, librarians of Judson College, Marion, Alabama. I am especially grateful to the Franciscans of Washington, D.C., for allowing their valu-able copy of the seventeenth-century life of Pierre de Thomas by Luke Wadding to come to Philadelphia and remain for a month, so that I could study it thoroughly.

I wish also to express my appreciation to President John Ingle Riddle (now president-emeritus), of Judson College, Marion, Alabama, and to the late Dean Robert Bowling for their interest in my work and especially for allowing me, for a period of two years, to teach a smaller number of hours than was customary at that school, so that time might be available to me for research and writing.

# Contents

# Abbreviations

For full bibliographical data, see the Bibliography

AASS      *Acta sanctorum bollandiana.*

ACG      Wessels (ed.), *Acta capitulorum generalium.*

AOCD      *Analecta Ordinis Carmelitarum Discalceatorum.*

*Bibl. Carm.*      Villiers, *Bibliotheca carmelitana.*

*Bull. Carm.*      Monsignanus and Ximenez (eds.), *Bullarium carmelitanum.*

LC      Predelli (ed.), *I libri commemoriali della Repubblica di Venezia, regesti.*

LMLU      Lecacheux and Mollat (eds.), *Urbain V. Lettres secrètes et curiales se rapportant à la France.*

MHC      Zimmerman, *Monumenta historica carmelitana.*

| | |
|---|---|
| MHSM | Ljubic, *Monumenta spectantia historiam Slavorum meridionalium.* |
| RISS | Muratori, *Rerum italicarum scriptores.* |
| *Spec. carm.* | Daniel a Virgine Maria, *Speculum carmelitanum.* |
| TCDD | Theiner, *Codex diplomaticus dominii temporalis S. Sedis.* |
| TMUE | Theiner and Miklosich, *Monumenta spectantia ad unionem ecclesiarum.* |
| TVMH | Theiner, *Vetera monumenta historica Hungariam sacram illustrantia.* |
| TVMS | Theiner, *Vetera monumenta Slavorum meridionalium historiam illustrantia.* |

# Pierre de Thomas
# Scholar, Diplomat, and
# Crusader

# 1
# Introduction

PIERRE DE THOMAS IS NOT RECKONED AMONG THE FAMOUS
men of his day, but his work in the papal diplomatic service
in the middle years of the fourteenth century was of great importance and merits serious study. It is impossible to obtain
a complete picture of the church union negotiations in this
period without considering his missions to Serbia and Constantinople. He was a key figure in the papal efforts to defend
Christendom against the rising power of the Ottoman Turks.
As has been more frequently recognized, he was also an outstanding leader in the crusading movement of the later Middle
Ages. The story of his life is colorful and full of variety. Born
into a poor peasant family, he rose in the service of the church
until he was received in honor by kings and emperors and
popes.

There are ample sources for the study of the life of Pierre
de Thomas. The contemporary biography of Philippe de Mézières is an excellent account and has been available to historians

for three centuries in the *Acta Sanctorum*.[1] While this edition
is not based on the best manuscript and contains some significant errors, it is nevertheless of real value. In 1954, an excellent
critical edition was published by Joachim Smet, O. Carm.[2]

Mézières was a friend of Pierre de Thomas in the important
period in which the latter was papal legate in the East or
worked to promote the crusade in Europe. His biography is
written in a flowing and vivid style.[3] Comparison with other
sources reveals that it includes most major incidents of Pierre's
life and is usually accurate. Yet it must be used with caution.
Not only is Mézières vague or inaccurate in discussing some
events of Pierre's earlier life with which he was not completely
familiar, but even in relating events of which he was an eyewitness he sometimes shows surprising lapses of memory. Furthermore, it should be noted that Mézières biography is a eulogy
written to extol the virtues of Pierre de Thomas, probably with
a view to his canonization. Therefore it frequently exaggerates
the importance of Pierre's work and the contrast between his
motives and those of persons who from time to time opposed
him.

The necessary corrective to Mézières' account is supplied by

---

[1] Philippe de Mézières, *Vita Sancti Petri Thomasii*, in *Acta Sanctorum bollandiana*, new edition, ed. Jean Carnadet, vol. III (Paris,
Rome, 1863). This was originally published in 1643 under the edi-
torship of Gottfried Henschen, S.J. He published a separate edition of
the same basic text at Antwerp in 1659. This separate edition is quite
rare and is not commonly cited.

[2] Philippe de Mézières, *The Life of Saint Peter Thomas*, ed. Joachim
Smet, O. Carm. (Textus et studia historica carmelitana, vol. II; Rome,
1954).

[3] Neculai Jorga, *Philippe de Mézières, 1327–1405, et la croisade au
XIVe siècle* (Bibliothèque de l'École des Hautes Études, vol. 110; Paris,
1896), p. 345, says about Mézières' biography, "c'est un très beau livre
de propagande pour la croisade que Pierre Thomas représenta pendant
de longues années, en Occident, . . ." He considers the account in it
of the crusade against Alexandria as one of the most beautiful bits of
Latin literature of the period.

the references to the work of Pierre de Thomas in documentary sources, especially those in the archives of the Vatican and the Venetian Republic. They make it possible to obtain accurate information about his diplomatic activities. Some of these documents have long been available to historians through the appendix to Luke Wadding's life of Pierre de Thomas[4] and in the *Annales ecclesiastici* of Raynaldus.[5] Virtually all the important ones appeared in the various source collections published in the nineteenth and twentieth centuries, although no large proportion of them can be found in one place.[6] More recently Joachim Smet, O. Carm., has made a fresh study of these materials, and many of his findings are mentioned in the footnotes and appendices in his edition of Mézières' biography. Father Smet has kindly made the pertinent materials from the Vatican archives available to me in a microfilm which he arranged to have prepared there. This has been an invaluable aid in tracing the life of Pierre de Thomas.

Although Pierre played a significant role in his own day and the sources for studying his life have long been available, his career as a whole has not been discussed extensively by critical historians. To be sure, as will become apparent in the course of this study, virtually every one of his missions hàs been treated to some degree by critical scholars, and their writings have contributed significantly to our understanding of these events.

No full-length biography of Pierre de Thomas has been written hitherto from the scholarly viewpoint. The better ones have been based almost exclusively on Mézières, while the less

[4] Luke Wadding, O. F. M., *Vita et res gestae B. Petri Thomae Aquitani, ex ordine B. Mariae Virginis a Monte Carmelo, patriarchae Constantinopolitani et sedis apostolicae legati* (Lyons, 1637).

[5] Odoricus Raynalus, *Annales ecclesiastici ab anno quo desinit Caesarius Cardinalis Baronius MCXCVIII usque ad annum MDXXXIV continuati* (Cologne, 1690–94. 9 vols., numbered XIII–XXI.

[6] See Bibliography. These collections of documents are too numerous to list at this point.

reliable ones are little more than historical romances. Even a second contemporary biography by Juan Carmesson, Franciscan provincial of the Holy Land, seems to be based largely on Mézières, for it contains only one episode not found in Mézières.[7] Three centuries later, the noted Franciscan historian Luke Wadding wrote a life of Pierre de Thomas in classical Latin,[8] but it also adds little to Mézières, although it includes some material from the documents which Wadding had discovered in the papal archives. In the late nineteenth century, a French clergyman, A. Parraud,[9] wrote a biography of Pierre, which also follows the Mézières tradition and makes little use either of other sources or of modern critical methods. A slightly later life in English by a Discalced Carmelite friar, Peter Thomas Burke, is a mere paraphrase of Parraud's work.[10] Recently a biography of Pierre de Thomas in a popular style was written by Daphne Pochin-Mould.[11] It is based on Smet's edition of Mézières' life. Therefore, while it also follows Mézières quite closely, it profits from Smet's own careful study and includes some facts from the archival materials which have not hitherto appeared in a biography of Pierre de Thomas. It is a great improvement over all earlier works on the subject but still has not provided a scholarly biography.

An exception to the general neglect of Pierre de Thomas

---

[7] Juan Carmesson, *Vita sancti Petri Thomae, patriarchae Constantinopolitani, legati apostolici,* in Daniel a Virgine Maria, *Speculum carmelitanum,* II (Antwerp, 1680), 171–95, also published separately (Antwerp, 1666). The episode not found in Mézières is in *Spec. carm.,* II, 180.

[8] See note 4 above.

[9] A. Parraud, *Vie de Saint Pierre Thomas de l'ordre des Carmes, fervent serviteur de Marie, patriarche titulaire de Constantinople, légat de la croisade de 1365* (Avignon, 1895).

[10] Peter Thomas Burke, O. C. D., *A Medieval Hero of Carmel* (Dublin, 1901).

[11] Daphne Pochin-Mould, *The Life of Saint Peter Thomas* (New York, 1961). This book is published by the Scapular Press.

by critical historians is in the work of Neculai Jorga, who published a definitive biography of Philippe de Mézières in 1896.[12] In some detail, he discussed the part of the life of Pierre de Thomas in which he was working with Mézières. Jorga was a careful scholar, who made extensive use of the archives as well as of Mézières. He was the first to make significant additions to the material about Pierre which is found in Mézières' biography.[13]

A. S. Atiya in *The Crusade in the Later Middle Ages* (London, 1938) noted that the life of Pierre de Thomas would be a suitable subject for a monograph.[14] His judgment has been fully sustained in the present study. Pierre has emerged as a man of greater versatility and wider achievements than has previously been recognized. As Jorga and Atiya have emphasized, he was a great promoter of the crusade. In working for that cause, he reached the pinnacle of his career. Yet he had done significant work in other areas before concentrating on the crusade. Most notably, he was a truly great diplomat, whose services were valued not only by the papacy but also by such able secular rulers as King Louis the Great of Hungary and the leaders of Venice.

[12] See note 3 above.

[13] This is Smet's conclusion in his edition of Mézières, *Life,* pp. 32, 48.

[14] On p. 129, n. 2. In this work, Pierre's career is discussed on pp. 128–36.

# 2

# Boyhood and Youth

PIERRE DE THOMAS WAS BORN ABOUT 1305 IN A HUMBLE
peasant cottage in the county of Périgord, a part of the duchy
of Aquitaine in southwestern France.[1] When he was born, his
native village was in the diocese of Périgueux, but in 1316 it
was included in the newly organized diocese of Sarlat, in which
it remained until the French Revolution.[2] This much is certain

[1] The approximate date of Pierre de Thomas' birth can be deter-
mined from the information given in Mézières, *Life,* ed. Smet, pp. 54–
57; AASS, Jan. 29, III, 611–12 (secs. 1–7). According to Mézières,
about twenty years elapsed between the time of Pierre's first stay in
Agen and his election as procurator general of the Carmelite Order.
This election took place in 1345, as recorded in Gabriel Wessels,
O. Carm., ed., *Acta capitulorum generalium Ordinis Fratrum B. V.
Mariae de Monte Carmelo,* I (Rome, 1912), 39 (hereafter abbreviated
ACG). Thus his first stay at Agen may be dated about 1325. Since
Mézières states that he was about twenty years old at that time, Pierre's
approximate birth date may be established as 1305. This date is cited
as early as 1680 in *Spec. carm.,* II, 173, note (a), and it has been com-
monly used since then.

[2] Mézières, *Life,* ed. Smet, p. 53; AASS, Jan. 29, III, 611 (sec. 1),
states that Pierre was born in the diocese of Sarlat. However, the
diocese of Sarlat was not created until 1316, when it was divided from
the diocese of Périgueux, as noted in Jean Joseph Escande, *Histoire du
Périgord,* I (Cahors, 1934), 131–32.

20

from the information given by Pierre's friend and biographer, Philippe de Mézières, but there is some uncertainty about the precise location of his birthplace. Mézières says that Pierre was born in Salimaso de Thomas,[3] but no trace of this precise name has been found elsewhere in medieval or modern sources.[4] Tradition favors the village of Lebreil in the parish of Salles-de-Belvès, and local veneration of Pierre de Thomas has centered around that locality. This tradition dates at least from the middle of the seventeenth century. In 1662 Armand Gerard, canon of Sarlat, visited the parish of Salles, where he found an altar dedicated to Pierre de Thomas in the parish church of St. Sacerdos and a chapel in the village of Lebreil which was believed by the local people to be Pierre's birthplace.[5] In the nineteenth century A. Parraud, who published a biography of Pierre de Thomas in 1895, visited this locality and found that

[3] Mézières, *loc. cit.;* the form Salimaso is from Smet's edition. The Bollandists knew only the form Salimosa, which appears to be incorrect.

[4] The other principal biographers of Pierre de Thomas do not give any significant help on this problem. The contemporary Juan Carmesson gives the form Salisinaso, or possibly Salismaso, as noted in the critical apparatus in Smet's edition of Mézières, *Life,* p. 53, where the Carmesson manuscripts are designated as y and z. Wadding, *Vita,* p. 1, also in *Spec. carm.,* II, 199, gives Pierre's birthplace as "vicus Salinarum," a designation which is no clearer than the others.

[5] Armand Gerard, in a letter to Gottfried Henschen, S.J., dated April 29, 1662 (Brussels, Koninklijke Bibliotheek, Ms. 8495, fol. 132v), tells of a visit made to Salles and Lebreil the preceding month. He notes that the chapel in Lebreil did not look as though it had been built originally for a chapel. Thus he insinuates that this was Pierre's actual birthplace, as local legend maintained. He also wrote that he had found traces of people in the village by the name of Thomas. Since this name is common, this fact proves nothing. According to other letters written by Gerard to the Bollandists, Brussels, Kon. Bib., Ms. 20614, fols. 187r-189v, cited by Smet in his edition of Mézières, *Life,* p. 53, n. 1, the canon of Sarlat learned from the curé of Salles that "a certain ecclesiastic," while searching the parish archives for a legacy, had come across a document from which it appeared that Pierre de Thomas had left a legacy to Salles as his native parish. The curé could not recall where the document was located, and the ecclesiastic who had found it was no longer in the vicinity.

the tradition was still strong.[6] Most writers who have touched upon Pierre's life have accepted Salles-de-Belvès as his birthplace.[7]

[6] Parraud, *Vie,* p. 1, n. 1; p. 2, n. 2; p. 3, n. 2; pp. 348–51. Parraud derives the name Salinoza, Salimosa, or Salina from the Latin phrase "salit Noza," referring to a stream, la Noze, which bounds the parish of Salles. Since it now appears that the correct reading of this name is not Salimosa but Salimaso, Parraud's derivation loses much of its force. (See note 3 above.) Parraud declares that the present church of Salles, a small romanesque structure of the tenth or eleventh century, is the one in which Pierre was baptized. From the Abbé Brugeaud, curé of Salles, he learned that there is a local tradition that the lords of the property cultivated by Pierre's father were the ancestors of the modern family Laporte, long resident in that country. A lady of this family, who had been born in the village of Lebreil in 1792, had talked to Brugeaud about the chapel there, said to be Pierre's birthplace, and had declared that this chapel had been in her family's possession from time immemorial. Since under the *ancien régime* rural properties, especially seignorial lands, rarely changed hands, this testimony was presumed to reach back at least to the sixteenth century. The Abbé Brugeaud, who had examined many of the local documents of Salles, told Parraud that he had never found anything to contradict this claim. The little chapel at Lebreil was destroyed in the French Revolution, but efforts were under way in 1895 to restore it. At that time the parish church of Salles still cherished the simple baptismal font where, according to tradition, the local saint was baptized, and in 1891 a stained glass window representing Pierre de Thomas as patriarch of Constantinople was placed in that church.

[7] There is some dissent from this opinion. Louis de Mas Latrie, *Histoire de l'île de Chypre sous le régne des princes de la maison de Lusignan,* II (Paris, 1852), 281, n. 2, says that Pierre's birthplace is Salignac de Thomas in the *arrondissement* of Sarlat. He apparently has no reason for adding "de Thomas" to the name Salignac other than his identifying it with the Salimaso de Thomas of Mézières. Mas Latrie's viewpoint has been accepted by Jean Baptiste Magnan, *Histoire du B. Urbain V et de son siècle d'après les manuscrits du Vatican* (second edition, Paris, 1863), p. 225, and more recently by Atiya, *Later Crusade,* p. 130. J. D. Gourges, *Dictionnaire topographique du département de la Dordogne, comprenant les noms de lieu anciens et modernes* (Paris, 1873), p. 307, gives a number of medieval forms of Salignac. None of them resembles Salimaso, Salimosa, or Salisinaso, and "de Thomas" is in no case appended. It should also be noted that, when Pierre first left home to seek an education, he went to Monpazier, according to Mézières, *Life,* ed. Smet, p. 54; AASS, Jan. 29, III, 611 (sec. 2). Monpazier is only five and one-half miles from Salles, whereas

Pierre de Thomas' name, like his birthplace, has given rise to much discussion. Scholars disagree both about its form and its meaning. From the writings of four contemporaries, Philippe de Mézières, Juan Carmesson, Jean Trissa, and Johann of Hildesheim, and from the archives of the Carmelites and the papacy, it is clear that the correct Latin form of the name is *Petrus Thomae* (usually spelled *Thome* in the fourteenth century).[8] This name is rendered into French either as Pierre

---

it is much farther from Salignac. It is probable that a country boy seeking an education would have gone to a town near home. If his home was Salles, Monpazier was relatively near it, but to reach Monpazier from Salignac Pierre would have had to travel through Sarlat, the episcopal seat, and several other towns where he could have received his education. A more fantastic theory about Pierre's birthplace was advanced by A. Plieux in an article, "Les Deux derniers abbés de Condom," *Revue de Gascogne,* XXII (1881), 32–35, in which he stated that Pierre was born in Condom. He derived his evidence for this theory from statements made in the Carmelite breviary and in the dedicatory preface addressed to the king of France in Elisée de Saint-Bernard's translation of the works of Saint Theresa into French, published in Paris in 1630. Neither of these sources is historically reliable. Plieux's article is analyzed and refuted in Pierre Feret, *La faculté de théologie de Paris et ses docteurs les plus célèbres—moyen âge,* III (Paris, 1896), 530, n. 4. The theory that Pierre was born in Condom was already old in the seventeenth century. Wadding, *Vita,* pp. 67–68, mentioned it in 1637 but recognized it as an error.

[8] Mézières, *Life,* ed. Smet, pp. 51, 53–54, 57; AASS, Jan. 29, III, 611–12 (secs. 1, 2, 6), also *ibid.,* ed. Smet, pp. 162, 169 (these parts not in AASS); Carmesson, *Vita* in *Spec. carm.,* II, 172; ACG, I, 39; Jean Trissa, *De magistris parisiensibus* in Benedict Zimmerman, *Monumenta historica carmelitana* (Lerins, 1907), p. 390, also in Heinrich Denifle, O. P., "Quellen zur Gelehrtengeschichte des Carmelitenordens im 13 und 14 Jahrhundert," *Archiv für Litteratur und Kirchengeschichte,* V (1889), 376, and in Bartholomaeus Maria Xiberta, O. Carm., *De scriptoribus scholasticis saeculi XIV ex ordine Carmelitarum* (Bibliothèque de la revue d'histoire ecclésiastique, fasc. 6; Louvain, 1931), p. 35; Johann of Hildesheim, *Defensorium Ordinis Fratrum gloriossissimae Dei Genetricis Mariae de Monte Carmelo per modum dialogi,* in *Spec. carm.,* I (Antwerp, 1680), 149. References to the full name in papal bulls may be found in Wadding, *Vita,* pp. 81–83; *Bullarium carmelitanum,* I, ed. Eliseo Monsignano, O. Carm. (Rome, 1715), 80–81; III, ed. Joseph Albert Ximenes, O. Carm. (Rome, 1768), 76–77, 81; Karl H. Schäfer, ed., *Die Ausgaben der apostolis-*

Thomas or Pierre de Thomas and often into English as Peter Thomas.[9] While the name Peter Thomas or Pierre Thomas is now taken as a double given name, especially in the religious names taken by members of the Carmelite Order, it is obvious that Thomas was a surname and not a part of his given name. In his biography, Philippe de Mézières normally calls his friend simply Petrus, reserving the fuller Petrus Thomae only for more formal references. The papal documents issued after he became a bishop, and thus, according to custom, using only the baptismal name, refer to him simply as Petrus, followed by his current title, while those issued before his elevation to the

---

chen *Kammer unter Benedikt XII, Klemens VI und Innocenz VI* (1335–1362) (Paderborn, 1914), p. 525. On the basis of a register of the church of Sarlat, allegedly cited by Daniel a Virgine Maria, Neculai Jorga in his *Philippe de Mézières*, p. 131, n. 3, asserts that the correct form of Pierre's surname in Latin is Thomas or Thomasius. I have found but one contemporary bit of evidence for Thomasius. This is in the letter of Cardinal Pierre de Monteruc, papal vice-chancellor, to Archbishop Raymond of Nicosia, May 21, 1368, in Mézières, *Life,* ed. Smet, p. 188. The only contemporary evidence for Thomas is in certain variant readings in one of the manuscripts of Mézières' biography. However, it should be noted that Joachim Smet has not accepted this reading in his edition of the biography, even though it is found in manuscript D, which he usually prefers. (See the critical apparatus in that edition, pp. 53, 54, 57.) As Smet notes, *ibid.,* p. 53, n. 2, Mézières' spelling is inconsistent, and no strong argument can be based upon it.

[9] In this study the form Pierre de Thomas is being used as the standard one, following Atiya, *Later Crusade,* pp. 129 ff., as against Jorga, *Mézières,* pp. 131 ff., where Pierre Thomas is used. In the fourteenth century names were somewhat flexible. As a member of a lower class of society in his youth, Pierre's name was probably spoken without the preposition "de," which was a mark of social standing, but in the more important part of his life, when he ranked as a doctor of theology and a dignitary of the church, the form "Pierre de Thomas" was most likely used. In the contemporary Greek of Leontios Makhairas, *Recital concerning the Sweet Land of Cyprus, entitled "Chronicle,"* ed. and tr., R. M. Dawkins, 2 vols. (Oxford, 1932), I, 90, 92, where the name is transliterated from the French (with a Greek case ending in one instance) both the forms Pierre de Thomas (Πιέρην τε Τουμας) and Pierre Thomas (Πιερ Τουμας) appear.

episcopate address him as Petrus Thomae.[10] The origin of his surname Thomas is not certain. In giving Pierre's birthplace as Salimaso de Thomas, Philippe de Mézières seems to imply that his surname came from his birthplace, and some modern scholars have taken this viewpoint.[11] On the other hand, Luke Wadding seems to believe that the name Thomae came from the given name of Pierre's father.[12] This is probably the correct view, since Thomas is a very common name. If Pierre de Thomas' surname were taken from his birthplace, one would expect it to be derived from Salimaso rather than from Thomas, since Salimaso was the primary element in its name, and, if used at all, the phrase "de Thomas" was added merely to distinguish the parish from others of similar name. It is probable that this particular Salles or Salimaso was popularly called "de Thomas" only after Pierre's fame had added distinction to his birthplace. The appellation Salimaso de Thomas must have been ephemeral, for no other trace of it has been found in the area of Salles-de-Belvès or elsewhere. It should be noted that the name Petrus Thomae was not an uncommon one, and other men of this name are mentioned in documents of the fourteenth century.[13]

[10] For references to the earlier, longer form of the name in papal documents see note 8 above. The form Petrus alone, followed by Pierre's current ecclesiastical title, may be found in Wadding, *Vita,* pp. 83 ff.; *Spec. carm.,* II 213; *Bull. carm.,* I, 81 ff.; Schäfer, *op. cit.,* pp. 556, 607; and in other places too numerous to mention.

[11] Atiya, *Later Crusade,* p. 129, n. 1; Smet in his edition of Mézières, *Life,* p. 53, n. 2.

[12] Wadding, *Vita,* p. 66.

[13] The most famous man of the fourteenth century who had the same Latin name as our Petrus Thomae was the Catalan Franciscan theologian, Pere Tomas, who was born about 1280 and died about 1350. See Am. Teetaert, "Pierre Thomas," in *Dictionnaire de théologie catholique,* eds., A. Vacant, E. Mangenot, et E. Amann, XII, part 2 (Paris, 1935), 2046–48, and Marti de Barcelona, O. F. M. Cap., "Fra Pere Tomas," in *Estudis franciscans,* XXXIX (1927), 90–103. He is probably the Petrus Thomae who is referred to as an official in the papal court at Avignon in records for the years 1330 ff. in Karl H.

Pierre de Thomas' father was a simple peasant farmer. He was, according to Philippe de Mézières, "a cultivator of lands not his own and a tender of animals, the poorest in his class." [14] He may have been a domestic serf, attached to the personal service of a lord and having no right in the land,[15] but serfdom was relatively rare in southern France in the fourteenth century, and it is therefore more probable that he was one of a numerous class of landless peasants who were not serfs but had to obtain land by leasing it for a term of years. The most common form of lease was that in which the cultivator paid a certain portion of the crop, and sometimes of the natural increase of the livestock, to the owner of the land. The proportion was not always the same, but it was commonly one-half, and the lessee was thus called a *métayer*. The leases usually ran for three years or for a multiple of three years, and at the close of this term the landlord would try to exact a higher rent if conditions seemed to warrant it. It was probably under a system such as this that Pierre's father obtained the

Schäfer, ed., *Die Ausgaben der apostolischen Kammer unter Johann XXII nebst den Jahresbilanzen von 1316–35* (Paderborn, 1911), pp. 595–99 *passim*. He is probably the one referred to in the records of 1317, *ibid.*, pp. 336–42, and of 1335 in Karl H. Schäfer, ed., *Die Ausgaben der apostolischen Kammer unter Benedict XII, Klemens VI und Innocenz VI (1335–62)* (Paderborn, 1914), p. 24. This Catalan Petrus Thomae has often been confused with Pierre de Thomas from Périgord. A third Petrus Thomae is recorded as having been transferred from the rectorate of the parish church of St. Gervase in Paris to the position of prebendary, canon, and archdeacon in the church of Fréjus in a three-way exchange of benefices approved by the Pope on July 29, 1365, in Alphonse Fierens, *Lettres d'Urbain V (1362–70)*, I (Analecta Vaticano-Belgica, vol. IX; Rome, Brussels, Paris, 1928), 712, 895; and Alphonse Fierens, *Suppliques d'Urbain V (1362–70)* (Analecta Vaticano-Belgica, vol. VII; Rome, Brussels, Paris, 1914), p. 572. In Fierens, *Suppliques d'Urbain V*, p. 523, there is a record of a cleric of Clermont named *Petrus de Thomas de Carluso* (under date of July 23, 1364).

[14] Mézières, *Life*, ed. Smet, p. 53; AASS, Jan. 29, III, 611 (sec. 2): "Pater suus massarius et terrarum non suarum cultor, animalium nutritor in gradu suo pauperrimus,..."

[15] Jorga, *Mézières*, p. 132, calls him a serf.

land on which he raised his crops and pastured his animals and was thus able to eke out a meagre subsistence for himself and his family.[16]

We know little of Pierre's childhood. He lived in a pleasant, fertile country with an excellent climate, neither uncomfortably hot nor uncomfortably cold, and he must have enjoyed many a happy day in the open countryside. Pierre had a brother and a sister. His brother died in early childhood, but his sister remained at home after Pierre had gone away to school.[17] It is reasonable to assume that from his earliest youth Pierre learned reverence for God and for the Virgin Mary through his home training and the ministrations of his parish priest. Since we have no record that Pierre de Thomas ever had a dynamic conversion experience, it is probable that he was a pious child, whose spiritual development was gradual and orderly.[18] One dark cloud blighted his childhood and left bitter memories. This was the extreme poverty of his family, and the uncertainties which it brought.[19]

When Pierre de Thomas was little more than a boy, he de-

[16] François Louis Ganshof, "Medieval Agarian Society in Its Prime—France, the Low Countries, and Germany," *Cambridge Economic History,* eds. J. H. Chapman and Eileen Power, vol. I (Cambridge, 1941), pp. 305–10; Henri See, *Les Classes rurales et le régime domanial en France au moyen âge* (Paris, 1901), pp. 204–06.

[17] Mézières, *Life,* ed. Smet, pp. 53–54; AASS, Jan. 29, III, 611. In a will drawn up at Venice, dated January 20, 1369, published by Neculai Jorga, "Le Testament de Philippe de Mézières," *Bulletin de l'Institut pour l'étude de l'Europe sud-orientale,* VIII (1921), 128, Philippe de Mézières mentioned a nephew of Pierre de Thomas, Raymond Robert, archdeacon of Nicosia in Cyprus, and gave him leave to retain whatever personal effects of Mézières he had in his possession. Raymond Robert was apparently Pierre's sister's son.

[18] Carmesson, *Vita,* in *Spec. carm.,* II, 172, says that Pierre's father taught him from infancy to fear God and abstain from all sin. Mézières says little about Pierre's childhood, probably because Pierre talked little about it.

[19] This is the dominant note in the few lines written about Pierre's childhood in Mézières, *Life,* ed. Smet, p. 54; AASS, Jan. 29, III, 611 (sec. 2). Carmesson, *loc. cit.,* and Parraud, *Vie,* pp. 5–6, paint too idyllic a picture of the childhood of Pierre de Thomas.

cided to leave home to pursue an academic career. This was the only way in which a boy of his class could hope to rise above his family's wretched and hopeless condition.[20] He went to the little city of Monpazier, probably because it was closest to his home. There he obtained his living and the money for his education by begging from door to door or on the streets of the town.[21] This life was by no means an easy one. In fact, it may at first have been even harder than his life at home. The mortality rate among such students was high. Some of the poor scholars were cared for by the mendicant orders. In their houses, they frequently provided simple lodgings and food for a certain number of students. Pierre de Thomas probably availed himself of their assistance as often as he could.[22]

At Monpazier, Pierre first had to learn to read and write. In his day, these skills required a knowledge of the Latin language and of the complicated system of abbreviations then in use. In a short time, he had progressed so well in his studies that he was able to become a teacher of less advanced students. After securing his elementary education in Monpazier, he went to the city of Agen, where he studied grammar and logic for several years. There he also became a teacher, first of grammar and then of logic. He stayed at Agen until he was about twenty years old. In both cities he was supported wholly by alms and

[20] There is no record that Pierre ever returned home for a visit after he left to go to school, although he may have done so. Parraud, *Vie,* pp. 7–8, cites a local legend of Salles-de-Belvès that Pierre once returned home in his later life when he was Latin patriarch of Constantinople and was with his mother at her deathbed. It is reported that she could not recognize her son in the great dignitary of the church except by the peculiar shape of his left foot, which resembled a goose's foot in a vague way.

[21] Mézières, *Life,* ed. Smet, p. 54: AASS, Jan. 29, III, 611 (sec. 2). Monpazier was then a relatively new town, founded in 1270.

[22] Benedict Zimmerman, O. C. D., "Les Carmes aux universités du moyen âge," *Études carmelitaines,* XVII, part 1 (1932), 84–85.

by his teaching and never received as much as twenty florins from home.[23]

While teaching in Agen, Pierre became acquainted with the prior of the Carmelite convent at Lectoure,[24] who was impressed by his teaching ability and invited him to join the staff at his house. There Pierre spent a year teaching grammar and logic in a school for boys. At this time the Carmelites, like other mendicant orders, frequently maintained schools not only for aspirants for membership and for promotions in the order but also for other qualified students. These ranged from elementary schools to schools of theology, the queen of medieval sciences. In the Carmelite house at Lectoure, Pierre was teaching the same subjects which he had been teaching as a secular teacher at Agen.[25]

At Lectoure, Pierre de Thomas first came into close acquaintance with the life of the religious order in which he was to spend most of his life, but he entered the Carmelite Order not at Lectoure but at Bergerac.[26] After he had spent a year at Lectoure, the prior of the Carmelite house at Bergerac saw

[23] Mézières, Life, ed. Smet, p. 54; AASS, Jan. 29, III, 611 (sec. 2); Carmesson, Vita, in Spec. carm., II, 172; Wadding, Vita, pp. 2–3, also in Spec. carm., II, 199; Parraud, Vie, pp. 7–9. Mézières, who knew Pierre de Thomas best, does not state the length of his stay at Monpazier. Carmesson states that it was three years.

[24] According to Ambrosius a St. Theresa, O. C. D., "Monasticon carmelitanum, seu lexicon geographicum omnium fundationem universi Ordinis Carmelitarum ab initio eiusdem Ordinis usque ad nostra tempora," Analecta Ordinis Carmelitarum Discalceatorum, XXII (1950), 587–88, the Carmelite convent at Lectoure was founded in 1296 outside the walls of the city. The convent was destroyed in the French Revolution, but its church still exists as the parish church du Saint-Esprit.

[25] Mézières, Life, ed. Smet, p. 54; AASS, Jan. 29, III, 611 (sec. 3); Heinrich H. Koch, Die Karmelitenklöster der niederdeutschen Provinz 13. bis 16. Jahrhundert (Freiburg im Breisgau, 1889), pp. 17–19.

[26] Ambrosius, "Monasticon carmelitanum," AOCD, XXII (1950), 132, says that the founding date of the convent of Bergerac is unknown. It was in existence as early as 1325.

him and admired his keen intellect and holy life. He brought him to Bergerac, where he began his novitiate in preparation for membership in the order.[27]

According to the information given by Mézières, Pierre de Thomas was twenty-one years old when he entered his novitiate.[28] The Carmelites were always glad to welcome a bright young man like him into their order, and he had much to gain by joining it, since he would thus be assured of receiving his daily bread and support for further education.

Before the Carmelite Order would accept him as a novice, Pierre de Thomas had to answer many questions to determine his eligibility for entrance into the order. A prospective novice was first asked whether he was of free status and legitimate birth, then whether he was married, burdened with debts, or a member of any other order, whether he had lost any member or the use of any of his senses, and whether he had any deformity in his body or suffered from any disease. Finally the Carmelite authorities inquired whether he had been expelled

[27] Mézières' testimony on the question of where Pierre entered the Carmelite Order is inconsistent. In the *Life of Saint Peter Thomas,* ed. Smet, pp. 54–55; AASS, Jan. 29, III, 611 (sec. 3) he says that it was the prior of Condom who invited Pierre to join the order at his house. On the other hand, in his account of the efforts of Pierre I of Cyprus to secure the canonization of Pierre de Thomas (published in Smet's edition of Mézières, *Life,* p. 187) and in his testament of 1369 (Jorga, "Le Testament," p. 129) Mézières stated that Bergerac was Pierre's native convent. This fact is confirmed in the work of a contemporary Carmelite Jean Trissa, *De magistris parisiensibus,* published in MHC, p. 390, and elsewhere as noted in n. 8, above. Trissa was well informed on Carmelite affairs. It must therefore be accepted that in this instance Mézières, *Life,* is incorrect. This is not the only place where it is known to be incorrect and therefore indeed it may be incorrect in some places which cannot be verified from other sources and therefore must be used in the absence of other evidence.

[28] Mézières, *Life,* ed. Smet, p. 54; AASS, Jan. 29, III, 611 (secs. 2, 3). He was in Agen until he was twenty years old and afterward was at Lectoure for one year before going to the convent where he joined the Carmelite Order.

from the Carmelite Order at some other place or from a laxer order. If he was not free of the impediments suggested in these questions, he could not be admitted into the order, and if it was subsequently discovered that he had been admitted with some hidden defect, he was at once expelled. Novices could be received only by the prior general or a provincial prior or by persons designated by one of them.[29]

In the constitutions of the Carmelite Order approved at the Chapter General of 1324, perhaps a few years before Pierre's entrance into the order, a ceremony is prescribed for the reception of novices. When a novice was to be received into the order, he was first shaved and provided with shoes such as were worn by the brethren. Then, wearing the tunic of the order with some secular garment over it, he was led into the chapter, where all the members of the convent were gathered. Usually a group of novices were received together.

When they came into the chapter, the prospective novices prostrated themselves in the midst of the friars. The presiding officer, usually the prior, then asked them, "What are you seeking?" They answered, "The mercy of God and of the order." Then they rose to their feet in the presence of the chapter, and the presiding officer explained to them the severity of the Carmelite Order and its poverty, and especially the three principal requirements of religious orders that, after the reception of the habit, for all time they were required to live in obedience and chastity and without personal property. He asked them their intention in view of these requirements. If they answered that they were willing to observe all these things and to renounce the world, the president then said, "May God who has made a beginning in you, himself perfect you among us." The brethren of the chapter answered, "Amen." Then the presiding officer took from each of the novices the secular

[29] MHC, pp. 5, 42–43.

garment that concealed the tunic of the order, saying over
each of them the words, "May God take from you the old
man with his deeds." The brethren again answered, "Amen."
The secular clothes were kept by the prior of the convent until
the day when the novice was finally received into the full membership of the order.

After the secular clothing had been removed from the novices, if the more lengthy and solemn form of the service was
used, the prior or other presiding officer said a number of
prayers over them, asking God to bless them and give them
the strength to persevere in the good work which they had
begun. Following these prayers he invested them with the
full habit of the order, making the sign of the cross over each
one and saying, "May the Lord endue you with the new man
who according to God is created in justice and true holiness,
in the name of the Father and of the Son and of the Holy
Spirit, Amen." Then the prior sprinkled each of them with
holy water and again prayed as follows: "Attend, O Lord, to
our supplications and deign to bless this, thy servant, upon
whom we place the habit of holy religion, that by thy favor he
may merit both to remain devout in thy church and to receive
eternal life, through Jesus Christ, our Lord, Amen."

Thus received and invested the novices were led in a solemn
procession to the choir of the church, where they prostrated
themselves before the altar while the other brothers stood in
their places. Then the prior began the solemn hymn, "Veni
Creator." After a number of ritual observances and prayers the
novices were raised to their feet and were again sprinkled with
holy water. Each of them kissed the altar reverently, then the
prior, and finally the brothers, after which they took their
stations in the last place in the choir.[30]

From the time when he was received as a novice in the

30 MHC, pp. 42-49.

Carmelite Order until the end of his life, the habit of the order was Pierre de Thomas' only form of clothing, except when in later life he was called upon to wear the vestments of his ecclesiastical offices. The first part of the habit to be put on was the tunic, a dark-colored woolen robe, which reached to the ankles. Over it was placed the scapular of the same color. A scapular is a long, narrow woolen garment which covers the shoulders equally in the front and back. According to the constitutions of 1324, the Carmelite scapular was to reach to the shin bone. In modern times the scapular and tunic of the Carmelites are brown in color. Over the tunic and scapular the cloak and hood of white wool were and are worn by members of the order. To the Carmelites the scapular is the essential element of the habit, but the white cloak and hood made a greater impression upon the people. Hence the Carmelites were known in England as the White Friars.[31]

The probation period, through which Pierre de Thomas had to pass in the convent of Bergerac, lasted one full calendar year, computed by fixed dates and not by movable feasts. During this time, Pierre and the other novices were under the tutelage of one of the brothers, who was responsible for teaching them the ways of the order and for correcting them for any breach of its rules. No one except this novice-master was permitted to reprimand them. The chief responsibility of a novice

---

[31] MHC, pp. 41–42; ACG, I, 8–12; Discalced Carmelites of Boston and Santa Clara, *Carmel, Its History, Spirit, and Saints* (New York, 1927), pp. 218–19; Benedict Zimmerman, "Carmelite Order" in *The Catholic Encyclopedia,* eds. Charles G. Herbermann *et al.,* III (New York, 1908), 356. Zimmerman's article in *The Catholic Encyclopedia* is the best account on general Carmelite history which I have discovered in any language. It is based upon an intimate knowledge of the constitutions, which Zimmerman had just edited in the *Monumenta historica carmelitana,* published at Lerins, 1907. My description of the Carmelite habit is based not only upon these readings but also upon observation of the modern Carmelite habit at Whitefriars Hall in Washington, D.C.

was to acquire a knowledge of the divine office, and no one was permitted to occupy him with any other task. Novices were not permitted to mingle freely with the rest of the community nor with the boys of the convent school. The purpose of the novitiate was not only to teach a prospective member the lore of the order, but also to give the members of the order an opportunity to learn about his morals and his fitness for the life of a friar.

Before his profession, or final admittance, into the Carmelite Order, Pierre de Thomas was required to request it three times of the members of the convent individually and collectively. A week or two before his profession, an inquiry was made among the brethren by the local prior or someone designated by him, to evaluate Pierre's worthiness for membership in the order. If they had found him unworthy, he would have been ejected immediately, without further ceremony. The minimum age for profession was fourteen, and no one could be admitted to this step without having served a full year's novitiate.[32]

The ceremony of profession is given in some detail in the constitutions of 1324.[33] Apparently, it was performed for each individual separately, in contrast to the ceremony of receiving novices. Whenever possible, the prior general of the Carmelite Order presided. At the time of Pierre's profession, presumably in 1327, this was Jean d'Alerio.[34] If he could not be present at a profession, as must have frequently been the case, the prior general designated someone else to act in his stead.

[32] MHC, pp. 49–50; Zimmerman, "Carmelite Order," *Catholic Encyclopedia*, III, 358; Parraud, *Vie*, pp. 12–14.

[33] MHC, pp. 50–52.

[34] According to the records in ACG, I, 20, 24, 26, 30, Jean d'Alerio was elected as prior general in 1321 and served until his resignation in 1330. See also MHC, pp. 114, 197, 206, 233, 237, 251, 380, 395.

For his profession, Pierre de Thomas entered the church of his convent clad in the tunic of the order without the scapular or the cloak and hood. After reaffirming that there was no canonical impediment to his admittance into the Carmelite Order, he placed his hands between the hands of the presiding officer and promised lifelong obedience to the prior general and to his lawful successors. Subsequently, with many prayers, he was invested first with the scapular and then with the cloak and hood. At the close of the ceremony, he took his place in the choir as a full-fledged member of the order.

In making his profession of lifelong obedience to the Carmelite Order, Pierre de Thomas surrendered much of his personal freedom, but he made the sacrifice gladly for a cause in which he believed with all his heart. In return, he gained the fellowship of a company of like-minded souls and the assurance that the order would care for his physical needs, though he himself would possess no personal property. He also received the support of the order for his further education and the guarantee that a place of service would be assigned to him when it was completed.

For the next quarter century, Pierre lived wholly within the Carmelite Order. Only in his later life, as a prelate of the church, was he exempted from its rules, and even then he lived by them as much as he could. It is therefore appropriate in a study of his life that some attention be given to the nature of the Carmelite Order and the major features of its way of life.

The Carmelite Order was one of the four mendicant orders of the Roman Catholic Church at this time. The two large and noted orders of this group were the Franciscans and the Dominicans, but the Carmelites and the Hermits of St. Augustine, though smaller, were organized on the same principles.

Unlike the other mendicant orders, "The Order of the Brothers of the Blessed Mary of Mount Carmel" had its origin in the East. It was founded about 1154 or 1155 by a Latin monk Berthold, a relative of Aymeric, Latin patriarch of Antioch. Its members received their first rule from Albert of Vercelli, patriarch of Jerusalem, about 1220. The early Carmelites were a community of hermits living on Mount Carmel on the Mediterranean coast of Palestine, a site made famous by the contest between the prophet Elijah and the priests of Baal in Old Testament times. They lived under a very strict rule, which required them to live largely in their cells, to own no personal property, to abstain from flesh meat at all times, and to fast from the middle of September until the following Easter. They were to keep silence from vespers until terce and at all times to guard against useless talk.[35]

As the situation of the Latins in Palestine became more and more precarious in the thirteenth century, some of the Carmelites began to form colonies in Europe. In 1238, colonies were founded in Cyprus, Sicily, Marseilles, and Valenciennes. In 1241, some of the brothers of English nationality went back to their native land with returning crusaders. In 1254, St. Louis, king of France, visited Mount Carmel and brought six French hermits to Charenton near Paris, where he established them. The first Chapter General of the Carmelite Order in the West was held at Aylesford, England, in 1247, and St. Simon Stock

---

[35] Zimmerman, "Carmelite Order," in *Catholic Encyclopedia,* III, 354–55; Discalced Carmelites, *Carmel,* pp. 3–32; Patrick R. McCaffrey, O. Carm., *The White Friars, an Outline Carmelite History with Special Reference to the English-Speaking Provinces* (Dublin, 1926), xiii-xiv, 10–30; Andrew of Saint Mary, O. C. D., *The Order of Our Lady of Mount Carmel* (Bruges, Courtray, 1913), pp. 3–13. There is an old tradition of the Carmelite Order that the prophet Elijah was actually its founder and that there was an actual, or a least a moral, succession of holy men on Mount Carmel from his time until the period of the crusader states, when they first came into the clear light of history. This tradition is no longer supported by the scholarly historians of the Carmelite Order, but it still appears in some works of Carmelite origin.

was elected prior general. At this time, the order was having some difficulty in the West. Some prelates were refusing to acknowledge it on the ground that it had been formed in contravention of the act of the Lateran Council of 1215 which forbade the establishment of new orders.

The new prior general immediately set about the task of putting the Carmelites on a firm footing. Before the close of 1247, he had secured an interim approbation of the order from Pope Innocent IV and certain modifications of the rule. The solitary life was changed for a community life. Meals were now to be taken in common. There was a relaxation of the abstinence from flesh meat, and silence was required only in the period between compline and prime. The brethren were permitted to keep donkeys and mules for traveling and for the transportation of goods, and fowl for the needs of the kitchen. With these modifications of its rule, the order ceased to be eremitical and took its place among the mendicant orders of the Catholic Church. In order to secure the advantages of higher education for members of the order, and to increase the number of vocations among undergraduates, St. Simon led in the establishment of Carmelite houses in the great centers of learning, such as Paris, Bologna, and Oxford.[36]

Though the enthusiasm of the people of Western Europe for mendicant orders had already begun to wane, the Carmelites grew rapidly after their establishment there. By the time of the Chapter General of 1324, the order was organized into fifteen provinces: the Holy Land, Sicily, England, Narbonne, Tuscany, France, Lower Germany, Lombardy, Aquitaine, Spain,

---

[36] Zimmerman, "Carmelite Order," *Catholic Encyclopedia,* III, 355–56; Discalced Carmelites, *Carmel,* pp. 33–42; McCaffrey, *White Friars,* pp. 31–70; Andrew of St. Mary, *Order of Carmel,* pp. 14–41. The modification of the Carmelite rule issued in 1247 is published in MHC, pp. 12–19.

Ireland, Upper Germany, Apulia, Provence, and Scotland.[37] In this same chapter general a revision of the constitutions of the order was approved. Since Pierre de Thomas entered the order at about this time, it is possible to form a picture of Carmelite life in his day by studying these constitutions of 1324 and the amendments made at subsequent Chapters General during his lifetime.[38]

The head of the order was the prior general, who was elected by the Chapter General. This body was made up of representatives from the provincial chapters. In the lifetime of Pierre de Thomas it usually met triennially. At each Chapter General, the prior general was required to give an account of his administration, after which the group voted either to approve his continuance in office or to remove him and elect a successor. The prior general was supported by a tax levied on the provinces for the administration of the order. In theory, his power was unlimited, but he dared not disregard the wishes of other leading members of the order.

At the head of each province was a provincial prior, who likewise had to give an account to the Chapter General. He was expected to call a meeting of the provincial chapter, made up of representatives of all houses in the province, at least once a year. On the local level, each convent was presided over by a prior or, in his absence, by a vicar. The prior administered the convent together with three guardians, who held the keys to the common chest and countersigned all financial transactions. Complaints against the prior might be taken to the provincial

[37] MHC, p. 21; ACG, I, 24–25.
[38] Until very recently the constitutions of 1324 were the oldest available complete set of Carmelite constitutions. In the summer of 1956 I was informed by Keith Egan, O. Carm., then librarian of Whitefriars Hall, Washington, D.C., that the constitutions of 1281 and 1294 have now been discovered. They were, of course, enacted before the time of Pierre de Thomas.

prior or the provincial chapter. Such was the organization of the Carmelite Order.[39]

The rules for the daily life of a Carmelite friar, which were to govern Pierre de Thomas for the rest of his life, were very rigorous. In fulfillment of the vow of poverty, no brother was allowed to have any property of his own, but all goods were held in common and were distributed to each member of the convent according to his need. The members of the order received all their sustenance by begging. According to the constitutions of 1324, each convent had its own territory for begging, and anyone who encroached on the territory of another house was punished. Even within the same convent, each brother was allotted a certain territory in which to do his begging, and no one might enter another's territory without the permission of the local prior. This local division of territory was probably made merely to avoid alienating the people of the community by too many appeals from the same house and to insure greater effectiveness in begging, for all the brothers were required to give the proceeds of their begging to the prior and the guardians of the conventual treasury, who had charge of all property of the house.[40] For Pierre de Thomas, going out among the people to ask for alms was no new experience, and he probably found it far less embarrassing to solicit gifts for a religious order than for himself, as he had had to do in his early student days.

Each brother in a Carmelite house had a separate cell in the dormitory. These cells were assigned by the prior with the assent of the other brothers or of the more discreet part of them. Each brother was required to stay in his cell or near it

[39] MHC, pp. 62–86 (constitutions of 1324); 116, 122–23, 128–30, 142–43, 156–57, 165, 172–75, 184–85 (amendments made at Chapters General from 1327–1362); Zimmerman, "Carmelite Order," *Catholic Encyclopedia*, III, 357–58.

[40] MHC, pp. 14, 22, 105.

day and night, meditating on the law of the Lord, unless occupied in some other proper occupation. During the night, the brothers were to remain in their cells and not to leave until the bell sounded in the morning. They were to make no noise that would disturb the quiet of the dormitory. Even when sleeping, they were required to wear the tunic and scapular. This last requirement was evidently imposed as a penitential practice and was evidently very distasteful, for penalties were provided for those caught sleeping without the scapular and severer ones for those who slept wholly naked, although exceptions were made for weakness and sickness. That these rules might be enforced, it was provided that brothers must keep their cells open at all times, to permit inspection. In 1345, it was further enacted that such an inspection be made nightly in each convent by the prior, the subprior, or the vicar.[41] Philippe de Mézières reports that Pierre de Thomas after his entrance into the order always slept in his tunic and scapular and never used a pillow.[42]

According to the rule given by Innocent IV in 1247, the Carmelite friars were required at all times to engage in some useful occupation and to guard against idle talk. They were to maintain silence from compline each evening until prime the next morning. The constitutions of 1324 reaffirmed these rules and required that silence be maintained at all times in the cloister, the dormitory, and the cells, except in the choir, the refectory, and the prior's cell. Brothers were enjoined especially against vain talk near the church and especially in it. Severe penalties were provided for swearing profanely by Christ, the Virgin Mary, or by the saints.[43]

At mealtime, the Carmelites were required to eat together

---

[41] MHC, pp. 13, 31, 148.
[42] Mézières, *Life,* ed. Smet, p. 56; AASS, Jan. 29, III, 612 (sec. 5).
[43] MHC, 16–17, 29–30, 172.

in the refectory and to remain silent; at this time the Holy Scriptures were read to them. It was required that the prior's cell be nearest to the entrance of the refectory, so that he could readily enter the room first and supervise the brothers there. No brother was permitted to change his place without the consent of the prior. At all times, the Carmelites were required to abstain from flesh meat unless permitted to eat it as a remedy for sickness or infirmity. An exception was made for those who were outside the convent on business of the order. They were permitted to eat stews made with meat, in order to avoid being burdensome to outsiders who might minister to their needs, but under no circumstances might they eat meat itself or hairs or blood or entrails. Even this concession was denied to friars traveling in advent or on ember days. At such times, however, they were permitted to eat eggs and milk products, according to the custom of the region where they were. The rules of 1247 required that the brothers fast every day except Sundays from the feast of the Exaltation of the Holy Cross (September 14) until Easter, except in case of sickness or infirmity. In the constitutions of 1324, this rule was relaxed, and daily fasting was required only in seven weeks from Quinquagesima Sunday until Easter and in advent. Fasting was also required on the eve of certain religious holidays, on ember days, and on some other designated days.[44]

The constitutions of 1324 provided certain exceptions to compulsory attendance in the refectory at mealtimes and compulsory silence. The higher officers and teachers were permitted to eat outside the refectory, provided that they ate the same food as those in the refectory. Even the priors and teachers were to eat in the refectory at least two days a week. No brother might join those eating outside the refectory except the person or persons designated by the prior to wait on

[44] MHC, pp. 13, 15, 27–28.

them. Whether outsiders were present or not, those eating outside the refectory were to maintain silence during the meal, except the one who presided at the table. However, anyone presiding might dispense with this rule with one other brother. A local prior might dispense with it with two brothers, and a provincial prior or the prior general might permit all the brothers with him at the table to engage in conversation without loud talking and commotion, which were never permitted. When no persons outside the order were present, masters, bachelors, and lectors (lecturers), and prelates or officers of the order were allowed to speak freely, for it was assumed that they would say nothing except what was permissible and honorable. In the Chapter General of 1345, it was evidently thought that these rules were too lenient, and it was enacted that no brother might eat outside the refectory without a special license, to be given only for due cause, except the masters of theology at all convents and bachelors lecturing at the University of Paris, who were to have this privilege without reservation. Pierre de Thomas did not take advantage of these concessions. Even in his later life, when as a bishop and papal legate he was exempt from the rules of his order, he never ate outside the refectory in a convent of his order, nor did he desire any food other than what the poor friars ate.[45]

All members of the Carmelite Order who had sufficient education were required to say the seven canonical hours of the divine office. A bell was rung at each of these hours, and the friars were expected to come to the service with due haste. When entering and leaving the choir, the chapter, or the refectory, the brothers were required to bow their heads reverently. They were always expected to bow at the name of Jesus or of Mary. Each of them was designated to lead the

[45] MHC, pp. 28–30, 146–47; Mézières, *Life,* ed. Smet, p. 61; AASS, Jan. 29, III, 613 (sec. 11).

divine office in turn, and in each convent there was a common tablet, listing the names of the friars and the duties assigned to each. In each house an oratory was constructed in the midst of the cells, where its members were expected to assemble each morning for mass. No brother who was a priest might refrain from celebrating mass for more than one day without the license of the prior. All Carmelites must take the eucharist at least ten times a year at times specified in the constitutions.[46] Pierre de Thomas was always faithful in the observance of these religious duties. Even after he reached a high rank in the church, he always arose for matins. Except for the two days before his death, when prevented from doing so by bodily weakness, he said the divine office every day from his entrance into the order until the end of his life.[47]

The patron saint of the Carmelites was the Virgin Mary, the mother of Christ, and they were ardent in venerating her. Pierre de Thomas shared in this devotion to the fullest. Mézières says that Pierre had great devotion to the glorious Virgin from his boyhood and served her devoutly. Luke Wadding declares that the name of Mary was always on his lips. Throughout his life, Pierre looked to her for strength and protection in times of need and danger.[48]

When members of the Carmelite Order found it necessary to travel, as Pierre de Thomas often did, they were required to observe certain rules. They were to go forth only on business of the order and to carry letters from their local prior, stating the time of their departure and of their expected return and the places where they were authorized to go. They were expected to

[46] MHC, pp. 13–14, 24, 27, 40–41.
[47] Mézières, *Life,* ed. Smet, pp. 60–61, 149; AASS, Jan. 29, III, 612–13, 634 (secs. 10, 11, 119).
[48] Mézières, *Life,* ed. Smet, pp. 55–56; AASS, Jan. 29, III, 611 (sec. 4); Carmesson, *Vita,* in *Spec. carm.,* II, 173, Wadding, *Vita,* pp. 5–6, also in *Spec. carm.,* II, 200.

go only to such places and to return at the specified time, unless prevented by reasonable cause. Normally no brother might travel alone, but one who left the convent was accompanied by another friar designated by the prior. Carmelites were not to travel on horseback, except in cases of great necessity. Without the license of the prior general or provincial or (after 1336) of the local prior, no Carmelite might lodge in a place other than a convent of his order, if he was able to reach one in a day's journey. If a traveling friar came to a Carmelite convent other than his own, he was required to show its prior his letter from his own prior. The host prior was then obliged to receive him and give him victuals according to his need and labors. The traveler was to eat in the refectory of the host convent unless he received permission from its prior to do otherwise, and he was not permitted to leave its portals that night. Without the license of the prior general or provincial, no friar might eat with persons outside the order in any place where there was a Carmelite house, except with members of other religious orders, prelates, kings, princes, patrons, or magnates. However, a local prior could license brothers to eat in a town with notable and honorable persons, provided that he saw that no occasion of scandal would arise.[49]

All infractions of the rules of the order were considered at the local chapter, which met in each convent every Sunday, or oftener if necessary, to enforce monastic discipline and to conduct the other business of the house. The local prior, or the person acting in his stead, presided at these meetings. No one was permitted to speak except to confess his faults or to answer a question put to him by the presiding officer. Each brother was expected to confess his own faults. He would then be assigned due penance by the leader. Accusations might be made by one brother against another if they could be proved. If an

[49] MHC, pp. 29, 33–36, 124, 167.

accusation could not be proved, the accuser must pay the penalty for the offense. For lighter offenses, a friar was required
to say a psalm or a number of psalms as penance. For more
serious offenses, a brother might be put on bread and water
for a number of days and confined to his cell in silence. For
the gravest offenses, a brother could be committed to the prison
maintained in each convent. In prison one received only bread
and water on Monday, Wednesday, and Friday each week.[50]
There is no evidence that Pierre de Thomas was ever subject to
any of these penalties, but they are of interest as forming part
of the system of life to which he belonged.

The entrance of Pierre de Thomas into full membership in
the Carmelite Order and into the way of life noted above at
the age of twenty-two marks the close of the early years of his
life, the years of childhood and adolescence. He had come
a long way in his first twenty-two years. In an age when inher-
ited wealth and social position were the normal prerequisites to
success in life, he began his days with neither. As the son of
a poor peasant, his only endowments were his natural ability
and his willingness to venture into the unknown. With courage, determination, and a willingness both to work and to endure hardship, he sought and obtained an education which led
to his acceptance into the Carmelite Order and prepared the
way for the great accomplishments of his later life.

[50] MHC, pp. 14–15, 30, 81–86, 106–10.

# 3

# Carmelite Student and Professor

WHEN PIERRE DE THOMAS BECAME A MEMBER OF THE CAR-
melite Order, the support and direction of his education was
assumed by the order. His program of studies, according to
the constitutions of 1324, came under the direction of the
provincial prior of his province, Aquitaine,[1] together with the
definitors of the provincial chapter.[2] If his own convent did
not offer the studies which he needed, a friar was sent to
another house. Certain convents in each province were designated as centers for advanced study in philosophy and theology.

[1] ACG, I, 24–27; Parraud, *Vie,* p. 14, n. 1. This was probably
Pierre de Casa, provincial prior of Aquitaine from 1324 to 1327.
Later (1330–42) he served as prior general of the Carmelite Order.
[2] These were an executive committee of four men regularly chosen
by each provincial chapter to transact its important business. See MHC,
pp. 75–81, 90; Zimmerman, "Carmelite Order," *Catholic Encyclopedia,*
III, 357–58.

For the most advanced students, the order maintained *studia generalia,* of which there were eight when Pierre de Thomas entered the order. This educational system was supported, along with other provincial and general expenses of the order, by a tithe levied on all income of each convent. Sometimes an alternate system of taxation was used instead of the tithe.[3]

After his profession, Pierre de Thomas was first assigned to teach "young brothers" at Bergerac or Condom. Apparently he taught on a more elementary level than before he had entered the order. He probably taught grammar to those who needed such instruction. In the Carmelite Order, teachers were required to hold classes on each of the days ordinarily designated for lecturing in the schools of the day.[4]

After Pierre had spent two years teaching on the elementary level, his superiors took notice of his ability and devotion and sent him for higher studies to Agen, where he had studied and taught before entering the order. Apparently Agen was something of an educational center in Aquitaine. In the Carmelite convent there he taught logic, as he had done before his profession, while he himself studied philosophy. He stayed at

[3] MHC, pp. 53, 56, 59–62, 128; Zimmerman, "Carmelite Order," *Catholic Encyclopedia,* III, 358; Benedict Zimmerman, "Les Carmes aux universités du moyen âge," *Études carmelitaines mystiques et missionaires,* XVII (1932), vol. I, pp. 92–93. In 1336, the tithe system was abolished, and each province was directed to work out a system of contributions by which the local convents might provide for the officers and work of the order.

[4] Mézières, *Life,* ed. Smet, pp. 54–55; AASS, Jan. 29, III, 611 (sec. 3). Mézières says that Pierre remained at Condom, where he entered the order, and "docuit fratres juvenes per duos annos." Since it is clear, as noted above, that Pierre entered the order at Bergerac rather than Condom, it is not clear whether he actually remained at Bergerac or was sent to Condom for his first teaching position as a member of the order. On Carmelite rules for teachers, see MHC, pp. 60–61. Koch, *Die Karmelitenklöster,* pp. 17–18, declares in reference to the province of Lower Germany, that many Carmelite houses had elementary schools as well as Latin schools. Elementary school teachers had the title *informator iuniorum.*

Agen for three years, the normal length of the philosophy course taken by a Carmelite friar.[5] In this period or at its close he was ordained to the priesthood, about 1331. Before taking this step he had to obtain the approval of his provincial prior or of the prior general.[6] Pierre was considered worthy of ordination, for he was free in his body from all the contaminations of youth and was fervently devoted to the Virgin Mary.[7]

In connection with his second stay in Agen, Pierre's biographer tells about the first miracle reported in his life. Some time after his ordination he is said to have fallen into such a state of poverty that he could scarcely provide himself with clothing, candles, oil for lamps, and other small necessities. One day in the early morning after matins, he was in his cell brooding over his poverty and praying for help to the Virgin Mary. He feared that he would be forced to give up his studies for lack of funds. At this time the Virgin appeared to him, visibly walking through the dormitory and watching over him. She took him by the cloak, led him through the dormitory, and said to him, "My son, have no fear because of your poverty, for I will not desert you. Study earnestly and serve my Son and me." When she had said this, she vanished from his sight. After daybreak, Pierre celebrated mass in honor of the Virgin Mary and thanked her for her promise. After this mass, a knight of that country appeared and said to him, "I want to say my confession to you." At the close of his confession, the knight

[5] Koch, *Die Karmelitenklöster,* p. 20; Zimmerman, "Carmes aux universités," pp. 92–93.

[6] MHC, p. 53.

[7] Mézières, *Life,* ed. Smet, p. 55; AASS, Jan. 29, III, 611 (sec. 3). According to Ambrosius, "Monasticon carmelitanum," AOCD, XXII (1950), 64, the convent at Agen was founded in 1270 outside the walls of the city in the region which today is between the rue Belfort and the rue Lassaigne. Some time in the fourteenth century it was moved within the city.

gave the young friar sixteen *royaux* of gold, and from that day Pierre was never again troubled by poverty.[8]

After studying philosophy for three years at Agen, Pierre de Thomas was sent to the Carmelite house at Bordeaux [9] to give lectures on the "new logic," and there he stayed for a year. The "new logic" included the more advanced logical works of Aristotle which had become known in Europe only in the twelfth century and were contrasted with the more elementary works included in the sixth-century translations of Aristotle by Boethius, known as the "old logic." The "new logic" presented logic as the science of concepts, whereas the old had presented it merely as a method of reasoning. After his stay at Bordeaux, Pierre lectured on natural philosophy for a year at the convent of Albi and then returned to Agen to lecture on philosophy for a year.[10]

About 1335, after these years of studying and teaching, Pierre de Thomas received one of the highest honors that could come to a young Carmelite friar. He was sent to the Carmelite

---

[8] Mézières, *Life,* ed. Smet, pp. 55–56; AASS, Jan. 29, III, 611 (sec. 4). The Bollandist edition says that the knight gave Pierre fifteen gold *royaux,* but "sixteen" is the better reading. Carmesson, *Vita,* in *Spec. carm.,* II, 173–74, clearly states that this vision occurred at Agen, but Mézières, the better source, is more vague. He may have discussed the vision at this point in the biography simply because the account of Pierre's ordination reminded him of a miracle so intimately connected with priestly duties. There is certainly some confusion in the story as told by Mézières, for at this time, as a member of the Carmelite Order, Pierre was assured of support for his education and would have had no cause to worry, unless as suggested by the Carmelite breviary and the writer Saracenus, both cited in Wadding, *Vita,* p. 68, the treasury of the local convent was badly depleted at the time of his vision.

[9] According to Ambrosius, "Monasticon carmelitanum," AOCD, XXII (1950), 143, the convent of Bordeaux was founded about 1264.

[10] Mézières, *Life,* ed. Smet, p. 56; AASS, Jan. 29, III, 611–12 (sec. 5). On the convent of Albi see Ambrosius, "Monasticon carmelitanum," AOCD (1950), 69–70.

college at the University of Paris, the chief theological school
of Christendom, to take the customary three-year course of
study. The decision to send him there was probably made by
the provincial prior of Aquitaine.[11] The constitutions of 1324
required each province to send a specified number of students
to the Carmelite *studium* at Paris. Some provinces were to send
one student; others, including Aquitaine, two. For each student
the province paid 150 *gros tournois* to the convent of Paris,
whether or not the students were sent there, and seventy *gros
tournois* to the student for vestments. Aquitaine was one of a
limited number of provinces which might send one additional
student to Paris without charge. Other students might be sent
there if supported by their provinces or by friends or relatives.
Each provincial prior sought to send his best students to Paris.[12]

The Carmelite convent at Paris, where Pierre de Thomas
now went to live was one of the oldest in Europe and had
originally been founded with the aid of St. Louis. Pierre lived
in the new convent, established in the period 1321 to 1324
on land granted by kings Philip IV and Philip V, after the
old site had been found unsuitable because it was too far from
the university and frequently flooded by the Seine in the spring-
time. The new convent, where the Carmelites remained until
the French Revolution, was located near the place Maubert along
the great rue de Sainte-Geneviève. In this convent there were
normally three hundred students from all provinces of the

[11] The provincial priors of Aquitaine in this period, according to
ACG, I, 32, 33, 35, were Jacques Dalzo (1333–36) and Élie Seguini
(1336–42).
[12] Mézières, *Life,* ed. Smet, p. 56; AASS, Jan. 29, III, 612 (sec. 5);
MHC, pp. 53–56, 59, 125–26. A constitution of 1336 stated that no
scholar might be sent to Paris unless he had given a complete course
of lectures on the philosophy or metaphysics of Aristotle and had
lectured on one of the four books of natural philosophy. Pierre had
fulfilled these requirements, although he probably went to Paris before the enactment of this constitution.

order who came to study at the University of Paris. Here Pierre was able to match his wits with the keenest thinkers of Christendom, both within and without his own order.[13]

At the University of Paris, Pierre de Thomas began his formal training in theology. He heard the lectures of the masters and bachelors and attended their disputations and determinations, where they discussed and argued the theological issues of the day. He remained at Paris for three years, making excellent progress in his studies. This was the normal period for a Carmelite to attend one of the higher schools.[14] At its close, he returned to Aquitaine where he was appointed as lector in the convent of Cahors.[15]

The office of lector, or lecturer in theology, in a Carmelite convent was a highly honored one. In addition to required studies in theology, which Pierre had apparently completed at Paris, a lector had to have the license of the prior general, the Chapter General, or a provincial chapter. A lector assigned to lecture in any convent of the order had his travel expenses and the expenses of transporting his books paid by that convent. Within the local house he ranked immediately below the bachelors, masters, subprior, and prior in the conduct of the business

[13] Alfred L. Franklin, *Les Anciennes bibliothèques de Paris, églises, monastères, collèges,* II (Paris, 1870), 1–2; Pierre Feret, *La Faculté de théologie de Paris et ses docteurs les plus célèbrés—moyen âge,* II (Paris, 1895), 33–34; III (Paris, 1896), 2; Bartholomaeus Maria Xiberta, O. Carm., *De scriptoribus scholasticis saeculi XIV ex ordine Carmelitarum* (Louvain, 1931), pp. 18–19; Michel Felibien, *Histoire de la ville de Paris,* III (Paris, 1725), 215–21. There is a map of Paris in the later Middle Ages which shows the location of the Carmelite convent in Lynn Thorndike, *University Records and Life in the Middle Ages* (Columbia University Records of Civilization, no. 38; New York, 1944), facing p. 448.

[14] MHC, pp. 59, 126, 142. In 1336 this term was reduced to two years, but this plan apparently was found inadvisable, for the longer term was restored in 1342.

[15] Mézières, *Life,* ed. Smet, pp. 56–57; AASS, Jan. 29, III, 612 (sec. 5); Wadding, *Vita,* pp. 7–8, also in *Spec. carm.,* II, 201.

of the house. Lectors were entitled to have an official seal. Like
other higher officers in the convent, a lector was entitled to the
assistance of a *socius* appointed by the local prior. According
to a constitution of 1342 those who had been lectors and had
been removed from office honorably ranked just below the
practicing lectors in the choir and refectory.[16] As lector in the
convent of Cahors, Pierre de Thomas was one of the principal
instructors in the school and may have been its supervisor. He
was required to lecture at least once a week and to perform
other academic duties between All Saints' Day and Whitsuntide
each year. If he was faithful to his duties, he was entitled to
receive a sum of money annually from his convent for vestments.[17]

In 1339, while Pierre de Thomas was lector at Cahors, there
was a severe drought in the region. All the crops were wither-
ing in the fields. A procession of all the clergy and people of
the city was formed to pray for rain. Pierre de Thomas was
asked to preach on the day of the procession. He led the clergy
and people half a league out of the city, perhaps to the shrine
of Notre Dame de Pont-Vieux. There he preached in the open

[16] MHC, pp. 57–58, 60, 92, 142. The term *lector* was used in two
senses by the Carmelites: (1) It was the title given to any lecturer in
theology, whether or not he held a degree; (2) As a rank in the order
it signified those who had held the office of lector but did not have the
degree of bachelor or master and who ranked immediately below
bachelors. The full title seems to have been *lector in theologia,* but,
although these men were required to have completed certain theological studies, they often taught natural or moral philosophy.

[17] MHC, p. 60. According to Ambrosius, "Monasticon carmelitanum,"
AOCD, XXII (1950), 222, the convent of Cahors was founded outside the city by one Eugène de Jean about 1262 and moved within
the city in 1273 or 1323, when it was located near the river Lot
on a street now called the Boulevard Cavaignac. Ambrosius states incorrectly that Pierre was prior, rather than lector, at Cahors from
1339 to 1341. The source of this error seems to be Antoine Marie de
la Présentation, O. C. D., *Le Carmel en France, étude historique,* VI
(Toulouse, 1939), 264, where no evidence is cited to prove that
Pierre was prior of Cahors.

air. He began his sermon with words of comfort, promising the people that they would have rain that day if they should have enough faith in the Virgin Mary. When he began to preach, there was not a single cloud in the sky nor any other sign of rain, but before his sermon was completed, it began to rain a little, and before long the people were struggling back to the city in a heavy downpour. The people interpreted these events as examples of Pierre's miraculous power, and they regarded him as a saint.[18]

Thus at Cahors, Pierre de Thomas first appeared prominently before the public, and here we first hear of his outstanding ability as a preacher. After he attained this fame at Cahors, he is reported to have requested a transfer from the city, because he regarded all worldly glory as an abomination. His request was not granted, and he remained in Cahors for three years, "lecturing, preaching, and performing miracles." [19]

About 1341, the Carmelite authorities in Aquitaine decided to send Pierre back to the University of Paris to complete his studies for the degree of bachelor of theology. Members of religious orders were normally required to study six years for this degree. They spent four years attending lectures on the Bible and two attending lectures on the *Sentences* of Peter Lombard. Since Pierre de Thomas had already studied for three years at Paris, only three years were required to complete his work. According to Mézières, he spent four years at Paris in this period. It is difficult to determine whether Mézières is in

[18] Mézières, *Life,* ed. Smet, p. 57; AASS, Jan. 29, III, 612 (sec. 6); Carmesson, *Vita,* in *Spec. carm.,* II, 175–76; Parraud, *Vie,* pp. 25–27. The date 1339 is given in *Spec. carm.,* II, 176, note a, and by Parraud, *Vie,* p. 25, n. 2, who cites as his source Raymond Foulhiac, "Annales de la ville de Cahors" (manuscript of the seventeenth century in the library of Cahors), fol. 73v, where the drought and procession are mentioned but not Pierre de Thomas. This is the earliest date in Pierre's life which can be cited with any approach to accuracy.

[19] Mézières, *loc. cit.*

error or whether Pierre studied for a year beyond the bac-
calaureate level.[20]

At the close of his second period of study in Paris, Pierre
de Thomas again returned to Aquitaine. Apparently he was
not there very long before the General Chapter of the Carmelite Order was held in Milan at the feast of Pentecost, May
15, 1345. The Chapter General was composed of three delegates from every province. One of these was the provincial
prior; the others were his *socii,* elected by the provincial chapter. In the election of the prior general all members of the
Chapter General took part, but its other business was entrusted
to a group of definitors, composed of one delegate from each
province, designated by his provincial chapter to serve in this
group.[21] It is not known whether Pierre de Thomas was a
delegate to the Chapter General of 1345,[22] but this session
was of great importance to him, for in it he was elected to the
high office of procurator general of the Carmelite Order.[23]

The procurator general was in charge of the temporal affairs

[20] Mézières, *Life,* ed. Smet, p. 57; AASS, Jan. 29, III, 612 (sec.
6); Feret, *Faculté de théologie,* II, 41–42, III, 171–72.

[21] MHC, pp. 67–75, 116, 122, 128. Zimmerman, "Carmelite Order,"
*Catholic Encyclopedia,* III, 357.

[22] According to a constitution adopted in 1336, published in MHC,
p. 131, the membership of the Chapter General of the Carmelites was
limited to masters, bachelors, lectors, local priors, or former priors.
As a bachelor, Pierre was eligible. Many friars who were not delegates
also attended these sessions to hear the brilliant disputations and eloquent preaching that accompanied them.

[23] Mézières, *Life,* ed. Smet, p. 57; AASS, Jan. 29, III, 612 (sec.
7). Since Mézières mentions no task committed to Pierre de Thomas
between his return from Paris to Aquitaine and the Chapter General
of 1345, it was probably a brief period. How long he does not say.
Pierre's election as procurator is recorded in the minutes of the Chapter General of 1345, which are published (in part) in ACG, I, 38.
This is the earliest date in the life of Pierre de Thomas which is recorded in a contemporary source. It is interesting to note that this
Chapter General was one in which an unusually large number of revisions to the constitutions of the order were made. They are published
in MHC, pp. 145–63.

of the order, under the direction of the prior general. He was required to live in Avignon, the seat of the papacy. Through his office passed all correspondence between the order or any of its members and the papal court. As one of the chief officers of the order he, with the provincial priors and the local priors at Paris and Avignon, was officially inducted into office by the prior general at the closing session of the Chapter General. At this time he was given a letter testifying to his election and his seal of office.[24]

The position and duties of the procurator general are clearly defined in a constitution adopted at the Chapter General of 1345, the same one at which Pierre was elected to the office. It is made clear in it that the procurator was to serve always as an assistant to the prior general. Although the procurator was normally chosen or confirmed by the Chapter General, the prior general was given the power to remove him at will and to appoint another in his place. Another constitution of 1345 provided that the procurator should receive fifteen florins annually from the treasury of the order, the same amount as was provided for the regent masters of theology at the chief Carmelite schools, those in Paris and Avignon.[25]

It would be difficult to overestimate the importance of his election as procurator general in the life of Pierre de Thomas. Hitherto he had lived in a quiet academic world, far removed from the practical politics of his day. His new office took him to Avignon, à great center of political activity. In promoting the interests of his order there, he had his first opportunity to discover and develop the diplomatic ability that was to serve him so well in later missions. At this time, he became personally acquainted with the leaders of the church and the prob-

[24] MHC, pp. 74–75, 93, 112, 163. The office of procurator of the Carmelite Order still exists.

[25] MHC, pp. 155-57. However, the master at Paris also received fifteen florins from his province.

lems of the Roman Curia. His later importance as a diplomat stemmed largely from contacts made in this period, and it is this diplomatic activity which proved to be his life's major work, by which he earned his place in history.

In the early summer of 1345, Pierre de Thomas established his residence in the beautiful and magnificent city of Avignon, the capital of Western Christendom. He lived in the Carmelite house, called the Carreterie, which had been founded in 1267 and had become the headquarters of the order when the seat of the papacy was established in the city. The prior general lived there. The local prior of the convent of Avignon, like the prior at Paris, was elected by the Chapter General, and authority over him was divided between the prior general and the provincial prior of Provence.[26]

As procurator general, Pierre de Thomas was expected to work very closely with the prior general. At this time the general of the order was Pierre Raymond de Insula Grassa. He was originally from the province of Narbonne. He had been elected to the highest office in his order at the Chapter General of 1342 and served until his death in 1357. His contemporary Jean Trissa pictured him as a simple man, able to keep the expenses of the order to a minimum, because his wants were few. He is reported to have treated all friars alike, from the greatest to the least.[27]

According to Philippe de Mézières, relations between the prior general and Pierre de Thomas were anything but cordial; when Pierre Raymond saw that the new procurator was of

[26] MHC, pp. 74–75, 164–67, 173, 177; Ambrosius, "Monasticon carmelitanum," AOCD, XXII (1950), 106; Parraud, *Vie*, p. 35.

[27] Jean Trissa, O. Carm., *Catalogus priorum generalium,* in MHC, p. 234. Other accounts of Pierre Raymond are found in MHC, pp. 237, 252, 385–86, and Mariano Ventimiglia, O. Carm., *Historia chronologica priorum generalium latinorum Ordinis beatissimae Virginis Mariae de Monte Carmelo* (Naples, 1773, and fascimile reprint, Rome, 1929), pp. 85–86. In the 1773 edition, facing p. 85, there is a picture supposed to represent Pierre Raymond. It is not in the reprint.

slight build and mediocre appearance and that the men of his province had ordained him to serve in that office, he despised Pierre de Thomas in his heart and because of embarrassment did not want to present him to the cardinals.[28] This story presents some difficulties. The men of Pierre's province lacked the power to make him procurator, since this officer was elected by the Chapter General, in which all seventeen provinces of the order had an equal voice.[29] Also, the attitude of Pierre Raymond toward Pierre de Thomas as reported by Mézières is not in harmony with other accounts of the general's character, though admittedly these are meager. Even though there is probably some confusion in Mézières' story, the emotional overtones which can be felt in reading it suggest that it is a repetition of some authentic recollection confided to Mézières by Pierre de Thomas.

If his relations with his general were not happy, Pierre de Thomas was not friendless in Avignon. The powerful and famous Cardinal Talleyrand de Périgord heard that the new procurator of the Carmelite Order was a native of Périgord and an able man. He invited Pierre to have dinner with him and the other cardinals at his great palace. After dinner that night, as was their custom, the cardinals entered into a theological discussion. Pierre's participation impressed the cardinals with his brilliance and erudition. Subsequently he began to preach and take part in theological disputations in Avignon so that his ability was widely recognized in the papal capital.[30]

[28] Mézières, Life, ed. Smet, pp. 57–58; AASS, Jan. 29, III, 612 (sec. 7): "Tunc generalis Ordinis sui, existens in curia, et videns ipsum Fratrem Petrum parvum corpore et modicae apparentiae, et quod illi de provincia sua ordinaverant illum procuratorem Ordinis, despexit eum in corde suo et nolebat ipsum ducere in praesentia cardinalium prae verecundia." This passage is especially interesting for the information it gives about Pierre's personal appearance.

[29] MHC, pp. 67–68, 140.

[30] Mézières, Life, ed. Smet, p. 58; AASS, Jan. 29, III, 612 (sec. 7); Carmesson, Vita, in Spec. carm., II, 177; Parraud, Vie, pp. 43–44. Carmesson says that Talleyrand asked the general of the Carmelites

An amusing incident is reported to have occurred on one occasion when Pierre de Thomas was an invited guest at a dinner in Talleyrand's palace. In the customary after-dinner talk, a discussion arose concerning apostates. Talleyrand praised the order of cardinals because there were no apostates in it. To this Pierre de Thomas quickly replied, "Of what sort those may be who abandon other orders I do not know, but indeed I certainly know this, that those who apostasize from your order are manifestly the holiest of men." [31]

The friendship of Cardinal Talleyrand was a great boon to Pierre de Thomas, for it was at his prompting that the general of the Carmelites, Pierre Raymond, decided to send the procurator to Paris to study for the master's degree in theology. This was an extraordinary action, for it was the normal custom for Carmelite students for the master's degree at Paris to be appointed at the triennial meetings of the Chapter General.[32] It is probable that Pierre Raymond, using the authority given

to bring Pierre de Thomas to dinner, but the more reliable Mézières does not mention the general's presence on that occasion, as he surely would have done if he had been there, since it would have been a victory for Pierre de Thomas. At this time Talleyrand was living in a palace built by Arnaud de Via, nephew of Pope John XXII. In the 1890's this building was still standing, according to Parraud, and housed the Petit Seminaire. For the life of Talleyrand see Norman P. Zacour, *Talleyrand: the Cardinal of Périgord (1301–1364)* (Transactions of the American Philosophical Society, new series, vol. 50, part 7; Philadelphia, 1960).

[31] Reported by Johann of Hildesheim in a lost work quoted in John Bale, *Scriptorum illustrium Maioris Brittaniae ... catalogus ...*, 2 parts (Basel, 1557–59), I, 464, cited by Smet in his edition of Mézières, *Life,* p. 58, n. 19. This passage is also reproduced in *Bibl. carm.,* II, 5–6.

[32] Mézières, *Life,* ed. Smet, p. 59; AASS, Jan. 29, III, 612 (sec. 8). In Smet's edition it is made clear that the (prior) general of the order sent Pierre de Thomas to Paris, and not the Chapter General, as stated in the AASS edition. This is confirmed by the fact that in the minutes of the Chapters of 1345 and 1348, the only pertinent ones, published in ACG, I, 38–41, his name does not appear in the lists of lecturers on the Bible and the *Sentences,* which were prerequisites for the master's degree in theology.

to him in 1345, relieved Pierre de Thomas of the procurator-ship during the interval between the Chapters General of 1345 and 1348 and appointed another in his place so that Pierre de Thomas could go to Paris to study. If the relations between the two men were strained, the prior general was undoubtedly all the more receptive to the suggestion of Talleyrand that Thomas be given the opportunity to complete his education at Paris.[33]

Pierre de Thomas began his studies for the degree of master of theology in the usual way, by giving lectures on the Bible in the Carmelite convent of Paris.[34] An aspirant for this degree was required to give these lectures for two years. Each year, they lasted from the lecturer's inception, usually in November, until the eve of the Nativity of the Blessed Virgin (September 7) the following year.[35] Juan Carmesson reports that he was a very popular lecturer and that even the masters admired him greatly for the truth and subtlety of his teaching.[36] While lecturing at Paris, he received sixteen florins annually, half from the general treasury of the order and half from his home province.[37]

During his busy days as a lecturer at Paris, Pierre de Thomas never failed to observe the religious exercises that were an important part of his monastic life. According to his own testimony, he never missed a single mass before lecturing nor

[33] In his edition of Mézières, *Life,* p. 60, n. 20, Joachim Smet suggests that Pierre de Thomas probably completed his term as procurator of the order, which extended to the next Chapter General at Metz on June 8, 1348, before resuming his studies at Paris. To the present writer it seems more probable that the general's extraordinary action occurred between the Chapters General of 1345 and 1348 and that Pierre de Thomas therefore served only a part of his term as procurator, perhaps only a small part. In the Chapter General of 1348, Jacobus Martini was chosen as procurator, as recorded in ACG, I, 41.

[34] Mézières, *Life,* ed. Smet, p. 59; AASS, Jan. 29, III, 612 (sec. 8).

[35] MHC, p. 152 (a Carmelite constitution of 1345).

[36] Carmesson, *Vita,* in *Spec. carm.,* II, 177.

[37] MHC, p. 155 (a constitution of 1345).

did he neglect to say matins.[38] His faithful fulfillment of these obligations at a time when he might well have been tempted to neglect some of them is an indication of the spiritual integrity which would characterize his entire life.

After his two years of lectures on the Bible, Pierre de Thomas normally would have had five years additional study and exercises to complete before receiving his master's degree.[39] It is unlikely that Pierre de Thomas completed more than a year of this work, since he was graduated, according to Mézières, in the third year of his study for the master's degree at Paris. In that year, a dispute is said to have arisen between the chancellor of Paris, who normally had the final say in granting degrees, and fourteen students of the university who were expecting to receive their degrees that year. Some of these were from the secular clergy, and some were from the religious orders. It was finally decided that one additional student from the religious orders should receive his degree that year. Because of his ability, Pierre de Thomas was chosen for that honor by the unanimous vote of thirty-two masters of theology from all religious orders at Paris, and even the chancellor agreed to his graduation, although he had not completed his studies according to the statutes of the university.[40]

[38] Mézières, Life, ed. Smet, pp. 60–61; AASS, Jan. 29, III, 612 (sec. 10).

[39] Hastings Rashdall, The Universities of Europe in the Middle Ages, 3 vols. (revised edition, ed. F. M. Powicke and A. B. Emden, Oxford, 1936), I, 19, 474–81; Feret, Faculté de théologie, III, 73–81. The normal length of the course was seven years. In the fourth year, the student lectured on the Sentences. In the other years, after the first two, he spent his time in studies, disputations, and other academic exercises, culminating in the Sorbonnic, a twelve-hour disputation in which he defended a thesis against all challengers.

[40] Mézières, Life, ed. Smet, pp. 59–60; AASS, Jan. 29, III, 612 (sec. 8); Carmesson, Vita, in Spec. carm., II, 177–78. According to Feret, Faculté de théologie, II, 44, dispensations from the ordinary course requirements at the University of Paris could be granted either

In spite of his effort to explain Pierre de Thomas' extraordinary graduation in detail, Mézières does not appear to understand what happened, and his account is vague and quite confused. He does not tell what was the issue in the dispute between the chancellor and the fourteen prospective graduates. Neither does he explain how a dispute between the chancellor and a group of students from both the regular and the secular clergy could be settled by granting a concession only to the latter group, a development that can hardly be considered self-explanatory. Furthermore, it seems preposterous that the university authorities would first make an agreement to graduate one more member of the regular clergy and then leave it to the masters of that group to choose the most qualified one, as Mézières seems to say. On the contrary, the university officials could scarcely have agreed to an additional graduation until they were assured that a qualified candidate was available, for it was their responsibility to uphold the standards of their school. It therefore appears that, even if there is some element of truth in Mézières' story, the background of Pierre's graduation must have been different from his account of it.

Perhaps the real basis for Pierre's graduation is found in the special concessions granted to the Carmelite Order in this period by Pope Clement VI. Each of these gave the Carmelites privileges which were already enjoyed by other mendicant orders, especially the Dominicans and Franciscans. In August, 1342, Clement decreed that students presented to the University of Paris by the Carmelites as lecturers on the *Sentences* should be exempt from the normal residence requirements for

---

by the faculty or by the pope. Mézières erroneously states that the normal length of the course for the master of theology degree at Paris was five years, whereas it was actually seven. He may have been thinking about the fact that Pierre would normally have had five more years of study after completing his lectures on the Scriptures.

that position.[41] In May, 1343, he granted a similar concession for those Carmelites who were presented as lecturers on the Bible at Paris. The normal prerequisite for this position was six years of study at the University of Paris or twelve at other *studia generalia*.[42] Finally, on July 2, 1349, Clement VI granted Carmelite students the right to receive the degree of master of theology at Paris without any prescribed residence requirement, provided that the student could pass whatever examination the chancellor should give him. If in doubt about the student's qualifying for the degree, the chancellor might give him an unusually rigorous examination, but if he passed it, he was entitled to the degree.[43]

It is quite possible that the last-named concession made to the Carmelites by Clement VI in the summer of 1349 furnished the real background for Pierre's early graduation. The traditional date for his graduation is 1349, and though this tradition cannot be traced beyond the seventeenth century, it is by no means improbable.[44] It is therefore quite possible that

[41] Bull of August 23, 1342, published in Michel Felibien, *Histoire de la ville de Paris*, III (Paris, 1725), 221–22; summary in *Chartularium universitatis Parisiensis*, eds. H. Denifle and E. Chatelain, 4 vols. (Paris, 1889–1907), II, 529.

[42] *Chartularium universitatis Parisiensis*, II, 537. Since Pierre de Thomas had spent seven years at Paris before going there to give lectures on the Bible, he qualified under the old rule.

[43] The petition of the Carmelite Order, presented to the pope at this time, is published in *Chartularium universitatis Parisiensis*, II, 651. Clement VI's bull granting the concession is published in *Bullarium carmelitanum*, III, 65–66, and in Felibien, *Histoire de Paris*, III, 222.

[44] The date 1349 for the graduation of Pierre de Thomas is given in Johannes Baptista Lezana, O. Carm., *Annales sacri, prophetici et eliani Ordinis Beatae Virginis Mariae de Monte Carmeli*, IV (Rome, 1656), 595–96. This date is quoted by no less authorities than Denifle and Chatelain in their edition of *Chartularium universitatis Parisiensis*, II, 536, n. 6. As Joachim Smet points out in his edition of Mézières, *Life*, p. 59, n. 20, there is no evidence that these editors had any firmer foundation for accepting the date than the calculations of Lezana. Nevertheless this date is a probable one. According to Mézières, *Life*, ed. Smet, p. 59; AASS, Jan. 29, III, 612 (sec. 8), Pierre de Thomas spent about three years in Paris. If he was sent there in the

Mézières' story of the dispute between the fourteen students and the chancellor of Paris is really a badly garbled account of a dispute between the Carmelites of Paris and the chancellor in which the Carmelites insisted that their candidates for the master's degree in theology should enjoy the same exemption from the residence requirements of the university as members of other religious orders. The chancellor resisted their demands, as he commonly resisted all efforts to relax the rules. When they could make no headway with him, the Carmelites appealed to the Pope, and after some consideration, he granted their request on July 2, 1349. We may conjecture that the Carmelites believed that Pierre de Thomas could qualify for the degree and therefore acted to take advantage of their new privilege. Though he had completed less than half of the normal curriculum, they presented him to the faculty for the degree of master of theology. He took his examination, passed it, and received the degree.

Pierre de Thomas was probably in Paris in the summer of 1348, when the city was struck by the Black Death with its high mortality and attendant fear and distress among the people. There is no record of his activities in this time of trial. Judging by his own conduct during a later plague in Cyprus and by the general record of the friars in this period, we may assume that he was faithful in giving spiritual comfort to the sick and fearful, hearing the confessions of the dying, and giving the last rites of the church.[45]

---

spring of 1346, after a relatively short period as procurator, as suggested on p. 59 above, his graduation could well have taken place in 1349.

[45] Parraud, *Vie,* p. 64, discusses the work of Pierre de Thomas during the Black Death. He places Pierre in Avignon at the time. The Black Death in Paris is discussed with citation of sources in Francis Aiden Gasquet, *The Great Pestilence (A.D. 1348–49), Now Commonly Known as the Black Death* (London, 1893), pp. 46–48, and in Anna Montgomery Campbell, *The Black Death and Men of Learning* (New York, 1931), pp. 157–58.

After Pierre received his master's degree at Paris, he was designated to serve as regent master of theology, or headmaster, at the Carmelite *studium generale* of the Roman Curia at Avignon.[46] This was one of thirteen Carmelite *studia generalia* listed in the records for 1345. Among the teaching positions in the Carmelite Order, that of regent master at the Roman Curia was second only to a similar position at Paris. By an act of 1345, the regent master at Avignon received fifteen florins a year from the treasury of the order and had two assistants paid by the order, a bachelor to lecture on theology and a lector in philosophy. Teachers at other *studia generalia,* except Paris, had less prestige and were supported wholly by provincial treasuries.[47] The Carmelite school at Avignon was probably affiliated with the University of the Roman Curia. This was founded by Pope Innocent IV in 1244 or 1245. It held its sessions wherever the papal court was located and was distinct from the Universities of Rome and Avignon.[48]

While he was serving as master of the Carmelite school at Avignon, Pierre de Thomas was often present at the dinner meetings of the cardinals, preached to them, and took part in their disputations, as he had done in his earlier stay in Avignon. At times, he preached before Pope Clement VI. As a good friar was expected to do, he also preached among the people of the city. Sometimes he preached two or three times a day in addition to participating in the disputations of the

---

[46] Mézières, *Life,* ed. Smet, p. 60; AASS, Jan. 29, III, 612 (sec. 9); Wadding, *Vita,* p. 10, also in *Spec. carm.,* II, 201. Mézières says that Pierre was made *regens in theologia in curia,* which is similar to the title *magister regens in Romana curia,* used in reference to the master of the Carmelite school in Avignon in a constitution of 1345 published in MHC, p. 155. Parraud, *Vie,* pp. 47–50, and others have misinterpreted Mézières' statement to mean that Clement VI appointed Pierre de Thomas as master of theology in his own court.

[47] MHC, pp. 53, 56–57, 59, 121–22, 126–27, 150, 155.

[48] Heinrich Denifle, O. P., *Die Universitäten des Mittelalters bis 1400,* I (Berlin, 1885), 301–10; Rashdall, *Universities,* II, 28–29.

cardinals. In the luxurious papal capital, he preached boldly against customs which he considered sinful. Among other things, he criticized the extravagant use of pearls in women's headdresses and other superfluous ornaments. It is said that his sermons spared no one, not even the Pope. He frequently held his listeners spellbound. One moment, he had them laughing at a funny story, and the next moment he could move them to tears. Thus he kept their attention, and people left his presence strengthened and edified. According to Mézières, he was very popular, especially among the citizens, the merchants, and the women, and his preaching had great effect upon them. The latter statement no doubt should be accepted with some reservations. Pierre's preaching was supported by the example of a life that was consistent with his teachings.[49]

As a priest, it was also the duty of Pierre de Thomas to hear the confessions of the people, prescribe penances, and grant absolution. He was often able to bring sinners to repentance. In the confessional, he revealed unknown sins to the laity and minute ones to the clergy. His love for souls was so great that Mézières ventured to say that Pierre would gladly have suffered martyrdom for one soul returning to God through him, though the person had been previously unknown to him. All the more was his love manifested to his friends.[50]

Pierre's popularity was beneficial to himself and his fellow Carmelites. Once when disturbed about the poverty of the Carmelite house in Avignon, especially in view of the devotion of the friars, he went out alone to beg and in just one

[49] Mézières, *Life* ed. Smet, pp. 60–61; AASS, Jan. 29, III, 612–13 (secs. 9, 11, 13). Carmesson, *Vita,* in *Spec. carm.,* II, 174–75, also has a passage in which he praises Pierre's preaching in a conventional, exaggerated style. Mézières' account is not wholly without such characteristics, but it shows a greater touch of realism.

[50] Mézières, *Life,* ed. Smet, p. 62; AASS, Jan. 29, III, 613 (sec. 14); Carmesson, *Vita,* in *Spec. carm.,* II, 185.

day returned with the sum of one thousand florins. He was so loved and admired for his virtue that no one denied his requests for funds. Thus he nourished the brethren of his order wherever he was residing.[51]

Johann of Hildesheim, a Saxon, who belonged to the Carmelite province of Lower Germany, studied under the direction of Pierre de Thomas at this time and acted as his assistant, as he later recalled in his *Defensorium Ordinis Fratrum gloriosissimae Dei Genetricis Mariae de Monte Carmelo per modum dialogi,* a defense of the order's traditions written in 1370.[52] In this passage Johann claims to have been eyewitness of a second appearance of the Virgin Mary to Pierre de Thomas. He says that one year on the holy night of Pentecost, while sleeping near Pierre, as was his custom, he was awakened by the sound of sweet voices and mysterious movements. He arose at once and found that his master was also awake. He inquired what had happened. Pierre at first declined to tell him, but after Johann persisted in asking on bended knee, he agreed to tell him on condition that he would reveal it to no one

[51] Mézières, *Life,* ed. Smet, p. 61; AASS, Jan. 29, III, 613 (sec. 12); Carmesson, *Vita,* in *Spec. carm.,* II, 175; Wadding, *Vita,* pp. 13–14, also in *Spec. carm.,* II, 202. Carmesson associates this story with Pierre's first stay in Avignon. Mézières relates it shortly after his account of his second stay, but in a section which is not strictly chronological in arrangement.

[52] Hildesheim's *Defensorium* is published in *Spec. carm.,* I, 145–59. The passage about Pierre de Thomas is on p. 149: "Tempore foelicis recordationis Domini Clementis Papae Sexti fui studens in Avinione: servivique pro tunc, recolendae memoriae, Magistro Petro Thomae, tunc scholas regenti, viro magnae scientiae, magnae famae, magnaeque opinionis, quoad sanctitatem vitae." On the life of Johann of Hildesheim see MHC, p. 431; Zimmermann, "Carmes aux universités," p. 98; Trijntje Jantine Annette Scheepstra, *Van den heilighen drien Conighen: Middlenederlandse Teksten* (Groningen, 1914), pp. 1–14. Hildesheim was later lecturer on the Bible at Paris (1359), prior of Cassel (1361), provincial definitor (1362), and prior of Marienau, where he died in 1375. He is known chiefly for his work on the legend of the Three Kings of Cologne, which was fairly popular in the later Middle Ages.

during Pierre's lifetime. Pierre then reported that he had been sleeping with sadness of mind and fervent yearnings, desiring from the Virgin Mary the protection and preservation of his order, perhaps because of its dimunition in the Black Death. The Virgin appeared to him and said, "Do not worry, Pierre, for our Carmelite Order will endure to the end, because Elijah, the founder of the order, entreated for it at the transfiguration, and his request was granted." [53]

It is most probable that this vision was a dream of Johann of Hildesheim himself. It represents the faith of a medieval Carmelite, especially in the inclusion of the legend that Elijah founded the order. It is improbable that Pierre de Thomas himself had such a vision without revealing it to his close friend Philippe de Mézières, who would surely have included it in his biography. No trace of the story is found in that work, except as an addition to the least reliable of the manuscripts.[54]

Parraud, late nineteenth-century biographer of Pierre de Thomas, believed that he made a visit to Spain during his term of service as regent master at Avignon. This is not impossible, but it is not based upon any reliable source.[55] It has also been alleged erroneously that his first bishopric was that of Badajoz in Spain and that he was appointed by Clement VI in 1346. This assertion is the result of a double error. Pierre de Thomas' first bishopric was Patti (*Pactensis*) in Sicily, not Badajoz (*Pacensis*) in Spain. He was appointed to the see of

---

[53] Lezana, *Annales,* IV, 590, 599 (bis); Carmesson, *Vita,* in *Spec. carm.,* II, 178, note g; Wadding, *Vita,* pp. 68–71; Parraud, *Vie,* pp. 69–70.

[54] Mézières, *Life,* ed. Smet, p. 39. The addition is given as note d in AASS, Jan. 29, III, 638, where it is said to have occurred in Bologna rather than in Avignon. See also Wadding, *Vita,* p. 69.

[55] Parraud, *Vie,* pp. 72–73. His authority is a statement by Elisée de Saint Bernard, O. C. D., in a dedicatory preface to a French translation of the works of St. Theresa published in 1630.

Patti in 1354 but is sometimes confused with his predecessor, Petrus Theutonicus, a Franciscan, who was appointed as bishop of Patti in 1346.[56]

As regent master of the Carmelite school in Avignon, Pierre de Thomas reached the pinnacle of his academic career. It was probably in this period that he wrote two theological works which are known from their mention in contemporary sources, a commentary on the gospel of Matthew [57] and a treatise on the immaculate conception of the Virgin Mary.[58] Many other works have been attributed to him, but these were actually written not by Pierre de Thomas but by his namesake (in Latin) the Catalan Pere Tomas (c.1280–1350), a noted Franciscan theologian and doctor of Paris.[59] No copy of Pierre de

[56] Wadding, *Vita*, preface "Candido Lectori" and pp. 71–72, tells how he confused the two bishops of Patti named Petrus. In Pius Bonifacius Gams, *Series episcoporum ecclesiae catholicae* (Ratisbon, 1873), p. 11, Pierre de Thomas is wrongly listed as bishop of Badajoz in 1346. The bull of appointment of Pierre de Thomas to his first bishopric (*Reg Aven.* 126, fol. 75r; *Reg. Vat.* 225, fol. 57r) is published in Wadding, *Vita*, pp. 83–86, and in *Bull. carm.*, I, 81–82. The bull appointing his predecessor Petrus Theutonicus to the same bishopric on February 15, 1346, is published in *Bullarium franciscanum*, ed. Giovanni Giacinto Sbaraglia, *et al.*, VI (Rome, 1902), 173.

[57] Jean Trissa, O. Carm., *De magistris parisiensibus*, MHC, p. 390, also published as noted above, p. 23, n. 8; see also MHC, pp. 202, 377, 394. Trissa wrote about 1360.

[58] Alfonsus Pompei, O. F. M. Conv., "Sermones duo parisiensis saeculi XIV de conceptione Beatae Virginis Mariae et Scoti influxus in evolutionem sententiae immaculistae Parisiis," *Miscellanea francescana*, LV (1955), 542, where in a sermon preached at the University of Paris about the end of the fourteenth century, Gerard Rondel, a professor there, referred to a *Tractatus de Conceptione Virginis* written by Pierre de Thomas. In the same sermon "Quasi aurora consurgens," Rondel also mentioned a work of "Petrus Thomas hispanus" (*ibid.*, p. 544), whom he therefore distinguishes from Pierre de Thomas. Pompei discusses the date of this sermon, *ibid.*, p. 503.

[59] On the alleged works of Pierre de Thomas, see Cosmas de Villiers, *Bibliotheca carmelitana*, II (Lyons, 1752, and facsimile edition by Gabriel Wessels, O. Carm., Rome, 1927), 609; Trithemius, *De scriptoribus ecclesiasticis* in Johann Albert Fabricius, *Bibliotheca ecclesiastica*, III (Hamburg, 1718), 150, and Wadding, *Vita*, preface (no pagination) and p. 6. On the Catalan Pere Thomas, see above, p. 25, n. 13.

Thomas' theological writings is known to exist today. His only extant writings are letters.[60] Pierre seems to have been a frequent letter writer, for in one place Mézières refers to the many letters which he had received from him.[61]

The death of Pope Clement VI on December 6, 1352, marked the end of a period in the life of Pierre de Thomas. For more than a quarter of a century, he had lived and worked primarily within his order and had been primarily a schoolman. He had risen to a high place in the Carmelite educational system. As procurator of his order and later master of its school at Avignon, he was introduced to the world of practical politics. In this period, he won the friendship of powerful men in the Roman Curia, especially his countryman Talleyrand. Thus the way was prepared for the diplomatic activity which would soon become his principal field of service.

[60] There are two of these. One is merely a formal letter authorizing the preaching of the crusade (see below, pp. 177–78). The other is his appeal to the pope and the Holy Roman emperor to continue the crusade against Egypt; it is written in a highly literary style (see below, pp. 290–91).

[61] Mézières, Life, ed. Smet, pp. 164–65 (not in AASS). Villiers, Bibliotheca carmelitana, II, 609, published in 1752, mentions a collection of Pierre's letters in the Carmelite convent of Cologne. It is not known to be in existence today.

# 4

# Early Diplomatic Missions

ON DECEMBER 16, 1352, TEN DAYS AFTER THE DEATH OF Pope Clement VI, twenty-five cardinals met to elect his successor. They did not delay in selecting a new pope, partly because they feared that the king of France would seek to interfere in the election. On the morning of Tuesday, December 18, they elected Étienne Aubert, cardinal bishop of Ostia, who chose the title Innocent VI. The Cardinal Talleyrand de Périgord, friend and patron of Pierre de Thomas, was one of the most influential men in this conclave.[1]

This election marked a turning point in the life of Pierre de Thomas. The new pope's background and spirit were similar to his own. Both men had risen from the lower ranks of society through success in the educational world. Both were

[1] Martin Souchon, *Die Papstwahlen von Bonifaz VIII bis Urban VI und die Entstehung des Schismas 1378* (Brunswick, 1888), pp. 54–63. A fresh discussion of this election is Norman P. Zacour, "A Note on the Papal Election of 1352: the Candidacy of Jean Birel," *Traditio,* XIII (1957), 456–62.

conservative in their outlook, and neither had any time for extravagance or show. It may be, as Luke Wadding suggested three centuries later,[2] that Étienne Aubert was one of the cardinals who had already shown interest in Pierre, although this cannot be proved from a contemporary source. At any rate, it was not long before Innocent VI began to entrust diplomatic missions to Pierre de Thomas, who had been largely ignored by the worldly and aristocratic Clement VI.

Pierre was significantly honored by the papacy for the first time in the spring of 1353, when he was invited to preach a series of sermons in the procession which conveyed the body of Clement VI from Avignon to the Abbey of Chaise-Dieu in Auvergne, which the deceased had chosen for his final resting place. Although Philippe de Mézières asserts that the relatives of Clement VI joined with the college of cardinals in inviting Pierre to preach these sermons, it is probable that the invitation came primarily from the new Pope and his circle.[3]

The procession did not take place until the latter part of March, 1353. Meanwhile, after short funeral ceremonies on the day after his death, the body of Clement VI had lain in the cathedral of Notre Dame des Doms in Avignon. The procession, which included five cardinals who were relatives of the late Pope, three archbishops, and many other churchmen, took twelve days to go from Avignon to the Abbey of Chaise-Dieu. On each of these days Pierre de Thomas delivered a sermon to the crowds who gathered around Clement's bier. On April 6 the procession reached the town of Le Puy, and Clement's body was laid in state in the Carmelite church there. When it came time for Pierre to preach his daily sermon, he found that he was so hoarse from the fatigue of the journey and from the strain of earlier preaching that he could not

---

[2] Wadding, *Vita,* pp. 13–14, also in *Spec. carm.,* II, 202.
[3] Mézières, *Life,* ed. Smet, p. 62; AASS, Jan. 29, III, 613 (sec. 15).

speak above a whisper. He was deeply embarrassed. Looking
toward the image of the Virgin Mary, he prayed fervently to
her. Soon he was able to announce his text with a loud voice
and to preach as well as ever, for which he gave credit to the
Virgin Mary and to the merits of Pope Clement VI.[4] A few
days after this incident the procession reached its destination,
and the body of Clement VI was laid to rest in the magnificent
mausoleum which he had prepared for the purpose.

For the next six months, Pierre de Thomas probably continued to serve as regent master of the Carmelite school at
Avignon, since there is no record of other activities in this
period. Then in September, 1353, Innocent VI called upon
him to serve as a papal nuncio to Genoa, Milan, and Naples.
September 29 is the date of the earliest record of this mission.[5]

[4] Mézières, *Life,* ed. Smet, pp. 62–63; AASS, Jan. 29, III, 613 (sec.
15); Carmesson, *Vita,* in *Spec. carm.,* II, 175–76. Eugène Déprez, "Les
Funerailles de Clement VI et d'Innocent VI d'après les comptes de la
cour pontificale," *Mélanges d'archéologie et d'histoire de l'École française de Rome,* XX (1900), 235–39; Odoricus Raynaldus, *Annales
ecclesiastici ab anno quo desinit Cardinalis Caesar Baronius, MCXCVIII
usque ad annum MDXXXIV continuati,* XVI (Cologne, 1691), *ad ann.*
1352, chap. 24; S. Baluze, *Vitae paparum Avenionensium, hoc est
historia pontificum Romanorum qui in Gallia sederunt ab anno Christi
MCCCV usque ad annum MCCCXCIV,* ed. G. Mollat, I (Paris, 1914),
310; II (Paris, 1927), 423, 442; Louis Gallien, O. Carm., "De historia
priorum et procuratorum generalium et priorum provincialium," VI
(Ms. 787 in Bibliothèque de Besançon, paper, seventeenth century),
fol. 26v. Gallien reports that in the Carmelite church at Le Puy he saw
a very old tablet containing the following inscription: "Anno Domini
Mcccliii. vi. Aprilis—Jacuit in praesente Ecclesia corpus Clementis—
Papae VI comitantibus illud quinque Cardinalibus, Tribus Archiepis-
copis et pluribus aliis fratribus inter quos erat fr. Petrus Thome patriarcha Constantinopolitanus ac legatus sancti passagii Terrae Sanctae
tempore quo Alexandria fuit capta per Christianos, quique—electus
fuerat ab omnibus—ut qualibet die praedicare eis locis ubi pro exequiis
funeris contingeret celebrare. Arbitramur Coopertorium Ecclesiae etiam
Ligneum fuisse ex Eleemosinis D. D. Cardinalium conditum." Since this
tablet mentions the capture of Alexandria in 1365, it was evidently
erected after the death of Pierre de Thomas early in 1366.

[5] Letter of Innocent VI to the doge and commune of Genoa, *Reg.
Vat.* 235, fols. 193r–193v, published in *Bull. carm.,* III, 76–77, in
Raynaldus, *Annales ecclesiastici, ad ann.* 1353, chap. 11, in Eugène

On October 7, 1353, he received a letter requiring all ecclesiastics as far as Genoa and Milan to give him safe-conduct through their lands, to receive him hospitably, to give him two gold florins a day for his expenses and those of his company, and to aid him in enforcing any decrees against rebels which he might issue on the Pope's behalf.[6] Three days later, he received one hundred florins from the papal treasury for the expenses of his journey.[7] He did not leave Avignon before October 22, the date of one of the letters which he carried to Naples.[8]

Pierre de Thomas first went to Genoa to deliver a message from Innocent VI urging that city to make peace with Venice and Aragon. For three years, Venice and Genoa had been at war, largely because of their maritime rivalry in the East. Venice had induced the Byzantine emperor and Aragon to ally with her, but after a Genoese victory at the Bosporus in 1352, the Byzantines had been forced to withdraw. Before his death, Clement VI had tried to end this war, and this effort had been continued by Innocent VI in April, 1353, but neither pontiff had had any success. After a severe Genoese defeat in

---

Déprez, *Innocent VI (1352–1362). Lettres closes, patentes et curiales se rapportant à la France* (Bibliothèque des écoles françaises d'Athènes et de Rome, 3rd series, vol. IV, fasc. 1; Paris, 1909), no. 225, cols. 152–53, and in Pierre Gasnault and M.-H. Laurent, *Innocent VI (1352–1362). Lettres secrètes et curiales* (Bibliothèque des écoles françaises d'Athènes et de Rome, 3rd series, vol. IV, tome I; Paris, 1959–60), no. 569, pp. 184–85. A brief discussion of this mission is found in Smet's appendix I in his edition of Mézières, *Life,* pp. 189–93.

[6] *Reg. Vat.* 235, fols. 193v–194r; *Reg. Vat.* 244, fols. 55r–55v, published in Wadding, *Vita,* pp. 81–83; *Bull. carm.,* I, 80–81; Gasnault and Laurent, *Lettres d'Innocent VI,* no. 584, p. 192; no. 586, p. 193. Archival references to papal letters concerning this mission are based upon the microfilm mentioned in the Bibliography.

[7] *Reg. Vat.* 235, fol. 208v; K. H. Schäfer, *Die Ausgaben der apostolischen Kammer unter Benedikt XII, Klemens VI und Innocenz VI (1335–1362)* (Paderborn, 1914), p. 525.

[8] *Reg. Vat.* 235, fols. 207r–207v; Déprez, *Lettres d'Innocent VI,* no. 237, cols. 164–65; Gasnault and Laurent, *Lettres d'Innocent VI,* no. 606, pp. 200–01.

August at the battle of Lojera, off the coast of Sardinia, Innocent decided to make another effort for peace. When he sent Pierre to Genoa, he also sent representatives to Aragon and Venice urging them to send plenipotentiaries to Avignon by November 30 to talk peace.[9]

In his letter of September 29, 1353, to the doge and commune of Genoa, Innocent deplored the bitter conflict between Genoa and her two enemies. He expressed his deep sadness at hearing of the many lives lost at Lojera and his concern over the danger to souls that came through the war. He urged the doge to send ambassadors to Avignon by December 21 to discuss peace terms with the representatives of Venice and Aragon. The message of this letter was to be supplemented by an oral message given by its bearer, the Carmelite friar Pierre de Thomas.[10]

After delivering his message at Genoa, Pierre was to proceed to the court of Giovanni Visconti, archbishop and lord of Milan, to deliver a letter written to him by the Pope on October 12. It urged the archbishop to aid the nuncio in his mission to the Genoese by persuasion or, if necessary, by force.[11]

It is unlikely that Pierre de Thomas ever delivered the Pope's message to Giovanni Valente, the doge of Genoa, for a radical political change occurred in the city even before he left Avignon. Genoa was completely crushed by her defeat at Lojera. Since her enemies were now in control of the sea, she found it necessary to submit to the overlordship of Giovanni Visconti, who controlled the farmlands of north Italy, her

[9] Heinrich Kretschmayr, *Geschichte von Venedig,* II (Gotha, 1920), 207–09; Samuele Romanin, *Storia documentata di Venezia,* III (Venice, 1855), 151–70; Suzanne Duvergé, "La Rôle de la papauté dans la guerre de l'Aragon contre Gênes (1351–1356)," *Mélanges d'archéologie et d'histoire,* L (1933), 221–34.

[10] See note 5 above.

[11] *Reg. Vat.* 235, fol. 195r; *Bull. carm.,* III, 77–78; Gasnault and Laurent, *Lettres d'Innocent VI,* no. 596, p. 196.

only source of food. Under the new order, the Genoese continued to enjoy their own laws but yielded control over their foreign relations to the Visconti. On October 9, Valente resigned as doge, and Marquis Guglielmo Pallavicino of Cassano became governor of Genoa in the name of Visconti.[12] News of this development probably reached Avignon by October 26, 1353, when Innocent VI acknowledged receipt of a letter from Giovanni Visconti and expressed joy at the news which it contained.[13] Since this letter is dated only four days after the latest one in which Pierre de Thomas' name appears, it is possible that he had not yet left Avignon when it was written and that he carried it to Milan. Certainly upon his arrival in north Italy, he found it necessary to negotiate directly with Giovanni Visconti about the affairs of Genoa.

Pierre de Thomas' part in the peace negotiations between Genoa and Venice was limited to delivering the Pope's messages. Until the close of 1353, the papacy actively sought to bring the war to an end. Fair promises were made by all concerned, but nothing came of the negotiations.[14] The Visconti were ready for peace,[15] but the Venetians wanted to fight on to total victory. They formed an alliance with the more important princes of north Italy and the Holy Roman emperor against the Visconti, whose intrigues, however, prevented it from becom-

[12] Romanin, *Storia di Venezia*, III, 170; Agostino Giustiniani, *Annali della Repubblica di Genova*, 2 vols. (3rd. ed., Genoa, 1854), II, 93; Smet's note in his edition of Mézières, *Life*, p. 190.

[13] *Reg. Vat.* 235, fol. 210r; Gasnault and Laurent, *Lettres d'Innocent VI*, no. 608, p. 201.

[14] Letters of Innocent VI to Giovanni Visconti and to the doge of Venice, December 9–18, 1353, *Reg. Vat.* 235, fols. 227v–229r, 232v; Gasnault and Laurent, *Lettres d'Innocent VI*, nos. 663, 666, 668–69, 672, pp. 227–31. These letters are discussed by Joachim Smet in his edition of Mézières, *Life*, pp. 191–92.

[15] Giovanni sent Petrarch to Venice in November to plead for peace, as noted in Gustav Koerting, *Petrarcas Leben und Werke* (Leipzig, 1878), pp. 302–05. The Venetians were not interested.

ing very effective. Throughout 1354, the war went badly for
Venice. After a decisive defeat in November, Venice was
ready for peace. A treaty was signed on June 1, 1356, between
the republic and the three nephews of Giovanni Visconti,
Matteo II, Bernabo, and Galeazzo, as lords of Genoa. They
had succeeded their uncle at his death in October, 1354. The
Visconti continued to rule Genoa till 1356, when she regained
her independence.[16]

After delivering his message at Milan, Pierre de Thomas
proceeded to the court of King Louis and Queen Joanna of
Naples. His mission to them seems to have been the principal
purpose of his journey to Italy, for it alone is mentioned by
Philippe de Mézières.[17] This mission was occasioned by an
appeal to the Pope from Louis of Durazzo, a nephew of the
Cardinal Talleyrand,[18] against his cousin Louis of Taranto,
king of Naples. Ever since the accession of Queen Joanna in
1343, the Tarantini and the Durazzeschi had been contending
for pre-eminence in the kingdom. In 1347, the Tarantini had
gained the upper hand when their leader, Louis of Taranto,
had married Joanna and had been crowned as king. Louis of
Durazzo had been the head of his family since the death of his
brother Charles in 1348, during the Hungarian invasion.[19] He
was dissatisfied because he had received no princely estates,

[16] Kretschmayr, *Geschichte von Venedig*, II, 209–11; Romanin,
*Storia di Venezia*, III, 170–73, 178–95; Duvergé, "La Rôle de la papauté," pp. 235–43, 248–49; Giustiniani, *Annali di Genova*, II, 93–97.

[17] Mézières, *Life*, ed. Smet, p. 64; AASS, Jan. 29, III, 613 (sec. 16).
Mézières knew nothing about the true purpose of this mission to
Naples and said that Pierre went to that kingdom because of some
great business concerning the church of God and the kingdom of
Apulia.

[18] His mother was the cardinal's sister Agnes de Périgord.

[19] A good brief account of the earlier struggles of these families is
found in Guillaume Mollat, *Les Papes d'Avignon* (9th ed., Paris, 1949),
pp. 277 ff. A detailed account is Émile G. Léonard, *Histoire de Jeanne
Iʳᵉ, reine de Naples, comtesse de Provence (1343–1382)*, vols. I and II:
*La Jeunesse de la reine Jeanne Iʳᵉ* (Monaco, Paris, 1932).

such as the king had given to his brothers. He demanded the custody of his two nieces, daughters of Charles of Durazzo and Queen Joanna's sister Maria. His argument was based on an alleged will left by their father appointing him as their guardian. His real interest was in their lands and their rights to the throne. King Louis refused to grant his cousin's demands, whereupon Louis of Durazzo appealed to Pope Innocent VI.[20]

Innocent determined to seek justice for Louis of Durazzo. He knew that the king of Naples ruled only for the benefit of his family and friends and cared nothing for justice. The Pope was also probably influenced by Talleyrand, who naturally supported his nephew's cause. Innocent wrote to King Louis and Queen Joanna and urged them to deliver the two daughters of Charles of Durazzo and their lands to their paternal uncle Louis, as provided in their father's will. The rulers of Naples declined to do so on the ground that they knew of no will of Charles of Durazzo. In frequent letters, King Louis complained about Talleyrand's influence against him in Avignon.[21]

Pierre de Thomas carried Innocent's reply to the king's assertions. In a letter of October 5, 1353, the Pope again ordered that the two girls be surrendered to their uncle. He declared that, even if Charles' will had not been found, his wishes could easily be confirmed by witnesses worthy of confidence. It would have been easy for such a will to be lost in the disturbances of the Hungarian invasion, which struck especially at the house of Charles of Durazzo. He rebuked King

---

[20] Léonard, *Histoire de Jeanne I^re*, vol. III: *Le Règne de Louis de Tarente* (Monaco, Paris, 1936), pp. 31–46, cf. pp. 3, 10–11, 27.

[21] This information is known from a letter of Pope Innocent VI to Louis of Naples, October 5, 1353, *Reg. Vat.* 235, fols. 197v–198r; Gasnault and Laurent, *Lettres d'Innocent VI*, no. 581, p. 191; summary in Mézières, *Life*, ed. Smet, p. 192.

Louis for his complaints against the cardinal of Périgord, whom
Innocent had never heard say anything in public or in private
against the king of Naples, although he rightly supported the
legitimate claims of his nephews. The pontiff urged the king
to write to Talleyrand in kindly terms, for he could be of
assistance to him in many ways.[22] By Pierre de Thomas, the
Pope also sent letters to the archbishops of Capua and Naples
and to Niccolo Acciajuoli, seneschal of the kingdom of Naples,
urging them to aid Pierre in his mission.[23] Similar letters were
sent to the king's brother Robert of Taranto, titular emperor
of Constantinople and to Robert's wife, Marie de Bourbon.[24]

These messages accomplished nothing at the court of Naples.
The rulers of Naples now claimed to have discovered a will
of Charles of Durazzo in which he had appointed Queen
Joanna, their maternal aunt, as guardian of his two young
daughters. They sent a copy of this will to the Pope. They also
asserted that the girls' mother, Princess Maria, was opposed
to having them and their estates delivered to Louis of Durazzo
and had presented a petition to the royal court to that effect.
The royal court therefore did not execute the Pope's order.
The lands of the princesses had never been confiscated but
were in fact exempt from royal taxation.[25] Innocent replied to
King Louis the following July (1354). He acknowledged receipt of copies of Charles' will and Maria's petition. He noted
that, upon his return from Naples, Pierre de Thomas had
explained the viewpoint of King Louis and Queen Joanna. Innocent thanked the king for his prompt replies to his letters

[22] *Ibid.*

[23] Letters of October 7, 1353, *Reg. Vat.* 235, fol. 198v; Gasnault
and Laurent, *Lettres d'Innocent VI,* no. 585, pp. 192–93.

[24] Dated October 22, 1353, *Reg. Vat.* 235, fols. 207r–207v; Déprez,
*Lettres d'Innocent VI,* no. 237, cols. 164–65; Gasnault and Laurent,
*Lettres d'Innocent VI,* no. 606, pp. 200–01.

[25] Letter to Innocent VI in Naples, Archivio di Stato, Registro di
Nicolo d'Alife, fol. 94, cited by Léonard, *Histoire de Jeanne I^{re},* III,
47, and n. 4.

but showed that he was still not satisfied that King Louis was doing right by Maria and her children. He insisted that he could accept no petition from Maria as valid until she was released from the close custody in which she was being held.[26] In this quarrel, it is difficult to tell on which side justice lay, since both the king and Louis of Durazzo desired the guardianship of the two princesses purely for selfish reasons.

The mission of Pierre de Thomas to Naples also failed to bring about a reconciliation between King Louis and Cardinal Talleyrand, so desired by the Pope. On December 15, 1353, an envoy of King Louis, the Genoese knight, Goffredo Larchario, was in Avignon, and Innocent VI took the opportunity to talk with him about the king's attitude toward Talleyrand, so that the envoy could convey the message back to his master.[27] In February, 1354, Innocent arranged a meeting between two of Louis' ambassadors and Talleyrand, in spite of the king's express instructions to them to the contrary, in a further effort to improve relations between the cardinal and the court of Naples.[28]

Pierre de Thomas probably returned to Avignon to report

[26] Letter of July 1, 1354, *Reg. Vat.* 236, fols. 133r–133v, in *Bull. carm.,* III, 81, and in F. Cerasoli, "Innocenzo VI e Giovanna I di Napoli, documenti inediti dell'Archivio Vaticano," *Archivio storico per le province napoletane,* XXII (1897), 364–65 (document XXXII). Innocent also wrote to Queen Joanna and other important persons in the kingdom of Naples, requesting them to urge King Louis to obey the Pope's commands. These letters are in *Reg. Vat.* 236, fols. 133v–134r, published in Cerasoli, *op. cit.,* p. 366 (document XXXIII). The others were the chamberlain, Raymond des Baux, count of Soleto, the knights Giovanni Extrandi and Matteo de Porta of Salerno, the archbishops of Capua, Taranto, and Brindisi, and the bishop of Apt.

[27] Letter of Innocent VI to Louis of Naples, December 15, 1353, *Reg. Vat.* 235, fols. 230r–230v; Cerasoli, "Innocenzo VI e Giovanna I di Napoli," XXII, 356–57 (document XX); Déprez, *Lettres d'Innocent VI,* no. 272, cols. 199–200; Gasnault and Laurent, *Lettres d'Innocent VI,* no. 670, p. 230.

[28] Letter of Innocent VI to King Louis and Queen Joanna, February 15, 1354, *Reg. Vat.* 236, fol. 33v; Cerasoli, *op. cit.,* p. 357 (document XXI).

to Innocent before the close of 1353. Perhaps he made the journey at the same time as the Neapolitan ambassador Goffredo Larchario, who was at Avignon on December 14, as noted above. Pierre's first diplomatic mission had been a modest one, in which his task was merely to deliver letters and a supplementary oral message. There is no evidence that he had part in any negotiations. Since the principal purpose of the mission was so closely related to the interests of his friend the Cardinal Talleyrand de Périgord, he may have been appointed to it largely at the cardinal's suggestion. Although political conditions prevented his efforts from being successful, there can be no doubt that Pierre did his best, for he was soon entrusted with greater tasks.

Toward the end of 1354, after a silent year which followed his first mission, Pierre de Thomas was appointed as the chief ambassador of Pope Innocent VI to King Stephen Dushan (1331–1355), the most powerful medieval king of Serbia, to discuss the union of the Serbian Orthodox and Roman Catholic churches.[29]

Stephen Dushan had first expressed an interest in church union more than seven years earlier. In a letter to the Serbian monarch dated March 2, 1347, Pope Clement VI noted that he had been informed by the Latin bishop Marcus of Scutari that Dushan desired to abjure the schism which divided the Eastern Orthodox churches from the Roman church and to be received into the Catholic fold with his people. Clement urged King Stephen Dushan to preserve in his good intentions and to heed the advice which the bishop of Scutari would bring from the Holy See. The Pope expressed a desire to receive word directly from Dushan through letters which would confirm the king's in-

---

[29] Mézières, *Life,* ed. Smet, pp. 64–70; AASS, Jan. 29, III, 613–14 (secs. 17–22). Smet discusses this mission in Appendix II to his edition of Mézières, *Life,* pp. 193–96.

terest in church union.[30] Not until 1354 did Dushan send such a letter.

Meanwhile Stephen Dushan continued to follow the traditional policy of his family and to support the autonomous Serbian Orthodox church, normally in communion with Constantinople, as the state religion of his kingdom. In April, 1346, about a year before his first overtures to Avignon, he had led the clergy of Serbia to create a national patriarchate with its seat at Pech. The new patriarch of Serbia, Joannicius, then crowned Dushan as emperor of the Serbs and the Greeks. Thus the Serbian church asserted its equality with the Byzantine church, and Stephen Dushan assumed an equality with the emperor at Constantinople, whom he hoped some day to supplant.[31]

Stephen Dushan's Orthodox religious policy is clearly reflected in his great law code, the *Zakonik*, published in 1349, two years after he expressed interest in church union. In this code, the Roman Catholic faith is called "the Latin heresy." It was tolerated in regions where its adherents were in the majority and among foreign settlers in Orthodox territory, such as the numerous German miners and merchants, but all proselytism by Latins was forbidden. All apostates from Orthodoxy to Roman Catholicism were faced with exile and loss of property. Latin clergy who sought to convert the Orthodox were

[30] Raynaldus, *Annales ecclesiastici, ad ann.* 1347, chap. 30. On the same date, Clement sent a letter to Nicolaus Buche, prothojusticiar of the kingdom of Rascia, and to others in the Serbian court, asking them to encourage Stephen in his good intentions. These letters are published in Augustin Theiner, ed., *Vetera monumenta historica Hungariam sacram illustrantia*, 2 vols. (Rome, 1859–60), I, 734–35 (hereafter abbreviated TVMH), and in *Magyar Diplomacziai Emlékek az Anjou-Koraból (Monumenta Hungariae historica, Acta externa*, 4 osztály, part A), ed. Gusztav Wenzel, II (Budapest, 1875), 218–19. See also Josef Konstantin Jirecek, *Geschichte der Serben*, I (Gotha, 1911), 407.

[31] Jerecek, *Geschichte der Serben*, I, 387–88; Alois Hudal, *Die serbisch-orthodoxe Nationalkirche* (Graz and Leipzig, 1922), p. 26.

threatened with imprisonment, and their churches could be confiscated.[32]

Stephen Dushan pursued a militant anti-Latin program in this period. In May, 1350, Cardinal Guy d'Auvergne wrote from Padua to the doge of Venice, the king of Hungary, and the grand master of the Hospitallers that, according to the testimony of reliable witnesses, King Stephen was seeking to convert Latin Christians to Orthodoxy by force and violence. Catholics were forced to be baptized again in the Eastern rite, a practice which was contrary to canon law. Guy urged these rulers to protect the Catholics of Serbia as much as they could and to intercede with Stephen Dushan on their behalf.[33] Stephen Dushan was building a large empire of diverse nationalities, and he evidently sought to create a new national unity by inducing all his subjects, regardless of their background, to join the Serbian Orthodox national church.

In 1351, Pope Clement VI expressed concern about religious conditions in Serbia. He had learned that Catholics in that land were being forced to repeat the sacrament of confirmation as well as baptism in the Orthodox rite. He criticized the Orthodox for rejecting the *filioque* clause and for insisting upon the use of leavened bread in the eucharist. Sometimes they even tore apart the unleavened hosts of the Latins with their hands or even trampled them underfoot. Clement also

[32] S. Novaković, *Zakonik Stefana Dushana, tsara Srpskog, 1349 i 1354* (Belgrade, 1898), arts. 6–8, pp. 11–13, cf. art. 153, p. 120, which illustrates that special provisions were made for foreign nationals in Serbia. The provisions of the *Zakonik* involving Latins are discussed by Matthew Spinka, *A History of Christianity in the Balkans, a Study in the Spread of Byzantine Culture among the Slavs* (Studies in Church History, vol. I; Chicago, 1933), pp. 146–47. See also Hudal, *Die serbisch-orthodoxe Nationalkirche*, p. 27.

[33] Sime Ljubic, ed., *Listine o odnosajih izmedju juznoga slavenstva i mletacke republike*, III (Monumenta spectantia historiam Slavorum meridionalium, vol. III; Zagreb, 1872), 186 (hereafter abbreviated MHSM); *Mon. Hung. hist., Acta externa*, II, 383–84; Jireček, *Geschichte der Serben*, I, 407. Jules Gay, *Le Pape Clément VI et les affaires d'Orient (1342–1352)* (Paris, 1904), p. 160.

had heard of serious irregularities among the Catholics of Serbia. Some archbishops and bishops were conferring holy orders contrary to canon law. Dispensations for marriages within the prohibited degrees were being granted without proper authority. Certain members of mendicant orders in Serbia were pretending to be legates of the Holy See. On September 1, 1351, Clement appointed three nuncios to Serbia to seek to win schismatics to unity with Rome and to eliminate these irregularities among Catholics. These nuncios were the archbishops of Durazzo and Ragusa and Bartholomew, bishop of Trau.[34]

There is no further record of relations between the papacy and Serbia until Stephen Dushan again took the initiative in 1354. He sent three ambassadors who arrived at Avignon early in the summer. They had been in Venice on June 16, when they had received letters of recommendation to the Pope from the Venetian republic.[35] The three envoys were Bosidarius, *judex generalis* of the kingdom, Nestegus, governor of Serrai, and Damian of Cattaro. Innocent VI acknowledged their arrival in a letter of August 29 to King Stephen Dushan. They had brought letters from the king in which he had expressed a desire for union with the Roman church. Stephen Dushan acknowledged the church of Rome as the mother, teacher, and mistress of all Christians, and the Roman pontiff as the universal father and lord and the true successor of the Blessed Peter, chief of the apostles. On behalf of their master, the ambassadors besought the Pope to send some devout men to Serbia to continue the work of reformation, which they said was already begun.[36]

[34] TVMH, I, 802–03; Raynaldus, *Annales ecclesiastici, ad ann.* 1351, chaps 20–21. Gay, *Clément VI et les affaires d'Orient,* pp. 160–61.
[35] MHSM, III, 264.
[36] Letter of Innocent VI to Stephen, king of Rascia (old name for Serbia), August 29, 1354, *Reg Vat.* 236, fols. 154v–155v, in TVMH, II, 8–9, and in *Mon. Hung. hist., Acta externa,* II, 441–43; Jireček, *Geschichte der Serben,* I, 408.

Bartholomew, bishop of Trau, a member of Clement VI's embassy of 1351, apparently returned to Avignon with the king's ambassadors. In his letter to the Pope, Stephen Dushan praised Bartholomew for his effective work toward the union of Serbia with the Roman church. Bartholomew certified the king's good intentions. He also reported Stephen Dushan's concern about the afflictions which the Christians of the East were suffering from the ravages of the Turks and conveyed the Serbian king's request for a papal appointment as captain-general of the Christian forces against them.[37]

In his letter to Innocent VI, which is known to us from the Pope's reply, Stephen Dushan confessed that some Roman Catholics in Serbia had been forced to repeat the sacraments of baptism and confirmation in the Orthodox rite. He promised that this practice would not be repeated and petitioned the Pope to absolve those who had thus been constrained to violate canon law and to restore them to their rightful relationship to the Roman church. He admitted that some Latin clergymen, both regular and secular, had been imprisoned, perhaps for proselytism, and promised to release them and to permit them

---

[37] Letter of Innocent VI to Stephen of Rascia, December 24, 1354, *Reg. Vat.* 236, fols. 222v–224v; TMVH, II, 11–13; Wadding, *Vita,* pp. 87–97; Luke Wadding, *Annales Minorum seu trium Ordinum a Sancto Francisco Institutorum,* VIII (3rd ed., Quaracchi, 1932), 109–12; *Bull. carm.,* II, 84–86; Abraham Bzovius, *Annalium ecclesiasticorum post Caesarem Baronium continuatio,* XIV (Cologne, 1618), cols. 1170–72; Raynaldus, *Annales ecclesiastici, ad ann.* 1354, chaps 28–29; *Mon. Hung. hist., Acta externa,* II, 445–46. In the above publications, this letter is erroneously dated December 25 by Wadding, *Vita,* and *Bull. carm.* and January 6 by Bzovius. See also Oskar Halecki, *Un Empereur de Byzance à Rome, vingt ans de travail pour l'union des églises et pour la défense de l'empire d'Orient, 1355–1375* (Travaux historiques de la Société des Sciences et des Lettres de Varsovie, vol. VIII; Warsaw, 1930), pp. 22–25. According to C. Eubel, *Hierarchia catholica medii aevi,* I (2nd. ed., Münster, 1913), 177, 490, Bartholomew was a canon of Contantinople who was appointed bishop of Cattaro in 1348, translated to the see of Trau in 1349, and died before the close of 1361.

to function with complete freedom. Latins had also been subject to insults and injuries in Serbia, and Catholic prelates had been unjustly ejected from their churches and monasteries. Stephen Dushan pledged that all former Catholic churches and monasteries would be restored to their rightful occupants except for six monasteries that could not be restored without scandal and imminent danger.[38]

The precise reasons for the abrupt change in Stephen Dushan's religious policy in 1354 are unknown. In view of the general history of Serbian negotiations with the papacy,[39] it may be assumed that his motives were purely political. Since it is known that his chief ambition was to capture Constantinople, it is probable that he hoped to gain papal assistance for this project. Four years earlier, he had unsuccessfully sought Venetian aid for the capture of Constantinople and had been willing to give the republic either the despotat of Epirus or the Genoese colony of Pera if they had aided him.[40] His concern about the growing power of the Turks was unfeigned, since he would need to overcome them as well as the Byzantines in order to achieve the mastery of the East which he desired. It has also been suggested that by accepting Catholicism Stephen Dushan hoped to protect his realm against King Louis of Hungary, who was planning to invade it to gain more land for his kingdom under the guise of conducting a crusade against schismatics.[41] In fact, Louis did attack in June, 1354. However, it is difficult to believe that Stephen Dushan, a shrewd and practical statesman, expected Louis to be deterred by a change in Serbia's religious status. As will become evident in

[38] Letter of Innocent VI cited in previous note.
[39] Spinka, *Christianity in the Balkans,* pp. 81–84, 129–39.
[40] MHSM, III, 174–79, 181.
[41] This motive for Stephen's action is given in a life of Innocent VI by Werner, a canon of Bonn, published in Baluze, *Vitae paparum Avenionensium,* I, 333.

the following chapter, the common faith which he shared with them did not restrain Louis from making war against the Venetians in spite of the Pope's expressed displeasure.[42]

Stephen Dushan had little to lose by these overtures to Avignon, since he and his people were in the bad graces of the Byzantine church. The patriarch of Constantinople Callistus had excommunicated the Serbians because they had set up a new national patriarchate with full powers of appointment and supervision over the metropolitans and bishops of the kingdom, including some who were serving in regions which prior to recent Serbian conquests had long been subject to Constantinople. Thus they had ignored the traditional rights of the ecumenical patriarch.[43]

Although he had acknowledged receipt of Stephen Dushan's letter in August, Innocent VI did not take formal action upon it until December 24, 1354. On that date, he announced the appointment of two nuncios to Serbia to discuss the church union question. One of these was Pierre de Thomas, who was described as a man outstandingly religious, praiseworthy in life, manners, and conversation, and full of the fear of God. The other was Bishop Bartholomew of Trau, who was being sent back to Serbia to continue his good work, especially since

[42] Discussions of Stephen's motives by modern scholars are found in Neculai Jorga, "Latins et Grecs d'Orient et l'établissement des Turcs en Europe, 1342–1362," *Byzantinische Zeitschrift,* XV (1906), 217; Halecki, *Un Empereur,* pp. 9–10, 24–25; Gregorio Novak, "L'alleanza veneto-serba nel secolo XIV," *Archivio veneto-tridentino,* VIII (1925), 19–28, 35–39.

[43] Hudal, *Die serbisch-orthodoxe Nationalkirche,* p. 26; Jireček, *Geschichte der Serben,* I, 389; Joseph Müller, "Byzantinische Analekten," *Sitzungsberichte der philosophisch-historischen Classe der kaiserlichen Akademie der Wissenschaften,* IX (Vienna, 1852), 357–64, 403–10. Two documents first published in the foregoing article are also published in Franz Xavier Miklosich and Joseph Müller, *Acta et diplomata Graeca medii aevi sacra et profana collecta,* I (Vienna, 1860), 560–64.

Stephen Dushan had expressed affection for him. These men would promote sound doctrine in Serbia and endeavor to uproot schism and error. For the love of the Holy See and the remission of his sins, the king was urged to receive them and aid them in their labors. The Pope expressed the hope that he might one day be able to grant Stephen Dushan the office of captain-general of Christian forces against the Turks and all his other legitimate desires, but he did not grant him the office immediately.[44] In his correspondence, Innocent consistently addressed Dushan as king of Rascia, ignoring the imperial title which he had assumed with the compliance of the Serbian Sabor (Assembly) in 1346.

In preparation for his Serbian mission, to give him the necessary status, Pierre de Thomas was appointed bishop of Patti and Lipari on November 17, 1354, in the bull *Pastoralis officii*.[45] He succeeded Petrus Theutonicus, O. F. M., who had served from 1346 until his death early in 1354.[46] The payment of the *servitia communia* for this bishopric, two hundred florins, is recorded four days after his appointment.[47]

---

[44] See above, note 37. Novak, "L'alleanza," pp. 35–36, says that Innocent granted Dushan the title which he had requested, but the verb in the letter is subjunctive, expressing a hope. In his letter of August 29 (note 36 above), Innocent had promised to send some discreet men to Serbia.

[45] Mézières, *Life,* ed. Smet, p. 65; AASS, Jan. 29, III, 613 (sec. 17). Bull of appointment in *Reg. Aven.* 126, *fol.* 75r; *Reg. Vat.* 225, fol. 57r; Wadding, *Vita,* pp. 83–86; *Bull. carm.,* I, 81–82. The copy in the Avignon registers is illegible in part because of stains, as noted by Smet in his edition of Mézières, *Life,* p. 65, n. 6. This is also apparent in the microfilm mentioned in the Bibliography. Letters announcing his appointment to the clergy and people of his diocese and to the archbishop of Messina are in *Reg. Aven.* 126, fol. 75v, and *Reg. Vat.* 225, fols. 57r–57v.

[46] Eubel, *Hierarchia catholica,* I, 384.

[47] Hermann Hoberg, *Taxae pro communibus servitiis ex libris obligationum ab anno 1295 usque ad annum 1455 confectis* (Studi e testi, vol. 144; Vatican City, 1949), p. 91.

In addition to the letter to Stephen Dushan, the two ambassadors were entrusted with similar letters to his wife Queen Helena and his son Urosh, king of Serbia.[48] A general letter, dated December 25, 1354, was sent to all the princes, counts, and barons of Serbia, urging them to receive the papal nuncios favorably and to assist them in their efforts.[49] On the same date, specific letters with a similar message were sent to Deanus, sebastocrat of Serbia, to Gaycus, grand logothete, to the noble Oliverius, despot of Serbia, to Prelubus, caesar of Serbia, to Count Grulbe of Cattaro, chamberlain of Serbia, and to Palmann the German, captain of the mercenaries in the service of the king of Serbia.[50]

The Pope also wrote to the spiritual leaders of Serbia. In a letter to Joannicius, patriarch of Serbia, Innocent reiterated the claim of the Roman Catholic Church to be the only true faith founded by Christ himself. He mentioned King Stephen's interest in church union and announced the mission of his nuncios. He called upon him as the chief pastor of the Serbian people, although illicitly, to receive the nuncios as the ministers of God, to follow their teachings, and to assist them in their

[48] Reg. Vat. 236, fols. 224v–225r; Wadding, Vita, p. 97; Annales Minorum, VIII, 112; Bull. carm., II, 86–87; TVMH, II, 13. Urosh was crowned as king of Serbia when his father was crowned as emperor.

[49] Reg. Aven. 127, fols. 32r–32v; Reg. Vat. 227, fols. 4v–5r; Reg. Vat. 236, fol. 226v.

[50] Reg. Vat. 236, fols. 226r–227r; TVMH, II, 15–16; Wadding, Annales Minorum, VIII, 113. The letter to Palmann the German is published in Karl Heinrich Schaefer, Deutsche Ritter und Edelknechte in Italien während des 14 Jahrhunderts, 4 vols. (Quellen und Forschungen aus dem Gebiete der Geschichte herausgegeben von der Goerres-Gesellschaft, Bände 15, 16, 25; Paderborn, 1911–40), II, 157–58. (Vols. 3 and 4 of this work are both in Band 25 of the Quellen und Forschungen.)

[51] Letter of January 5, 1355; Reg. Vat. 236, fols. 225r–226r; Wadding, Vita, pp. 98–102; Annales Minorum, VIII, 112–13; Bull. carm., I, 82–83; Bzovius, Annales ecclesiastici, XIV, cols. 1174–75; TVMH, II, 13–14; partially in Raynaldus, Annales ecclesiastici, ad ann. 1354, chap. 27. The date of this bull is given erroneously in some of the

work.[51] Joannicius died before the nuncios reached Serbia.[52] A letter was also sent to the Orthodox clergy of Serbia.[53] and to the Roman Catholic clergy in that kingdom,[54] asking for their cooperation in the negotiations.

On December 27, 1354, Pierre de Thomas and Bartholomew of Trau received a commission to work to bring the Orthodox church of Serbia into full submission to the papacy and to correct certain abuses among the Catholics of Serbia. It was virtually identical with the one issued by Clement VI in 1351 to Bartholomew and two other prelates.[55]

On November 21, 1354, the nuncios received three hundred gold florins from the papal treasury.[56] On December 24, they received a safe-conduct from the papal chancery combined with an authorization to procure four gold florins a day from ecclesiastical persons or others through whose lands they should travel on their way to Serbia.[57] They also received numerous spiritual faculties for their own comfort and for the aid of

---

publications. The correct date is given above; it is based upon the microfilm mentioned in the Bibliography, as are all precise archival references and dates concerning this mission.

[52] Jireček, *Geschichte der Serben,* I, 409.

[53] *Reg. Aven.* 127, fols. 31v–32r; *Reg. Vat.* 227, fol. 4v; TVMH, II, 14–15; Wadding, *Annales Minorum,* VIII, 115. The letter is dated December 24, 1354.

[54] *Reg. Aven.* 127, fols. 32v–33r (date illegible); *Reg. Vat.* 227, fols. 5r–5v (December 25, 1354); *Reg. Vat.* 236, fols. 229r–229v (December 24, 1354).

[55] *Reg. Aven.* 127, fols. 31r–31v; *Reg. Vat.* 227, fols. 4r–4v; *Reg. Vat.* 236, fols. 227r–227v; Wadding, *Vita,* pp. 103–07; *Annales Minorum,* VIII, 113–14; *Bull carm.,* I, 87–88; Raynaldus, *Annales ecclesiastici, ad ann.* 1354, chap. 26; Bzovius, *Annales ecclesiastici,* XIV, cols. 1173–74; TVMH, II, 16–17. On the commission of 1351, see above p. 83.

[56] *Reg. Vat.* 237, fol. 69r. The same detail is given from another source in Schaefer, *Die Ausgaben der apostolischen Kammer unter Benedikt XII, Klemens VI und Innocenz VI,* p. 556.

[57] *Reg. Vat.* 236, fol. 230v, cited by Smet in his edition of Mézières, *Life,* p. 194, n. 2.

deserving Catholics whom they might meet in their travels.[58]

Though the latest of the letters concerning the Serbian mission is dated early in January, 1355, Pierre and Bartholomew remained in Avignon until at least February 1, the date of a letter carried by Pierre from the Pope to the Holy Roman Emperor Charles IV in the interest of Cardinal Talleyrand's nephew Robert of Durazzo,[59] younger brother of that Louis of Durazzo whose complaints against the king of Naples had occasioned Pierre's mission to that kingdom.

Innocent VI aimed to secure Robert's release from imprisonment by Jacopo of Savoy and commissioned Pierre de Thomas to work for this end while passing through Italy on his way to Serbia. Robert had been arrested on July 12, 1354, while traveling from Avignon to Milan. Jacopo's wife, Sibyl, was really responsible for his arrest. She was angry because her nephew Robert des Baux had been murdered in Naples at the instigation of his wife, Princess Maria, Queen Joanna's sister, and she at first believed that Robert of Durazzo had helped to plan the murder and was on his way to marry Maria. Too late she learned that he was actually planning to seek the hand of a niece of Giovanni Visconti. Sibyl's husband, hard-pressed to explain the arrest, blamed it on the fact that Robert's father

[58] *Reg. Aven.* 127, fol. 32v; *Reg. Vat.* 227, fol. 5r; *Reg. Vat,* 236, fols. 227v–229r. These faculties are summarized in Raynaldus, *Annales ecclesiastici, ad ann.,* 1354, chap. 27. For example, the nuncios were authorized to grant dispensations to twenty couples who had unwittingly married within the prohibited degrees. Thus they would be able to aid those who had been victimized by those in Serbia who falsely claimed the power to grant such dispensations, as noted in their commission (and in the one of 1351).

[59] *Reg. Vat.* 237, fols. 19r–19v, published in Francesco Cerasoli and Carlo Cipolla, "Innocenzo VI e casa Savoia, documenti dell'Archivio Vaticano," *Miscellanea di storia italiana,* XXXVIII (1902), 167–68; summary in Emil Werunsky, *Excerpta ex registris Clementis VI et Innocentii VI summorum pontificum historiam sancti romani imperii sub regimine Karoli IV illustrantia* (Innsbruck, 1885), p. 92, where no mention of Pierre de Thomas is made.

had despoiled his father of the principality of Achaia.[60] As early as a week after his arrest, Innocent VI had begun to work for Robert's release, but though he employed every stratagem at his command, he had thus far been unsuccessful.[61]

Pierre de Thomas and Bartholomew of Trau left Avignon early in February, 1355. They went first to Milan, where Pierre presented a papal letter to its rulers, Matteo, Bernabo, and Galeazzo Visconti, urging them to aid Innocent's efforts to secure Robert's release,[62] as their uncle Giovanni Visconti had done before his death the previous October.[63] The nuncios then went to the court of Charles IV, who was on his way to Rome to receive the crown of the Holy Roman Empire and was spending some time at Pisa.[64] Pierre also delivered papal letters to him urging him to intervene with Jacopo of Savoy on behalf of Robert of Durazzo.[65]

This time, Innocent's efforts achieved the desired effect. The

[60] Léonard, Histoire de Jeanne I^re, III, 91–96, cf. I, 130, II, 279–83, and III, 27–32; Gaudenzio Claretta, "Roberto di Durazzo dei reali di Napoli e la famiglia di Iacopo di Savoia principe d'Acaja," Atti della Reale Accademia delle Scienze di Torino, XV (1879), 750–51.

[61] Léonard, Histoire de Jeanne I^re, III, 96–99, 134–35; Gerolamo Biscaro, "Le relazioni dei Visconti di Milano con la Chiesa; l'archivescovo Giovanni, Clemente VI e Innocenzo VI," Archivio Storico Lombardo, LV (1928), 75–84. Papal documents related to this affair are published in Cerasoli and Cipolla, "Innocenzo VI e casa Savoia," pp. 152–66.

[62] Letter of January 13, 1355, Reg. Vat. 237, fol. 11r; Cerasoli and Cipolla, "Innocenzo VI e casa Savoia," p. 167. This letter is discussed in Biscaro, op. cit., p. 84.

[63] Léonard, Histoire de Jeanne I^re, III, 96–99; Cerasoli and Cipolla, "Innocenzo VI e casa Savoia," pp. 158–59.

[64] According to E. Werunsky, Der erste Römerzug Kaisers Karls IV (Innsbruck, 1878), pp. 46–148, Charles IV stayed in Pisa from January 18 to March 22, except for a brief visit to Lucca from February 13 to 15.

[65] In addition to the letter of February 1, mentioned above, there is a letter to Charles IV from Innocent VI dated January 13, found in Reg. Vat. 237, fols. 10v–11r, published in Cerasoli and Cipolla, "Innocenzo VI e casa Savoia," pp. 166–67. The two letters vary only in minor details.

emperor urged Jacopo to release Robert. As a result of papal and imperial intervention, the young prince was freed from imprisonment on March 18 in the presence of the imperial ambassador Sacramoro de' Pomerii.[66] Pierre de Thomas was therefore successful in these negotiations.

Although the papal letters which he delivered to Charles IV relate only to the affair of Robert of Durazzo, Pierre also discussed his mission to Serbia with the emperor. The absence of a letter from Innocent VI to Charles on the subject suggests that Pierre was instructed to feel out the emperor's attitude toward the church union negotiations with Stephen Dushan and to reveal only as much as seemed appropriate. Charles IV was enthusiastic about the prospect of church union. On February 19, 1355, he gave Pierre de Thomas a message to the king of Serbia in which he congratulated him for his desire to accept the Roman Catholic faith. He informed Stephen of his imminent coronation as emperor at Rome. He stressed the common bond which he shared with the Serbian monarch in the use of the "noble" Slav language." He promised to urge King Louis of Hungary to make peace with Serbia. He mentioned Stephen Dushan's recent conquests in Greece and wished him success in his further efforts in that direction, especially since they would now lead to the extension of the Catholic faith.[67]

[66] Act of Liberation, dated Pinerolo, March 18, 1355, Torino, Archivio di Stato, *Protocollo del notario Nassapore*, 132, published in Claretta, "Roberto di Durazzo e la famiglia di Iacopo di Savoia," pp. 787–88, cf. pp. 753–54.

[67] Published in Johann von Gelnhausen, *Collectarius perpetuarum formarum,* ed. Hans Kaiser (Innsbruck, 1900), pp. 167–69. Gelnhausen's edition is also published in J. W. Hoffman, *Sammlung ungedruckter Nachrichten, Dokumenten und Urkunden,* II (Halle, 1737), 185. A digest of the letter, which makes no mention of Pierre de Thomas, is published in J. F. Böhmer, *Die Regesten des Kaiserreichs unter Kaiser Karl IV, 1346–1378* (Regesta imperii, vol. VIII) ed. Alfons Huber (Innsbruck, 1877), p. 161.

It is probable that the last two statements reflect the desires of Stephen Dushan as revealed to Emperor Charles IV by Pierre de Thomas. It was natural that Charles IV should have a feeling of common interest with Stephen Dushan, since the lands of both rulers were threatened by the expansionist designs of Louis of Hungary. Halecki notes also that the Holy Roman emperor had a sincere interest in church union and founded a convent of Benedictines of the Slavic rite at Prague.[68]

After visiting Emperor Charles IV, Pierre de Thomas, together with his fellow ambassador Bartholomew of Trau, continued his journey to Serbia. The two men went through Venice[69] and delivered a letter from Innocent VI to the doge, informing him of their mission to Serbia and requesting his aid, especially in securing their passage across the Adriatic.[70] At this time, Marino Faliero was doge of Venice and was already plotting to make himself prince of that city after murdering its chief patricians. For this conspiracy, he was executed on April 18. There is no record of his reception of the nuncios.

Pierre and Bartholomew also carried a message to King Louis of Hungary, urging him to aid them in uniting the king and people of Serbia to the Roman Catholic Church.[71] This brief letter was to be supplemented by an oral message from the nuncios, in which they probably asked Louis to suspend hostilities with Serbia, at least during the period of church union nego-

[68] Halecki, *Un Empereur,* pp. 25–26.

[69] Mézières, *Life,* ed. Smet, pp. 65–66; AASS, Jan. 29, III, 613–14 (sec. 18).

[70] Letter of November 23, 1354, *Reg. Vat.* 236, fol. 238v; Wadding, *Vita,* pp. 109–10; *Bull. carm.,* I, 83–84. Both publications give erroneous dates but are otherwise correct.

[71] Letter of November 22, 1354, *Reg. Vat.* 236, fol. 238v; TVMH, II, 11; *Mon. Hung. hist., Acta externa,* II, 445; Wadding, *Vita,* pp. 108–09; *Bull. carm.,* I, 82. The date is incorrect in the last two publications.

tiations. Open war between Serbia and Hungary actually ceased in May, 1355, perhaps as a result of this intervention.[72] There has been some question about whether the nuncios visited Hungary on their way to Serbia, since it is known that they traveled there from Venice by sea,[73] but it is not impossible, since the way from Venice to Hungary by land was not a long one,[74] and they could have easily made a round trip before taking ship for Serbia.

On their voyage across the Adriatic, the nuncios found it necessary to sail on a small ship. According to Mézières, the prayers of Pierre de Thomas on two occasions were necessary to save them from disaster. On one occasion, their little ship was almost overtaken by a large Turkish pirate vessel, but a cloud or mist suddenly appeared out of a clear sky and hid them from its view so that they were able to escape. At another time, they ran into a severe storm and were saved by being tossed across a sand bar by a large wave into a lake which was somewhat removed from the sea. Both of these stories were originally told by Friar Pierre Roquette, a companion of Pierre de Thomas and perhaps a Carmelite, in the presence of the archbishop of Nicosia in Cyprus and many other witnesses.[75]

The messengers of Innocent VI arrived in Serbia about March, 1355. Pierre de Thomas was clearly the leader of the embassy and conducted the negotiations with the king of Serbia. Bartholomew's function was probably that of an inter-

[72] Ignaz Aurelius Fessler, *Geschichte von Ungarn,* III (Leipzig, 1816), 344; Jereček, *Geschichte der Serben,* I, 411; Smet's comments in his edition of Mézières, *Life,* p. 196.

[73] Joachim Smet in his edition of Mézières, *Life,* p. 65, n. 8, thinks that Pierre did not visit Hungary at this time.

[74] A year and a half later, Pierre traveled from Venice to Hungary within four days. See below, p. 112.

[75] Mézières, *Life,* ed. Smet, pp. 65–67; AASS, Jan. 29, III, 613–14 (secs. 18–19). The name of Pierre Roquette is totally lost in the *Acta Sanctorum* edition through a faulty reading in the manuscript on which it is based, as noted by Joachim Smet in his edition.

preter. As a Catholic bishop in Serbia, he knew the language of the country, while there is no evidence that Pierre de Thomas had any acquaintance with Serbian.[76] Bartholomew also had been to the court of Stephen Dushan before and had been commended by him in his letter to the Pope, but Innocent VI does not appear to have had real confidence in him. In the negotiations with the Visconti and Charles IV, where no interpreter was required, Bartholomew's name does not appear.

Unfortunately, Mézières' biography of Pierre de Thomas is the only available source of information for the negotiations of Pierre in Serbia. Though this account makes interesting reading, it is filled with generalizations and pro-Latin bias. In it no effort is made to understand the position of Stephen Dushan, who is presented as a capricious, malicious, and deceitful tyrant. On the other hand, Pierre de Thomas is depicted as a man of outstanding wisdom, without any recognition of the limitations he suffered in dealing with the affairs of a country which was so unfamiliar to him.

According to Mézières, Pierre and Bartholomew came into the presence of King Stephen Dushan some days after their arrival in Serbia. To Pierre, the king appeared larger than any other man of his day and of dreadful visage.[77] Pierre quickly ran afoul of Serbian court protocol, which required one who appeared before the king to kiss his feet before talking to him and to show other marks of respect which seemed excessive to the men of the West. Although he was repeatedly

[76] If Pierre had known Serbian, no ordinary accomplishment for a Latin of his day, Mézières surely would have mentioned it.

[77] Mézières, *Life,* ed. Smet, p. 67; AASS, Jan. 29, III, 614 (sec. 20): ". . . qui quidem rex inter omnes homines mundi suo tempore maior erat et terribili facie." These words of Mézières surely reflect the impressions of his friend Pierre de Thomas. According to Harold V. W. Temperley, *History of Serbia* (London, 1917), p. 65, Serbian sources agree that Stephen Dushan was a large man but portray him as handsome rather than ugly and terrifying.

warned that the death penalty could follow his failure to observe these customs, Pierre refused to comply with them, lest the honor of the church be sullied by the unbecoming behavior of a papal nuncio. Mézières says that he stood before the king's presence with politeness and dignity *sine inclinatione aut aliqua alia reverentia.* Perhaps the last phrase is somewhat of an exaggeration. The king received them surrounded by his knights and barons and spoke to them haughtily and with much boasting, if we may believe Mézières' report.[78]

On a later day appointed for the purpose, Pierre discussed the purpose of his mission clearly and forcefully in a speech before the king in which he set forth the advantages that Serbia would receive from union with the Roman church. In Stephen Dushan's replies, according to Mézières, Pierre could discern pride, craftiness, and deceit. This means that the king was not ready to make the immediate and complete declaration of obedience to the Pope which the nuncio desired and hoped for. The negotiations dragged on for months. Often Stephen Dushan appeared to accept agreements favorable to the papacy, and later he would change his mind.[79]

Severe friction at times developed between the king and the nuncio. Mézières tells of an occasion when Stephen Dushan became so incensed against Pierre de Thomas that he forbade any Catholic in his realm to attend any mass said by Pierre and threatened to put out the eyes of anyone who disobeyed the order.[80] There was much fear among the Catholics of Serbia,

[78] Mézières, *Life,* ed. Smet, pp. 67–68; AASS, Jan. 29, III, 614 (sec. 20).

[79] Mézières, *Life,* ed. Smet, p. 68; AASS, Jan. 29, III, 614 (secs. 20–21). Mézières says that many agreements were concluded to the honor of the Roman church and afterward maliciously broken by the Serbians.

[80] Mézières, *Life,* ed. Smet, p. 68; AASS, Jan. 29, III, 614 (sec. 21). In a letter to his nephew, Mézières declared that the penalty was death. See Neculai Jorga, "L'épître de Philippe de Mézières à son neveu," *Bulletin de l'Institut pour l'étude de l'Europe sud-orientale,* VIII (1921), 33–35.

but Pierre de Thomas refused to be intimidated. He had no fear of death but yearned to die for the exaltation of the Catholic faith. He comforted his people. He calmly announced that he would celebrate mass at the usual hour the next morning. He invited the faithful to attend but did not command them to do so. When the hour arrived, the Catholics of that place flocked to his mass. Three hundred Germans were there in addition to Catholics of other nations who braved the king's anger to attend.[81]

When Stephen Dushan heard that his edict had been broken, he was furious. He called the Germans before him, scowled at them, and said, "Why have you not been afraid to break my edict? Do you know that I announced that I would have your eyes put out if you should hear the mass of this enemy of mine?" The captain of the Germans, a devout and valiant soldier, spoke for the Germans. This was probably Palmann, to whom Innocent VI had addressed one of the letters brought by Pierre de Thomas to Serbia.[82] He answered the king, "My lord, it is indeed true that we heard your edict, but we fear God more than you. And how could we leave such a father to celebrate mass alone, without us? You know that we are all Catholics and faithful to the Roman church. If it is for this that you want to pluck out our eyes, we are ready to lose not only our eyes but also our lives in defense of the Catholic faith." When the king heard these courageous words from this brave and loyal soldier, his anger was assuaged, and he began to admire the great determination of the apostolic nuncio and the Germans, according to Mézières.[83]

[81] Mézières, Life, ed. Smet, pp. 68–69; AASS, Jan. 29, III, 614 (sec. 21).

[82] For other references to Palmann, who later in the year 1355 was commanding the Serbian garrison at the fortress of Klis, see Joannes Schafarik, Acta archivi veneti spectantia ad historiam Serborum et reliquorum Slavorum meridionalium, I (Belgrade, 1860), 165–66, 173–76.

[83] Mézières, Life, ed. Smet, p. 69; AASS, Jan. 29, III, 614 (sec. 22).

Although we do not know it with certainty, we may safely assume that Stephen Dushan reacted so violently against Pierre de Thomas because he sought to win individual Serbian converts from Orthodoxy to Catholicism. As is noted above, such proselytism was contrary to Serbian law as recently codified in the *Zakonik*. Stephen Dushan was willing to consider uniting his entire national church to the Roman church, but he was unwilling to have its members drawn off one by one. It is probable that his order actually forbade all persons in Serbia to go to Pierre's masses, not merely the Catholics, as Mézières has it. Mézières admits that Pierre engaged in proselytism and makes the questionable assertion that he won many Orthodox churches, including some metropolitan churches, in Serbia to the Roman allegiance.[84]

Pierre de Thomas remained in Serbia for the better part of a year. He did not leave until the early part of 1356.[85] Thus he remained in Serbia until after the death of Stephen Dushan, which occurred on December 20, 1355. As long as Stephen Dushan lived, Pierre continued to hope that the union of the churches might be effected. He faced serious opposition, although Mézières probably exaggerates in saying that the nuncio had to beware of many snares laid for him by the king and was able to get out of the country only with difficulty. Pierre probably left Serbia of his own accord, recognizing that there was no hope of winning Stephen Dushan's son and successor Urosh III to the Catholic faith.[86]

[84] Mézières, *Life,* ed. Smet, pp. 69–70; AASS, Jan. 29, III, 614 (sec. 22).

[85] According to the Venetian Senate, *Misti,* XXVII, 65v; MHSM, III, 312–13, he arrived in Venice shortly before March 25, 1356, after a visit to Hungary.

[86] Mézières, *Life,* ed. Smet, pp. 69–70; AASS, Jan. 29, III, 614 (sec. 22). The contemporary Carmelite writer Jean Trissa in the passage of his *De magistris parisiensibus* published in MHC, p. 390, and elsewhere as noted above p. 23, n. 8, states that the mission of Pierre de

Pierre de Thomas' church union negotiations in Serbia ended in failure primarily because Stephen Dushan saw no political value in a union with Rome, once he really explored the idea, and his only interest in church union was political. The negotiations brought him none of the advantages for which he had had reason to hope. His realm was not freed from the Hungarian menace, nor did he receive the desired commission as captain of all Christian forces against the Turks. Thus he had nothing to lose by remaining in the Orthodox communion. His own religious thinking and that of the majority of his subjects was Byzantine and Orthodox, not Western and Catholic. His pet project was the conquest of Constantinople, and the Greek inhabitants of that city would far more readily accept an Orthodox emperor, even though of another nationality, than a Catholic. Furthermore, the Serbian Orthodox church was autonomous and completely subject to his control, while, as he could clearly see from the sermons of Pierre de Thomas and from his bearing as a papal nuncio, the Roman Catholic Church expected rulers to recognize the authority of the Pope over the church in their countries. Stephen Dushan did not want to give up the traditional ecclesiastical independence of his realm. Hence he tried to curb every effort of Pierre de Thomas to build up the power of the Catholic Church in Serbia, which already had the allegiance of his subjects on the Adriatic coast. Stephen Dushan would have accepted church union only if the Pope had offered concrete political advantages in return for a purely nominal submission. This was contrary to papal policy.

---

Thomas to Serbia was a failure because Stephen Dushan died before his arrival in Serbia. While this statement is not true, it may reflect an impression within the Carmelite Order that the king's death brought an end to any hope of success of Pierre's mission to Serbia. This impression is probably true. Pierre's mission to Serbia is the last event mentioned in his biography in Trissa's work, which therefore must have been written shortly afterward.

Therefore Stephen Dushan rejected the union, and to all appearances his son and successor was even more adamant in refusing to accept Catholicism.[87]

Some authorities have blamed Pierre de Thomas for the failure of these negotiations. According to them he angered the Serbian monarch from the beginning by a strong bias in favor of King Louis of Hungary, Stephen Dushan's inveterate enemy. Louis was naturally unfavorable to the conversion of Serbia to Catholicism because he used the schismatic status of the Serbians in the eyes of the Latin church as an excuse for his frequent attacks on Serbia to annex border lands. It is also alleged that Pierre de Thomas went to Hungary immediately after the failure of his Serbian mission with the express purpose of stirring up the Hungarian monarch to begin a new crusade against Serbia.[88]

---

[87] Novak, "L'alleanza," pp. 36–37; Voinovitch, *Histoire de Dalmatie,* pp. 447–48; Halecki, *Un empereur,* pp. 26–27. William Miller, "The Balkan States: I. The Zenith of Bulgaria and Serbia (1136–1355)," *Cambridge Medieval History,* ed. J. B. Bury *et al.,* IV (New York, Cambridge, 1927), 546, suggests that the fall of John VI Cantacuzenus and the victory of John V Palaeologus in the Byzantine civil war on November 22, 1354, caused Stephen Dushan to have more confidence that he could win Constantinople unaided and hence made him less disposed to union with the Western church.

[88] The first mention of Pierre de Thomas' bias in favor of Hungary which I have found is in Raynaldus, *Annales ecclesiastici, ad ann.* 1356, chap. 24: "Hoc anno Ludovicus Ungariae Rex, cum Stephanus Rex Rasciae, qui antea ad Romanae ecclesiae conjunctionem Ungaricae potentiae terrore se rediturum spoponderat, in haeresi et schismate obduresceret, sacram, auctore B. Petro Thomae Episcopo Pactensi apostolico internuntio, qui e Rascia in Ungariam se contulerat, expeditionem in eum decrevit, ut regnum illud Ungarico imperio adjungeret, atque ex eo haeresim et schisma excinderet." Jireček, *Geschichte der Serben,* I, 411, develops the viewpoint still further. He says that Pierre de Thomas reached Serbia in the spring of 1355, when the country was threatened by a Hungarian invasion. This is correct. However, he assumes that Pierre de Thomas showed from the beginning that his real sympathies were with the king of Hungary and that he left Serbia after a brief and hopeless visit and immediately went to Hungary to stir up more trouble for the Serbians. His viewpoint is followed by

There is no contemporary evidence that Pierre de Thomas favored the king of Hungary against Serbia before the failure of his mission to Serbia. If he had visited him before going to Serbia, it was only to deliver the Pope's message, which presumably requested Louis to desist from his attacks against Serbia and to promote the church union negotiations.[89] Every bit of evidence points to the fact that Innocent VI believed that the union of Serbia with the Roman Catholic communion was a real possibility in 1355. He therefore could not have sanctioned a pro-Hungarian policy that would have assured the failure of this effort to bring Serbia into the fold, and Pierre de Thomas was unfailingly loyal to papal policy.

It is true that Pierre de Thomas visited King Louis of Hungary on his return journey from Serbia to the West. Thus it appears that he took the land route. He found Louis preparing a war against Serbia. The king asked him to convey his request to Innocent VI to appoint him as captain of a crusade against the enemies of the church, especially against the Serbian heretics, whose insults against the Redeemer vexed his pious soul. He also sent letters to the Pope and an ambassador, Stephen, bishop elect of Zagreb, to promote the same project. Pierre de Thomas agreed to take the king's message to the Pope.[90] He

Novak, "L'alleanza," p. 37, by Voinovitch, *Histoire de Dalmatie*, I, 447–48, and with some hesitation by Halecki, *Un Empereur*, p. 26. However, as noted above, Pierre de Thomas appears to have stayed in Serbia for the greater part of a year, apparently with some hope of success, and did not leave that country until after the death of Stephen Dushan.

[89] Joachim Smet in appendix II of his edition of Mézières, *Life*, p. 196. It is interesting to note that the Emperor Charles IV in his letter to Stephen Dushan promised to do all he could to induce Louis of Hungary to make peace with Serbia. Pierre carried this letter. See above, p. 92.

[90] Letter of Innocent VI to Louis of Hungary, August 11, 1356, *Reg. Vat.* 238, fols. 150r–152r; Wadding, *Vita*, pp. 110–19; *Annales Minorum*, VIII, 131–13; Raynaldus. *Annales ecclesiastici, ad ann.* 1356, chap. 27; *Bull. carm.*, I, 94–96; TVMH, II, 24–25.

may have agreed to do so merely as a courtesy, but it is also possible that at this time, after the failure of his best efforts to win Serbia to the Roman Catholic faith by peaceful persuasion, he approved Louis' plan to unite that nation to the Latin church by force of arms, believing that it was the only way to accomplish this objective. However, this does not necessarily mean that he supported such a policy while there was still hope of winning Serbia by negotiation or that he was the real author of Louis' plan, which was formulated before his arrival in Hungary.

At the time of Pierre's visit to the Hungarian court serious trouble was already brewing between Hungary and the republic of Venice. King Louis gave him letters and an oral message to the Venetian Senate. He professed to desire peace with Venice and offered a safe-conduct to any Venetian envoys who should be sent to him. Pierre carried this message to Venice, where he arrived shortly before March 25, 1356. On that date the senate considered it and voted to send the embassy which Louis had requested, lest they seem less inclined to peace than he.[91]

Pierre then continued his journey to Avignon, where he reported on his experiences in Serbia to Innocent VI and delivered the Hungarian king's messages.[92] His companion on the mission, Bartholomew of Trau, did not return with him. By May 1, 1356, he had not yet arrived at Avignon. Innocent wrote to him, requesting him to return and present his report, as Pierre de Thomas had done.[93] He forbade the bishop of

[91] *Misti*, XXVII, fol. 65v; MHSM, III, 312–13.

[92] Mézières, *Life,* ed. Smet, p. 70; AASS, Jan. 29, III, 614 (sec. 22). See also note 90.

[93] *Reg. Aven.* 132, fol. 538r; Augustin Theiner, *Vetera monumenta Slavorum meridionalium historiam illustrantia,* I (Rome, 1863), 234 (hereafter abbreviated TVMS); Tade Smičiklas, *et al., Codex diplomaticus regni Croatiae, Dalmatiae et Slavoniae,* XII (Zagreb, 1914), 345.

Trau to negotiate further concerning the question of church union in Serbia without further instructions from Avignon. Thus it appears that Bartholomew could not be trusted to follow papal policy but tended to develop plans of his own without adequate authority.

By the middle of 1356, Pierre de Thomas was well established in a career in the papal diplomatic service. In his second mission, which was his first really important one, he had clearly shown his ability in his negotiations with Charles IV and Stephen Dushan. King Louis of Hungary was obviously impressed with his ability and fidelity, for he entrusted him with important messages. Throughout the mission Pierre showed his complete and unwavering devotion to the Roman Catholic Church, even to the point of being willing to die for the faith. This sacrificial spirit proved of great benefit to him in later episodes of his life, when he needed strength for hard and dangerous tasks.

# 5

# Peace Negotiations between Venice and Hungary

THE NEXT MAJOR ACTIVITY OF PIERRE DE THOMAS WAS HIS part in the peace negotiations of 1356–57 between Venice and Hungary.[1] The chief issue in the war which broke out between these two states in 1356 was the control of the Dalmatian coast, especially the city of Zara. Venice desired to hold this area to protect her vital Adriatic sea lanes, while Hungary was interested in it as a maritime outlet to a large continental region. The Zaratines themselves were jealous of their local liberties and always ready to revolt against the power that held them, calling upon the other for aid. The struggle between Venice and Hungary had been going on for more than two centuries, and the territory had frequently changed hands. The most famous incident in this struggle is the capture of Zara from Hun-

[1] Mèziéres, *Life,* ed. Smet, pp. 70–74; AASS, Jan. 29, III, 615–16 (secs. 23–27). Smet reviews this mission in his edition of Mézières, *Life,* pp. 197–201 (appendix III).

gary for Venice by the men of the Fourth Crusade. In the early part of the reign of King Louis (1342–82), there was some fighting between the two nations from 1345 to 1348, in which the Venetians were generally victorious. It had been concluded by a truce for a period of eight years.[2] Meanwhile, because of the Hungarian menace which threatened them both, an alliance grew up between Venice and Stephen Dushan of Serbia.[3]

As the period of the truce drew to a close in the early months of 1356, fresh negotiations were undertaken between Venice and Hungary, in which Pierre de Thomas had a brief part, as noted at the close of the previous chapter. In this period, Venice seems to have desired peace sincerely, provided that it could be secured without loss of territory. Therefore she was willing to offer the Hungarians an annual payment of 6,000 to 7,000 ducats for Clissa and Almisium and other disputed places in Slavonia. Recognizing the danger of war, she nevertheless made provision for the defense of her territory.[4]

Meanwhile, Louis was ostensibly preparing for a campaign against Serbia. After a war against the Tatars in Poland, he came down to Zagreb in the mid-Lent of 1356 and began to assemble the forces needed to recover the territories which Stephen Dushan had earlier taken in the southern part of his kingdom.[5] Here Pierre de Thomas may have met him on his way back from Serbia. On June 4, in a letter to the Pope, Louis announced that he was making war against Serbia. He declared

[2] Louis de Voinovitch, *Histoire de Dalmatie,* I (Paris, 1934), 314, 323, 342, 346–445.
[3] Gregorio Novak, "L'alleanza veneto-serba nel secolo XIV," *Archivio Veneto-tridentino,* VIII (1925), 8–21.
[4] Venetian records in MHSM, III, 314–21. See also Voinovitch, *Histoire de Dalmatie,* I, 448–49.
[5] Ignaz Aurelius Fessler, *Geschichte von Ungarn,* III (Leipzig, 1816), 337–39; letter of Louis of Hungary to the doge of Venice, March 1, 1356, published in *Monumenta Hungariae historica, Acta externa,* ed. Gusztav Wenzel, II (Budapest, 1875), 467.

that Serbia rightfully belonged to him and was occupied by rebels and "schismatics." He promised to restore it to the Roman Catholic fold. He promised not to attack the lands of any faithful Catholic. He sent his chaplain, Stephen of Buda, to request the Pope to send a legate and to preach a crusade against the Serbians.[6]

Nevertheless it appears that Louis' letters about the Serbian crusade were, at least for the present, primarily a cloak for his hostile intentions against Venice. In the same month of June, 1356, he personally led his main force in a drive against Venice from the mainland. He penetrated into the March of Friuli, took the cities of Sacilu and Conegliano, and laid siege to Treviso. Under John Csuzy, a second Hungarian force attacked Dalmatia.[7] Many princes joined Hungary against Venice, including Emperor Charles IV, the count of Goritz, the duke of Austria, the patriarch of Aquileia, Bernabo Visconti of Milan, and the lord of Verona. Venice continued to negotiate with Hungary.[8] On July 9, 1356, the Collegio in Venice voted to give full freedom to other Dalmatian cities if the Hungarians would agree not to question the Venetian rights in Zara and Nona.[9]

[6] Letter of Louis of Hungary to Innocent VI from Zagreb, June 4, 1356, György Fejér, *Codex diplomaticus Hungariae ecclesiasticus et civilis*, tome IX, vol. II (Buda, 1833), pp. 471–75; Tade Smičiklas, et al., *Codex diplomaticus regni Croatiae, Dalmatiae et Slavoniae*, XII (Zagreb, 1914), 356–58; Raynaldus, *Annales ecclesiastici, ad ann.* 1356, chaps. 24–26.

[7] Fessler, *Geschichte von Ungarn*, III, 346–47; Bálint Hóman, *Gli Angioini di Napoli in Ungheria, 1290–1403*, translated from the Hungarian by Luigi Zambra and Rudolfo Mosca (Reale Accademia d'Italia, Studi e documenti, vol. VIII; Rome, 1938), pp. 366–71.

[8] Voinovitch, *Histoire de Dalmatie*, I, 449–50; Heinrich Kretschmayr, *Geschichte von Venedig*, II (Gotha, 1920), 215–16; Samuele Romanin, *Storia documentata di Venezia*, III (Venice, 1855), 368–69.

[9] MHSM, V, 279–80. The Collegio was composed of the chief officers of state and acted as the executive body in Venice. It proposed measures to the Senate.

As soon as Innocent VI learned of the outbreak of war between Venice and Hungary, he sought to re-establish peace. In April, 1356, he had made an effort to renew an earlier league of Christian powers against the Turks and had called a meeting in Avignon for November 1, but the support of Venice was necessary, and nothing could be done while she was distracted by war with Hungary.[10] On July 4, the Pope wrote to Louis of Hungary. He declared that he was unhappy because he had learned that Louis, who had begun well by attacking "schismatic" Serbia, had more recently turned his arms against his coreligionists of Venice. This letter was carried by Bongiovanni, bishop of Fermo, who was authorized to negotiate with the king.[11] This envoy reached Venice in the latter part of July. He continued his negotiations with both parties until September. As a result of these negotiations, Venice agreed to give up Nona, if her rights to Zara were recognized and the Hungarians surrendered their conquests in the area of Treviso. By the close of the period, the Venetians also agreed that both belligerents should send ambassadors to Innocent VI and should accept his mediation of their quarrel. It was suggested that a truce be arranged until Christmas or even until mid-Lent.[12] The king of Hungary insisted that he would conclude peace only if all Dalmatia, including Zara, were relinquished to him.[13]

In the summer of 1356, Innocent VI decided to send Pierre

[10] Oskar Halecki, *Un Empereur de Byzance à Rome* (Warsaw, 1930), pp. 28–29. Mézières, *Life,* ed. Smet, p. 70; AASS, Jan. 29, III, 615 (sec. 23) gives the crusade against the Turks as Innocent's chief motive for seeking this peace.

[11] *Reg. Vat.* 238, fol. 118; Raynaldus, *Annales ecclesiastici, ad ann.* 1356, chap. 29; Fejér, *Codex diplomaticus Hungariae,* tome IX, vol. II, p. 502; TVMH, II, 21–22; *Mon. Hung. hist., Acta externa,* II, 475–76.

[12] Venetian records from *Secreta collegii* in MHSM, V, 282–92.

[13] Statement in his letter from Zagreb, October 28, 1356, published in MHSM, V, 295.

de Thomas as his nuncio to Venice and Hungary to act as negotiator between them. He was also sending him to Constantinople to discuss the question of church union there,[14] and it was necessary for him to travel through Venice on his way to the East. It was not expected that the peace negotiations there would take much time.

By this time, Innocent VI had decided to support the Hungarian crusade against Serbia in an effort to divert King Louis from expanding his kingdom at the expense of Venice. The earliest mention of Pierre's new mission is in the Pope's letter of July 17 to the doge of Venice, in which he urged him to break his alliance with Serbia. Innocent reminded him that the Hungarian king was engaged in a crusade against Serbia to eradicate the evils of heresy from that land. Therefore the Veneto-Serbian alliance was serving to encourage heretics, as well as offering a further cause for war between Venice and Hungary, which the papacy was trying to bring to an end.[15] Though his name is not mentioned in it, Pierre de Thomas was probably commissioned to carry another letter to the prelates of the Adriatic area, authorizing them to excommunicate all who should aid the Serbian heretics.[16] In his letter of August 11, 1356, in which he officially granted Louis' request to be named as captain of a crusade against the Serbians, Innocent also offered some other suggestions to the Hungarian monarch.

[14] See Chapter 6.
[15] *Reg. Vat.* 238, fols. 153r–153v; Wadding, *Vita,* pp. 121–23; *Annales Minorum,* VIII, 134–35; *Bull. carm.,* I, 89; TVMH, II, 23. This letter is also published from the Venetian copy in *Libri Commemoralium,* V, 79, in MHSM, III, 327–28; *Mon. Hung. hist., Acta externa,* II, 478–79; Schafarik, *Acta archivi Veneti spectantia ad historiam Serborum et reliquorum Slavorum meridionalium,* I (Belgrade, 1860), 156–58.
[16] Letter of Innocent VI to the patriarchs of Aquileia and Grado and the archbishop of Salzburg, July 17, 1356, *Reg. Vat.* 238, fol. 152v; Wadding, *Vita,* pp. 119–21; *Annales Minorum,* VIII, 133–34; *Bull. carm.,* I, 88; TVMH, II, 22–23.

He reminded him that there were heresies in his own Bosnian lands, which he would do well to uproot before seeking to cleanse other nations. He also urged Louis to come to the aid of Cardinal Albornoz, who was defending the church's interests in Italy against Francesco Ordelaffi of Forli and Giovanni and Guglielmo de Manfredi of Faenza. In connection with this Italian project, Innocent granted the tithes of all ecclesiastical revenues in Hungary to the king for three years.[17] Thus Innocent tried in every way to divert Louis from his war with Venice.

At this time, Innocent wrote to the rulers of Venice and Hungary and urged them to make peace with each other. These letters were carried by Pierre de Thomas and announced his appointment as a nuncio to these lands. In his letter to the doge of Venice, written on August 10, 1356, the Pope announced that King Louis was willing to submit all questions between him and Venice to the Pope for arbitration and to remove his troops from conquered Venetian territory. He urged the doge to heed the oral messages which Pierre would deliver with the letter on behalf of the Holy See.[18] In his letter to King Louis of Hungary, written on the next day, Innocent commended the king for his gracious offers in the interest of

[17] *Reg. Vat.* 238, fols. 150r–152r; Wadding, *Vita*, pp. 110–19; *Annales Minorum*, VIII, 131–33; Raynaldus, *Annales ecclesiastici, ad ann.* 1356, chap. 27; *Bull. carm.*, I, 94–96; TVMH, II, 24–25. Other letters concerning these affairs are in *Reg. Vat.* 238, fols. 152r–152v, 162r–162v; TVMH, II, 26–27; *Mon. Hung. hist., Acta externa*, II, 479–80. Later papal correspondence concerning the Serbian crusade is published in TVMH, II, 28–35. Mézières, *Life,* ed. Smet, pp. 70, 72; AASS, Jan. 29, III, 615 (sec. 23, 25) errs in making the Holy Land the goal of this crusade.
[18] *Reg. Vat.* 238, fols. 153v–154r; Wadding, *Vita*, pp. 126–28; *Annales Minorum*, VIII, 135–36; Bull, carm., I, 92–93; Fejér, *Codex diplomaticus Hungariae,* tome IX, vol. II, pp. 504–05; TVMH, II, 23–24. In his edition of this letter Fejér erroneously designates Pierre de Thomas as *episcopus Portuensis* instead of *episcopus Pactensis*. The Venetian copy of this letter is published in MHSM, III, 329–30.

peace with Venice. The Pope expressed the hope that the peace negotiations would be successful. Innocent sent oral messages to Louis by Pierre de Thomas and also by Stephen, bishop elect of Zagreb, who had come to Avignon as a Hungarian ambassador.[19]

For his trip to Constantinople, in which his mission to Venice and Hungary was included, on August 11, 1356, Pierre de Thomas received five hundred florins from the papal treasury.[20] He was also authorized to procure six florins a day from ecclesiastics through whose lands he might pass,[21] and he received a safe-conduct addressed to all clergymen and secular rulers.[22]

Pierre de Thomas left Avignon in the late summer of 1356, and after crossing the mountains and the plain of Lombardy[23] arrived in Venice on September 20.[24] By this time, the Doge Giovanni Gradenigo, to whom the papal letters were addressed, had died. The letters were therefore received by his successor, Giovanni Delfino, who took office in August, 1356.

In Venice, Pierre de Thomas was received joyously and magnificently by the doge and the nobles. Not long after his arrival he delivered his message to the Venetian authorities in an effective address.[25] On September 23, 1356, three days after

[19] *Reg. Vat.* 238, fols. 152v–153r; Wadding, *Vita,* pp. 124–26; *Annales Minorum,* VIII, 135; *Bull. carm.,* I, 93; Fejér, *Codex diplomaticus Hungariae,* tome IX, vol. II, pp. 503–04; TVMH, II, 25–26.

[20] Karl H. Schäfer, *Die Ausgaben der apostolischen Kammer unter Benedikt XII, Klemens VI und Innocenz VI (1335–1362)* (Paderborn, 1914), p. 607.

[21] Letter of July 15, 1356, *Reg. Vat.* 238, fols. 129v–130v. The archival references for this letter and others concerning this mission come from the microfilm mentioned in the Bibliography.

[22] *Reg. Vat.* 238, fols. 130v–131r (same date). On fol. 131r the same privileges are given to Pierre's companion on his mission to the East, Guglielmo Conti, bishop of Sizebolu.

[23] Mézières, *Life,* ed. Smet, p. 71; AASS, Jan. 29, III, 615 (sec. 24).

[24] Letter of Doge Giovanni Delfino to Pope Innocent VI, November 16, 1356, MHSM, V, 301–02.

[25] Mézières, *Life,* ed. Smet, p. 71; AASS, Jan. 29, III, 615 (sec. 24). Mézières declares that Pierre de Thomas announced his mission to the doge and council in a remarkable speech, admonishing them to peace

he arrived in Venice, the Collegio voted to entrust him with the Venetian truce message to King Louis of Hungary. They proposed that both belligerents should agree to a truce until Easter Sunday, April 9, 1357. During the time of the truce, the warring powers should refrain from doing any damage against each other. If any damage was done by either party against the other, double indemnity was to be paid by the offending party within eight days after it was demanded and a bill of particulars given. However, each side was free to rebuild, to fortify, and to provision the places which it held at the beginning of the truce. Meanwhile both parties should send ambassadors to the Pope. These envoys should remain at Avignon until Christmas and present the causes of the war to Innocent VI. If he, as mediator, could succeed in reconciling the two parties before Easter, well and good. If not, they would be free at that time to resume hostilities. The Venetians were willing to conclude the truce on these terms either by an exchange of formal letters or through ambassadors at Conegliano or any other place. Whether or not the Hungarians agreed to the truce, the Venetians were willing to send an embassy to the Roman Curia if Hungary would do likewise. On the next day, September 24, the Venetians voted to give Pierre de Thomas gifts to the value of one hundred ducats. They also voted to offer him a reward of three thousand ducats, which they had earlier offered the bishop of Fermo if he could bring the peace negotiations to a successful conclusion,[26] for the Venetians knew that they were being defeated, and they wanted to salvage as many as possible of their Dalmatian possessions.

---

by many irrefutable arguments. This testimony is confirmed in the doge's letter to the Pope, dated November 16, 1356, MHSM, V, 301–02, in which he declared that Pierre de Thomas had expounded Innocent's message "cum multa maturitate et sapienter."

[26] Minutes of the Collegio, September 23 and 24, 1356, and letters of the doge of Venice to the king of Hungary, September 23, 1356, MHSM, V, 293–95.

On September 24, 1356, or shortly thereafter, Pierre de Thomas left Venice and made his way across the battle lines to Hungary, arriving in Zagreb on September 28.[27] Though this journey was a brief one, it was fraught with danger. The papal nuncio had to pass through the two warring armies, and his work was vigorously opposed by the mercenaries of both sides, who did not want peace, because they made their living by war. The dangers which Pierre underwent on this journey are mentioned not only by his friend Philippe de Mézières but also by the doge of Venice.[28]

At Zagreb, the king of Hungary received Pierre de Thomas with all due honor, and after some days had passed, the nuncio announced his mission to the king and delivered the papal letters to him. These named him as captain of a crusade against the Serbians and the enemies of the church in Italy and urged him to make peace with Venice. The king saw him frequently and heard him graciously, providing for his sustenance while in Hungary. The account of the negotiations between the king and the nuncio which Philippe de Mézières gives in his biography of Pierre de Thomas is remarkable both for its naïvité and its incredibility. According to this account, Pierre found the king as a raging lion, proposing the destruction of Venice, and by his preaching was able to convert him into a veritable angel of peace, who was willing to relinquish Zara and all Dalmatia to the Venetians and to become their friend if they would simply promise to present him with one white horse a year as a token

[27] Letter of Louis of Hungary, dated Zagreb, October 28, 1356, MHSM, V, 295–97.

[28] Mézières, *Life,* ed. Smet, p. 71; AASS, Jan. 29, III, 615 (sec. 24). Letter of the doge of Venice to Innocent VI, November 16, 1356, MHSM, V, 301–02: ". . . dominus Petrus dei gratia Pactensis episcopus . . . de nostris intencionibus informatus ad regem ipsum accessit, qui tandem post multos labores et pericula, que in itinere diversis ex causis multipliciter est perpessus, . . . die x mensis huius ad nos cum intencione regia est reversus."

of friendship.[29] In reality, the history of these negotiations is neither so simple nor so dramatic. They were lengthy and complicated, and there is no evidence that the king was ever so violent in his hatred of Venice or so willing to agree to peace at all costs. On the contrary, as a shrewd statesman and diplomat, he always professed a desire for peace, while refusing to conclude it until he was convinced that he had gained all that he could hope to gain for the expansion of his realm.

Pierre de Thomas stayed in Hungary from September 28 to the early part of November, 1356. He returned to Venice on November 10, bringing with him the proposals of the Hungarian monarch.[30] So far as the truce was concerned, King Louis agreed to the terms suggested by the Venetian government on September 23. He proposed that the truce should last from St. Martin's Day (November 11) until the following Easter and that it should be published and observed in the regions of Treviso and Caneta within four days, in Istria within ten days, and in Dalmatia and Croatia within twenty-two days.[31] This truce was formally ratified by the Collegio at Venice on November 16, and since St. Martin's Day was already past, it was dated from the present.[32]

The Hungarian terms for a definitive peace brought by Pierre de Thomas did not receive such an immediate acceptance at Venice. The proposals of King Louis, which were originally

[29] Mézières, Life, ed. Smet, pp. 72–73; AASS, Jan. 29, III, 615 (secs. 25–26).

[30] Letter of Doge Giovanni Delfino to the Pope, November 16, 1356, MHSM, V, 301–02. In the doge's letter of the same date announcing the truce with Hungary (MHSM, V, 299–301) the date of Pierre's arrival in Venice from Hungary is given as November 15. This is obviously an error, for already on November 14 the Venetians were discussing the Hungarian peace terms, according to the minutes of the Collegio (MHSM, V, 297–98).

[31] Letter of Louis of Hungary to the Venetian government, October 28, 1356, MHSM, V, 295–97.

[32] MHSM, V, 299–301.

written down by Pierre de Thomas himself, were presented in
six articles. (1) Louis desired to regain Spalato, Trau, Sebenico,
and Scardona [33] in return for relinquishing his conquests in
Treviso. (2) He was willing to surrender Zara to Venice, but
he demanded tribute for Nona and Zara and required that
Venice promise to allow those Zaratines who had been expelled for disloyalty to Venice to return with full restoration
of property and to remain there unmolested. If they declined
to return, the king would reimburse them elsewhere. (3) The
king wanted a war indemnity of 100,000 florins. Perhaps this
sum could be diminished. (4) He required that the Venetians
aid him with two galleys in his crusade against infidels and
schismatics, presumably the Serbians. (5) When Louis went
to war against the Pope's enemies in Italy, the Venetians were
to furnish him with three hundred archers for eight months
or with money sufficient to hire so many. (6) The Venetians
were requested to send ambassadors to Hungary to discuss terms
of peace. [34]

The Venetian Collegio, reinforced with additional members
two days previously, [35] discussed the Hungarian peace terms on
November 14, 1356. They decided to inform Pierre, bishop
of Patti, legate (sic) of the Holy See, that they did not wish
to declare their final intentions to the king of Hungary except
in case of extreme necessity. However, they placed full confidence in him and believed he would not reveal anything to
the king of Hungary except as desired by their ambassadors
and that he would secure all the good that he could for them.
Therefore they would reveal to him the maximum terms of

[33] According to Novak, "L'alleanza veneto-serba," pp. 34–35, Venice
had obtained Scardona less than a year before this (January 10, 1356)
by purchase from Serbia.

[34] These terms are discussed in a letter of instructions to the Venetian ambassadors on December 2, 1356, just before they went to
Hungary, MHSM, V, 303–04.

[35] MHSM, V, 297.

peace which their plenipotentiaries to the king of Hungary would be authorized to concede in the name of the republic. The Venetians were willing to surrender Spalato, Trau, Sebenico, and Scardona, provided that the king would surrender his conquests in Conegliano, Treviso, and Caneta and would promise not to discriminate against the Venetian partisans in the four cities. They were willing to pay tribute for Nona but not for Zara. They agreed to repatriate all exiled Zaratines who would be loyal to Venice in the future. They did not agree to pay the requested indemnity of 100,000 florins but gave their ambassadors authority to agree to an indemnity which seemed reasonable to the Collegio; its amount was not revealed. Because of their present condition, the Venetians asked to be excused from furnishing three hundred archers for the king's wars in Italy, but they were willing to give him two galleys whenever he should go on a crusade to the Sepulcher of the Lord or against the Turks or Saracens, or to furnish money to provide for them for a period of time to be mutually agreed upon. (Under these terms the galleys could not be used against the Serbians, allies of Venice, against whom Louis' proposed crusade was directed.) At the same session, the Collegio voted to give Pierre de Thomas expense money up to one hundred ducats.[36]

As they agreed to do in the meeting, the Venetian leaders soon arranged a conference with Pierre de Thomas to discuss their proposed reply to the Hungarian peace terms and to get his reaction. He was generally satisfied with it. He was especially pleased with their replies to the articles on the indemnity and on the aid requested by the Hungarian king for his wars in Italy, because he believed that Louis would readily accept the Venetian terms on these points. In reference to the other four articles, he hoped that the Hungarians would accept the Venetian modifications of the terms but he could make no

[36] Collegio minutes of November 14, 1356, MHSM, V, 297–98.

definite statement beyond what was written in the summary of
the terms which he had brought from Zagreb. He solemnly
swore that he would reveal nothing to anyone about the maximum Venetian terms of peace, except with the authorization of
the Venetian ambassadors. He was agreeable that the Venetians
should try to gain every advantage and every improvement in
the peace terms which they could secure, and he promised that
he himself would do his best to bring this about.[37]

Meanwhile, Pierre de Thomas was anxious to continue his
journey to Constantinople. Nevertheless, by the earnest request
of the doge of Venice and the king of Hungary he was persuaded to stay in the area and to make another trip to Hungary
in the hope that through his efforts peace might be concluded.
To explain Pierre's position to Innocent VI, Doge Giovanni
Delfino addressed a letter to the Pope on November 16, 1356,
requesting him to excuse the nuncio if he was unable to continue his journey to Constantinople more speedily, since his
mediation was of great value in the peace negotiations between
Venice and Hungary. The doge expressed the hope that the
negotiations would be concluded in a short time. He noted that
because of the severity of the winter, it would have been impossible for Pierre to find a ship to take him to Constantinople
after his return to Venice from Hungary. The doge promised
to help Pierre in securing passage to the East after the peace
negotiations with Hungary were concluded.[38] At this time,
by virtue of authority given to him by the Venetian government, Pierre officially announced the truce with Hungary in the
Venetian territories.[39]

[37] The meeting with Pierre de Thomas is discussed in the letter of
instructions given to the Venetian ambassadors to Hungary on December 2, 1356, MHSM, V, 304.

[38] Letter of Giovanni Delfino to Innocent VI, November 16, 1356,
MHSM, V, 301–02.

[39] Letters patent from the Doge Giovanni Delfino on behalf of
Pierre de Thomas, November 15, 1356, MHSM, V, 298–99. An in-
ferior but fairly good edition of this letter is also found in Giovanni

On November 24, the Venetian Collegio appointed three ambassadors to go to Hungary with Pierre de Thomas to continue the peace negotiations, Andrea Contareni, Michael Faletro, and Benintendi de Ravegnani, chancellor of Venice.[40] On December 2, they received their instructions from the Collegio. These reveal the terms which the Venetians hoped and desired to secure from Louis of Hungary at this time, in contrast to the terms earlier revealed to Pierre de Thomas as the severest they would accept in case of absolute necessity. The Venetians still desired to retain the four Dalmatian cities of Spalato, Trau, Sebenico, and Scardona, which Louis was demanding in return for his relinquishing the conquered Venetian lands. If the king would not leave them to Venice at present, they hoped that he could be induced to retain them only for a limited period for his honor's sake and then return them to Venice. If the ambassadors could not retain all of these cities, they should try at least to secure Sebenico. If the king refused all concessions, they might offer all that was contained in the schedule of maximum concessions given to Pierre de Thomas.

Concerning Zara the Venetians preferred that all the exiled (pro-Hungarian) Zaratines, especially the chief nobles, should remain outside the city, but they promised to restore all their property and also to make some adequate annual provision for them. The Hungarians wanted them admitted into the city. Instead of the galleys which the king of Hungary asked for his wars against Serbia, the Venetian ambassadors were instructed first to offer money for a term which seemed expedient to them. If the king absolutely demanded the galleys, they were instructed to grant them for as short a time as he would accept,

Battista Verci, *Storia della marca trivigliana e veronese,* XIII (Venice, 1789), appendix of documents, pp. 60–61. In the latter edition Pierre de Thomas is referred to as *Pactien. episcopus* instead of *Pacten. episcopus,* and the date of the letter is given as December 15 instead of the correct November 15.

[40] MHSM, V, 302–03.

provided that a crusade was officially preached against Serbia.[41] For Zara, the Venetians were willing to accept a compromise decision by Pierre de Thomas or the Pope, if the king demanded it for his honor's sake. The Venetian ambassadors were authorized to include the allies of the king of Hungary in the treaty so that their relations with Venice would be the same as before the war. The Venetians promised to restore certain lands of the patriarch of Aquileia which they had in their possession, as soon as he should return the relics of their saints which he had taken from Venice. If there was any question about these relics, the Venetians were willing to refer the issues to the Pope, his legate, or any other appropriate person. For the war indemnity the ambassadors could offer 20,000 to 25,000 florins, instead of the 100,000 asked by King Louis.

The ambassadors were given a fair amount of freedom to decide what to conceal and what to reveal to the king of Hungary. They were instructed to avoid saying anything that would anger him and thus endanger the peace. In minor details they were instructed to agree to terms not specifically authorized in their instructions if it seemed best to do so. They were directed to write back to the Collegio concerning any serious modifications of the authorized terms, giving the proposed changes and their advice concerning them. They were allowed five ducats a day for their expenses, beside what was required for Pierre de Thomas, his retinue, and guards.[42]

On Sunday, December 4, 1356, the Venetian ambassadors left their home city en route for Zagreb with Pierre de Thomas.[43] They remained in Hungary for about two months in

[41] On this point the Collegio allowed them to offer more than was allowed in the maximum terms given to Pierre de Thomas.

[42] MHSM, V, 303–06.

[43] On December 1 it was decreed that the ambassadors should leave Venice the following Sunday under penalty of one hundred pounds each (MHSM, V, 303). Their official authorization, giving them plenipotentiary powers, is dated December 3 (MHSM, V, 307–08).

the effort to make peace. They were unable to reach any agreement with King Louis, because he insisted that Zara be relinquished by Venice, and the ambassadors did not have the authority to grant his concession. At length the king requested that the negotiations be transferred to Venice, since the remaining disagreement could be resolved only by the Venetian home government. He declared that he had devised a reasonable way of settling the Zaratine question, and if that question were settled, the two parties could easily agree on other issues. Thus it was decided that the Venetian ambassadors should return home and that King Louis of Hungary should shortly send ambassadors to Venice to continue the negotiations.[44] By February 11, 1357, the Venetian envoys to Hungary returned to their home city. The Collegio voted to authorize two of them, Andrea Contareni and Michael Faletro, together with three other men to be elected by the Collegio, to negotiate with the Hungarian ambassadors when they should arrive at Venice.[45] It is probable that Pierre de Thomas returned to Venice with them.[46]

When the Hungarian ambassadors arrived in Venice, negotiations were resumed about the beginning of March.[47] The Hungarians did not live up to the promise of their king that the discussions should be centered around the question of Zara and that if agreement could be reached concerning Zara,

[44] Minutes of the Collegio, March 13, 1357, MHSM, V, 312; Archive of Udine, Historical Papers, codex 23, published in MHSM, III, 361, and in *Mon. Hung. hist., Acta externa,* II, 490.

[45] Minutes of the Collegio, February 11, 1357, MHSM, V, 311. This is the earliest recorded mention of their return.

[46] The first record of his presence in Venice after the journey to Hungary is found in the Collegio minutes of March 17, 1357, MHSM, V, 312. By this time the Hungarian ambassadors had arrived in Venice. Pierre may have returned to Venice with them, but it is more probable that he returned, as he had gone, with the Venetian embassy, with whom he worked most intimately during the negotiations.

[47] They were already in progress on March 13, 1357, MHSM, V, 312.

they would settle all other issues on the basis of the articles previously discussed by the two parties. Instead they demanded that Venice surrender the entire Dalmatian coast with all its cities and territories, which they said belonged to Hungary and had been held illegally by the Venetians. This demand was harsher than those contained in King Louis' original peace proposals, which Pierre de Thomas had brought to Venice in November. During the next several days, the negotiations continued, but the two parties were unable to agree on the major issues.[48] By March 13, the Venetians were beginning to lose patience, and they demanded that the discussions be carried on solely on the basis of the agreements made in Hungary between King Louis and the Venetian ambassadors. The Venetians considered further negotiations a waste of time as long as the Hungarians persisted in their unreasonable demands.[49]

At first, the Hungarians haughtily replied that their king desired to obtain more concessions than the Venetian ambassadors had offered him at Zagreb, or else he would not have asked that the talks be transferred to Venice. In a short time, however, they reduced their exorbitant demands, which had probably been made primarily to give them a good bargaining position. They continued to demand the cession of Spalato, Trau, Sebenico, and Scardona to Hungary. They agreed that Venice should retain control of Nona and Zara but should pay the king an annual quit-rent for Nona and a sum of money for Zara. They continued to demand a war indemnity of 100,000 florins. They also asked that the Venetians furnish King Louis with two galleys for a year, to be used in his projected crusade against the Serbians, and ten galleys if he

[48] The details of these negotiations are discussed in Archive of Udine, Historical Papers, codex 23, MHSM, III, 361–64; *Mon. Hung. hist., Acta externa,* II, 490–94. The editor, Ljubic, in MHSM, III, 361, n. 1, on the basis of internal evidence believes that this document was composed in 1356–57, and is therefore contemporary.

[49] Minutes of the Collegio, MHSM, V, 312.

should undertake a crusade to deliver the Sepulcher of the Lord. The Hungarians demanded that under Venetian control the Zaratines should enjoy the liberties which they had enjoyed in the time of the Ban Mladen.[50] This last demand led to much discussion, because the Venetians and the Zaratines could not agree on the extent of the liberties included under that formula. The Zaratines demanded full control of their city and of the adjacent island of Pago. They also insisted that they should not be required to pay taxes to support the Venetian garrison at Zara. The Venetians refused to grant these concessions.[51]

Thus the Venetians and the Hungarians could not agree to any peace terms, primarily because the latter would not make any final agreement until the Zaratines were satisfied. The Hungarians at length asked the Venetians to state their final intentions. This the Venetians would not do. They considered it useless to do so until some satisfactory solution to the Zaratine question was found. The Hungarians sought license to depart from Venice. This was granted to them. They went to Padua, probably to enlist the aid of Francesco Carrara, lord of Padua, as mediator between them and the Venetians. Pierre de Thomas accompanied them to Padua.[52] They apparently

[50] Voinovitch, *Histoire de Dalmatie,* I, 419–20, 423, 425–27. The Ban Mladen Subitch ruled Zara in the name of Hungary early in the fourteenth century.

[51] Archive of Udine, Historical Papers, codex 23, MHSM, III, 362–65; *Mon. Hung. hist., Acta externa,* II, 492–96. According to this source, the Venetians were ready to accept most of the Hungarian demands but sought some modifications. Instead of the 100,000 florins demanded by the Hungarians, they offered a war indemnity of 40,000 florins, the highest offer they had yet made. They sought to limit their participation in the crusade against Serbia to six months and agreed to provide ten galleys for Louis' proposed crusade to the Holy Land only if he went in person. Since the peace negotiations broke down on the Zaratine question, these issues, which were peripheral, were not resolved at this time.

[52] Archive of Udine, Historical Papers, codex 23, MHSM, III, 365; *Mon. Hung. hist., Acta externa,* II, 496. In this source Pierre de Thomas is erroneously called *episcopus Paretensis.*

made this journey within a few days after March 17, 1357. On that night, according to information received by the Venetian government, the Hungarian ambassadors sent a messenger to the lord of Padua to invite his mediation. The Venetians wrote to Stefano, their notary at Padua, and instructed him to go before the lord of Padua and urge him to do all in his power to bring the negotiations to a successful conclusion. The Venetians expressed their hope that he would consider his own welfare closely linked with that of Venice, even as they felt theirs linked with his.[53] At about this time, the Collegio voted that the five Venetians who had recently negotiated with the Hungarians should confer with the ambassadors who might be sent from the lord of Padua and with Pierre de Thomas. They were then to give their advice to the Collegio in writing.[54]

The lord of Padua sent his vicar to Venice, together with certain other knights in whom the Hungarian ambassadors had confidence. On his behalf, they were to offer their assistance in the peace negotiations between the republic and Hungary. Pierre de Thomas returned to Venice with them. The ambassadors from Padua had an interview with the doge, at which Pierre de Thomas was present. They asserted that their lord

[53] Letter of the Collegio to Stefano, Venetian notary at Padua, March 17, 1357, MHSM, V, 312. The historical manuscript in the archive of Udine, cited in note 52, declares that the Hungarian ambassadors went to Padua with the intention of returning home, but that the lord of Padua entered the negotiations on his own initiative in an effort to make peace between the two powers. This statement is probably incorrect in view of the finding of the Venetian Collegio that the Hungarians had called upon Carrara for help. Likewise, the fact that Pierre de Thomas accompanied the Hungarian ambassadors to Padua indicates that he expected further negotiations there. If the Hungarians were planning to break off the discussions and go home, Pierre would not have gone with them, for, as will appear below, the time for his journey to Constantinople was approaching.

[54] Minutes of the Collegio, March 17 or 18, 1357, MHSM, V, 312. This section of the minutes is not clearly dated. It appears between a letter of March 17 and a record of March 18, so apparently belongs to one day or the other.

desired to see peace restored between the two states for the
honor of both parties and for his own good, since his lands
were close to the battle area. They promised to work with the
papal nuncios to establish peace between the two powers if
the Venetians would inform them of the differences that were
obstructing the peace.[55] The Venetians declined to state their
position to the ambassadors from Padua either verbally or in
writing. On March 28, 1357, the Collegio voted to inform
Pierre de Thomas and the embassy from Padua that they
would present their views to the lord of Padua through a special
ambassador whom they would send to him. They were pleased
that he had entered the negotiations.[56]

Subsequently, the chancellor of Venice went to Padua with
two notaries. He explained to Francesco Carrara that he had
authority only to state the Venetian position, and not to conclude any agreements. He admitted that his government was
wary of entering into any further negotiations with the Hungarians, because they believed that they had been deceived in
the earlier discussions. On their part, the Hungarian ambassadors professed a sincere desire for peace. They felt that they
had erred in leaving Venice with the negotiations completely
disrupted through the discords arising from the Zaratine question. They offered to prolong the truce for an additional
month beyond Easter Sunday (April 9), the day of its expiration, which was rapidly approaching, provided that the Venetians and Hungarians could agree on the division of the Dalmatian coast between them, the principal issue in their dispute,
and only accessory issues remained. It appears that the Hungarians now actually wanted peace, but the Zaratines who were

[55] Archive of Udine, Historical Papers, codex 23, MHSM, III, 365;
Mon. Hung. hist., Acta externa, II, 496.
[56] Minutes of the Collegio, March 28, 1357, MHSM, V, 313–14;
Archive of Udine, Historical Papers, codex 23, MHSM, III, 365; Mon.
Hung. hist., Acta externa, II, 496–97.

in their embassy confused the issues and stirred up more dissension, because they saw that the Hungarians were disposed to peace and feared the conclusion of a treaty that was not to their liking. They reopened the question of the division of Dalmatia. At Padua, the ambassadors from Venice and Hungary met before Francesco Carrara. Pierre de Thomas and Bongiovanni, bishop of Fermo, were also present.[57] Again the negotiations failed to bring about the desired peace. The Hungarian ambassadors withdrew to the lands which their king held in the county of Treviso, and the Venetians returned to their home city, accompanied by Pierre de Thomas.[58]

Bishop Bongiovanni of Fermo accompanied the Hungarian ambassadors to their king's camp. He was able to induce the Hungarians to reveal their final intentions in the peace negotiations, which they would never do before, either in Hungary or in Venice. He received a written statement of these terms, signed by one of the chief Hungarian ambassadors. The Hungarians declared that they were prepared to conclude peace if the Venetians should give a satisfactory answer to all their demands. They renewed their offer to prolong the truce for another month for discussions on accessory points, provided that the Venetians accepted the principal Hungarian demands. With these terms Bongiovanni returned to Padua. The Hungarian ambassadors agreed to wait two days in their camp for the Venetian reply.[59]

[57] For the earlier work of Bongiovanni see above, p. 107. According to *Reg. Vat.* 239, fols. 22r–22v, published in Abraham Bzovius, *Annalium ecclesiasticorum post Caesarem Baronium continuatio,* XIV (Cologne, 1618), col. 1252, Innocent VI had recalled Bongiovanni to Avignon on February 8, 1357. In his edition of Mézières, *Life,* p. 200, n. 25, Joachim Smet suggests that he had obtained permission to remain in the Dalmatian region.

[58] Archive of Udine, Historical Papers, codex 23, MHSM, III, 365–66; *Mon. Hung. hist., Acta externa,* II, 497–98.

[59] Archive of Udine, Historical Papers, codex 23, MHSM, III, 367; *Mon. Hung. hist., Acta externa,* II, 498–99.

The bishop of Fermo and the vicar of the lord of Padua went to Venice and took the Hungarian peace terms to Pierre de Thomas, who had not yet sailed to the East. These three then went to the doge with them. They found him in a council of forty nobles which had been designated to carry on the war. The doge invited them to read and explain the new terms to the council. After he had discussed them with the group, the doge declared to the papal nuncios and the Paduan ambassador that the Venetians had always desired peace and still desired it. Furthermore, the doge and his council were willing to discuss peace with the Hungarians whenever they were willing to do it on the basis of the proposals already presented by the Venetians. However, they asserted that every time they had agreed to treat with the Hungarians concerning the peace, the Hungarians made demands which they knew the Venetians would not accept. The Venetians therefore believed that the Hungarian king did not really want peace but was merely trying to feel out the sentiments of the Venetians. They were out of patience and doubted that Louis would make peace, even if they accepted his so-called final terms. It was now about the beginning of April, and the truce was to run out on April 9. The Hungarian envoys, who were waiting in Conegliano, were notified of the unwillingness of the Venetians to enter into further negotiations. On April 5, they wrote to the bishop of Fermo that they were not surprised at the outcome of this final peace effort, for they had come to believe that the Venetians were not sincere in their professed desire for peace but were merely wasting time in the negotiations. By this time, neither party trusted the other.[60]

Philippe de Mézières probably refers to this closing stage of the negotiations when he tells of a time when Pierre ex-

[60] Archive of Udine, Historical Papers, codex 23, MHSM, III, 367–68; *Mon. Hung. hist., Acta externa*, II, 499–501.

pounded a plan for a peace treaty to a group of nobles in
Venice, and one of those who heard him speak broke forth in
words of blasphemy, denouncing Pierre de Thomas and the
church and urging others to reject the treaty. According to
this story, it was not long before God, the author of peace and
the lover of unity, punished that man for his wickedness, for
on that same day, while he was inciting others to war, he suddenly fell dead. Mézières blamed the Venetians for the failure
of the peace efforts of 1356–57 and accused them of prolong-
ing the war because they trusted in human power and in the
abundance of their riches.[61]

Mézières' account of these negotiations is of little value. He
gives only a misleading general summary of events, probably
because he knew nothing else about them. Most remarkable is
his anti-Venetian bias, especially in view of Pierre de Thomas'
generally favorable attitude toward the Venetians. Probably
Mézières' viewpoint, as expressed in his biography of Pierre
de Thomas, was colored by his indignation at the efforts of the
Venetians to make a separate peace with the Sultan of Egypt
just after the crusade of 1365.[62] His judgment that the Venetians were primarily responsible for the failure of negotiations
for peace in 1357 is not supported by other sources. They
worked for peace at least as diligently and sincerely as the
Hungarians, if not more so.

After the expiration of the truce between them on Easter
Sunday, April 9, 1357, the war between Venice and Hungary
broke out in full fury. It went badly for Venice. Treviso held
out, but its fall seemed imminent. At the instigation of the
king of Hungary, the Venetian subject cities of Spalato, Trau,

[61] Mézières, *Life,* ed. Smet, pp. 72–74; AASS, Jan. 29, III, 615–16
(secs. 26–27).
[62] See below, p. 292.

Sebenico, and Ragusa rose in rebellion and expelled their Venetian counts. Zara fell to the Hungarian armies on December 18. Venice was desperate. On January 12, 1358, the Senate met and discussed the situation. By now it was willing to give up Zara but still tried to retain Ragusa and some other possessions on the eastern shore of the Adriatic. It was too late. The king of Hungary would not give up his conquests on the mainland of Venetia unless the Venetians would surrender all claim to Dalmatia. There was no alternative for the republic. By the Treaty of Zara on February 18, 1358, she surrendered all claim to Dalmatia, including the cities of Nona, Zara, Scardona, Sebenico, Trau, Spalato, and Ragusa. The doge renounced the title *dux Dalmatiae et Croatiae*. In return, the Hungarians agreed to restore the Venetian territories which they had conquered in Istria, Treviso, and Caneta, and to renounce any rights which they may have acquired in those regions. These transfers of land were to be completed in three weeks. All prisoners of war were to be freed, and both governments promised to refrain from reprisals against those in their territories who had sided with the enemy, a stipulation that was subsequently violated on all sides. Free trade was to be allowed to the subjects of each of the powers in the lands of the other, and both parties promised to prevent their subjects from acts of piracy against subjects of the other. In the Treaty of Zara, the power of Venice on the Dalmatian coast was broken. It was a severe blow to her.[63] Philippe de Mézières naïvely presents the latter part of the Veneto-Hungarian War and the Treaty of

[63] Voinovitch, *Histoire de Dalmatie*, I, 451–54; Fessler, *Geschichte von Ungarn*, III, 353–59; Hóman, *Gli Angioini di Napoli in Ungheria*, pp. 370–71; Romanin, *Storia documentata di Venezia*, III, 201–06; Kretschmayr, *Geschichte von Venedig*, II, 216–18. The Treaty of Zara is published in MHSM, V, 368–71. Venice regained Zara in 1409 by purchase from King Ladislas of Naples for 70,000 ducats (Voinovitch, *Histoire de Dalmatie*, I, 481).

Zara as a judgment of God against Venice for breaking off the negotiations against the advice of Pierre de Thomas.[64]

In the effort to negotiate a peace settlement between Venice and Hungary, Pierre de Thomas' diplomatic ability was seen more clearly than ever before. He was active in most of the intricate negotiations. Through several months, he worked patiently for peace amid many discouragements and never despaired of gaining his object until the very end. A great tribute to his integrity is the confidence which was placed in him by both parties to the quarrel. If he worked more closely with the Venetians and seems to have favored them in some phases of negotiations, he did so because the Pope was especially concerned about Venice in view of the responsibilities which he wanted her to assume in the East. At no time was Pierre so pro-Venetian that he forfeited the confidence of the Hungarians. His peace efforts failed not because of anything which he did but because neither party was ready to make the compromises necessary for peace, since each of them hoped to improve their military position so as to be able to demand more favorable terms. In the end, Hungary was the winner.

[64] Mézières, *Life,* ed. Smet, pp. 73–74; AASS, Jan. 29, III, 616 (sec. 27).

# 6

# Mission to Constantinople and Travels in the East

AT THE COLLAPSE OF THE NEGOTIATIONS BETWEEN VENICE
and Hungary, Pierre de Thomas was already preparing to em-
bark for Constantinople to discuss the church union question.
In fact, he had expected to sail before this time, but the ship
on which he had planned to go had left Venice while he was
in Padua making a final effort to reconcile the warring powers.[1]
Thus he found it necessary to provide otherwise for his voyage.
Because of his many labors on behalf of the republic, the
Venetian Senate on March 28, 1357, voted to permit him to
arm a ship of sixty oars in Venice, provided that the crew be
made up of mariners who were neither Venetians nor in the
employ of Venetian ships. However, he might employ as many
as three Venetians to command his ship.[2]

[1] Archive of Udine, Historical Papers, codex 23, MHSM, III, 366;
*Mon. Hung. hist., Acta externa*, II, 497–98.
[2] *Misti*, XXVII, fol. 115r, quoted in Smet's edition of Mézières,
*Life*, p. 201, n. 26. In a letter to the doge on July 17, 1356 (*Reg. Vat.*
238, fol. 142v), Innocent VI had asked him to aid Pierre de Thomas

The mission of Pierre de Thomas to Constantinople was the response of Pope Innocent VI to a letter from the Byzantine Emperor John V Palaeologus expressing interest in church union. This letter had been brought by two ambassadors, Paul of Smyrna and Nicholas Sigeros. They had arrived at Avignon during the octave of Pentecost (June 12–19) in 1356, when they disembarked from a small galley near the church of Notre Dame des Miracles.[3] They were well received in Avignon, and Sigeros was given several rich gifts.[4]

Innocent VI was naturally quite interested in their message. Ever since the schism of 1054, the popes had been seeking to heal the breach between the Greek and Latin churches. From the 1330's, when both Latins and Greeks became aware of the growing Turkish menace in the Aegean which threatened them both, church union negotiations had been carried on with some frequency. Thus far, all efforts for union had failed, because neither party had entered into the discussions with a genuine desire for compromise and mutual understanding. The Byzantines, like Stephen Dushan, were interested only in political advantages, while the Roman Catholics demanded that the Greeks accept a theory of papal government generally accepted in the West but odious to the Orthodox. The union was also hindered by the mutual hatred between Latins and Greeks

in securing passage to the East. This and other letters concerning this mission from the papal archives are in the microfilm mentioned in the Bibliography.

[3] S. Baluze, *Vitae paparum Avenionensium*, ed. G. Mollat, I (Paris, 1914), 334. For the story of this church see Parraud, *Vie*, p. 118, n. 1.

[4] Karl Heinrich Schäfer, *Die Ausgaben der apostolischen Kammer unter Benedict XII, Klemens VI und Innocenz VI* (Paderborn, 1914), pp. 605–06. In the record the name of the Greek ambassador is given as Bayssaereartus. Halecki, *Un Empereur de Byzance à Rome* (Warsaw, 1930), p. 53, n. 1, suggests that this is a corruption of the Latin form of Sigeros' title, megateriarchis. The envoy received a silver water pitcher, gilded and enameled with a base and lid, weighing over thirteen marks, a similar pitcher weighing six marks and sixteen ounces, and a piece of scarlet cloth worth 140 florins.

which had resulted from many clashes of interest since the time of the First Crusade.[5]

The imperial chrysobull which the two envoys brought from John V was dated December 15, 1355.[6] Thus it had been issued a little more than a year after the coup d'état of November 22, 1354, by which the young emperor had regained his throne from John VI Cantacuzenus, who had usurped it for seven years. John V still faced serious difficulties. His rule was opposed by Matthew Cantacuzenus, son of the former emperor, who continued to wage civil war against him for three years after his father's abdication. A more serious menace faced him in the Ottoman Turks, who had been introduced into Europe in considerable numbers in the period of civil war. They had occupied almost all Thrace and in 1354 had captured the city of Callipolis (Gallipoli), which they fortified as a base for further expansion into the Balkans. The people of Constantinople were quick to recognize their danger.[7]

---

[5] An interesting discussion of the reasons for the failure of these discussions is found in M. Viller, "La Question de l'union des églises entre Grecs et Latins depuis le concile de Lyon jusqu'à celui de Florence (1274–1438)," *Revue d'histoire ecclésiastique*, XVII (1921), 280–303, 515–32. For a discussion of the fourteenth-century negotiations before 1354 with an extensive bibliography see Kenneth M. Setton, "The Byzantine Background to the Italian Renaissance," *Proceedings of the American Philosophical Society*, C (1956), 37, 40–45.

[6] The text of this chrysobull is published in Augustin Theiner and Franz Miklosich, *Monumenta spectantia ad unionem ecclesiarum graecae et romanae* (Vienna, 1872), pp. 29–33 (Greek) and 33–37 (Latin). This work is hereafter abbreviated TMUE. Comments on the document may be found in Halecki, *Un Empereur*, pp. 32–34, and in Smet's note in his edition of Mézières, *Life*, p. 202. Halecki, *op. cit.*, p. 52, notes that it did not take six months to travel from Constantinople to Avignon. He suggests that the departure of John V's embassy may have been delayed by the Orthodox opponents of the union. It is also a possibility that Stephen Dushan's death in December, 1355, caused the emperor to examine the Balkan situation anew before sending the ambassadors to the Pope.

[7] Halecki, *Un Empereur*, pp. 9–10; Neculai Jorga, "Latins et grecs d'Orient et l'établissement des Turcs en Europe, 1342–1362," *Byzantinische Zeitschrift*, XV (1906), 213–16.

In his chrysobull, John V, as several of his predecessors had done, combined a promise of future faithfulness to the Roman Catholic Church with an appeal for military aid against his enemies. An unusual feature of his letter is his effort to prove his sincerity by offering a detailed series of guarantees for the fulfillment of his promises. Doubtless, the plan which he proposed is an evidence of his good faith, but it is also a testimony to his naïveté and lack of understanding of world conditions in his day.

His letter began with John's solemn promise to be obedient to the Pope and his legitimate successors, to receive his legates and nuncios reverently, and to do all in his power to induce the people of his empire, both laity and clergy, to become faithful, obedient, reverent, and devoted to the papacy. However, he recognized that the long duration of the schism had hardened the hearts of his people so that they could scarcely be drawn from their accustomed ways unless by means of wisdom, moderation, and prudence. Therefore the emperor, in consultation with Archbishop Paul of Smyrna and Nicholas Sigeros, had devised a plan intended to surmount these difficulties. Upon the Holy Gospels, he had taken a solemn oath to carry out its terms to the best of his ability.

John V proposed that after receiving his letter Pope Innocent VI should send three galleys to Constantinople with the two Byzantine envoys. Upon the arrival of these ships, John promised to surrender his second son Manuel to Archbishop Paul of Smyrna, who should send him to the Pope in one of the galleys. The other two galleys John would retain for the defense of his empire, together with two others which Archbishop Paul should fit out in the East for this purpose, presumably with funds brought from Avignon. As soon as possible after the arrival of the emperor's son in Avignon, the Pope should send an army of 500 cavalry and 1,000 infantry

in fifteen transport ships. These troops and the five afore-
mentioned galleys were to be at the emperor's command for
six months to aid him against the Turks and his Greek enemies.
In assuming that the Pope could send such large forces to the
East at short notice, John V was clearly misinformed about
Innocent's true situation.

During these six months, according to John's plan, a papal
legate in consultation with the emperor was to confer benefices
and ecclesiastical dignities upon able Greeks who should spon-
taneously accept the union of the churches. John expressed
confidence that by the close of the period his people as a whole
would gladly accept the union in gratitude for the assistance
given by the papal forces. If they would not accept it, he was
prepared to enforce their obedience to it with the advice of
the papal legate, who would be given a large palace as a
permanent residence and a venerable and beautiful church. It is
difficult to conceive how John could have expected his people
to accept church union so readily or how he thought they
could be coerced into it. This detail he had apparently not
worked out. Nevertheless, there is reason to believe from studying his plan that, absurd as it seems, John really believed that
the Pope could raise forces of sufficient strength to defeat the
Turks decisively and to enforce any program agreed upon by
the emperor and the papal legate.

John promised to give his eldest son a teacher from the
West to instruct him in the Latin language and its literature
under the direction of the legate. He also offered to provide
three large dwellings in which a Latin school could be established and to encourage the Greek nobles to send their children there to learn Latin letters. The idea of providing such
teaching for children of the Greek leaders, which was not
original with John V, possessed real merit, for the difficulty
of communication, linguistic and otherwise, between Greeks

and Latins was one of the greatest barriers to political and ecclesiastical union between Christians of the East and the West.

To prove his good faith, the emperor offered certain guarantees. He declared that if he should fail to do his part to effect the union of the churches after receiving the requested aid from the West, he would consider himself unworthy of imperial power and would abdicate in favor of his eldest son. He would then relinquish to the Pope all parental rights over that son, so that the Pope could provide him with tutors and guardians of his own choosing and arrange a suitable marriage for him. The Pope could seize the Byzantine Empire in the name of that son as legitimate emperor. Just how John thought the Pope would be able to gain control of the empire or even of the heir, who was not the son to be sent to Avignon, was not discussed. John also proposed that if Innocent VI should send three or more galleys to the East with the archbishop of Smyrna and the emperor failed to send his son Manuel to Avignon as he promised, the Pope and his representatives should be entitled to exact 4,000 florins from the Byzantines for every galley sent to Constantinople. This sum could readily be secured by confiscating the property of Byzantine subjects in the Latin states of the East. On the surface, this proposal looks practicable, until it is recognized that the Pope was not the ruler of these Latin states and that their rulers probably would not permit exactions against Byzantines who were living in their midst by virtue of trade treaties or other mutually advantageous agreements.

If the emperor fulfilled his promises completely, Innocent was to be obligated to aid him against all his enemies, especially against the infidels, so that they could be expelled from Christian lands. The money for this purpose must come from the Pope, because the Byzantine Empire was too poor to bear the expense. The emperor requested that he be made the chief captain and standard-bearer of this crusade and therefore the commander of all the troops who should come from the West to participate in it. In this way, he apparently hoped to avoid any aggression by ambitious Western leaders against his empire and to minimize the danger of clashes between Greeks and Latins, such as had often marred earlier crusades. If he should lose power over his empire so that he should be unable to fulfill his promises, John V asked the Pope to absolve him of all blame and to aid him in regaining his throne. Thus he protected himself in the event of a victory of Matthew Cantacuzenus or an uprising of the Orthodox against the union.

John V's letter to Pope Innocent VI was the first to propose such a detailed program for bringing the schism to an end and securing Western help for Byzantium. Earlier Byzantine emperors had at times written to popes, but their letters contained only declarations of intentions and confessions of faith. John Palaeologus did not stop with such generalizations but sought to develop a practicable plan for church union. A study of his proposals and his later actions gives the impression that the emperor sincerely intended to do all he could to promote church union. Nevertheless, if he did not deliberately promise more than he could perform, he promised all that he could fulfill under the best possible circumstances and carefully left himself so many loopholes that he could always justify his actions somehow. Because his plan did not fit in with real conditions in West or East, it was virtually worthless and, as we shall see, in his reply Innocent VI wisely ignored it.[8]

[8] Halecki, *Un Empereur,* pp. 31–35. Halecki was the first scholar to make a careful study of these negotiations. While disagreeing with him on some points, I acknowledge the essential soundness of his work and my indebtedness to it. On p. 31, n. 2, Halecki notes that some historians have looked upon John V's letter to the Pope as a hoax perpetrated against the men of the West by an emperor who had a low opinion of their good judgment. He finds the most distinct expression of this viewpoint, which is found as early as the seventeenth

Among the persons in the East who shared John V's interest in church union were the two men who served as his envoys to the Roman Curia. The more important of these was Paul, archbishop of Smyrna, a Latin, who in the name of the Holy See had accepted the emperor's promises of fidelity and obedience to the Roman Catholic Church. Paul was originally from south Italy. He had been appointed to the see of Smyrna on July 10, 1345, shortly after the Latins had conquered that city from the Turks. He had a perfect command of both Latin and Greek and was well versed in Eastern affairs. It is generally agreed that he is the Latin bishop who about this time (1355–56) took part in a theological discussion between Gregory Palamas, chief of the Hesychasts, and the noted antipalamist writer Nicephoras Gregoras. He was then at the beginning of an extended period of work on behalf of church union.[9]

_____

century, in Berger de Xivrey, "Memoire sur l'empereur Manuel Paléologue," *Memoire de l'Academie des Inscriptions,* XIX/2 (1853), 22–23. On the other hand, Viller, "La Question de l'union des églises," *Revue d'histoire ecclésiastique,* XVIII, 58, n. 1, considers that this letter was inspired by great wisdom and prudence and marks notable progress in the relations between the Byzantines and the papacy. The truth lies between these extremes. Halecki himself takes a middle view.

[9] Letter of John V to Innocent VI, December 15, 1355, TMUE, pp. 29–37. Nicephoras, Gregoras, *Historiae Byzantinae,* lib. 29, chaps. 55–59, in Migne, *Patrologia Graeca,* CXLIX (Paris, 1865), cols. 229–32; also in *Corpus Scriptorum historiae Byzantinae,* vol. IV, part III, ed. Immanuel Becker (Bonn, 1855), pp. 262–65, where mention is made only of a Latin bishop who took part in the theological discussions. See also Giovanni Mercati, *Se la versione dall'ebraico del codice Veneto Greco VII sia di Simone Atumano, arcivescovo di Tebe* (Studi e testi, vol. 30; Rome, 1916), p. 30 and n. 7; Kenneth M. Setton, "The Byzantine Background to the Italian Renaissance," *Proceedings of the American Philosophical Society,* C, 45–46; Halecki, *Un Empereur,* pp. 36–38, 141–43, 149–57, 173–74, 188, 190, 206–07, 283, 407; C. Eubel, *Hierarchia catholica,* I (Münster, 1913), 206, 445, 456, 482. Paul was appointed to the see of Thebes in 1357, and on April 17, 1366, he was appointed as Latin patriarch of Constantinople in succession to Pierre de Thomas. Paul died about 1371.

It is probable, as Halecki recognizes, that Paul of Smyrna played a large part in the formulation of John V's plan of union, if indeed he was not its chief author, and was intended to be the papal legate to be appointed under its terms. In his chrysobull of 1355, John acknowledged that he consulted with Paul in drawing up the proposals contained in it, and Halecki sees a similarity in spirit and method between them and a plan of 1367 upon which Paul is known to have had profound influence.[10] Paul of Smyrna was therefore probably most responsible for the emperor's exaggerated views about the Pope's ability to give military and naval aid to the Byzantine Empire. Several years later, the Greek Demetrius Cydones complained about the unfulfilled promises made by the archbishop of Smyrna, including the promise of galleys for the defense of the empire.[11] It is difficult to see how Paul felt justified in making such promises. As archbishop of Smyrna, he should have been aware of the Pope's recent unsuccessful efforts to raise a fleet of galleys for the defense of that city.[12] Hence he should have recognized that it would be difficult, if not impossible, for Innocent to raise the galleys and other forces required in John's plan to effect the union of the churches. Because of his own great interest in church union, perhaps he expected news of the emperor's favorable declaration to arouse the leaders of the West as nothing else had done.

Paul's fellow envoy Nicholas Sigeros, grand hetairiarch of

[10] Halecki, *Un Empereur,* pp. 36–38, 149–51. The two plans both exhibit an effort to forsee all possibilities and to give detailed promises on both sides with effective guarantees to assure fulfillment.

[11] Demetrius Cydones, *Correspondance,* ed. Raymond J. Loenertz, O. P., I (Studi e testi, vol. 186; Vatican City, 1956), no. 93, p. 127, which Loenertz dates summer 1364; published with a French translation in Demetrius Cydones, *Correspondance,* ed. Giuseppe Cammelli (Paris, 1930), pp. 31–32. As noted below, p. 178, Cydones also complained of similar unfulfilled promises of "the legate," presumably Pierre de Thomas.

[12] See the beginning of Chapter 7.

the Byzantine Empire, was also of considerable importance in the negotiations of 1355. He had played a significant role in church union negotiations of John VI Cantacuzenus and had represented him in Avignon in 1348 and 1352. His importance in the political life of the empire is attested by his participation in the signing of treaties with Venice in 1349 and 1357. It is interesting to note that his collaboration with Cantacuzenus did not prevent his being called *dilectus familiaris* by John V in the chrysobull of 1355.[13]

Within a month after the arrival of John V's embassy in Avignon, Pope Innocent VI decided to send an embassy to Constantinople, headed by Pierre de Thomas, to discuss the church union question with the emperor.[14] Because of his earlier negotiations with King Stephen Dushan of Serbia, another Orthodox sovereign, Pierre was well qualified for the task. Actually this mission was of much greater importance, because, while Serbia was only an outpost of Orthodoxy, the Byzantine Empire was its ancient and traditional center, and the acceptance of church union there would have had a profound effect throughout the East.

As Pierre's traveling companion and fellow ambassador, Innocent appointed a Dominican friar, Guglielmo Conti, who at this time was appointed bishop of Sisopolis (Sizebolu) in Thrace, on the coast of the Black Sea northwest of Constanti-

---

[13] TMUE, p. 34; Halecki, *Un Empereur,* pp. 38–39; Thomas and Predelli, *Diplomatarium Veneto-Levantinum,* I, 344; II, 39–43; Franz Xavier Miklosich and J. Müller, *Acta et diplomata Graeca medii aevi sacra et profana collecta,* III, *Acta et diplomata res gestas Graecas Italasque illustrantia* (Vienna, 1865), 119, 126.

[14] The earliest letters which refer to this mission are dated July 14, 1356. They are found in *Reg. Aven.* 133, fols. 246r–246v, and are cited by Smet in his edition of Mézières, *Life,* p. 83, n. 46. They concern his proposed visit to his diocese of Patti on his way to or from the East.

nople.[15] Perhaps Conti's principal function on this mission was to act as interpreter for Pierre de Thomas, as Bartholomew of Trau apparently acted on his Serbian mission. There is no evidence that Pierre de Thomas knew Greek.

Through his ambassadors, Innocent VI sent a letter to Emperor John V in which he acknowledged receipt of the emperor's letter with his profession of obedience to the Roman church and his request for aid against the Turks and rebels. He expressed his joy and that of his brethren, the cardinals and prelates of the Roman Catholic Church, at the news of the emperor's good intentions, in which he urged John to persevere. He ignored the elaborate system of guarantees contained in the emperor's letter but simply promised to pray to God for him and to solicit the aid of Christian princes of the West against his enemies if he would persevere in his efforts to lead his people to accept the Catholic faith. The message contained in the letter was to be supplemented by an oral message to be brought by the nuncios.[16]

That Innocent actually intended to send military aid to John V in return for a definite profession of faith in Roman Catholi-

[15] Halecki, *Un Empereur*, p. 55; Eubel, *Hierarchia catholica*, I, 74, 188. Conti was appointed bishop of Sisopolis on July 20, 1356. He was translated to the see of Cittanova in Istria in 1359 and died before April 21, 1363. It was once supposed that he was a Franciscan, and hence the bulls relating to his mission to Constantinople with Pierre de Thomas are published in Wadding, *Annales Minorum*, VIII, 127–30. Girolamo Golubovich, O. F. M., *Biblioteca bio-bibliografia della Terra Sante e dell'Oriente Francescano*, series I, vol. III (Quaracchi, 1919), p. 300; V (Quaracchi, 1927), 94, shows that he was actually a Dominican. See also C. Eubel, ed., *Bullarium franciscanum*, VI (Rome, 1902), 227, n. 3.

[16] Letter of Innocent VI to John V, July 21, 1356, *Reg. Vat.* 238, fols. 140v–142r; Wadding, *Vita*, pp. 128–34; *Annales Minorum*, VIII, 127–28; *Bull. carm.*, I, 89–91; Raynaldus, *Annales ecclesiastici, ad ann.* 1356, chaps. 33–34; Abraham Bzovius, *Annalium ecclesiasticorum post Caesarem Baronium continuatio*, XIV (Cologne, 1618), cols. 1245–47.

cism is attested by letters which he sent to the four great Latin powers of the East. On July 17, 1356, he wrote to the rulers of Genoa and Venice, to King Hugues IV of Cyprus, and to the Knights Hospitaller of Rhodes. He told them about his negotiations with John V and required them to give the Byzantine ruler all possible aid as soon as they should be informed by one or both of the papal nuncios that he had orally ratified the confession of faith which he had professed in his letter.[17] A little later he wrote an additional letter to Genoa, releasing that republic from its alliance with the Turks, made while fighting against Venice, Aragon, and John Cantacuzenus. He reiterated his request that the Genoese aid John Palaeologus if he should renounce the schism.[18]

To aid him in his spiritual ministry in the East Pierre de Thomas received numerous faculties, chiefly for the benefit of Catholics in the lands through which he should travel.[19] He was authorized to employ four unmarried clerks who had not taken holy orders for secretaries.[20] As noted above,[21] he and his companion were granted ample financial provision for their journey. They received letters to the doge of Venice,[22] the kings of Hungary and Cyprus, and the grand master of the Hospitallers, requesting their aid and cooperation, if needed, during their travels in the East.[23]

As noted at the beginning of this chapter, the two envoys

[17] *Reg. Vat.* 238, fols. 142r–142v, published in Halecki, *Un Empereur*. pp. 358–59, summarized in Raynaldus, *Annales ecclesiastici, ad ann.* 1356, chap. 35, and Bzovius, *Annales ecclesiastici,* XIV, 1247.

[18] Letter of August 6, 1356, *Reg. Vat.* 238, fols. 157r–157v; Halecki, *Un Empereur,* pp. 359–60.

[19] *Reg. Aven,* 134, fols. 4v–6v.

[20] *Reg. Aven,* 134, 5r–5v.

[21] Page 110.

[22] *Reg. Vat.* 238, fol. 142v.

[23] *Reg. Vat.* 238, fols. 162v–163r. The letter to the king of Hungary, after which the others are patterned, is published in TVMH, II; 27–28.

sailed from Venice to Constantinople in the spring of 1357. When they arrived in the Byzantine Empire, they found that the emperor was with his army, fighting aagins tthe Turks and the forces of Matthew Cantacuzenus. The nuncios went to the emperor's camp and were received with great honor by John V and his nobles. Pierre de Thomas was the chief spokesman. He delivered Innocent's letter and explained the purpose of his message. Firmly but tactfully he insisted that the emperor declare whether he was prepared to swear his loyalty to the Roman Catholic Church. He dismissed John's elaborate plan for facilitating the union and dissuaded the emperor from sending his young son Manuel, then only five or six years old,[24] to Avignon, as had been suggested in John's letter.[25]

Pierre de Thomas also brought a papal letter addressed to the patriarch of Constantinople. In it, Innocent VI noted that he had received no letter from the patriarch, who he assumed was the emperor's chief counselor and the promoter of the church union negotiations. He charitably assumed that the patriarch had written such a letter and that it had been lost. He urged him to use his influence to promote the union.[26] There was no probability that this letter would be favorably received, for the incumbent patriarch, Callistus, was an avowed foe of Roman Catholicism. For example, in December, 1355, the very month in which John had written his subservient letter to the Pope, Callistus sent a message to the clergy of Bulgaria in which he took the opportunity to castigate the Pope of Rome for separating himself from "the Catholic and apostolic church

[24] Halecki, *Un Empereur,* pp. 32–33.
[25] Mézières, *Life,* ed. Smet, p. 74; AASS, Jan. 29, III, 616 (sec. 28), cf. also the letter of John V to Innocent VI in Mézières, *Life,* ed. Smet, p. 78; AASS, Jan. 29, III, 616 (sec. 30).
[26] Letter of Innocent VI to the patriarch "of the Greeks," August 18, 1356, *Reg. Vat.* 238, fols. 163r–164r; Wadding, *Vita,* pp. 135–38; *Annales Minorum,* VIII, 129; *Bull. carm.,* I, 96–97; excerpt in Raynaldus, *Annales ecclesiastici, ad ann.* 1356, chap. 35.

of Christ." He also declared that baptism by aspersion, practiced by the Latins, was invalid.[27]

In addition to his letters to the emperor and the patriarch, Pierre de Thomas brought letters to others in the East who were interested in church union. Important among these was Filippo de Bindo Incontri, O. P., inquisitor in the East, whom the Pope requested to assist Pierre de Thomas and Guglielmo Conti with helpful advice.[28] Filippo was of Italian descent. He was perhaps born at the Genoese colony of Pera near Constantinople, where he almost certainly entered the Dominican Order. About 1333 he commenced his theological disputes with the Greeks. In 1351 he was appointed as chaplain of the Holy See and inquisitor in Romania. In 1359 his inquisitorial authority was extended to the empires of the Golden Horde and Persia. Pierre de Thomas arrived in the East in the period of Filippo's greatest activity. His four polemical treatises were written in this period. Filippo undoubtedly worked closely with Pierre de Thomas while he was in the East. It is probable that Pierre was the *Reverendissime pater et domine* to whom Filippo addressed his first polemical treatise, the *Libellus qualiter Graeci recesserunt ab oboedientia Ecclesiae Romanae,* which is chiefly an account of the Photian Schism.[29]

Pierre de Thomas also brought papal letters to several other persons resident in the Orient, some Greeks and some Latins, who had written to Innocent VI testifying to the emperor's

[27] Halecki, *Un Empereur,* pp. 49–52.

[28] *Reg. Vat.* 238, fol. 163r; chief parts published in Raymond J. Loenertz, O. P., "Fr. Philippe de Bindo Incontri, O. P., du couvent de Péra, inquisiteur en Orient," *Archivum Fratrum Praedicatorum,* XVIII (1948), 269.

[29] Raymond J. Loenertz, "Fr. Philippe de Bindo Incontri, O. P., du couvent de Péra, inquisiteur en Orient," *Archivum Fratrum Praedicatorum,* XVIII (1948), 265–80; Thomas Kaeppeli, O. P., "Deux nouveaux ouvrages de Fr. Philippe Incontri de Péra, O. P.," *ibid.,* XXIII (1953), 161–83.

good will and expressing their own interest and willingness to cooperate in the cause of church union.[30]

Of the Roman Catholics who encouraged John V in his desire for church union, four were Genoese. The most important of these was Francesco Gattilusio, who had recently received the island of Lesbos as a fief in return for aid given to John V in his struggle against Cantacuzenus.[31] Other Genoese supporters of church union were Lancilotto de Castro, podestà of the Genoese citizens in the Byzantine Empire, Percivallo de Lomellini, a member of a prominent merchant family in the East, and Rafaelo de Fuoneto, podestà and governor of the Genoese colony of Chios.[32] The two other Roman Catholic collaborators in the plan of union are obscure men. Gabriel, bishop of "Azaron," probably of Maronia in Thrace, is otherwise unknown. Henry, "duke of Glagonia," is probably duke of Glagovia in Silesia.[33]

A number of Greeks, still Orthodox, similarly favored the union of the churches and received papal letters.[34] Three of them belonged to the noble family Metochites, which was closely related to the imperial family. Two of the Metochitai mentioned in the papal letters were brothers, Nicephoras, who

---

[30] Letter of Innocent VI to Francesco Gattilusio, duke of Lesbos, August 18, 1356, *Reg. Vat.* 238, fol. 164r; Wadding, *Vita,* pp. 138–39; *Annales Minorum,* VIII, 130; *Bull carm.,* I, 96. A list of persons to whom similar letters were sent is preserved in *Reg. Vat.* 238, fols. 164r–165r. published in Halecki, *Un Empereur,* p. 45, n. 1.

[31] Halecki, *Un Empereur,* pp. 44, 150, 167–68, 190, 195–96, 259; William Miller, "The Gattilusj of Lesbos, 1355–1462," *Byzantinische Zeitschrift,* XXII (1913), 406–10, also published in his *Essays on the Latin Orient* (Cambridge, 1921), pp. 313–17.

[32] Halecki, *Un Empereur,* pp. 44–46.

[33] Halecki, *Un Empereur,* pp. 46–47.

[34] *Reg. Vat.* 238, fols. 164v–165r; Halecki, *Un Empereur,* p. 45, n. 1. As Halecki notes (*ibid.,* p. 47, n. 3), their Orthodox status is shown by the fact that the Pope did not address them as *"dilecti filii"* nor send them the *"salutem et apostolicam benedictionem,"* a formula reserved for Catholics and replaced for others by *"gratiam in presenti que perducat ad gloriam in futuro."*

held the office of grand logothete, and Demetrius, a grand stratopedarch. It is not known whether Alexis Metochites, grand domestic of the empire, was a brother of the other two. Two other lay nobles of distinguished lineage likewise favored church union. These were George Tagaris, grand stratopedarch, and Thomas Palaeologus, uncle of the emperor.[35] Most surprising among the Greek supporters of the union is Maximus Calopherus, who was a caloyer, or member of the Orthodox regular clergy, a group who were normally bitterly opposed to all things Latin. Maximus, also a member of one of the leading families of the empire, belonged to a minority of Greek monks who were favorable to church union.[36]

After delivering his letters, Pierre de Thomas remained in the Byzantine Empire for several months. He discussed the question of church union with all who would listen and induced as many as he could to join the Roman Catholic church. He was well treated by the Greek emperor and nobles, who provided bountifully for his needs. He prayed fervently to God and mortified his body with fastings and afflictions on behalf of the conversion of the Greeks to Catholicism. He put himself in touch with those Greeks who were most favorable to the union of the churches.[37]

At least two Greeks were converted to Roman Catholicism through his preaching. The most important of these was John Lascaris Calopherus, a brother of the Greek monk Maximus who favored church union. This convert later fell into the bad graces of John V because of his secret marriage to the emperor's niece Maria Cantacuzena and fled to the West, where in 1365

[35] Halecki, *Un Empereur,* pp. 47–49; Thomas Kaeppeli, O. P., "Deux nouveaux ouvrages de Fr. Philippe Incontri de Péra, O. P.," *Archivum Fratrum Praedicatorum,* XXIII (1953), 173; R. J. Loenertz, O. P., "Théodore Métochite et son père," *ibid.,* XXIII, 184–94.

[36] Halecki, *Un Empereur,* pp. 49, 274.

[37] Mézières, *Life,* ed. Smet, pp. 74–75; AASS, Jan. 29, III, 616 (secs. 28–29).

Pope Urban V gave him letters of reference addressed to John V and other princes.[38] In that year, he joined the crusade against Alexandria, on which Pierre de Thomas served as papal legate, and afterward continued in the service of Pierre I of Cyprus. He was active in efforts for church union as late as 1374.[39] Pierre de Thomas' other known convert, Demetrius Angelus, a knight of Thessalonica, was the traveling companion of John Lascaris Calopherus in 1365.[40]

It would be interesting to know whether Pierre de Thomas had any significant influence upon Demetrius Cydones, the illustrious Greek statesman and writer of the fourteenth century, who later became a Roman Catholic and one of the most ardent supporters of church union. He accompanied John V on his famous visit to Rome in 1369.[41] It is probable that Cydones was in Constantinople at the time of Pierre de Thomas' visit and that the two men discussed the question of church union, in which Cydones was already interested. Raymond J. Loenertz, O.P., who is preparing an edition of Cydones' correspondence, of which the first volume has ap-

---

[38] Letters of Urban V to John V, to King Pierre I of Cyprus, to the grand master of the Hospitallers, and to the doges of Venice and Genoa, April 18, 1365, *Reg. Vat.* 247, fols. 80r–81v, published in Halecki, *Un Empereur*, pp. 360–63.

[39] Halecki, *Un Empereur*, pp. 91–98, 272–85, 298–99, 326, 360–64; Neculai Jorga, *Philippe de Mézières (1327–1405 et la croisade au XIV^e siècle* (Paris, 1896), pp. 280, 285.

[40] We know of these men as converts of Pierre de Thomas through a letter of Urban V to Pierre on their behalf, April 18, 1365, *Reg. Vat.* 247, fol. 78 [bis] r; *Bull. carm.,* I, 125–26 (where it is erroneously dated April 19). See also Giovanni Mercati, *Notizie di Procoro e Demetrio Cidone* (Studi e testi, vol. 56, Vatican City, 1931), pp. 437–38.

[41] Halecki, *Un Empereur,* pp. 95–98, 143–45, 178, 188–207; Demetrius Cydones, *Correspondance,* ed. Giuseppe Cammelli (Paris, 1930), pp. v–xxxiv; Setton, "The Byzantine Background to the Italian Renaissance," *Proceedings of the American Philosophical Society,* C, 53–54.

peared,[42] believes that Cydones is the noble Greek with whom the inquisitor Filippo de Bindo Incontri argued on a point of textual criticism in 1358, which was during or shortly after Pierre's visit to Byzantium.[43] Pierre de Thomas is undoubtedly the papal legate mentioned in three of Cydones' letters.[44]

Though some of the Byzantines accepted Pierre's message gladly, or at least listened to it sympathetically, others were bitterly opposed to the religion of the West. On one occasion, according to Juan Carmesson, while the papal nuncio was speaking before the emperor about the dignity and wisdom of the Pope and cardinals, and many Catholics were present, a certain important Greek noble burst into a tirade against the Pope and the cardinals and reported some dishonorable things which he claimed to have seen at the Roman Curia. Pierre de Thomas could not bear this and spoke in defense of the leaders at Avignon, revealing the many laudable things which they were always doing, such as celebrating the divine office, securing justice, distributing alms to the poor, and other virtues publicly exhibited by the cardinals. He prophesied that the wrath of God would soon overtake that nobleman because of his blasphemies. On the following night that man was seized

---

[42] Demetrius Cydones, *Correspondance*, ed. R. J. Loenertz, O. P., vol. I (Studi e testi, vol. 186, Vatican City, 1956).

[43] Loenertz, "Fr. Philippe de Bindo Incontri," *Archivum Fratrum Praedicatorum*, XVIII, 267, 270–71; R. J. Loenertz, *Les Recueils de lettres de Démétrius Cydonès* (Studi e testi, vol. 131, Vatican City, 1947), pp. 109–10.

[44] Cydones, *Correspondance*, ed. Loenertz, no. 31, p. 61; no. 93, p. 127; no. 97, p. 134. Loenertz dates these letters 1362, 1364, and 1365. According to him the first and third are addressed to George the Philosopher, the second to Simon Atumano. On the latter see Setton, *op. cit.*, pp. 47–52. Loenertz' letter no. 31 is summarized in his article "Fr. Philippe de Bindo Incontri," *Archivum Fratrum Praedicatorum*, XVIII, 274–75, and by Smet in his edition of Mézières, *Life*, p. 209. Loenertz' letter no. 93 is published with a French translation in Cydones, *Correspondance*, ed. Cammelli, pp. 29–33, where it is dated 1362–70 and is said to be without address.

by internal ailment characterized by much inward pain and swelling. He lingered until the next day and died miserably. The people considered this an evidence of divine judgment, and as a result three Greek nobles were converted to Catholicism and later journeyed to Avignon to be confirmed in the Latin rite.[45] This could be the occasion of the conversion of John Lascaris Calopherus and Demetrius Angelus, both of whom later went to Avignon, and it is possible that Demetrius Cydones was the third.

In the Byzantine Empire, the chief interest and mission of Pierre de Thomas was to discuss the question of church union with Emperor John V. The progress of these negotiations is best known through a letter of the emperor to Pope Innocent VI dated November 7, 1357, which is included in both contemporary biographies of Pierre de Thomas.[46] In it, the emperor reports that Pierre de Thomas discussed the Catholic faith with him while they traveled with the imperial armies and urged him to make a public declaration, but he did not feel able to make a commitment until he could return to Constantinople. Perhaps he was not ready to take any action until he should gain at least a partial victory over his enemies. Upon his return to Constantinople, the emperor made a public profession of the Catholic faith, promising in the presence of many bishops that he desired to observe the same fidelity to the Pope as was observed by other Catholic princes. He declared that with the advice of his nobles he swore to Pierre de Thomas that he held everything which was held by the Roman

---

[45] Carmesson, *Vita,* in *Spec. carm.,* II, 180. This passage is of special interest because it is only one I have found in Carmesson's biography which has no real parallel in Mézières' work.

[46] Mézières, *Life,* ed. Smet, pp. 76–79; AASS, Jan. 29, III, 616–17 (secs. 30–32); Carmesson, *Vita,* in *Spec. carm.,* II, 181–82; *Bull. carm.,* I, 91–92. Smet's edition is a complete critical edition with all the variant readings from both Mézières and Carmesson. The text of this letter is known only from these manuscripts.

Church and wished to live and die in that faith. If this is true, at least the circle of nobles which was closest to him favored the union at this time. Mézières adds the detail that John V at this time devoutly received the Eucharist from the hands of Pierre de Thomas.[47]

In his letter, John did not seek to paint an unduly favorable picture of the prospects for church union. He admitted that he could not induce all his people to obey the Roman Church, because they were not all faithful to him, and many were lying in wait, seeking an occasion against him. However, if the Pope would send him the aid which he had requested, John assured him that all the people of the East would be subject to the Pope and faithful to him. The emperor reminded Innocent of his family's loyalty to Roman Catholicism, especially that of his great-great-grandfather Michael VIII, who had remained true to the Catholic faith to the end of his life.[48] John reiterated his desire to fulfill all the promises made in his letter of December, 1355. Only the advice of Pierre de Thomas had prevented him from sending his son to Avignon. The emperor expressed his desire to visit the Pope and express his fidelity in person. He assured the Pope that he need not be discouraged because the patriarch of Constantinople was hostile to church union, for he would depose him and replace him by a proponent of church union.

The emperor thanked Innocent VI for sending so wise and prudent a man as Pierre de Thomas as his nuncio, for his empire was greatly encouraged through his ministry, and through his teaching both Greeks and Latins had been turned to a better life. John also attributed certain temporal blessings to the efficacy of Pierre's benediction. For example, soon after

[47] Mézières, Life, ed. Smet, p. 75; AASS, Jan. 29, III, 616 (sec. 29).

[48] John wrote of his proavus but obviously was referring to Michael VIII rather than to Andronicus II, who was consistently Orthodox in his policy.

receiving it he had captured a great Turkish prince, and many fortified towns acknowledged his lordship.[49] Matthew Cantacuzenus, contender for the imperial title, was captured with his wife, two sons, and two daughters.[50]

Was John V actually converted to Catholicism at the time of Pierre de Thomas' mission as nuncio? Scholars have not agreed in their answers to this question. Halecki asserts that John V was not officially converted to Catholicism at this time. He says that the only evidence of his conversion was his reception of Communion in the Latin rite, an act which he considers merely an evidence of the emperor's personal good will and not an official acceptance of Catholicism.[51] On the other hand, Viller and Smet take the view that the emperor's actions are evidence of a full conversion to the Roman Catholic faith.[52] This view is clearly the correct one. When the emperor swore fidelity to the Pope and the Roman Catholic Church in the presence of many bishops, declared his full acceptance of Catholic teachings, and took Communion in the Latin rite, there can be little doubt that he became a member of the Roman Church. As will appear below, when Pierre de Thomas

[49] Halecki, Un Empereur, p. 67. This Turkish prince was probably Khalil, son of the Ottoman Sultan Orkhan and Theodora, daughter of Emperor John Cantacuzenus. He was actually captured by the Genoese governor of Phocaea. Orkhan later forced John V to pay half Khalil's ransom and to go and bring him from Phocaea, also to betroth his daughter to Khalil.

[50] Nicephoras Gregoras, Historiae Byzantinae, lib. 37, chap. 16, in Migne, Patrologia Graeca, CXLIX (Paris, 1865), cols. 499–502; also in Corpus Scriptorum historiae Byzantinae, vol. IV, part III, ed. Immanuel Becker (Bonn, 1855), pp. 564–67. Joannes Cantacuzenus, Historiarum libri IV, chaps. 45–49, in Migne, Patrologia Graeca, CLIV (Paris, 1866), cols. 335–66; also in Corpus Scriptorum historiae Byzantinae, vol. XX, part III, ed. Ludovicus Schopenus (Bonn, 1832), pp. 327–60.

[51] Halecki, Un Empereur, p. 62, and n. 2.

[52] Viller, "La Question de l'union des églises," Revue d'histoire ecclésiastique, XVIII, 58, n. 2; Smet in his edition of Mézières, Life, p. 204.

was commissioned as papal legate in 1359, Innocent VI wrote
to John V as a Catholic and made provision for aiding him
against the Turks.

When his business in Constantinople was completed, Pierre
de Thomas bade farewell to the emperor,[53] about the end of
1357, and sailed to the kingdom of Cyprus, intending from
there to make a pilgrimage to the Holy Land. He landed at
Famagusta, on the southeastern coast of the island. When King
Hugues IV heard about his arrival in his kingdom, he went
to meet him. He received him with all the honor due to a dignitary of the church and brought him to his capital, Nicosia.
Pierre de Thomas refused these honors as much as he could.
In a kindly way he said to the king, "I am not a nuncio or a
legate of the Pope, but just a poor pilgrim friar, desiring to
visit the Sepulcher of the Lord, and therefore may it please
your majesty not to show me these honors, because I am not
worthy of them." The king replied, "Lord bishop, we know
you well and what the Lord has been pleased to do by your
hands. Even if you were not a papal nuncio nor a bishop, nevertheless we would want to honor you as a master of theology
and because of your virtues." Pierre responded humbly, again
asserting his own unworthiness and citing Holy Writ, so that
a pious struggle arose between him and the king. At length
Pierre de Thomas preached before the king, who praised him
greatly and continued to heap honors upon him.[54] In this incident, Pierre's true humility is seen. When he felt that the
honor of the church was at stake, he insisted upon being treated
with the greatest respect and honor, but he did not seek or
expect recognition for himself.

It was natural that Pierre de Thomas should visit Cyprus

[53] Mézières, *Life,* ed. Smet, p. 80; AASS, Jan. 29, III, 617 (sec.
34), says that he bade farewell to the emperor with tears.
[54] Mézières, *Life,* ed. Smet, p. 80; AASS, Jan. 29, III, 617 (sec.
34).

on his way to the Holy Land, for that kingdom was the farthest outpost of Latin Christendom in that direction and a center of the pilgrim traffic, as well as for trade between East and West. Hugues IV was a member of the French house of Lusignan, which had ruled the island for a century and a half. Since 1269 they had also held the crown of Jerusalem, now an empty dignity since the Moslem reconquest of all Palestine. Hugues was an able ruler, who kept the peace in his land. Though he had contributed to the Christian fleet which had captured Smyrna from the Turks in 1344, he was generally content to maintain the defense of his own island and was not interested in offensives against the Moslems.[55] During this visit to Cyprus Pierre de Thomas may have discussed the defense of the Byzantine Empire with Hugues IV, but there is no record of such a discussion.[56]

While he was visiting at the court of Cyprus, Pierre de Thomas was struck with a serious illness. The king and all his people were greatly concerned. The queen of Cyprus, Alice d'Ibelin,[57] prepared his food with her own hands throughout his illness, and he ate no other food. His illness lasted many days, after which he recovered and was able to continue on his journey.[58]

After thanking the king for all his kindness, Pierre sailed from Cyprus to the Holy Land against the advice of the king,

[55] Sir George Francis Hill, *A History of Cyprus*, 4 vols. (Cambridge, 1940–52), II, 301–05.

[56] Such a discussion is suggested by Smet in his edition of Mézières, *Life*, p. 80, n. 43. Pierre de Thomas carried a letter to Hugues IV as well as to other Latin rulers of the East urging them to aid Palaeologus if his conversion should prove to be genuine (*Reg. Vat.* 238, fols. 142r–142v; Halecki, *Un Empereur*, p. 359). Pierre thus had the authority to organize an alliance to help Byzantium but seems to have taken no action until he could again confer with the Pope in Avignon.

[57] Hill, *History of Cyprus*, II, 283.

[58] Mézières, *Life*, ed. Smet, p. 81; AASS, Jan. 29, III, 617 (sec. 35).

who warned him that his presence there would be divulged
to hostile Saracen authorities by merchants who were false
Christians. He arrived safely in Palestine, probably in 1358,
and was received with joy by the faithful Christians in Jerusalem. He visited the Sepulcher of the Lord and other holy
places with much devotion and effusion of tears. He celebrated
mass over the Holy Sepulcher. He prayed earnestly for the
Christians of the Holy Land and urged them to stand for Christ
even unto death. Very many of these Christians said to him,
"Father, you cannot escape bodily death, for you are known
as a papal nuncio." Pierre was little alarmed at these words,
for he earnestly desired martydom if it should be God's will
for him. He assembled as many Christians as he could from all
nations on Mount Zion at the hour of terce and fearlessly
preached in the presence of all the Saracens who were coming
and going at that mid-morning hour. These Saracens murmured
against him, and the Christians present grew fearful, but no
one laid a hand on him. When his pilgrimage was completed,
Pierre de Thomas returned without hindrance to Cyprus, where
he was received with admiration by King Hugues.[59] Later
Hugues learned and reported to the Pope in a letter that the
sultan of Egypt, overlord of Palestine, had ordered the emir
of Jerusalem beheaded when he learned that a papal nuncio
had been allowed to preach publicly in Jerusalem and to
escape alive.[60]

While preparing for his return to the West, Pierre de
Thomas remained in the Carmelite house at Famagusta, Cyprus,
for some time. During this period several evidences of his
unusual devotion are reported. Every night at about midnight,
he prostrated himself upon the floor of his cell and prayed so

[59] Mézières, *Life,* ed. Smet, pp. 81–82; AASS, Jan. 29, III, 617–18
(secs. 36–37).
[60] Mézières, *Life,* ed. Smet, p. 83; AASS, Jan. 29, III, 618 (sec.
38).

intently that he was oblivious of all that was going on about him. On one occasion, his chaplain was walking through Pierre's room without a light and walked over him without Pierre's even knowing it. It is reported that Armenians and others who lived near the house said that they often saw fire from heaven hovering over his room during the hours when he was at prayer.[61]

Pierre de Thomas' visits to the Holy Land and Cyprus at this time were of great importance in his life. He is remembered as one of the great promoters of the crusade against the Moslems in the fourteenth century. Yet there is no evidence of his interest in the crusade before 1358, although the question of church union, which he had discussed with the rulers of Serbia and Byzantium, was closely related to the defense of Europe against the Turks. His real interest in the crusade as such dates from the time of his visit to Cyprus and the Holy Land. He was deeply stirred when he actually saw the places associated with the life of Christ ruled by Moslems. Then too, although there is no record of it, it is probably during this period that he became acquainted with Pierre de Lusignan, son and heir of Hugues IV, who for ten years had been interested in promoting a crusade to rescue the Holy Land from the Moslems and to restore the Latin kingdom of Jerusalem, which was his legal heritage.[62]

At length, Pierre de Thomas left Cyprus for Avignon.[63]

[61] Mézières, *Life,* ed. Smet, p. 82; AASS, Jan. 29, III, 618 (sec. 37).

[62] Aziz Suryal Atiya, *The Crusade in the Later Middle Ages* (London, 1938), pp. 319–23. Atiya credits Pierre de Thomas as a principal influence in causing Prince Pierre of Cyprus to be interested in the crusade. The reverse is probably true, for Atiya himself admits that Pierre de Lusignan was interested in the crusade for ten years before this time, whereas there is no evidence of Pierre de Thomas' interest in it prior to his visit to the Holy Land and Cyprus.

[63] Mézières, *Life,* ed. Smet, pp. 82–83; AASS, Jan. 29, III, 618 (sec. 38).

Perhaps on his homeward journey he visited his diocese of Patti and Lipari in Sicily. He had hoped to make such a visit either on his way to Constantinople or on the return journey, for he had obtained an indulgence from Innocent VI permitting him to grant holy orders in his diocese or in the city of Messina, even though the island of Sicily was under interdict, provided that the ceremonies were held privately and no excommunicated or interdicted persons were admitted. At the same time, he received an indulgence permitting him to celebrate the divine office publicly with open doors three times in Messina and three times in his own diocese, provided that no excommunicated person were admitted, though persons merely under interdict might be permitted to attend.[64] Since Pierre went to Constantinople by way of Venice and was long occupied in negotiations there, his visit to Sicily must have been made on the return journey, if at all.

Pierre de Thomas returned to Avignon from his visit to the East in the latter part of 1358 or early in 1359. He was received by the Pope and cardinals and reported to them about the state of affairs in the East.[65] It may have been only after his return to Avignon that he delivered the oral messages given to him by the Byzantine emperor,[66] though he may have sent this information to the Pope in a confidential letter, no longer extant, before embarking on his dangerous pilgrimage to the Holy Land.

Pierre de Thomas must have returned to Avignon from Constantinople with a happier spirit than he had on his return

---

[64] Letters of July 14, 1356, *Reg. Aven.* 133, fols. 246r–246v, cited by Smet in his edition of Mézières, *Life,* p. 83, n. 46.

[65] Mézières, *Life,* ed. Smet, pp. 82–83; AASS, Jan. 29, III, 618 (sec. 38).

[66] Letter of John V to Innocent VI, November 7, 1357, Mézières, *Life,* ed. Smet, p. 79, lines 5–7; AASS, Jan. 29, III, 617 (sec. 32); Carmesson, *Vita,* in *Spec. carm.,* II, 182.

from Serbia a few years earlier. In Serbia, he had been able to accomplish little or nothing in the cause of church union. In Constantinople, he found the emperor and many of the nobles sympathetic to church union, though the majority of the clergy and people remained hostile to all things Latin. Through the information which he brought from the East and the letters of the Byzantine emperor and the king of Cyprus, Pope Innocent VI became increasingly aware of Pierre de Thomas' ability as a diplomat and his knowledge of Eastern affairs. Thus the stage was set for the humble Carmelite friar to play a role of increasing importance in the next seven years.

# 7

# The League Against the Turks

PIERRE DE THOMAS DID NOT REMAIN IN AVIGNON FOR LONG after his return from the East. On May 11, 1359, Pope Innocent VI, recognizing his unusual knowledge of that region, appointed him as papal legate in the East, primarily to lead the Christian powers in their defense against the Turks.[1] This was an important point in Pierre's life. While his interest in the crusade had probably been aroused during his visit to Cyprus and the Holy Land, it was only with this appointment that he assumed an active role in this movement, which occupied the major part of his attention for the remainder of his life. In his day the idea of the crusade against the infidel included two major interests, the traditional crusader's goal of rescuing the Holy Land from the Moslems and the newer

[1] *Reg. Aven.* 140, fols. 54r–55r; *Reg. Vat.* 234, fols. 2r–2v; Wadding, *Vita,* pp. 144–50; *Bull carm.,* I, 100–02.

objective of defending Christendom against the Turkish menace. In 1359 Pierre was most intimately concerned with this
newer phase of the crusade. Later the reconquest of the holy
places became his chief objective, especially after further talks
with Pierre de Lusignan in Cyprus.

By 1359, the Latin powers in the Levant, and the papacy
as well, had been concerned with the Turkish menace for
about thirty years. They first began to sense the danger about
1330. Their first concrete action was taken in 1343, when,
with the encouragement of Pope Clement VI, the Venetians,
the Knights Hospitaller of Rhodes, and the king of Cyprus
joined in equipping a fleet which captured the city of Smyrna
from the Turks in the following year. After this first flush of
enthusiasm, the others gradually withrew from the venture,
so that by 1349 the Hospitallers were left as the sole cham-
pions of the Latins against the Turks. In 1350, Clement VI
induced the three powers to renew their earlier league against
the Turks for ten years. In the treaty, a squadron of eight
galleys was established, three from Venice, three from the
Knights of Rhodes, and two from Cyprus. A papal legate was
to be in command. The Pope and each of the three powers was
to contribute 3,000 florins annually for the defense of Smyrna.[2]

The league of 1350 came to nothing. Hugues IV of Cyprus

---

[2] Jules Gay, *Le Pape Clément VI et les affaires d'Orient (1342–
1352)* (Paris, 1904), pp. 119–21; Delaville le Roulx, *Les Hospitaliers
à Rhodes jusqu'à la mort de Philibert de Naillac (1310–1421)* (Paris,
1913), pp. 110–11; Raynaldus, *Annales ecclesiastici, ad ann.* 1350,
chap. 33; *ad ann.* 1351, chap. 22. Published sources concerning this
league may be found in the following: Louis de Mas Latrie, *Histoire
de l'île de Chypre sous le règne des princes de la maison de Lusignan*
II (Paris, 1852), 217–18; LC, II, 184; Thomas and Predelli, *Diplomatarium Veneto-Levantinum,* 2 vols. (Venice, 1880–99), I, 349–50;
II, 2–3; Eugène Déprez, ed., *Innocent VI (1352–1362). Lettres closes,
patentes et curiales se rapportant à la France,* fasc. 1 (Paris, 1909),
no. 44, col. 28; no. 55, cols. 34–35; no. 246, cols. 173–74; nos. 248–
49, cols. 175–76. Venice and the papacy paid their 3,000 florins for the
defense of Smyrna in 1351 and the papacy also paid this sum in 1353.

gave no evidence of real interest in it. Venice was soon diverted for five years by her naval war against Genoa. Clement VI sought in vain to activate the league. Before his death in 1352, he admitted defeat and released the Hospitallers from their oaths.[3] Soon after his accession, Pope Innocent VI sought to renew the league against the Turks[4] but made no progress until March, 1357, when Venice, Cyprus, and the Hospitallers agreed to a new alliance against the Turks for five years from September 8, 1357. Its terms were similar to those of the league of 1350, except that the contributions of Venice and the Hospitallers were reduced from three galleys to two galleys from each.[5] The formation of the new league made no real change in the situation in the East. The active defense of the Latins in this region continued to be carried out solely by the Hospitallers.[6] The papacy received no cooperation from the Latin maritime powers for the defense of Smyrna. They even avoided paying the 3,000 florins expected annually from each of them for this purpose.[7]

Thus by the spring of 1359, Innocent had come to the realization that he could not rely upon the Latin powers of the East to defend Christendom against the Turks without

[3] Thomas and Predelli, *Diplomatarium Veneto-Levantinum*, II, 1–3; Gay, *Clément VI et les affaires d'Orient*, pp. 121–24; Delaville le Roulx, *Les Hospitaliers à Rhodes*, pp. 110–12; Raynaldus, *Annales ecclesiastici, ad ann.* 1351, chap. 22.

[4] Déprez, *Lettres d'Innocent VI*, no. 44, col. 28; no. 55, cols. 34–35; no. 246, cols. 173–74; nos. 248–49, cols. 175–76; nos. 260–65, cols. 184–93; Mas Latrie, *Histoire de Chypre*, II, 221–22; Raynaldus, *Annales ecclesiastici, ad ann.* 1355, chaps. 38–41; 1356, chap. 36; Delaville le Roulx, *Les Hospitaliers à Rhodes*, pp. 125–26; Oskar Halecki, *Un Empereur de Byzance à Rome* (Warsaw, 1930), p. 29; Thomas and Predelli, *Diplomatarium Veneto-Levantinum*, II, 26–28.

[5] Thomas and Predelli, *Diplomatarium Veneto-Levantinum*, II, 35–39; Mas Latrie, *Historie de Chypre*, II, 218–19; LC, II, 261–62.

[6] Delaville le Roulx, *Les Hospitaliers à Rhodes*, pp. 139–40.

[7] LC, II, 264; Neculai Jorga, *Philippe de Mézières et la croisade au XIVe siècle* (Paris, 1896), p. 101.

more positive leadership from the papacy. The fleet provided by the treaty of 1357 existed only on paper, and the power of the Turks was growing. At this time, the Ottomans were beginning their systematic conquest of the Balkan peninsula.[8] The Byzantine emperor had professed his adherence to the Roman Catholic faith and was appealing for assistance through Pierre de Thomas, who was in the West to plead the emperor's cause. Innocent decided to intervene more actively in the affairs of the East by sending Pierre as his legate to promote the papal policy there.

In his new office, Pierre's mission was primarily to promote the crusade against the Turks. In his commission, dated May 11, 1359, Innocent noted his concern about the afflictions and annoyances to which the Christian people of the East, and especially of Smyrna, were subjected by the Turks, who were now spreading into more and more territory with the purpose of blotting out the Christian name. To fulfill his mission, Pierre de Thomas was given full power to negotiate with kings, princes, and other authorities, both ecclesiastical and secular, to make and confirm alliances between the Christian powers of the area, and to make peace between warring groups. He could proceed with ecclesiastical censures against all who obstructed his efforts. His legatine authority extended throughout the patriarchate of Constantinople, the kingdom of Cyprus, and the archbishoprics of Crete, Smyrna, Patras, Athens, Thebes, Corinth, Rhodes, Naxos, Corfu, Durazzo, Lepanto, and Neopatras. In this region, he was directed to work for the reformation of churches and ecclesiastics and the improvement of the morals of the people, in addition to promoting the crusade. Innocent expressed his full confidence in Pierre de Thomas, describing him as "a devout and prudent man, learned in the Catholic faith and frequently proven in arduous labors, espe-

[8] Halecki, *Un Empereur*, pp. 73–74.

cially in those parts (i.e. the East), distinguished in wisdom and filled with many virtues." [9]

At the same time, Innocent issued letters to Pierre de Thomas and to other Latin prelates authorizing the preaching of a crusade against the Turks throughout Pierre's jurisdiction [10] and in all the territories of Genoa and Venice.[11] In these letters, he enumerated some additional complaints against the Turks. When they occupied new territories, they frequently massacred Christians. Others they sold like brute beasts, and when they had reduced them to bitter servitude, forced them to abjure the Christian faith and trample the cross underfoot; they also burned churches and other buildings which they were not able to hold. Pierre de Thomas and the prelates associated with him were authorized to confer the crusader's cross upon all who should request it. To anyone who should spend a year in the service of the league against the Turks, at his own expense or with the support of another, a plenary indulgence was offered, just as to crusaders going to the Holy Land. This indulgence was also offered to anyone who would support another in this service for a year. In a letter of May 12, 1359, Pierre de Thomas was authorized to excommunicate all Christians who traded with the Turks or made agreements with them. He was also given the power to dissolve alliances between Christians and Turks, releasing the Christian parties from their oaths.[12]

[9] *Reg. Aven.* 140, fols. 54r–55r; *Reg. Vat.* 234, fols. 2r–2v; Wadding, *Vita,* pp. 144–50; *Bull carm.,* I, 100–02. Raynaldus, *Annales ecclesiastici, ad ann.* 1359, chap. 16, quotes the part of the commission which lists Pierre's virtues.

[10] Letter to Pierre de Thomas and to the chief prelates of his jurisdiction, May 11, 1359, *Reg. Aven.* 140, fols. 62v–63v; *Reg. Vat.* 234, fols. 7v–8r; Wadding, *Vita,* pp. 150–57; *Bull. carm.,* I, 102–04; partial text in Raynaldus, *Annales ecclesiastici, ad ann.* 1359, chap. 16.

[11] Letter of the same date to Pierre de Thomas and to the archbishop of Genoa and the bishop of Castello, *Reg. Aven.* 140, fol. 63v; *Reg. Vat.* 234, fol. 8r.

[12] *Reg Aven.* 141, fols. 22r–22v.

To give him the added prestige which befitted his new mission, Innocent VI translated Pierre de Thomas· from the see of Patti to the more important bishopric of Coron, a Venetian city in southern Greece.[13] The Pope ordered all prelates and nobles of the East to receive Pierre kindly and grant him safe-conduct.[14] For his support, he was entitled to procure six florins a day from ecclesiastics through whose lands he might pass. If he needed to stay in any one place for an extended period, neighboring prelates were also to help defray his expenses.[15] He might threaten with ecclesiastical censures any clergyman, even a member of a religious order, who would not grant him the support that was due.[16] To aid him in his work, he was authorized to appoint seven unmarried clerks not in holy orders to serve as notaries.[17] He could require the services of Franciscans, Dominicans, and members of other religious orders, even those residing outside the bounds of his jurisdiction.[18] He was permitted to reserve eight benefices of an annual value of not more than twenty gold florins to be given by him to able men.[19] Thus he could reward his associates.

As was customary in the case of legates who were to exercise their office far from the Roman Curia, Pierre de Thomas

[13] Letters of May 10, 1359, *Reg. Aven.* 140, fols. 97v–98v; *Reg. Vat.* 234, fols. 28r–29v. These include the letter of appointment and letters of notification to the people of his diocese, the archbishop of Patras, and the doge of Venice. The letter of appointment is published in Wadding, *Vita,* pp. 140–43, and *Bull. carm.,* I, 100. According to Hermann Hoberg, *Taxae pro communibus servitiis ex libris obligationum ab anno 1295 usque ad annum 1455 confectis* (Vatican City, 1949), p. 43, the *servitia communia* of this bishopric, amounting to 650 florins, were paid on May 21, 1359.

[14] *Reg. Aven.* 140, fols. 55r–56r; *Reg. Aven.* 141, fol. 23v; *Reg. Vat.* 234, fols. 2v–3r. References for these and other papal letters concerning this legation were obtained from the microfilm mentioned in the Bibliography.

[15] *Reg. Aven.* 141, fols. 17v–18r, 20v–21r.

[16] *Reg. Aven.* 141, fol. 17r.

[17] *Reg. Aven.* 141, fols. 17r–17v.

[18] *Reg. Aven.* 140, fol. 62v; *Reg. Vat.* 234, fol. 7v.

[19] *Reg Aven.* 141, fols. 18v–19r.

was given much spiritual authority and responsibility. Through able priests of his retinue, he was to see that the Catholics of his jurisdiction confessed regularly.[20] He was appointed as inquisitor in his territory with full power to investigate and prosecute heresy and to call upon the secular arm to deal with serious offenders.[21] He had full power to strike all persons with ecclesiastical censures, to relax such censures, and to negotiate with excommunicated persons when desirable.[22] He received numerous faculties and privileges for the benefit of his own retinue and of the Catholics of his jurisdiction.[23]

At the time of Pierre's appointment as legate in the East, Innocent also made a new arrangement for the defense of Smyrna. Since 1356, Archbishop Orso Delfino of Crete had been acting in a dual capacity as legate and as papal vicar and captain of Smyrna.[24] Now in 1359 the Pope separated the two offices. While he appointed Pierre de Thomas as legate, the vicarate and captaincy of Smyrna were entrusted to Niccolo Benedetti, preceptor of the Knights Hospitaller in Venosa. Since the Hospitallers were the nearest Latin power to Smyrna and most interested in its defense, the choice was a wise one. Benedetti's commission was for eight years. During this period,

[20] *Reg. Aven.* 141, fol. 23v.

[21] *Reg. Aven.* 140, fol. 64r; *Reg. Vat.* 234, fols. 8v–9r; Wadding, *Vita,* pp. 161–63; *Bull carm.,* I, 105–06, partially published in Raynaldus, *Annales ecclesiastici, ad ann.* 1359, chap. 18.

[22] *Reg. Aven.* 140, fols. 61r-62v; *Reg. Vat.* 234, fols. 6v–7v; *Reg. Aven* 141, fols. 19v–20r.

[23] *Reg. Aven.* 140, fols. 60v–62r; *Reg. Vat.* 234, fols. 6v–7r, 9r; *Reg. Aven.* 141, fols. 21r–21v. Among these are the right to grant a certain number of dispensations to illegitimate persons, to those married within the prohibited degrees, and to those who had traded with the infidel or gone to Jerusalem without the license of the Holy See.

[24] Jorga, *Mézières,* p. 139, n. 5; Eubel, *Hierarchia catholica,* I (Münster, 1913), 215, 266, 288, 351; Sir George Francis Hill, *A History of Cyprus,* 4 vols. (Cambridge, 1940–52), II, 302, n. 4; Raynaldus, *Annales ecclesiastici, ad ann.* 1356, chap. 36.

he was to maintain a force of 150 Latin mercenaries to guard
the city and two papal galleys to patrol the seas. Within seven
years, he was to fortify the city with walls and towers.[25] It
thus appears that the Pope decided to add two galleys of his
own to those which were to be supplied by the maritime powers
according to the treaty of 1357.

For his support, Innocent ordered that Benedetti should receive the 3,000 florins annually which the papacy had been
providing for the defense of Smyrna.[26] Presumably he was also
expected to receive the like sums that were due from Venice,
Cyprus, and the Hospitallers, whenever they should be paid.
He was authorized to send two galleys and another ship as
often as he desired to trade at Alexandria and in other overseas
territories of the sultan, except in iron and wood products and
other forbidden merchandise.[27] All Catholic clergy and nobles
were required to give Benedetti safe-conduct as he traveled to
Smyrna. He was permitted to secure as many as ten members
of religious orders to give him spiritual aid during his term
of office. He was authorized to grant certain indulgences to
those who would aid the war against the Turks.[28] Niccolo and

[25] Benedetti's commission, dated May 11, 1359, is in *Reg. Aven.*
140, fols. 60r–60v; *Reg. Vat.* 234, fols. 6r–6v. The essential facts
concerning this commission are stated in a papal letter to Orso, archbishop of Crete, of the same date, *Reg. Aven.* 140, fols. 63v–64r; *Reg.
Vat.* 234, fol. 8v, published in Wadding, *Vita,* pp. 157–61; *Bull. carm.,*
I, 104–05; and Raynaldus, *Annales ecclesiastici, ad ann.* 1359, chap. 16.

[26] Letter to the papal nuncio, Pietro Damandi, May 25, 1359, *Reg.
Vat.* 241, fols. 63r–63v, ordering him to pay this sum annually to
Benedetti from papal funds. Benedetti was informed of this action
in a letter of the same date, *Reg. Vat.* 241, fols. 63v–64r. This letter
is confused by Halecki, *Un Empereur,* p. 69, n. 1, with his original
commission, issued two weeks previously.

[27] Two letters of May 11, 1359, *Reg. Aven.* 140, fols. 56r–56v;
*Reg. Vat.* 234, fols. 3r–3v. These letters are identical except that the
one permits him to send *una navis* and the other *duo galeae.* The captains of the ships and all merchants traveling on them were required
to swear that they would not engage in any illicit trade.

[28] *Reg. Aven.* 141, fols. 18r–18v, 22v–23r.

his two brothers Francesco and Pace were entitled to retain any land which they should conquer from the Turks,[29] and the two brothers, in the order named, were granted the right of succession to the vicarate of Smyrna during his eight year term of office.[30]

Innocent VI also made provision in 1359 to assist the Byzantine emperor John V. It was impossible for him to send as much aid as John had requested in his letter of December, 1355, but he ordered the forces of the league against the Turks to assist the emperor. In one of his letters to Pierre de Thomas, the Pope reminded him that according to his own testimony John V had sworn henceforth to obey the Roman Church, to profess its tenets, and to do all in his power to induce his people to accept the same viewpoint. Therefore Innocent called upon Pierre to aid the emperor and to urge the faithful to help him recover his lands from the Turks and other enemies of the Christian name, so that as he should receive aid from the Roman Church, he might be impelled to adhere more firmly to his laudable purpose. In this letter, Innocent spoke of the emperor as *carissimus in Christo filius noster,* indicating that he considered him a Catholic.[31]

In this period, Innocent VI also wrote to King Hugues IV of Cyprus. He informed him of the new arrangements for

[29] *Reg. Aven.* 141, fols. 23r–23v.

[30] Letter to Francesco and Pace Benedetti, May 11, 1359, *Reg. Aven.* 140, fol. 57r; *Reg. Vat.* 234, fols. 3v–4r. Francesco Benedetti was a Hospitaller, like his brother Niccolo. Pace is simply called a Florentine citizen. Smet in his edition of Mézières, *Life,* pp. 206–07, calls the first of these brothers Giovanni.

[31] Letter of May 11, 1359, *Reg Aven.* 141, fols. 20r–20v; another copy dated May 12, *ibid.,* fols. 21v–22r, in which Pierre de Thomas was authorized to proceed against anyone who should oppose his efforts to assist the emperor. These letters are cited by Smet in his edition of Mézières, *Life,* p. 208, n. 12. Innocent's successor, Urban V, did not, however, accept John V as a Catholic. In writing to him on April 18, 1365 (*Reg. Vat.* 247, fols. 80r–80v, published in Halecki, *Un Empereur,* pp. 360–61), Urban addressed him as a non-Catholic.

the defense of the East. He required him to receive Pierre de Thomas kindly when he should visit his kingdom and to accept the advice which he should give. He called upon Hugues and the other members of the league of 1357, Venice and the Hospitallers, to aid Pierre de Thomas and Niccolo Benedetti in the defense of Smyrna and of the entire East against the Turks.[32] At this time, the members of the league made a real effort to fulfill their commitments, probably because of the initiative which the Pope had taken. On June 8, 1359, the Venetian Senate voted that the two galleys required by the treaty be placed in the service of the league. For their maintenance in Crete, 2,000 ducats were assigned and 4,000 additional ducats for the convoys of March and September. Furthermore, a crew of oarsmen and some equipment were to be sent to Crete for the legate's galley.[33] By the fall of 1360, the king of Cyprus and the Knights Hospitaller had each provided two galleys for the league, and Pierre de Thomas had one of his own.[34]

By July 14, 1359, Pierre de Thomas and Niccolo Benedetti arrived in Venice on their way to the East. They requested the Venetian government for a larger contribution to the league than had been asked when the treaty of 1357 was signed. The

[32] Letter of Innocent VI to Hugues IV of Cyprus, May 10, 1359, *Reg. Aven.* 141, fols. 23v–24r.

[33] Senato, *Misti,* XXIX, fol. 7v (June 8, 1359). This and the following references to the *Misti* were called to my attention in the footnotes in Smet's edition of Mézières, *Life,* pp. 208, 210, and have been verified in the microfilm at the Lea Library of the University of Pennsylvania.

[34] Senato, *Misti,* XXIX, fol. 90r (October 14, 1360). By this time Hugues IV of Cyprus had died and his son Pierre I, who was greatly interested in the crusade, had ascended the throne. Perhaps Cyprus did not contribute her galleys to the league until after the young king's accession. Mézières, *Life,* ed. Smet, p. 84; AASS, Jan. 29, III, 618 (sec. 39), does not mention the galleys of Cyprus in his account of the fleet which Pierre de Thomas assembled in the summer or autumn of 1359.

Senate replied that it would hold strictly to its earlier commitments. Its members even contested their obligation to pay 3,000 ducats a year for the defense of Smyrna. They claimed that an earlier payment of such a sum was purely a voluntary contribution, and not due to any obligation which they had assumed. However, the Senate voted to furnish a galley to the legate and the captain of Smyrna.[35] This was probably the galley which Pierre had at his own command a year and a half later, as noted above.

Pierre de Thomas arrived in the East about the late summer of 1359. He gathered the galleys which were available and visited the city of Smyrna and other places in his jurisdiction.[36] He appears to have gone rather quickly to Constantinople. Here he found the emperor fighting against the Turks and in need of help. According to Mézières' account Pierre de Thomas quickly aroused all the Christians of his jurisdiction to war against the Turks, promising them many spiritual and temporal benefits. He strengthened the Byzantine emperor and all the magnates and people of the empire by his preaching, his holy life, and his assistance in war. He endured many physical dangers and labors for the exaltation of the faith. He sustained many reproaches from the envious and also from detractors and false Christians, but God gave him many victories against the Turks.[37]

One recorded event in this struggle is an attack directed

[35] Senato, *Misti,* XXIX, fol. 14v (July 14, 1359). Halecki, *Un Empereur,* p. 69, states incorrectly that the Venetians provided only one galley for the league against the Turks. This galley was for the personal use of Pierre de Thomas and of Niccolò Benedetti. As noted above, the Senate had already voted two galleys as its contriubtion to the league.

[36] Mézières, *Life,* ed. Smet, p. 84; AASS, Jan. 29, III, 618 (sec. 39).

[37] Mézières, *Life,* ed. Smet, pp. 84–85; AASS, Jan. 29, III, 618 (sec. 39). Mézières' chronology for this period cannot be accepted with assurance, but in the absence of contradictory evidence it seems best to follow it.

against the Turkish fortress town of Lampsacus, situated at some distance from the sea on the Dardanelles opposite Gallipoli. Pierre de Thomas himself joined in this expedition with the galleys of the Latin league and some Byzantine galleys. The Christian forces landed and stormed the city. The legate was in the thick of the battle, urging on the forces. After many dangers and toils they captured the city, sacked it, and burned it. Then they held a council and decided to return to their ships. Meanwhile the main body of the Turks, who had been absent from the city at the time of its capture, returned in time to see it in flames. Heartsick and angry, in large numbers they lay in ambush to block the escape of the Christian forces from the town to the sea. Ignorant of the true state of affairs, Pierre de Thomas led his company in an orderly march to their galleys. He had fifty of the Knights Hospitaller and very many Venetians, Genoese, Englishmen, Greeks, and other Christians. Suddenly the Turks jumped from their hiding places. Howling and shouting, they made an attack on the Christians. Most of the Christian mariners and fighters fled helter-skelter to the galleys, each one trying to get ahead of the other, deserting their standards to the reproach of their faith.

Pierre de Thomas did not run away with the others. He was grieved at their cowardice. With the Knights Hospitaller and a few other Latins, he resisted the Turks and did not turn his back. Fighting with great difficulty against superior numbers, these few Christians gradually made their way to the galleys. By strenuous effort, they drove the Turks back so that the Christian forces could reach the ships. In this skirmish, according to Mézières' exaggerated account, only seven of the legate's band were killed, bravely making their defense, while many of the other Christians lost their lives in their flight. The Turks are reported to have lost about three hundred men, including their captain. In this episode Pierre de Thomas

showed great bravery and presence of mind, which would later
serve him well in the crusade of 1365 at Alexandria.[38]

Thus a genuine effort was made by the forces of the Latin
league under the leadership of Pierre de Thomas to aid the
Byzantine emperor in his struggle against the Turks. This effort
was a concrete answer to John V's appeals of 1355 and 1357.
This fact has not always been recognized. Halecki takes the
view that the promising negotiations of 1357 came to naught.
He says that the papal registers are silent on relations with
Byzantium for eight years after 1356. He believes that Pierre de
Thomas, in the case of the Byzantine Empire as in the case of
Serbia, resorted to a policy of forceful repression to compel
the Eastern Orthodox population to accept Catholicism.[39] His
evidence for this repressive policy is drawn from the bulls in
which Pierre was given inquisitorial power in his jurisdiction
and the power to proceed against heretics and schismatics
with ecclesiastical censures and the aid of the secular arm.
He notes that Pierre was able to put this program into opera-
tion only in the island of Crete, where those who would not
be converted were threatened with the stake.[40]

This view represents a complete misunderstanding of the
policy of Innocent VI and Pierre de Thomas toward the Byzantine Empire in 1359. Unfortunately, in his research Halecki

[38] Mézières, Life, ed. Smet, pp. 85–86; AASS, Jan. 29, III, 618–19
(sec. 40). Parraud, Vie, pp. 152–53, says that Pierre de Thomas actually waged corporal war at this time. From Mézières' account it is difficult to tell whether Pierre participated in the fighting or merely stood
by to encourage and bless the soldiers. Mézières speaks not only of
Pierre's benedictio but also of his strenuitas, the same word which he
uses for the efforts of the Knights Hospitaller and other fighting men
who were present on this occasion.

[39] As noted above, pp. 100–02, this is an incorrect view which
some scholars have taken concerning the attitude of Pierre de Thomas
after the failure of his mission to Serbia.

[40] Halecki, Un Empereur, pp. 60, 70–71. R. M. Dawkins echoes
this view of Pierre's activity in Crete in a note in his edition of Leontios Makhairas, Recital concerning the Sweet Land of Cyprus entitled
"Chronicle," II (Oxford, 1932), 94–95.

failed to find the letters in which the Pope recognized John V as a Catholic and directed his legate to assist him against the Turks. There is no evidence that the routine powers to prosecute heretics and schismatics given to Pierre de Thomas at the beginning of his legation mark the beginning of a policy of forcibly converting the people of the Greek East to Catholicism. These powers applied chiefly, if not solely, to the Latin territories in the East. Pierre's proceedings in Crete were directed not against the Orthodox faith of the native Greeks but against a heresy among the Venetian overlords.[41] Pierre de Thomas not only aided the Byzantines at the Battle of Lampsacus but continued to include their empire in his field of interest throughout his service as legate in the East.[42]

While Pierre de Thomas was performing the many duties of his office, word came to him that a serious heresy was springing up in the island of Crete. He was greatly disturbed by this news and at once went to Crete with one small galley in the hope of uprooting the heresy before it should gain strength. Mézières, whose work is the sole source of information about this episode, tells nothing about the nature of the heresy, nor does he give any precise indication of the time when Pierre learned about it. The position of his account of these events in his biography suggests that they occurred in 1359, probably in the autumn.[43]

It is reported that Pierre de Thomas went to Crete against

[41] Mézières, *Life,* ed. Smet, pp. 87–89; AASS, Jan. 29, III, 619 (secs. 42–46). Even John Hackett, *A History of the Orthodox Church of Cyprus* (London, 1901), pp. 128–29, though generally hostile to Pierre de Thomas, does not cite his actions in Crete as evidence of persecution of the Orthodox.

[42] Mézières, *Life,* ed. Smet, pp. 85–86; AASS, Jan. 29, III, 618–19 (secs. 39, 41). For this criticism of Halecki's viewpoint I am indebted to Joachim Smet, O. Carm., who discusses it in his edition of Mézières, *Life,* pp. 211–12. His reasoning is fully supported by the sources, the most important of which he was the first to discover.

[43] Mézières, *Life,* ed. Smet, pp. 87–90; AASS, Jan. 29, III, 619 (secs. 42–47).

the advice of his friends, who warned him that he would face serious trouble there for two reasons. First, the leader of the heresy was a first cousin of the duchess of Crete and had many powerful friends who could obstruct the legate's efforts. Second, Pierre de Thomas by his marvelous preaching had kept some Venetian galleys in the service of the league against the Turks beyond the term for which they had been given by the Venetian government. His friends feared that the duke of Crete would demand the hire of these ships, which Pierre was unable to pay.[44] It is difficult to accept the truth of this last assertion. The galleys contributed by Venice to the league were subject to the terms of the treaty of 1357, by which they were to be in its service until September, 1362, very shortly before Pierre de Thomas returned to Western Europe. Thus their term of service could not have ended by the time of Pierre's visit to Crete, even if it did not occur as early as 1359.

When Pierre arrived at the city of Candia, it is reported that the duke of Crete, probably Pietro Baduario,[45] received him neither as a papal legate nor as a friend but as an enemy. As Pierre's friends had feared, the duke demanded the hire of the galleys rudely, proudly, and with threats. The legate wisely ignored these demands and cautiously began to inquire about the heresy. He learned that it had already spread throughout the island and had led many to forsake the Catholic faith. He summoned all the heretics in the city of Candia, including their leader, the duchess' cousin. They came before him with boldness, arrogance, and anger. In a kindly way, he examined them

---

[44] Mézières, *Life,* ed. Smet, p. 87; AASS, Jan. 29, III, 619 (sec. 42).

[45] Ernst Gerland, *Das Archiv des Herzogs von Kandia im königlichen Staatsarchiv zu Venedig* (Strassburg, 1899), p. 32. Pietro Baduario was duke of Crete from 1358 to 1360. If Pierre's visit to Crete occurred later in his legation than appears from its position in Mézières' biography, perhaps Marino Grimani (1360–62) was duke when he arrived.

in a doctrinal discussion. They answered him insolently and evaded his questions. Later he examined them individually and learned more about their errors. He called upon the duke, as representative of the secular arm, to aid him in suppressing the heresy. At his wife's instigation, the duke answered him angrily, heaped reproaches upon him, denied him aid, and uttered threats against him. A murmur arose in the city and throughout the island for the death of Pierre de Thomas and his associates, so prevalent had the heresy become. The legate comforted his fearful retinue. He showed his usual willingness to die for the exaltation of the Catholic faith.[46]

On the next day, so the story continues, Pierre de Thomas excommunicated the duke of Crete with solemn ringing of bells and placed an interdict upon the city of Candia. The observance of the divine office was suspended and all church doors were shut. Pierre spoke to the duke so boldly that everyone was amazed. He reminded the duke that the Catholic Church gave kingdoms to the faithful and took them away from the unfaithful. If they continued to support heresy and disobbedient men, the lord Pope would take the government of Crete away from the Venetians and give it to some other authority.[47] When one remembers the traditional friendship between the papacy and the Venetian government, Innocent VI's reliance upon the republic as one of the chief supporters of his Eastern policy, and the cordial relations which Pierre de Thomas had recently had with the leaders at Venice, it is difficult to believe that he addressed the duke of Crete in this way. There are undoubtedly elements of truth in Mézières' account, but exaggeration is apparent in almost every detail.

The story concludes in the same manner. We are told that

---

[46] Mézières, *Life,* ed. Smet, pp. 87–88; AASS, Jan. 29, III, 619 (secs. 42–43); Wadding, *Vita,* pp. 30–31, also in *Spec. carm.,* II, 206.
[47] Mézières, *Life,* ed. Smet, p. 88; AASS, Jan. 29, III, 619 (sec. 44).

the duke's heart was gripped by the fear of God when he heard the pronouncements of Pierre de Thomas. He feared the loss of his government and sought pardon from the legate. Pierre received him with humility and induced him and the others to renounce all evil. Afterward in a public ceremony, Pierre officially condemned the duke and his council to be burned as heretics, whereupon they confessed their heresy and begged for pardon, which was granted to them.[48] The duchess' cousin persisted in his heresy and was burned at the stake by order of the duke. And now, wonder of wonders, the inhabitants of Crete, who previously had gnashed their teeth against him, almost venerated Pierre de Thomas, and he was greatly honored by the duke and the nobles. When the heresy was stamped out in Candia, Pierre de Thomas traveled to the city of Canea, where he had the bones of an adherent of the same heresy dug up and burned.[49] Apparently the leaders of Crete harbored some malice against Pierre de Thomas, for in 1360 they lodged a complaint against him at Venice.[50] Of this Mézières was probably unaware.

After a time, Pierre left Crete and sailed for Smyrna, where he underwent many labors and dangers for the defense of the city. Sometimes he paid the mercenaries there from his own funds. He regularly admonished them and preached to them and often went with them to fight against the Turks. He used all the money which he could obtain from his own revenues, from preaching, or otherwise to support the garrison of Smyrna and the war against the Turks.[51]

During this period, the war against the Turks was carried

[48] This detail is at variance with the earlier part of Mézières' story, in which the duke is not himself guilty of heresy but merely of refusing to help Pierre stamp it out.

[49] Mézières, *Life,* ed. Smet, pp. 88–89; AASS, Jan. 29, III, 619 (secs. 45–46).

[50] Senato, *Misti,* XXIX, fol. 90r (October 14, 1360). The nature of this complaint will be discussed below.

[51] Mézières, *Life,* ed. Smet, p. 89; AASS, Jan. 29, III, 619 (sec. 46).

on so effectively under Pierre's leadership that the Turks generally lost ground. One of the chief Turkish princes, the emir of Ephesus (Altoluogo), rendered tribute, which he had never done before to any other legate or Christian leader, and ever afterward he honored the Christians in his territory. The emir's submission greatly simplified the task of defending Smyrna.[52] This emir was probably Khidr Bey, who led the Turkish forces on the western coast of Asia Minor after the death of his brother, 'Umar Bey, emir of Smyrna.[53]

There are a few references to Pierre de Thomas and affairs in the East in the papal archives for the latter months of 1359. On October 28, Innocent instructed Pierre to look into the condition of the monastery of St. Catherine in Crete of the Order of St. Basil, which was said to have become vacant and to have been occupied by infidels or schismatics. He was instructed to make provision for it.[54] In November, the Pope planned to arm new galleys at the expense of the Apostolic Camera and other Catholics for a term of three years. He again ordered the crusade to be preached in Cyprus and in the Latin East in general, as well as in Italy and certain other countries. The tithe of all ecclesiastical revenues for three years was provided to support the cause.[55]

From the beginning of 1360, the interest of Pierre de Thomas shifted increasingly toward the affairs of the kingdom of Cyprus and the plans of King Pierre I to drive the Moslems from the Holy Land, which will be discussed in chapter 8. Nevertheless, he continued to travel widely in the fulfillment

---

[52] Mézières, *Life*, ed. Smet, p. 86; AASS, Jan. 29, III, 619 (sec. 41); Halecki, *Un Empereur*, p. 72.

[53] Gay, *Clément VI et les affaires d'Orient*, pp. 86–93.

[54] *Reg. Aven.* 140, fol. 124v; *Reg. Vat.* 234, fol. 47v; cited by Smet in his edition of Mézières, *Life*, p. 210 and n. 20.

[55] Letter of November 23, 1359, minute in *Reg. Vat.* 244L, fol. 48r (no. 130), cited by Halecki, *Un Empereur*, p. 73, n. 1, and by Smet in his edition of Mézières, *Life*, p. 210, n. 21; letter to the king of Cyprus, October 26, 1359, *Reg. Vat.* 244L, fol. 18r, cited by Halecki, *loc. cit.*

of his legatine duties. Sometimes he was in Smyrna, sometimes in Cyprus, Crete, or Turkey. Sometimes he had many galleys at his command, sometimes few or even only one. Regularly he engaged in preaching and teaching. He made war, converted and baptized Moslems and induced a few Greek Orthodox people to unite with the Latin church. He gave unsparingly of his time and energy to this work.[56]

In the midst of these labors, while traveling from Rhodes to Cyprus on a French ship, Pierre de Thomas is reported to have performed a miracle. During the voyage a storm arose, and the vessel was badly tossed about, so that the seamen feared for their safety. When they came near Paphos in Cyprus, instead of going into port the ship was driven into a very dangerous place. The mariners called upon God for help and cast sixteen anchors[57] into the sea, all to no avail. Then they went to Pierre de Thomas for assistance. He prayed for the safety of the ship and took a certain cross which he had,[58] fastened it to a rope and lowered it into the sea. Immediately the sea became calm, and all those on board thanked him for saving their lives.[59]

---

[56] Mézières, *Life,* ed. Smet, p. 86; AASS, Jan. 29, III, 619 (sec. 41).

[57] It is interesting to note that they used as many as sixteen anchors. Though modern ships use only two or three anchors, Auguste Jal, *Archéologie navale,* II (Paris, 1840), 168–72, shows from contemporary records that it was common for medieval ships to use many anchors. They were manipulated by hand and were therefore much lighter than modern anchors operated by machinery.

[58] This was probably the jeweled processional cross of Pierre de Thomas which was said to contain a piece of the true cross. It is mentioned by Philippe de Mézières in a will drawn up in January, 1369, published in Neculai Jorga, "Le Testament de Philippe de Mézières," *Bulletin de l'Institut pour l'étude de l'Europe sud-orientale,* VIII (1921), 132.

[59] Mézières, *Life,* ed. Smet, p. 96; AASS, Jan. 29, III, 621 (sec. 54); Carmesson, *Vita, Spec. carm.,* II, 186, also published in Mas Latrie, *Histoire de Chypre,* II, 284. Mézières calls the ship *navis magna Franciae* and Carmesson, *magna navis Provincialium.*

A little information about the activities of the Latin league against the Turks in 1360 is found in the records of the Venetian government and the papacy. In March, 1360, the Venetian government learned that Zelabi, lord of Sinope, was arming galleys on the Black Sea. It was decided that the captain of the Gulf, Bertucio Civrano, should go to Constantinople with four galleys to consult the Venetian bailie there about the advisability of the Venetian forces' entering the Black Sea to do battle against Zelabi. It was left to the decision of these men whether to invite the Genoese and the Byzantine emperor to join such an expedition. If they decided upon action against the lord of Sinope, Civrano was to invite Pierre de Thomas to join him with the galleys of the Latin league or at least to permit the two Venetian galleys in the allied fleet to participate in the expedition.[60] There is no evidence that Pierre de Thomas was ever approached concerning this affair.

On October 12, 1360, Innocent VI granted faculties to Pierre de Thomas to proceed against the Saracens and other infidels,[61] thus broadening his original commission to lead the crusade against the Turks. Perhaps in this grant the Pope aimed to show his recognition and approbation of the growing interest of his legate and of Pierre I of Cyprus in the reconquest of the Holy Land from the Saracens.

At about the same time, a complaint arrived in Venice from the duke of Crete and his council that Pierre de Thomas had deserted the league against the Turks, the salvation of Christians, and had gone to Cyprus with one of the Venetian galleys and two furnished by the kingdom of Cyprus. They asserted

---

[60] Senato, *Misti*, XXIX, fol. 54r (March 31, 1360). For this and other archival references, papal and Venetian, concerning the Latin league I am indebted to the research of Joachim Smet, O. Carm., as presented in his edition of Mézières, *Life,* pp. 210–11. All of them have been checked in the microfilms noted in the Bibliography.

[61] *Reg. Aven.* 144, fol. 563r.

that he had disarmed his own galley and the two galleys of the Hospitallers. Thus, according to their report, only one Venetian galley remained in the service of the union against the Turks. The doge reported these things to Avignon.[62] The background of this complaint is unknown. Perhaps it grew out of the resentment of the leaders in Crete against Pierre de Thomas for prosecuting the heresy in which so many of them or their associates were involved.[63] Their complaint was not valid. As papal legate, Pierre was leader of the league and was authorized to use its forces as he thought best. All his energies were absorbed in promoting the interests of the church, and it is difficult to believe that he had disarmed any of the galleys of the league unless for some good reason.

The Venetians themselves did not hesitate to use for their own purposes the two galleys which they had contributed to the league. Thus on December 26, 1360, after Venetian relations with the Byzantine Empire had become strained because several Venetians had been murdered in a church, orders were given to the two Venetian galleys of the league stationed in Crete to go to the waters of Coron and Modon and remain there until March.[64] Subsequently they were used to convey ambassadors to Constantinople.[65] On July 22, 1361, the Venetian merchant fleet was authorized to use these galleys as their convoy to Constantinople if they deemed it necessary.[66] Therefore the Venetians had no just cause for complaint if Pierre de

[62] Senato, *Misti*, XXIX, fol. 90r (October 14, 1360), quoted in part in Halecki, *Un Empereur*, p. 73, n. 3.

[63] If this was the background of the complaint made by the Cretan leaders in the autumn of 1360, its date tends to confirm the inference of Mézières' biography that Pierre's visit to Crete occurred in the closing months of 1359.

[64] Senato, *Misti*, XXIX, fol. 101v. The fact that two Venetian galleys of the Latin league were apparently still in Crete belies the assertion of the Cretan leaders that Pierre had taken one of them to Cyprus.

[65] *Ibid.*, fols. 107v, 108v, 109r, 111r, 113v–114v, dated from January 30 to March 16, 1361.

[66] *Ibid.* XXX, fol. 10r.

Thomas used these galleys at his own discretion in his legatine activities.

As late as September 28, 1361, Pierre continued to promote the crusade against the Turks. On that date, he wrote a letter from Nicosia, Cyprus, in which he appointed his chaplain Cosma de Castro Rosa, a Franciscan of the province of the Holy Land, and the incumbent lector of the Dominican house of Venice as his vicars to promote the crusade against the Turks in Venice.[67] He gave them full authority to preach the cross against infidels and Turks and to grant the authorized indulgences to crusaders. An indulgence of forty days could be granted to anyone who listened to them preach the crusade. With the license, aid, and counsel of the doge and council of Venice, to whom he recommended them, they were to do whatever seemed best for promoting the defense of Smyrna, the honor of his legation, and the ruin of infidels. Any money collected for the defense of Smyrna was to be committed to two honorable men who should be appointed by the doge of Venice. These treasurers should forward the money to Candia, where Pierre intended to assemble an armada at some future date against the enemies of the faith. Pierre authorized his vicars to excommunicate anyone who attempted to obstruct their efforts to carry out his commission, including their superiors or other dignitaries of the church.[68]

[67] This letter is published in Flaminio Cornaro, *Ecclesiae venetae antiquis monumentis, nunc etiam primum editis, illustratae ac in decades distributae,* VII (Venice, 1749), 280–82 (discussed on pp. 244–45). This edition is taken from a copy in the archives of the Dominican convent of SS. John and Paul in Venice. It was not the original letter, which by its own testimony was sealed with Pierre's pontifical seal, but a copy made at the convent on Saturday, August 20, 1362, by the notary Manfredo Magistri Drachini. In the letter Pierre de Thomas styled himself "Frater Petrus, Dei gratia episcopus Coronensis, Apostolicae Sedis in Venetiis & janua usque ad locum vulgariter nuncipatum *la Tana* inclusive legatus."

[68] In a letter of May 11, 1359, *Reg. Aven.* 140, fol. 62v; *Reg. Vat.* 234, fol. 7v, Innocent VI gave Pierre full power to enlist members of religious orders in his service without securing permission of their

This same letter of Pierre de Thomas reveals that he had earlier authorized Cosma de Castro Rosa to preach the crusade in the kingdom of Naples, although Pierre's papal commission did not include that land.[69] This unauthorized preaching aroused the displeasure of Pope Urban V a few years later. In a letter of February 2, 1363, to Cardinal Gil d'Albornoz, papal legate in Italy, he ordered it forbidden and all monies collected in Naples for the crusade against the Turks to be confiscated and applied to the defense of the lands of the church in Italy.[70]

There is no record that Pierre de Thomas carried out his intention of raising a fleet against the Turks at Candia. He was hampered by lack of interest on the part of others, and his attention was increasingly diverted toward the crusade to win the Holy Land for Christendom. He accomplished little against the Turks after his effort at Lampsacus, despite his many labors. By this time, the Byzantines were beginning to despair of getting any real help from the West. Their viewpoint is expressed by Demetrius Cydones in a letter which was probably written in the summer of 1364, almost two years after Pierre de Thomas had left the East to prepare in the West for the crusade against the Saracens. Cydones complained that the Byzantines no longer had any inclination to implore aid from the papacy, because they had received so little real help in the past. The Greeks remembered the galleys and promises of the archbishop of Smyrna (Paul) and the legate (Pierre de

---

superiors, and on the same date Pierre received power to excommunicate anyone who should attempt to hinder his work (*Reg. Aven.* 140, fols. 62r–62v; *Reg. Vat.* 234, fols. 7r–7v).

[69] As noted above, p. 160, he was commissioned to preach the crusade only in his own jurisdiction and in the territories of Genoa and Venice.

[70] *Reg. Vat.* 245, fol. 76r, published in P. Lecacheux and G. Mollat, *Urban V (1362–70), Lettres secrètes et curiales se rapportant à la France* (Bibliothèque des écoles françaises d'Athènes et de Rome, 3rd series, vol. V; Paris, 1902–54), no. 197, p. 23.

Thomas), but they were not followed by the type of help which was really needed, so they concluded that the Pope's promises were nothing but bombast.[71] However, it should be noted that the Byzantines had a tendency to overestimate the power and resources of the papacy.[72]

Undoubtedly Pierre de Thomas spent much time in the routine work of his legation. On June 3, 1362, Innocent VI granted him the authority to dispense six couples who had entered into marriage within the prohibited degrees.[73] This would seem to indicate that he had already granted all the dispensations of this type which were permitted in the faculties granted to him at the beginning of his legation.[74]

Part of his responsibility as legate was to exercise general supervision over the Latin clergy in the East. In carrying out this phase of his work, he sought to prevent Latin priests in this region from wearing beards. Although the canons of the Roman Catholic Church forbade priests to grow either long hair or beards, many of the Latin clergy in the East had found it desirable to let their beards grow, as the Greek clergy did, since the Christians of the Orient had little respect for a shaven priest. Pierre de Thomas was determined to see that the canons were obeyed. He issued an edict forbidding Latin priests to wear beards, under pain of excommunication. Several years later, upon the appeal of some of these priests, Pope Urban V annulled this edict and granted pardon to those who had trans-

[71] Demetrius Cydones, *Correspondance,* ed. Raymond J. Loenertz, O.P. I (Vatican City, 1956), no. 93, p. 127, which Loenertz dates summer, 1364; published with a French translation in Demetrius Cydones, *Correspondance,* ed. Giuseppe Cammelli (Paris, 1930), pp. 31–32.

[72] See above, pp. 132–34, 137.

[73] *Reg. Aven.* 148, fol. 520v, cited by Smet in his edition of Mézières, *Life,* p. 211 and n. 29.

[74] He was authorized to grant six of them in a letter recorded in *Reg. Aven.* 140, fol. 62r, and in *Reg. Vat.* 234, fol. 7r, and eight of them in a letter found in *Reg. Vat.* 141, fol. 21v.

gressed it.[75] He saw, as Pierre evidently could not see, that it was wise for the Catholic clergy in the East to yield in matters incidental to the customs of the region. One of Pierre de Thomas' greatest weaknesses was his legalistic bent, which led him to insist upon the observance of every detail of the canon law, without taking account either of extenuating circumstances or of the distinction between essentials and incidentals.

Pierre de Thomas continued to serve as papal legate in the East until the autumn of 1362, when he left for the West with the king of Cyprus, as will appear at the beginning of chapter 9. Meanwhile for more than two years his attention had been focused increasingly upon the affairs of the kingdom of Cyprus and the crusading plans of King Pierre I.

[75] Letter of Urban V to the regular and secular clergy in the Genoese colony of Pera, in Caffa, and in other Orthodox and Moslem lands, June 12, 1365, published in *Bullarium franciscanum,* VI, ed. Conrad Eubel (Rome, 1902), 392.

# 8

# Activities Centering in Cyprus

LATE IN 1359, KING PIERRE I OF CYPRUS INVITED PIERRE DE Thomas to come to his kingdom and officiate at his coronation as king of Jerusalem.[1] The young king had just ascended the throne of Cyprus on October 10 at the death of his father, Hugues IV.[2] He had been crowned as king of Cyprus on November 24, 1358, a year before his father's death, presumably to assure his quiet succession.[3] It was significant that Pierre I called upon the papal legate in the East, the official promoter of the crusade, to crown him king of Jerusalem, a title which signified his claim to be the lawful ruler of the Holy Land, now actually under Moslem rule. Thus he proclaimed to all

---

[1] Mézières, *Life,* ed. Smet, p. 90; AASS, Jan. 29, III, 620 (sec. 47).
[2] Leontios Makhairas, *Recital concerning the Sweet Land of Cyprus entitled "Chronicle,"* ed. and trans. R. M. Dawkins, 2 vols. (Oxford, 1932), I, 79.
[3] *Ibid.,* pp. 77–79.

the world that he took this title seriously and planned to promote the holy war against the infidel.[4] He had been interested in the crusade for many years and had been longing for the day when he would be able to take a more active part in it, but hitherto he had been hindered by his father's cautious policies.[5]

This invitation of Pierre I of Cyprus was a significant event in the life of Pierre de Thomas. During the first six months of his legation he had been traveling from place to place and seems to have had no center for his activities. After he went to Cyprus for the coronation, the island kingdom became his headquarters for the remainder of his stay in the East. Likewise in this period, Pierre de Thomas and King Pierre I began their extended association and collaboration in promoting a crusade to capture the Holy Land, although their friendship probably began during the legate's earlier visit to Cyprus. Toward the close of this time, Pierre de Thomas found another kindred spirit in Philippe de Mézières, also an enthusiast for the crusade. Through these associations, the legate's interest shifted from the crusade against the Turks in Asia Minor and the Balkans to the crusade against the Saracens in Palestine and Egypt. Thus the foundations of the crusade of 1365 were being laid.

For a time it appeared doubtful that Pierre de Thomas would reach Cyprus alive. When he received the king's invitation, he was on the island of Rhodes, the headquarters of the Knights Hospitaller. He was suffering from a serious illness, which kept him confined to bed from Christmas, 1359, until near Easter,

---

[4] Mézières, loc. cit., says that the king called upon Pierre de Thomas to perform this ceremony because of his mighty works and great fame.

[5] Sir George Francis Hill, A History of Cyprus, 4 vols. (Cambridge, 1940–52), II, 301–05, 319; Aziz Suryal Atiya, The Crusade in the Later Middle Ages (London, 1938), pp. 319–23; Neculai Jorga, Philippe de Mézières et la croisade au XIVe siècle (Paris, 1896), p. 104.

1360, the date appointed for the coronation. As the time approached, he decided in spite of his sickness to go to Cyprus for the coronation, because he greatly desired the church to receive honor through his performing that ceremony. Since he was unable to stand upon his feet, he had himself carried into a galley bound for Cyprus. His friends feared that he would die on the way.[6]

After his ship reached the port of Paphos in Cyprus, Pierre de Thomas regained his health so rapidly that it was considered miraculous. When the galley reached port, the legate appeared on his bed as if dead. Bérenger Grégoire, dean of Nicosia, who was his traveling companion, left the ship and went into the city to find lodgings for him. He secured a place and returned to the galley within an hour. About this time Pierre de Thomas' sickness left him, and he arose from his bed and went joyfully up to the stern of the ship, thanking God for restoration to health. Bérenger was more than a little surprised to see him standing there and asked, "How are you?" Pierre answered, "Very well, and how are you?" Then the legate said, "The Blessed Gregory has healed me." He left the galley and went to the lodging prepared for him and after that suffered no more sickness.[7]

From this account it is evident that Pierre de Thomas arrived in Cyprus a few weeks before Easter Sunday, April 5, 1360, the coronation date.[8] It is probable that he quickly

[6] Mézières, *Life,* ed. Smet, pp. 89–90; AASS, Jan. 29, III, 620 (sec. 47).

[7] Mézières, *Life,* ed. Smet, pp. 90–91; AASS, Jan. 29, III, 620 (secs. 47–48).

[8] This chronology is that of Mézières' biography as documented in the two previous notes. Makhairas, *Chronicle,* I, 89–91, gives a different chronology. He says that Pierre arrived in Cyprus on December 8, 1359, at Kerynia rather than Paphos. This account is repeated by the later chroniclers Amadi and Strambaldi, published in *Chroniques d'Amadi et de Strambaldi,* ed. René de Mas Latrie, I (Paris, 1891), 409

traveled from Paphos, at the western end of the island, to the capital, Nicosia, in the center of the island, where he was received by King Pierre I, by his wife Eleanor of Aragon,[9] by his mother Alice d'Ibelin, who had cared for Pierre de Thomas when he was ill on his earlier visit to Cyprus, and by all the nobles, both lords and ladies. He was received with great joy and with the splendor and magnificence due to a papal legate.[10]

The coronation festivities began with a royal procession from Nicosia to Famagusta, on the southeast coast where, since the fall of the last strongholds in Palestine to the Saracens, the kings of Jerusalem were customarily crowned. Of all cities in Cyprus, Famagusta was nearest to the Holy Land. With great pomp and ceremony, the king, the queen, and the papal legate, together with the army of Cyprus and a crowd of people of both sexes, journeyed toward Famagusta. According to the chronicler Makhairas, the king left Nicosia on March 23, 1360, and reached Famagusta four days later. The procession was attended by many sermons and holy admonitions of Pierre de Thomas, probably delivered to the royal family and nobles at various stops along the way. His eloquent preaching, which

---

(Amadi), and II (Paris, 1893), 39 (Strambaldi). Makhairas' account cannot stand against the information given by Mézières, which claims to be based upon the eyewitness testimony of Bérenger Grégoire and confirms the claim by many exact details. Mézières tends to be vague when he is unsure of his information. Makhairas' chronology is nevertheless accepted by John Hackett, *A History of the Orthodox Church of Cyprus* (London, 1901), p. 130, and by Hill, *History of Cyprus*, III, 1081 (who gives Makhairas' date incorrectly as 1358). Jorga, *Mézières*, pp. 105–06, accepts Mézières' chronology.

[9] Hill, *History of Cyprus*, II, 308 and n. 3; note by Dawkins in Makhairas, *Chronicle*, II, 94.

[10] Mézières, *Life*, ed. Smet, p. 91; AASS, Jan. 29, III, 620 (sec. 48), in his account of the royal reception of Pierre does not say where it occurred. He does mention that Pierre afterward joined the king and nobles in the grand coronation procession to Famagusta, which, according to Makhairas, *Chronicle*, I, 93, began at Lefkosia or Nicosia.

even the cardinals had heard with interest, must have added to the procession.[11] On the day after his arrival in Famagusta, King Pierre made a number of appointments to offices in the kingdom of Jerusalem which had become vacant through death.[12]

The coronation of Pierre I as king of Jerusalem took place on Easter Sunday, April 5, 1360, in the cathedral church of St. Nicholas at Famagusta.[13] Each of the estates of the realm were asked concerning their willingness to acknowledge Pierre as king. When the barons and nobles and all the people there assembled gave him their acclamation, Pierre de Thomas, assisted by the clergy of the realm, by virtue of his legatine office anointed the king with the holy oil, solemnly consecrated him to his royal office, and placed upon his head the crown of Jerusalem. Afterward his wife Eleanor was crowned as queen of Jerusalem. The coronation was followed by other solemnities for many days in Famagusta[14] and afterward in Nicosia. Thus Pierre I dedicated himself to the magnifying of the Christian faith and the destruction of its enemies, and there was, accord-

[11] He probably preached in French, the language of the court of Jerusalem and Cyprus. Therefore the majority of the common people of the kingdom, who were Greeks, could not have understood him.

[12] Makhairas, *Chronicle,* I, 93; Mézières, *Life,* ed. Smet, p. 91; AASS, Jan. 29, III, 620 (sec. 48). In most of his dates Makhairas has the day of the week one day in advance of what it should be, as Sunday, March 28, 1360, instead of Saturday.

[13] Makhairas, *loc. cit.;* Mézières, *Life,* ed. Smet, pp. 90–91; AASS, Jan. 29, III, 620 (secs. 47–48). Both sources agree on the coronation date. The cathedral of St. Nicholas is described in George Jeffery, *A Description of the Historic Monuments of Cyprus* (Nicosia, 1918), pp. 116–27, and in Rupert Gunnis, *Historic Cyprus, a Guide to its Towns and Villages, Monasteries and Cities* (London, 1936), pp. 90–95. This cathedral is a magnificent example of early fourteenth century Gothic architecture and resembles the cathedral at Rheims.

[14] Makhairas, *loc. cit.,* tells of a noble assembly which lasted for eight days at Famagusta. He mentions the coronation of the queen, omitted by Mézières.

ing to Philippe de Mézières, universal rejoicing among the Christians of the East.[15]

Some time after the coronation, Pierre de Thomas determined to win the Greeks of Cyprus to full obedience and loyalty to the Latin church. He was disturbed because the Orthodox population, bishops, priests, and people alike, had little respect for the Roman Catholic Church and whenever possible, they induced Latins to attend Greek services. This was a period of growing friendship between the Latin ruling class of Cyprus and the Greek population. In 1368, only eight years later, Pope Urban V, upon the complaint of King Pierre I, wrote that many Latin women of Cyprus were attending Greek churches.[16] As a strict Catholic with a legalistic bent and little appreciation of other forms of Christianity, Pierre de Thomas was alarmed at this trend, so much so that Mézières says that he feared the ruin of the Latin church in Cyprus.[17]

Pierre's fear was, of course, exaggerated. The Latin church was dominant on the island, and the ruling family was loyal to it. Through most of the period since the Latin conquest of 1191, the Orthodox clergy had been severely restricted, and occasionally they had been cruelly persecuted. The number of Orthodox bishops had been reduced from fourteen to four, and in 1260, the Greeks were forbidden to have an archbishop in Cyprus after the death of the one who then held the office. All Orthodox ecclesiastical appointments on the island were subject to the Latin primate, and the Greek bishops were re-

[15] Mézières, *Life,* ed. Smet, pp. 91–92; AASS, Jan. 29, III, 620 (sec. 48).

[16] Hackett, *Orthodox Church of Cyprus,* p. 138; Hill, *History of Cyprus,* III, 1082–83.

[17] Mézières, *Life,* ed. *Smet,* p. 92; AASS, Jan. 29, III, 620 (sec. 49). Mézières dates Pierre's efforts to deal with the religious situation in Cyprus "many days" after the coronation. Makhairas, *Chronicle,* I, 89–91, places these events between the legate's arrival in the island in December, 1359, and the coronation, but as has been noted above, the best evidence indicates that Pierre de Thomas did not arrive in Cyprus till shortly before the coronation.

quired to take an oath to recognize the paramount authority of the Roman Catholic authorities in the kingdom.[18]

In general, the Greeks accepted these humiliating conditions quietly, since the services in the local Orthodox churches were permitted. At times, however, the resentment of the people led to the outbreak of disturbances. The most serious of these prior to 1360 occurred in 1313 when an angry mob tried to burn down the palace of the Latin archbishop to destroy a papal legate whom they suspected of insulting their prelates.[19] Pierre de Thomas therefore faced no easy task when he decided to seek to bring the Greek Christians of Cyprus into closer union with the Latin church, but he was not deterred by the dangers he faced.

With the permission of the king, he assembled the Greek clergy in the cathedral church of St. Sophia in Nicosia.[20] This meeting was attended by the chief bishop of the Orthodox and also by their other bishops, abbots, and lesser clergy.[21] Seated before the high altar of the cathedral under its vault painted

[18] Hackett, *Orthodox Church of Cyprus*, pp. 59–70, 74–77, 81–85, 90–95, 101–27, 141–48, cf. p. 658; Hill, *History of Cyprus*, III, 1042–51, 1056–81, 1085–88. By the early fifteenth century, the Greek church in Cyprus was in poor standing with the patriarchate of Constantinople because of its subjection to the Latin church. In 1405–12, the Greeks of Cyprus sought union with the church of Constantinople, but it was refused for that reason.

[19] Hackett, *Orthodox Church of Cyprus*, p. 126; Hill, *History of Cyprus*, III, 1071–72.

[20] Mézières, *Life,* ed. Smet, p. 92; AASS, Jan. 29, III, 620 (sec. 49); Makhairas, *Chronicle*, I, 91. Both sources agree on the place where the assembly was held, though on little else. For a description of the cathedral of St. Sophia, see Jeffery, *A Description of the Historic Monuments of Cyprus,* pp. 64–80, and Gunnis, *Historic Cyprus*, pp. 47–55. It is built after the plan of a thirteenth century French cathedral.

[21] Mézières, *loc. cit.,* says only that the chief bishop of the Greeks and all his priests were at the meeting, while Makhairas, *loc. cit.,* says that bishops, abbots, and priests were present. *Episcopus major,* the term used by Mézières, is correct. The Greeks were not allowed to have an archibishop, but one of their bishops evidently acted as primate, probably the one whose see was coterminous with the Latin archbishopric of Nicosia.

with golden stars on a blue field, Pierre de Thomas as papal legate presided over the assembly. He was assisted by a large number of Latin clergy and learned men. The doors of the church were closed by the Latins to discourage interruptions from outside. The Greeks did not know what to expect. We know little of the actual content of the discussions. Pierre probably chided the Greeks for failure to show sufficient respect to the Latin church and especially for welcoming Latins to their services. Perhaps he complained of other practices which seemed objectionable to him. He probably sought to win them to a more scrupulous observance of the customary subordination of the Greeks to the Latin church in Cyprus,[22] but he may also have sought to persuade them to a full acceptance of the Latin rite. For the most part, he sought to win them by argumentation, but he may well have threatened to use his ecclesiastical powers against them if they would not do as he required. It is difficult to believe that he tried to seize them and confirm them by force in the Latin rite, as Makhairas would have us believe.[23]

At first, Pierre de Thomas' assembly went smoothly. According to Mézières, many Greeks confessed their errors and were reformed.[24] This means that they renewed their customary

---

[22] Giovanni Francesco Loredano, *Histoire des rois de Chypre de la maison de Lusignan,* I (Paris, 1732), 385, reports that Pierre de Thomas in a conversation with the king after the riot which followed this assembly insisted that he was not seeking to make any innovation.

[23] Mézières, *Life,* ed. Smet, p. 92; AASS, Jan. 29, III, 620 (sec. 49); Makhairas, *Chronicle,* I, 91. Makhairas says that the Greeks were uninformed of Pierre's intentions, which were to confirm them by force in the Latin rite. Mézières treats the assembly purely as an effort to convert the Orthodox to Catholicism, without taking into account the peculiar conditions arising out of the subjection of the Greeks to the Latins in Cyprus. He says that Pierre sought to win the Greeks by expounding the Scriptures "dulciter and demonstrative." However, a little later in his narrative, Mézières admits that Pierre sometimes used threats in seeking to convert the Greeks of Cyprus. See Smet's edition, p. 93; AASS, Jan. 29, III, 620–21 (sec. 51).

[24] Mézières, *Life,* ed. Smet, p. 92; AASS, Jan. 29, III, 620 (sec. 49).

submission to the Latins and agreed to desist from certain practices. They did not really have any greater reverence for the Latin church nor did they accept its doctrines as superior to their own. They merely accepted the inevitable, recognizing that they must make this submission whenever it was demanded as long as the Latins were the rulers of Cyprus. Only under such circumstances would they be permitted to minister to their people and preserve their faith in the island kingdom.

Even this nominal submission was too much for one hot-head among the Greek clergy, whose name was Mantzas. In a loud voice, he burst out in a denunciation of the legate and the Roman church. His boldness encouraged others to take a stand, and soon there was an uproar in the cathedral. Meanwhile, some Greeks were hanging around outside the doors of the church and heard the commotion within. They began to murmur and shout against the legate. Rumors began to spread throughout the city that the Latins were mistreating the Orthodox clergy in the cathedral, and soon an angry mob was rushing to the church shouting, "Kill the Legate!" The people tried to get into the building to attack the Latins and rescue the Greeks, but the Latins had bolted the door to keep them out. Some of the people secured a great beam and tried to break down the door with it.[25]

When the Latin churchmen in the cathedral recognized what

---

[25] Mézières, *Life,* ed. Smet, p. 92; AASS, Jan. 29, III, 620 (sec. 50); Makhairas, *Chronicle,* I, 91. Mézières tells of a Greek priest who spoke against Pierre de Thomas. His name is supplied by Makhairas, who says that he was one whom the Latins seized to confirm by force. Both sources mention the uproar in the church and the coming of the mob to the cathedral. Makhairas tells about their trying to break down the door with a great beam. He adds that they also tried to set fire to the cathedral. This detail I doubt, because both Greek and Latin clergy were in the building, and the Greeks probably would not have wanted to endanger the lives of their own clergy. Perhaps the story of the fire was introduced into this account as a result of confusion between this riot and the one directed against the papal legate Pierre, archbishop of Rodez, in 1313. See above, p. 187 and n. 19.

was happening outside, many of them were afraid, and perhaps some found a way to escape. Pierre de Thomas stood firm. To those around him he said, "Let us be comforted in the Lord. Bear the cross with me, and we will gladly die for the Catholic faith." Not moving from the spot where he had been sitting, he rose to his feet before the high altar and calmly awaited whatever fate should befall him.[26]

Meanwhile, news of the riot reached the king's palace. As soon as Pierre I learned about it, he sent his brother Jean de Lusignan, prince of Antioch, with the admiral Jean de Sur and the vicomte (sheriff) of Nicosia to the cathedral to quell the riot. They armed themselves at once, mounted their horses, and with a band of soldiers came to the church of St. Sophia. They restrained the people, who withdrew to one side, ordered the church doors to be opened, and permitted both Latin and Greek clergy to go in peace.[27]

After the tumult had been quieted, it is reported that Pierre

[26] Mézières, *Life,* ed. Smet, p. 93; AASS, Jan. 29, III, 620 (sec. 50); Makhairas, *loc. cit.* Mézières says that a Greek priest opened the door, and the mob rushed into the church, whereupon many of the Latin clergy fled, while Pierre de Thomas stood his ground, as noted in the text. Makhairas says that the mob did not succeed in entering the church. His story seems more reasonable. The Latins surely had the bolted doors well guarded. Mézières' story of Pierre de Thomas' standing calmly at the altar while the mob rushed in lacks the ring of truth, especially since he says nothing about the crowd's reaction to this unusual courage, though Pierre quite clearly escaped unharmed.

[27] This account is based upon Makhairas, *Chronicle,* I, 91. His account is repeated in summary by Amadi, *Chroniques d'Amadi et de Strambaldi,* I, 409–10, and by Florio Bustron, *Chronique de l'île de Chypre,* ed. René de Mas Latrie (Paris, 1884), p. 258. They add the name of the admiral, which Makhairas does not give. Mézières, *Life,* ed. Smet, p. 93; AASS, Jan. 29, III, 620 (sec. 50), tells essentially the same story, except that he says that the royal officers expelled the crowd from the church. Makhairas gives the impression that the royal officers came primarily to rescue the Greek clergy, while Mézières says that they came to save Pierre de Thomas and his associates from the Greeks. Actually, they came to restore order and to protect the safety of all concerned.

de Thomas urged the king to punish those who were most responsible for the insurrection, especially because the honor of the Holy See had been offended in the affront which he had received. He avowed that in his assembly in the cathedral, he had not tried to make any innovation but merely to secure the recognized rights of the Roman Church in Cyprus. Very politely, the king refused to take any action against the rioters, partly because in such popular uprisings it is difficult to assess blame among individuals. Pierre I also pointed out that it was against his interest at the beginning of his reign to arouse the hatred of the Greeks, who formed the majority of his subjects. He could not punish the rioters without seeming to attack their religion and to take the legate's part against his own people, and such an impression he did not want to create.[28] Thus he followed the traditional policy of his house. The Lusignans were loyal Catholics but did not want to make life unbearable for their Greek subjects, lest they be encouraged to flee in large numbers or invite a Byzantine reconquest of the island. They recognized that the Greeks could neither be converted quickly nor left without spiritual guidance. Therefore they protected the Orthodox clergy against the more zealous Latin prelates.[29]

Even after the trouble in Nicosia, the courageous and unyielding Pierre de Thomas desired to continue preaching among the Greeks of Cyprus and seeking to instruct them in the Catholic faith, regardless of personal danger. Opposition never intimidated him; it spurred him on to greater efforts. There can be little doubt that King Pierre I dissuaded him from further

[28] This account comes from Loredano, *Histoire des rois de Chypre,* I, 385–86, which was published in the eighteenth century, and is not based upon any known contemporary source. Nevertheless, the account is true to what is known about the attitudes of the two men and if it is not based on an unknown source, it represents a good understanding of the situation.

[29] Hackett, *Orthodox Church of Cyprus,* pp. 85, 123–26; Hill, *History of Cyprus,* II, 1042, 1044–45, 1047–48, 1052–53, 1058, 1062.

activity, at least for the present. Perhaps he even suggested the wisdom of Pierre de Thomas' leaving Cyprus for a while, until popular unrest should have an opportunity to subside. The king, nevertheless, remained a close friend of the legate.[30]

The efforts of Pierre de Thomas to convert the Orthodox believers of Cyprus to the Latin church seem to have accomplished little. Makhairas reports that the royal officials who brought the Greek clergy out from Pierre's assembly "bade them continue to act as they were accustomed." [31] Philippe de Mézières tries hard to make Pierre's work in Cyprus sound like a great success story. He says that the legate was able to establish the chief bishop of the Greeks, the other bishops, and almost all the priests on the island in obedience to the Pope and the Roman Catholic Church, so that at the time when Mézières was writing Pierre's biography, about the spring of 1366,[32] the Greeks were regularly confirmed by the archbishops of Nicosia.[33] All this sounds good, but the Greeks had been forced

[30] The two principal sources are extremely biased at this point and therefore unreliable. Mézières, *Life,* ed. Smet, p. 93; AASS, Jan. 29, III, 620–21 (secs. 50–51), reports that the legate had no fear, even after the riot, but against the advice of his friends continued his ministry among the Greeks "now with threats, now with good words . . . and with the most devout and Catholic king consenting and showing favor." On the other hand, Makhairas, *loc. cit.,* says that when the king's men quelled the riot and freed the Greek clergy from the cathedral, they ordered the legate to leave the island. According to this account, Pierre I shortly afterward sent an embassy to Avignon among other things "to tell the most holy Pope not to send legates to cause dissensions." It is unlikely that the king offended either his personal friend Pierre de Thomas or the Pope, whose representative the legate was, in this manner. At this period, as noted below, Pierre I had to defend his claim to the throne of Jerusalem and Cyprus against his nephew Prince Hugues of Galilee before the Pope and therefore had a special reason to try to keep in his good graces.

[31] Makhairas, *Chronicle,* I, 91. From this passage, Hackett, *Orthodox Church of Cyprus,* pp. 132, 135, and Hill, *History of Cyprus,* III, 1081, conclude that Pierre's efforts to convert the Greeks were a total failure.

[32] Mézières, *Life,* ed. Smet, pp. 31, 184–85.

[33] Mézières, *Life,* ed. Smet, p. 93; AASS, Jan. 29, III, 621 (sec. 51).

to accept such Latin ecclesiastical overlordship since the 1220's. The evidence does not show that Pierre de Thomas accomplished any more than to enforce the customary submission of the Greeks to the Latins. Undoubtedly the Greeks commonly ignored it whenever supervision by the Latin clergy became lax, as it sometimes did, since the archbishops of Nicosia were often nonresident.

Other references to the activities of Pierre de Thomas at this period are found in the letters of Demetrius Cydones. About 1362, he wrote from Constantinople to his friend George the Philosopher in Cyprus. He advised him not to remain in Cyprus, where they would not tolerate his violent anti-Latin views. At one time, according to the letter, George had been quite favorable to the Roman Catholic Church and had given good reason to believe that he was one of its adherents when he had confessed to the inquisitor Filippo de Bindo Incontri, a member of the Dominican Order. Later George expressed a change of heart and returned to the Orthodox faith, for which he underwent imprisonment and a beating. In a letter to Demetrius Cydones, which had accidentally been opened and made public, George had attacked "the legate," apparently Pierre de Thomas, and had also accused Filippo de Bindo Incontri of shameful vices. Thus it can be seen that the position of Pierre de Thomas as a leading proponent of church union sometimes made him a target for hatred among the Greeks. George the Philosopher later left Cyprus for Rhodes.[34]

[34] Demetrius Cydones, *Correspondance*, et. Raymond J. Loenertz, O. P., I (Vatican City, 1956), no. 31, pp. 60–62, also published in J. C. Boissonade, *Anecdota Graeca* (Paris, 1844), pp. 299–302. This letter is summarized in French in Raymond J. Loenertz, "Fr. Philippe de Bindo Incontri, O. P., du couvent de Péra, inquisiteur en Orient," *Archivum Fratrum Praedicatorum*, XVIII (1948), 274–75, cf. p. 276. In the same article, p. 278, Loenertz connects the beating and imprisonment of George the Philosopher mentioned in this letter with the efforts of Pierre de Thomas to enforce the union of the churches in

Pierre de Thomas probably left Cyprus not long after the riot at Nicosia, perhaps in the summer of 1360. He took leave of the king, who had conferred so many honors and tokens of friendship upon him, and directed his steps toward Rhodes and Turkey.[35] Perhaps he paid another visit to Smyrna, to encourage the garrison there.

In this period Pierre de Thomas decided to visit his bishopric of Coron and the neighboring principality of Achaia. When his friends learned about his plans, they urged him not to go there. At this time. Marie de Bourbon, princess of Achaia, was claiming the throne of Jerusalem and Cyprus for her son Hugues de Lusignan, prince of Galilee, and they feared that she would make some reprisal against Pierre de Thomas because he had crowned Pierre I as king of Jerusalem. She held certain strong castles near the lands of the church of Coron and thus was in a position to strike at him.[36]

Ignoring these warnings, Pierre de Thomas sailed to Coron. There he was well received by the people of his diocese. He also visited the principality of Achaia, where he was received

---

Cyprus. It is by no means clear that George suffered these persecutions in Cyprus. He seems to have traveled widely in the East, and there were many places under Latin control where he may have been punished for being too outspoken against the Catholic Church. Except at the time of the assembly held by the legate at the cathedral church of Nicosia, no instance of persecution of the Cypriotes is mentioned by Makhairas, who was certainly no partisan of the legate.

[35] Mézières, Life, ed. Smet, p. 94; AASS, Jan. 29, III, 620 (sec. 51).

[36] Mézières, Life, ed. Smet, p. 94; AASS, Jan. 29, III, 621 (sec. 52). Marie was princess of Achaia through her second husband, Robert of Taranto, prince of Achaia and titular (Latin) emperor of Constantinople. Her first husband, the father of the prince of Galilee, was Guy de Lusignan, eldest son of Hugues IV of Cyprus and half brother of Pierre I. On the role of Marie de Bourbon in Achaia see William Miller, The Latins in the Levant (London, 1908), pp. 285, 287; Sir Rennell Rodd, The Princes of Achaia and the Chronicles of Morea, a Study of Greece in the Middle Ages (London, 1907), pp. 191–92. The claims of Hugues of Galilee to the throne of Cyprus are discussed below, pp. 208–09.

with great joy and honor by the barons and nobles. He encountered no sign of hostility from the princess or her agents. He preached and taught in the province of Achaia, reformed the Latin churches and rectors in that region and brought some Orthodox Greeks into the Roman Catholic fold. Through his preaching and his holy life, the nobles of the province were led to more devout living. Though these stories of Pierre's success must be discounted somewhat, there is undoubtedly some truth in them.[37]

On this visit to Achaia, Pierre de Thomas received an unusual appeal from the lord of Arcadia, one of the chief barons of the principality. This rich and powerful noble was blessed with a good and devout wife and many daughters, but although they had been married for many years, he and his wife had no son. He invited Pierre de Thomas to a banquet in his castle and showed him great honor. In the presence of all the guests, he told his problem to the legate and expressed his faith and that of his wife that if Pierre would bless the lady, she would have a son. At the close of the banquet, Pierre called the lady of Arcadia to him and on bended knee in the presence of her husband and the others who were there said a lengthy benediction over her, tearing out his hair, as he earnestly entreated God to grant her desire. At the close of the prayer, he assured the lady of Arcadia that God would give her a son. Some days later, as Mézières reports, she conceived and in due time gave birth to a baby boy, as Pierre had predicted.[38]

While Pierre de Thomas was engaged in his varied work as legate, King Pierre I of Cyprus was beginning his advance

[37] Mézières, *Life,* ed. Smet, pp. 94–95; AASS, Jan. 29, III, 621 (sec. 52). It is not clear whence Pierre de Thomas sailed to Coron. Perhaps it was from Rhodes or Asia Minor *(Turchia),* which are mentioned by Mézières immediately before this journey.

[38] Mézières, *Life,* ed. Smet, pp. 95–96; AASS, Jan. 29, III, 621 (sec. 53).

against the Moslems. Even before he was crowned as king of Jerusalem, he had seized his first opportunity to gain territory on the mainland of Asia when in January, 1360, he had accepted the invitation of the men of Gorighos, a town on the southern coast of Asia Minor, to become their overlord and defender. They had been subjects of the king of Armenia, but the current ruler of that land was too weak to defend them from the growing power of the Turks. Gorighos was an important center for trade with central Asia Minor, and its occupation was a real diplomatic victory for the king of Cyprus.[39]

The immediate result of the occupation of Gorighos was an alliance against Pierre I by four Turkish rulers of Asia Minor, who began to fear for their own safety. This did not deter the king of Cyprus, who prepared at once to take the offensive against them. In the summer of 1361, he attacked and captured the rich and well-fortified city of Adalia. After this victory, two of those who had allied against him, the emirs of Alaya and Monovgat, accepted his overlordship, which, however, never became more than nominal.[40]

By the time Pierre I returned from his conquest of Adalia, on September 22, 1361,[41] Pierre de Thomas had probably returned to Cyprus from his travels, for he wrote a letter from

[39] Makhairas, Chronicle, I, 99–101; Amadi in Chroniques d'Amadi et de Strambaldi, I, 410–11; Hill, History of Cyprus, I, 320; Jorga, Mézières, pp. 111–12; Atiya, Later Crusade, pp. 323–24. Makhairas says that Pierre I asked permission of the Pope to use the two galleys furnished by Cyprus for the league against the Turks in the defense of Gorighos. He intimates that this permission was granted.

[40] Makhairas, Chronicle, I, 101–13, 347, II, 99; Amadi in Chroniques d'Amadi et de Strambaldi, I, 411; Bustron, Chronique, p. 259; Guillaume de Machaut, La prise d'Alexandrie, ou chronique du roi Pierre Ier de Lusignan, ed. Louis de Mas Latrie (Geneva, 1877), pp. 20–21; modern accounts in Hill, History of Cyprus, II, 321–22; Jorga, Mézières, pp. 114–15, 121–23; Atiya, Later Crusade, pp. 324–27. The Christians held Adalia until 1373.

[41] Makhairas, Chronicle, I, 109.

Nicosia only six days later.[42] Needless to say, the legate was overjoyed at the news of the Christian occupation of Adalia. After the king's return to Cyprus, he went to the newly conquered city to organize the Latin church there, perhaps in October, 1361. He consecrated the church to Latin worship and appointed priests and members of religious orders to celebrate the divine office in Adalia. He gave spiritual encouragement to the defenders of the city and conferred many spiritual privileges on them. Afterward, he returned to Cyprus and continued to encourage the king in the cause of the crusade. He instituted processions and solemn masses of thanksgiving for the victory at Adalia.[43]

The joy which prevailed in Cyprus because of the success of the expedition to Adalia was soon overshadowed by a visitation of the Black Death in the closing months of 1361 or in 1362.[44] The Cypriotes recognized that they were in danger

[42] Flaminio Cornaro, *Ecclesiae venetae antiquis monumentis nunc etiam primum editis, illustratae ac in decades distributae*, VII (Venice, 1749), 244–45, 280–82. See above, pp. 177–78.

[43] Mézières, *Life*, ed. Smet, p. 96–97; AASS, Jan. 29, III, 621 (sec. 55).

[44] Makhairas, *Chronicle*, I, 61, 119, tells of two visitations of the plague in Cyprus, one in 1348 and another in 1363. The second plague is said to have started in March, 1363. Amadi in *Chroniques d'Amadi et de Strambaldi*, I, 412, follows Makhairas. There are also records of a severe attack of the plague at Naples in the summer of 1363, as noted in Kenneth M. Setton, "Archbishop Pierre d'Ameil in Naples and the affair of Aimon III of Geneva (1363–1364)," *Speculum*, XXVIII (1953), 651. However, since Mézières, *Life*, ed. Smet, pp. 97–101; AASS, Jan. 29, III, 622–23 (secs. 56–60), states that he and Pierre de Thomas were both in Cyprus at the time of the plague, it must have broken out before their departure for the West with Pierre I on October 24, 1362. Hill, *History of Cyprus*, II, 323, n. 2, suggests that the plague may have appeared in 1362, died down in the autumn of that year, and reappeared in March, 1363. He notes that the plague had appeared in the West in 1361; for example, the Second Pestilence in England extended from August 15, 1361, to May 3, 1362. Records of a visitation of the plague in Constantinople from September, 1361, to August, 1362, are found in S. Lampros, Βραχέα Χρονικά (Μνημεῖα τῆς ἑλληνικῆς ἱστορίας), I, Athens, (1932–33),

as they heard that the pestilence was raging everywhere else in the eastern Mediterranean, although it had not yet come to Cyprus. It was especially severe in Rhodes, Asia Minor, and Syria. They considered the plague an evidence of the wrath of God. Pierre de Thomas went to the king and urged him to descend from his royal throne and unite the people to do penance and cry to heaven to see if God would abate his anger and save the people. Pierre I followed this advice. The legate gave himself to penance. He assembled the clergy in a solemn procession. He instituted masses to appease the wrath of God.[45]

Then the terrifying news came to Nicosia that the plague had penetrated to Cyprus and had struck at Famagusta. Men afflicted by it died after two or three days of illness. The fear of death touched every heart. Pierre de Thomas was touched with grief, yet confident in God. He assembled the king, the queen, the nobles, and the people and began to preach to them, urging them all to penitence and declaring that if they really desired to be right with God and to live better lives the pestilence would depart from the kingdom. Pierre's preaching ordinarily had a powerful effect upon his hearers, and in this time of fear the people were all moved to tears.[46]

When he saw the devotion of the king and his people, Pierre de Thomas decided upon an additional measure to persuade God to spare Nicosia from the plague. He appointed a day on which everyone, regardless of rank, was to participate in a solemn penitential procession, barefooted and fasting on bread and water. As the day of this procession approached, tension

---

no. 15, lines 12–14; no. 52, lines 26–27, cited by Loenertz, "Fr. Philippe de Bindo Incontri," *Archivum Fratrum Praedicatorum,* XVIII, 276. Raynaldus, *Annales ecclesiastici, ad ann.* 1361, chap. 9, assigns Mézières' account of it, which he quotes, to 1361, probably because it follows the capture of Adalia.

[45] Mézières, *Life,* ed. Smet, p. 97; AASS, Jan. 29, III, 622 (sec. 56).
[46] Mézières, *Life,* ed. Smet, p. 98; AASS, Jan. 29, III, 622 (sec. 57).

in Nicosia mounted, for news from Famagusta indicated that
the force of the plague was increasing. Gone was the glory
of the coronation festivities and the thrill of victory over the
infidel. Even the bitter hostility between the Latins and Greeks
was forgotten, as every heart was conscious of being under the
judgment of God.

On the appointed day, all the people of Nicosia joined in
the penitential procession. The king was there with his wife
and children, his mother, and all the ladies of the palace, the
merchants of the city, and all the common people. All were
fasting on bread and water. All were wearing simple clothing.
All walked with bare feet in great humility and devotion.
Marching by companies, praying as they went, they came to
the great cathedral church of St. Sophia, where two years before Pierre de Thomas had been mobbed by the Greeks. Now,
still endowed with papal authority, he was leading the procession, barefooted like all the rest. With him were associated
all the clergy of the city from the various nations of Christians.
In the cathedral, the people gathered together and knelt before
the crucifix. Then, with Pierre de Thomas leading in as loud
a voice as he was able and the clergy responding and the people
weeping, they all began to cry to heaven and to chant the hymn,
*"Sancte Dominus, sancte fortis, sancte misericors."*[47]

After these ceremonies at the cathedral, the procession continued through the streets of the city. It came to a place which
Mézières calls "the cemetery." This was perhaps the abbey of
St. Dominic, where most of the kings and queens and many
nobles and churchmen of Cyprus were buried. It is thought
to have been the finest building in Nicosia.[48] At "the cemetery,"

[47] *Ibid.*
[48] Gunnis, *Historic Cyprus,* pp. 35–38. The abbey of St. Dominic
stood near the Paphos Gate of Nicosia. It was totally destroyed by the
Venetians in remodeling the city walls in 1567, and its precise location is not now known.

Pierre de Thomas preached to the people. The occasion is described by Philippe de Mézières as follows: "When we were all seated and silence had been obtained, the legate opened his mouth and began to preach. He declared marvelous things and things beyond what should cause men to marvel, as God, the king, and all who heard were witnesses. Very briefly by his sermon—no, not by it but by the Holy Spirit—he moved everyone to tears, comforted everyone concerning the plague, and turned the hearts of his hearers to spiritual joy. Why should I multiply words concerning the sermon? For if it is right to say, had Augustine or some one of the holy doctors preached the same sermon, it would have been enough." [49]

After the sermon, when the fear of death had departed from the people, the legate, the king, and all the people returned to the cathedral church, and Pierre de Thomas celebrated mass. The people thanked God for his mercy and for the teaching of the legate. When the people had returned to their homes, Pierre de Thomas had hardly enough strength to sustain himself and almost passed away, but when he had taken some bread and water, his strength was renewed.[50]

After he had called the city of Nicosia to repentance and comforted its people, Pierre de Thomas left it to the mercy of God and courageously turned his steps toward Famagusta, "the furnace of pestilence and death." Here the pestilence was increasing in violence every day. Thirty or forty persons a day were dying. Pierre grieved at the death of so many Christians and implored God for mercy. As in Nicosia, he organized a penitential procession. Since Famagusta was a commercial city with a more cosmopolitan population, a greater number of

[49] Mézières, *Life,* ed. Smet, p. 99; AASS, Jan. 29, III, 622 (sec. 58). The translation in the text follows Smet's edition. There are quite a few verbal differences in the AASS, but the general tenor of the passage is the same. Since the word *coemeterium* does not appear in AASS, it is not clear in that edition just where Pierre preached this sermon.
[50] *Ibid.*

nationalities participated in this procession than in the one at Nicosia. Greeks, Armenians, Nestorians, Jacobites, Georgians, Nubians, Indians, and Ethiopians, as well as Latins and Jews, assembled in national or religious groups. All moved in an orderly procession toward the church with hymns and songs and lamentations, each in his own mother tongue. An innumerable array of candles was carried. Here where the people were living daily in the midst of death, Pierre's ministry was even more effective than in Nicosia, if that were possible. In a short time he moved the people to such devotion that infidel Saracens, Turks, and Jews who were present burst into tears and with bare feet devoutly joined the Christian procession. Not only the Latins, who belonged to the Catholic Church and understood him, but even people of other nations, who could not understand him, were brought to the point of tears by his preaching.[51]

After this procession had been held, the force of the plague abated. At that time, two hundred persons in Famagusta were lying on their beds without hope of recovery, and it was the last quarter of the moon, a fatal period according to the physicians of the day. "But," says Mézières, "Jesus Christ, our great physician, paid no attention to the waning of the moon, that is to the sins of the people, and healed all the sick, and not even one of them died, while on the preceding days, as noted above, thirty or forty had died." From that day of compassion the plague withdrew from Famagusta and from all Cyprus.[52]

The sojourn of Pierre de Thomas in Cyprus at this time was

---

[51] Mézières, *Life,* ed. Smet, pp. 99–100; AASS, Jan. 29, III, 622 (sec. 59). Though Mézières does not indicate the language in which Pierre de Thomas preached on this occasion, it was probably French, the court language of Cyprus, which could have been understood by most of the Latins who were present. He may have preached in Latin, which could have been understood by all men of the West who had sufficient education.

[52] Mézières, *Life,* ed. Smet, p. 100; AASS, Jan. 29, III, 622–23 (sec. 59).

especially important because it was then that he met Philippe de Mézières, who soon became his closest friend, his faithful fellow laborer in the cause of the crusade, his spiritual son, and eventually his biographer.[53] Mézières then about thirty-five years old. He had been born in 1326 or 1327 to a minor noble family of Picardy. He began his military service in 1345 under Lucchino Visconti in Lombardy. In the following year, he went to the East. Apparently he went first to Cyprus and from there sailed to Smyrna, where he served for a time under Humbert II, dauphin of Viennois, and was knighted after a fierce battle near Smyrna. Upon the failure of Humbert's crusade, he went on a pilgrimage to the Holy Land and there was inspired to dedicate his life to the liberation of that country from the Moslem yoke. In this period, he conceived the idea of a new order of chivalry dedicated to this purpose. From Palestine, he returned to Cyprus, where he met the young Prince Pierre, who had already become greatly interested in the cause of the crusade. Mézières became one of the earliest members of Prince Pierre's new crusading order, the Order of the Sword. A close friendship grew up between the two youths, which later became the basis of their collaboration, together with Pierre de Thomas, in the crusade of 1365. Mézières did not remain long in Cyprus; he left for the West before September, 1349, and spent many years there.[54] He did not return to Cyprus until the time of the capture of Adalia or shortly afterward. Pierre I then appointed him as chancellor of the kingdom.[55]

In the following words, Philippe de Mézières expressed his

[53] A brief biography of Mézières can be found in Atiya, *Later Crusade*, pp. 137–54. The definitive work on his life is Neculai Jorga, *Philippe de Mézières (1327–1405) et la croisade au XIV^e siècle* (Paris, 1896).

[54] Jorga, *Mézières*, pp. 9–92; Atiya, *Later Crusade*, pp. 137–38.

[55] Jorga, *Mézières*, p. 109.

recollection of his first impressions of Pierre de Thomas and the closeness of their friendship: "But when the legate was working such marvelous divine works from God in Cyprus, I, the chancellor of the kingdom of Cyprus, an unworthy man, seeing and hearing the foregoing miracles of God through the hand of his servant the legate and considering his sanctity, I, though unworthy, was occasionally and frequently the messenger of my lord, the king, to the legate and of the legate to my lord in secret and important affairs. But to the legate I declared my condition and my intention, and indeed I found such great charity in his gracious fatherly spirit, which, should I wish to write it, I would have neither the time nor the ability to express my mind fully with the pen, and therefore I will pass on to the works of God done through him. I will write one thing, and God being my witness, I will speak the truth, that from that time henceforth by the grace of God I chose him to be my very special father and he chose me, in spite of my unworthiness, as a son. And would that I had fully known the grace of God in him and that I had completely repaid my debt to him, as his most ardent love imparted to me and embraced me, which will clearly appear in his passing from this world." [56]

[56] Mézières, *Life,* ed. Smet, p. 101; with some variations in AASS, Jan. 29, III, 623 (sec. 60). The awkward repetition in the early part of the passage reflects the deep emotion which Mézières felt in writing it.

# 9

# The Preaching of the Crusade and the Pacification of Bologna

ON OCTOBER 24, 1362, A NEW CHAPTER IN THE LIFE OF
Pierre de Thomas began when he sailed from Cyprus to the
West with the fleet of King Pierre I. Especially since his occupation of Adalia, the king had been planning a great crusade
to win the Holy Land from its Moslem rulers, the Mamelukes
of Egypt. In this project, he was consistently encouraged by
Pierre de Thomas and Philippe de Mézières. Pierre I knew
that his kingdom lacked the men and resources for such a crusade and therefore he decided to go to the West to enlist the
aid of the knights in that region. In this venture, he was accompanied by a goodly number of nobles, among them Mézières. Pierre de Thomas left his legatine work in the East to
go with them to Europe and to use his influence to promote

the crusade at Avignon.[1] Some of the ships in the fleet may have belonged to the Latin league, which was under his direction.[2]

The king and his company first sailed to the island of Rhodes, seat of the Knights Hospitaller. They were well received by the grand master, Roger de Pins, who had lent Pierre I some galleys for the expedition against Adalia. During their brief stay on the island, the king and Pierre de Thomas persuaded the grand master and the chapter of the Hospitallers to agree in writing to support the crusade. Two knights from the garrison at Adalia joined the king's company at Rhodes in response to his summons.[3]

From Rhodes, the company of Pierre I sailed to Venice, where they arrived on December 5, 1362. They were received with great honor and magnificence by Doge Lorenzo Celsi, who went out with all his nobles in the *Bucentaur,* the state galley of Venice, as far as the port of San Niccolo di Lido to meet them. The king was lodged in the house of Andrea Zane,

[1] Mézières, *Life,* ed. Smet, pp. 102–03; AASS, Jan. 29, III, 623 (secs. 61–62); Leontios Makhairas, *Recital concerning the Sweet Land of Cyprus entitled "Chronicle,"* ed. and trans. R. M. Dawkins, 2 vols. (Oxford, 1932), I, 113–15; Chronicle of Amadi, published in *Chroniques d'Amadi et de Strambaldi,* ed. René de Mas Latrie, I (Paris, 1891), 412; Florio Bustron, *Chronique de l'île de Chypre,* ed. René de Mas Latrie (Paris, 1884), pp. 260–61; Matteo Villani, *Cronica,* XI, 35, ed. Ignazio Moutier, V (Florence, 1826), 189. The fundamental modern account for the departure is Neculai Jorga, *Philippe de Mézières et la croisade au XIV* siècle (Paris, 1896), pp. 142–43. Especially from this point, Jorga's work is an invaluable aid in tracing the life of Pierre de Thomas. Its worth is recognized by Joachim Smet in his edition of Mézières, *Life,* p. 27, n. 1, pp. 32, 48.

[2] Although other chroniclers, cited above, report the whole fleet as that of Pierre I, the Venetian chronicler Caroldo cited by Jorga, *Mézières,* p. 143, n. 2, reports that at his arrival in Venice the king had two galleys of his own, while three others formed the fleet of the legate of Smyrna (Pierre de Thomas).

[3] Mézières, *Life,* ed. Smet, p. 103; AASS, Jan. 29, III, 623 (sec. 62); Makhairas, *Chronicle,* I, 115; Jorga, *Mézières,* p. 144. The two knights were Pierre de Sur and Jacques le Petit.

podestà of Treviso, by the grand canal. The doge presented many gifts to the king and his company. Lorenzo Celsi, a comparatively young man, had been doge of Venice for more than a year at this time. He had been elected on July 16, 1361, after the death of Giovanni Delfino.[4]

Pierre I discussed his plans for the crusade with the doge, who encouraged him to persevere in his efforts. Celsi promised that the republic in accordance with her traditions would give him ships and provisions and offer her own forces for the crusade. Nevertheless, until the king should return from his journey, the enterprise should be kept secret. Otherwise the success of the expedition, and Venetian trade as well, would be endangered.[5] Some Venetian ambassadors who were about to leave for Avignon were directed to support Pierre I's project at the Roman Curia.[6] Much of the king's success in Venice was due to the efforts and influence of Pierre de Thomas, who spoke before the doge on the king's behalf and received an eloquent response from Celsi.[7] Ever since his mediation in their war with Hungary, the Venetians had held Pierre de Thomas in high esteem. At this period, they urged the Pope to confirm his appointment of the Venetian citizen Niccolo Verde as dean of his diocese of Coron.[8]

[4] Mézières, *Life,* ed. Smet, p. 103; AASS, Jan. 29, III, 623 (sec. 62); Jorga, *Mézières,* pp. 145–47. Jorga gives copious references to the sources.

[5] Mézières, *loc. cit.;* Caroldo, "Cronaca di Venezia," Bibliothèque nationale de Paris, ms. italien 320, fols. 195r–195v, cited by Jorga, *Mézières,* p. 149 and n. 1.

[6] Senato, *Misti,* XXX, fols. 124r, 128v, cited by Jorga, *Mézières,* p. 149 and n. 2.

[7] Mézières, *loc. cit.;* Caroldo, "Cronaca di Venezia," fol. 191v, cited by Jorga, *Mézières,* p. 150 and n. 2.

[8] Action of the Senate, December 27, 1362, *Misti,* XXX, fol. 124r. They spoke of Pierre de Thomas as one "qui devotionem et amorem multum ostendit ad istud dominium." This reference was called to my attention in Jorga, *Mézières,* p. 150, n. 1, and checked in the microfilm in the Lea Library, University of Pennsylvania.

After he had obtained assurances of aid from Venice, Pierre I and his men departed from that city on January 2, 1363,[9] and in the next month they made their way across north Italy to Genoa, receiving magnificent receptions from the principal rulers of the area.[10] Pierre de Thomas remained with the group. By his eloquent preaching, he supported Pierre I's appeal for aid against the Moslems of Palestine and Egypt. His efforts bore much apparent fruit, as the Visconti and other rulers made solemn promises to support the crusade.[11] Although Mézières wrote enthusiastically about these promises, it is almost certain that their makers did not take them seriously. Unlike the rulers of Venice, who could hope to gain valuable commercial advantages from participation in a successful crusade, these despots of north Italy had no personal interest in the holy war. Yet it was a venerable cause, which they dared not flatly reject. Hence they humored the idealistic king of Cyprus by making promises which they had no intention of fulfilling.

Soon after the arrival of Pierre I in Genoa early in February,[12] Pierre de Thomas left him and Philippe de Mézières and went to Avignon to prepare for their reception at the papal court. [13] A new pope was now reigning. Innocent VI had died on September 16, 1362. Twelve days later, the cardinals elected as his successor Guillaume de Grimouard, abbot of the monastery of St. Victor in Marseilles, who took the name

---

[9] Louis de Mas Latrie, *Histoire de l'île de Chypre sous le règne des princes de la maison de Lusignan*, 3 vols. (Paris, 1852–61), II, 247, published the authorization of the Grand Council on January 1, 1363, for the doge to accompany Pierre I as far as Mestre the following day.

[10] The journey is related with abundant references to the sources in Jorga, *Mézières*, pp. 149–52.

[11] Mézières, *Life*, ed. Smet, pp. 103–04; AASS, Jan. 29, III, 623 (sec. 62).

[12] Jorga, *Mézières*, pp. 150–51.

[13] Mézières, *Life*, ed. Smet, p. 104; AASS, Jan. 29, III, 623 (sec. 63).

Urban V. Pierre de Thomas must have approved their selection. The new Pope was even more austere than Innocent VI had been. He was a foe of pomp and luxury and a lover of justice, austere living, and education.[14] On November 7, 1362, the day after his coronation, Urban V sent letters to the principal rulers and churchmen of the Latin world to notify them of his accession.[15] Among these, was one to Pierre de Thomas requesting him to continue in his office of legate.[16] It may be assumed that he received it in north Italy.

The decision of Pierre de Thomas to precede Pierre I of Cyprus to Avignon and prepare the way for him was wise. While the legate had many friends in the Roman Curia, the king's position there was uncertain. In a letter written November 29, 1362, which Pierre I had presumably received in north Italy, the new Pope wrote to him concerning the claims of the king's nephew Hugues de Lusignan, prince of Galilee, to the throne of Cyprus.[17] Since the time of Pierre's accession, these claims had been pressed at the papal court by the prince's mother, Marie de Bourbon, and by his cousin King John II of France.[18] Pope Innocent VI had accepted the validity of these claims, and Pierre I had sent ambassadors to attempt to make a settlement, but no final agreement had been made in Inno-

[14] G. Mollat, *Les Papes d'Avignon* (Paris, 1949), pp. 105–11.

[15] Many of these are published or summarized in P. Lecacheux and G. Mollat, *Urbain V (1362–70), Lettres secrètes et curiales se rapportant à la France* (Bibliothèque des écoles françaises d'Athènes et de Rome, 3rd series, vol. V; Paris, 1902–54), pp. 1–10. (Hereafter this work is abbreviated LMLU.) There are three fascicules in this work, published in 1902, 1906, and 1954, but only one pagination and one series of numbers for the documents.

[16] *Reg. Vat.* 245, fols. 5r–5v, summary in LMLU, no. 5, p. 3. A letter to Pierre I is noted in LMLU, no. 41, p. 6.

[17] *Reg. Vat.* 245, fols. 16v–17r, LMLU, no. 119, p. 12.

[18] According to a note by Dawkins in Makhairas, *Chronicle,* II, 96, King John II and Prince Hugues were third cousins. Their common ancestor was Louis IX. Hugues' descent ran: Louis IX, Robert of Clermont, Louis I de Bourbon, Marie de Bourbon, Hugues of Galilee.

cent's time.[19] Urban V now urged the king of Cyprus to fulfill his obligations to Marie de Bourbon and to deal benevolently with his nephew, Prince Hugues. He offered to act in a friendly manner as a mediator in their dispute but reminded King Pierre that he had not answered certain letters about it addressed to him by Innocent VI. Urban urged that replies to these should now be sent to him. At the same time, the Pope urged the king's brother, Jean de Lusignan, and Pierre de Thomas to intercede with Pierre I on behalf of his sister-in-law and nephew.[20] Pierre de Thomas therefore faced the task of presenting the king's viewpoint not only concerning the crusade but also in reference to the claims of Prince Hugues.[21]

When Pierre de Thomas arrived in Avignon, he was received with favor by Pope Urban V, who had heard about his ability and holy life. He was likewise greeted with joy and affection by the cardinals and his other friends in the curia. He reported to the Pope concerning his labors in the East for

[19] The fullest source on the case of Hugues of Galilee is Makhairas, *Chronicle*, I, 93–97, 113–15. Some relevant letters are published in Raynaldus, *Annales ecclesiastici, ad ann.* 1360, chaps. 13–16. Modern accounts are Hill, *History of Cyprus*, II, 309–10, and Jorga, *Mézières*, pp. 117–19. Makhairas claims that a provisional settlement was made in Innocent's time whereby Hugues of Galilee should receive an annual pension of 50,000 white bezants of Cyprus, that King John II of France would not agree to it, and that, in addition to his desire to promote the crusade, a desire to make a final settlement of Hugues' claims at Avignon prompted Pierre I to make his visit to the West. However, it is possible that the king actually hoped that he could avoid further discussion of the issue until it was raised again in Urban's letter, written after Pierre I had left Cyprus.

[20] *Reg. Vat.* 245, fols. 17r–17v, LMLU, nos. 120–21, pp. 12–13.

[21] As is pointed out in Aziz Suryal Atiya, *The Crusade in the Later Middle Ages* (London, 1938), pp. 322–23, these two topics were not unrelated. The interest of Pierre I in the crusade, a cause dear to the heart of the papacy, was a very strong point in his favor in his dispute with Hugues of Galilee, who was an untried youth According to Makhairas, *Chronicle*, I, 115, the dispute was settled at Avignon by confirming the plan by which Prince Hugues received an annual pension of 50,000 white bezants of Cyprus.

the exaltation of the Catholic faith and also described the sad conditions in that part of the world, where the Catholic faith was being threatened by Saracens and Turks, so that churches were being profaned and Christian people sold into slavery. He informed the Pope of the great interest of Pierre I in finding a remedy for these conditions, which really were a threat to all Christendom. A good beginning was made by the king in the capture of Adalia, and the infidels were struck by fear. Now, despite the perils of a long journey, Pierre I had come to the West to show the Pope, the cardinals, and the princes of the West how he believed the power of the Saracens could be broken and the Holy Land restored to the Christians.[22]

In the few short months of his pontificate, Urban V had already shown much interest in the crusade. On the day after his coronation, in his letter announcing his accession to the grand master of the Hospitallers, he had urged him to continue the war of God against the enemies of the faith.[23] Several days later, he wrote to the archbishop of Nicosia and his suffragans that, following the examples of Clement VI and Innocent VI, he was imposing a tithe on the church revenues of Cyprus for three years for the defense of Smyrna and other regions against the Turks.[24] Therefore, with no difficulty, Pierre de Thomas persuaded the Pope and cardinals to support a general crusade against the Moslems.[25] Urban expressed his desire

[22] Mézières, *Life,* ed. Smet, pp. 104–05; AASS, Jan. 29, III, 623 (secs. 63–64). Pierre de Thomas' report to Urban V is summarized in a papal letter of May 25, 1363, published in LMLU, no. 487, pp. 63–64.

[23] LMLU, no. 21, p. 4.

[24] Letter of November 19, 1362, published in LMLU, no. 113, p. 11; Jorga, *Mézières,* pp. 157–58. The money was to be collected by a nuncio, Pietro Damandi, archdeacon of Limassol.

[25] That the decision to proclaim a *passagium generale* was due to the persuasion of Pierre de Thomas is stated in Urban V's letter of May 25, 1363, to the grand companies of France published in LMLU, no. 487, pp. 63–64, in which Pierre de Thomas is called by the title

to confer with the king of Cyprus, and the way was thus prepared for him to be favorably received at Avignon.[26] The Pope honored Pierre de Thomas on March 6, 1363, by promoting him from the bishopric of Coron to the archbishopric of Crete although, according to Mézières, Pierre did not seek the promotion.[27]

In a letter to the king of Cyprus, Pierre de Thomas informed him of the favorable developments at Avignon.[28] Pierre I left Genoa for Avignon about the middle of March.[29] He arrived in the papal city on Holy Wednesday, March 29, 1363. At this time John II, king of France, was also in Avignon.[30] King Pierre was well received by the Pope, the cardinals, and the king of France, who was anxious to see the chivalrous ruler of Cyprus. Urban V gave Pierre I two golden rings and an *Agnus Dei* medal. In return, the king gave the Pope a silver lantern, which the latter gave to the abbey of St. Victor at Marseilles.[31]

---

archbishop of Crete. Concerning the bad conditions in the East, this letter says (p. 64): "que omnia venerabilis frater noster Petrus, archiepiscopus Cretensis, dudum in partibus ultramarinis apostolice sedis legatus, nobis et fratribus nostris asserens esse vera, contra infideles eosdem indici generale passagium persuasit."

[26] Mézières, *Life,* ed. Smet, p. 104; AASS, Jan. 29, III, 623 (sec. 63).

[27] Mézières, *Life,* ed. Smet, p. 105; AASS, Jan. 29, III, 623 (sec. 63); D. Rattinger, S. J., "Der liber provisionum praelatorum Urbani V," *Historisches Jahrbuch der Goerres Gesellschaft,* XV (1894), 58. The bull appointing Pierre de Thomas archbishop of Crete is recorded in *Reg. Aven.* 155, fols. 33v–34r, and the usual letters of notification on fols. 34r–34v. Joachim Smet in his edition of Mézières, *Life,* p. 105, n. 6, cites the reference for the bull of appointment and states that he found no copy in the Vatican registers. According to Hermann Hoberg, *Taxae pro communibus servitiis* (Vatican City, 1949), p. 44, the *servitia communia* for the archbishopric of Crete (500 florins) were paid on March 23, 1363.

[28] Mézières, *Life,* ed. Smet, p. 105; AASS, Jan. 29, III, 623 (sec. 64).

[29] Mas Latrie, *Histoire de Chypre,* II, 239, n. 1.

[30] Jorga, *Mézières,* pp. 160–62.

[31] E. Müntz, "L'argent et le luxe à la cour pontificale d'Avignon," *Revue des questions historiques,* LXVI (1899), 400.

King Pierre reported on conditions in the East much as Pierre de Thomas had done.[32]

The king's words confirmed the decision of Urban V to proclaim a general crusade to win the Holy Land from the infidel and aroused many knights to take up the cause. On Good Friday, March 31, 1363, the Pope celebrated mass in the presence of John II, Pierre I, and the Cardinal Talleyrand de Périgord and of many nobles and conferred upon them the crusader's cross. Afterward, he gave a dinner in honor of the kings of France and Cyprus. There can be little doubt that Pierre de Thomas was present at these festivities, which had come to pass largely as a result of his efforts. Yet we hear nothing of him, so greatly was he outshone by the illustrious men around him.[33]

On the same day, the papal plans for the crusade were announced in a series of letters. King John II of France was appointed as captain general of the crusade. The date set for the departure of the *passagium generale* was March 1, 1365, and King John swore upon the gospels that he would begin his journey then or earlier unless prevented by a legitimate impediment. To finance this crusade, the king was authorized for the next six years to collect a tithe of all the ecclesiastical revenues of France other than those of the cardinals, the mili-

---

[32] His outline of the situation is summarized in Urban's commission to Pierre de Thomas as legate of the crusade more than a year later (July 10, 1364), *Reg. Aven.* 156, fols. 45r–46r; *Reg. Vat.* 246, fols. 271r–273r; *Reg. Vat.* 253, fols. 27r–27v. published in Wadding, *Vita,* pp. 164–71, and *Bull. carm.,* I, 116–18.

[33] Mézières, *loc. cit.* The names of the prominent nobles are given in the account of this meeting in Jorga, *Mézières,* pp. 165–66, where most of the significant sources are cited. Another modern account is Maurice Prou, *Étude sur les relations politiques du pape Urbain V avec les rois de France Jean II et Charles V (1362–1370)* (Bibliothèque de l'École des Hautes Études, sciences philologiques et historiques, vol. 76; Paris, 1888), p. 25.

tary orders, and clergymen authorized to go on the crusade.[34] He was also to receive all donations, legacies, fines, and penances not specifically designated to some other cause.[35] Absolution was offered to thieves, usurers, and authorities, lay and ecclesiastical, who had taken bribes to permit usurers to operate in their lands if they would disgorge their ill-gotten gains to be used for the king's crusade, unless restitution could be made to rightful possessors.[36] A similar provision was made in the archdioceses of Crete, Corfu, and Rhodes for the support of Pierre I of Cyprus.[37] As archbishop of Crete, Pierre de Thomas was charged to carry it out in his province.

In a letter to the archbishop of Rheims and his suffragans, which was probably sent to other provinces as well, Urban V authorized the preaching of the crusade. A plenary indulgence was offered to anyone who should go on the crusade to recover the Holy Land or should support another in this enterprise. Lesser indulgences were offered to clergymen who should preach the crusade and to their listeners. Each week, a mass was to be said for the liberation of the Holy Land. The Pope pronounced anathema against anyone who should seek to dissuade the king of France from his good intentions.[38]

About two weeks after the initial proclamation of the cru-

[34] Papal letter to John II, published in Prou, Étude sur les relations politiques, pp. 95–102; partially published in Raynaldus, Annales ecclesiastici, ad ann. 1363, chap. 15; summary in Alphonse Fierens, Lettres d'Urbain V (1362–70), I (Analecta Vaticano-Belgica, vol. IX; Rome, Brussels, Paris, 1928), 276. A similar letter to the archbishop of Rheims is published in Fierens, op. cit., pp. 276–85.

[35] Prou, Étude sur les relations politiques, pp. 91–94; Fierens, Lettres d'Urbain V, I, 269–76.

[36] Ibid., pp. 293–96; LMLU, nos. 344–47, pp. 40–41.

[37] Letter to the archbishops of Crete, Corfu, and Rhodes, Reg. Aven. 155, fols. 241v–242r; Reg. Vat. 261, fol. 6r.

[38] Fierens, Lettres d'Urbain V, I, 285–92; Raynaldus, Annales ecclesiastici, ad ann. 1363, chaps. 16–18.

sade, on April 14, 1363, Urban V preached the crusade in a public sermon before the kings of France and Cyprus and many others. The Cardinal Talleyrand de Périgord, long a friend of Pierre de Thomas, was appointed as legate of the crusade.[39] The next day, Urban informed King Charles of Navarre about the crusade and urged him to make peace with John II of France and with Peter IV of Aragon, with whom he was then at war.[40] Toward the end of May, Urban wrote to the principal leaders of Europe, urging them to terminate all quarrels between Christian princes and to take the cross against the enemies of the faith.[41]

At first King Pierre I of Cyprus, who had done so much to arouse interest in the crusade, had no official position in it. He was not satisfied with the plan to delay the beginning of the crusade until March 1, 1365, but expressed a desire to return to the East as soon as possible. Therefore on May 25, 1363, Urban V appointed him as precursor general of the crusade. He was authorized to assemble two hundred armed knights from the kingdom of France, together with two thousand knights and six thousand infantrymen from other lands, to sail with him on his expedition. He was permitted to draw freely from the bands of mercenary soldiers and to enlist any

[39] Mézières, Life, ed. Smet, pp. 105–06; AASS, Jan. 29, III, 623–24 (sec. 64). The date April 14 comes from two of the lives of Urban V in S. Baluze, Vitae paparum Avenionensium, ed. G. Mollat, 4 vols. (Paris, 1914–27), I, 384, 396. A variant reading of the second of these lives gives the date April 12, which seems to be inaccurate. It is published in Raynaldus, Annales ecclesiastici, ad ann. 1363, chap. 14, and accepted by Jorga, Mézières, p. 166.
[40] LMLU, no. 354, p. 42. Jorga, Mézières, p. 169, discusses this letter, which he dates April 16.
[41] Letters of May 25, 1363, listed in LMLU, nos. 476–87, pp. 62–64. The letter to Emperor Charles IV is published in J. Prochno, ed., Acta Urbani V (1362–70) (Monumenta Vaticana res gestas Bohemicas illustrantia, vol. III; Prague, 1944), pp. 95–97, and in Raynaldus, Annales ecclesiastici, ad ann. 1363, chaps. 20–22, and the letter to King Louis of Hungary in TVMH, II, 55–56.

persons from the patriarchates of Aquileia and Grado, the archbishopric of Salzburg, and the lands of Sicily, Hungary, and the East who desired to go on the crusade. Those who should go with him were promised the same indulgences as were offered to those who should go on the principal expedition.[42] On the same date, Urban wrote a letter to the doge of Venice in which he hailed Pierre I as *precursor magnificus* of the crusade and urged that the republic aid him with ships, sailors, victuals, and other necessities for the voyage.[43]

There has been some discussion about the attitude of Pope Urban V toward Pierre I of Cyprus at this time, since he passed over the king of Cyprus with all his enthusiasm and knowledge of the East and appointed John II of France as captain general of the crusade. Halecki suggests that Pierre I was rejected because his interest was centered too exclusively upon the reconquest of the Holy Land, whereas the Pope desired a more comprehensive plan which would include the defense of the East against the Ottoman advance as well as the Palestinian expedition.[44] This contention is not supported by the sources. It is true that Urban V was interested in the defense of Smyrna and other regions threatened by the Turks, as is evidenced by the fact that on May 12, 1363, he appointed a new captain for Smyrna and made some provisions for strengthening its defenses.[45] However, Urban's letters of March 31 and May 25, 1363, cited above, make it perfectly clear that the principal goal of the crusade was the recovery of the

---

[42] LMLU, nos. 488–89, p. 65; Raynaldus, *Annales ecclesiastici, ad ann.* 1363, chap. 19. The title *precursor generalis passagii* is given by Mézières, *Life,* ed. Smet, p. 106; AASS, Jan. 29, III, 623 (sec. 64).

[43] LC, III, 14; Raynaldus, *Annales ecclesiastici, ad ann.* 1363, chap. 23.

[44] Halecki, *Un Empereur de Byzance à Rome* (Warsaw, 1930), pp. 80–83.

[45] LMLU, nos. 458–61, pp. 60–61; Jorga, *Mézières,* p. 158, n. 2, and *addenda,* p. xxviii.

Holy Land, notwithstanding the mention of the depredations of the Turks as a part of the background of the crusade. On this point there was no difference of opinion between the two kings. King John II of France was appointed as leader of the expedition because he was the highest ranking military leader among the crusaders and it was hoped that the support of the cause by a man of his prestige would induce others from the West to join it. Pierre I's rank among the monarchs of Christendom was much lower, and it would have been unthinkable for Urban to have asked John II to serve under him.

Although he had expressed a desire to return to the East without delay, Pierre I did not return to that region at once. He stayed in Avignon until May 31, 1363, and then went on a journey into northern Europe to solicit support for the crusade. He traveled in France, England, Germany, Bohemia, and Poland. Everywhere he was received with great honor and entertained with magnificent festivities, but he found few who could be interested in the cause which he represented, although he extended his journey to seventeen months.[46] Pierre de Thomas did not accompany the king on this journey. He stayed in southern France and Italy aiding Urban V in his efforts to prepare the way for the crusade by making peace among the princes of Europe. For much of this time, his friend Philippe de Mézières stayed with him and aided in this work.

Their first assignment was to end the war between the lord of Milan, Bernabo Visconti, and the papal forces in Italy. This war was regarded as one of the principal obstacles to the crusade. For more than a decade, the Visconti had been seeking to build a good-sized state in north Italy, partly at the expense of

---

[46] Mézières, *Life,* ed. Smet, pp. 106, 120–21; AASS, Jan. 29, III, 624, 627 (secs. 65, 83); Baluze-Mollat, *Vitae paparum Avenionensium,* I, 384–85, 396, 400; Jorga, *Mézières,* pp. 172–201. Mas Latrie, *Histoire de Chypre,* II, 239, n. 1.

the papal territories. They especially wanted possession of the city of Bologna, which could be used as a center from which to reduce Florence to impotence and as a springboard for further expansion into the states of the church. Since the beginning of the pontificate of Innocent VI, they had faced a strong opponent in the papal legate and commander, Cardinal Gil d'Albornoz, who was seeking to restore the authority of the church in her Italian lands. When Albornoz gained possession of Bologna in March, 1360, Bernabo Visconti determined to win the city by force. In the war which ensued, Albornoz was generally successful, for he was an able general and diplomat, like Bernabo willing to use deceit to gain his objectives.[47]

When Urban V ascended the papal throne, he found this war still in progress and strongly supported the efforts of Albornoz in Italy. He ordered Bernabo Visconti to appear at the Roman Curia by March 1, 1363, to state his case. When he failed to appear by that time, Urban renewed the ban of excommunication declared against him by Innocent VI and proclaimed a crusade against him, in which his neighbors were invited to participate.[48] Albornoz continued to press the war against the forces of the Visconti in Italy and completely defeated them at the Battle of Solara on April 6, 1363. In this battle, the cardinal lost his nephew, Garcia Albornoz, but Ambrogio Visconti, natural son of Bernabo, was taken pris-

[47] Mollat, *Papes d'Avignon*, pp. 204–31; Jorga, *Mézières*, pp. 206–10. For longer accounts see Hermann Joseph Wurm, *Cardinal Albornoz, der zweite Begründer des Kirchenstaates; ein Lebensbild* (Paderborn, 1892), pp. 3, 25–178, and Francesco Filippini, *Il Cardinale Egidio Albornoz* (Bologna, 1933), pp. 7–303.

[48] Urban's letters are published in Augustin Theiner, *Codex diplomaticus dominii temporalis S. Sedis,* II (Rome, 1862), 403, 405, 407–08 (hereafter abbreviated TCDD) and in LMLU, no. 1, p. 1; nos. 222–29, pp. 27–28; no. 239, pp. 30–34. See also Jorga, *Mézières,* pp. 210–11, and Wurm, *Cardinal Albornoz,* pp. 181–85.

oner. It looked as though the church would soon be fully victorious.[49] When the Pope learned of the victory at Solara, he congratulated the leaders of the church's forces.[50] On May 1, he wrote to the doge of Venice and urged that no salt, foodstuffs, or other goods be sent from Venetia to the lands of Bernabo Visconti.[51]

Meanwhile, at Avignon the crusade had been preached, and the kings of France and Cyprus were planning an expedition. They recognized that the church's war in Italy was one of the major obstacles to their getting support in the West. Already during his visit to Milan on his way from Cyprus to Avignon, Pierre I had talked to Bernabo Visconti about the possibility of his making peace with the church. Now Pierre and John II of France offered to act as mediators between the Pope and the lord of Milan.[52] Urban accepted their plan with reservations. On May 1, he wrote to Albornoz and gave him permission to make peace with Bernabo and his allies, subject to the approval of the allies of the church. If a satisfactory treaty could be made, the Pope would release Bernabo, his followers, and his lands from all ecclesiastical censures.[53] In another letter, he announced to Albornoz that the kings of France and Cyprus intended to send ambassadors to Italy to aid in the peace

---

[49] Matteo Villani, *Cronica*, XI, 44 (ed. Moutier, V, 197–99); Albano Sorbelli, ed., *Corpus chronicorum Bononiensium*, 3 vols. (Muratori, *Rerum italicarum scriptores*, new edition, tome XVIII, part 1; Città di Castello, 1938–39), III, 156–58; Jorga, *Mézières*, pp. 211–12; Smet's appendix VI in his edition of Mézières, *Life*, p. 213; Wurm, *Cardinal Albornoz*, pp. 183–84. Villani dates the battle April 16, while the *Corpus chronicorum Bononiensium* has April 6. Filippini, *Il Cardinale Albornoz*, p. 317, asserts that the earlier date is correct on the basis of a letter of April 12 from Albornoz to the bishop of Orvieto.

[50] LMLU, nos. 377–78, p. 48; TCDD, II, 408.

[51] LMLU, no. 396, p. 54; TCDD, II, 409.

[52] Mézières, *Life,* ed. Smet, p. 107; AASS, Jan. 29, III, 624 (sec. 66).

[53] LMLU, no. 386, pp. 52–53.

negotiations. If Visconti would surrender the fortress of Lugo and all the lands of the church which he held in the territory of Bologna, they and Albornoz might make peace with him. However, Urban V promised to support Albornoz in the further prosecution of the war if he felt it wise to continue the struggle to the destruction of the perfidious Bernabo.[54] These letters were sent by Niccolo Spinelli, doctor of laws, who was to explain the Pope's position more completely.[55]

For the embassy to Bernabo Visconti, King John of France chose Roger de St. Severin, count of Milet, Pierre Aycelin de Montaigu, bishop of Nevers, and Philippe de Moulins, licentiate in laws. Moulins seems to have played a lesser part in the negotiations.[56] Pierre I sent Pierre de Thomas and Philippe de Mézières. These ambassadors left Avignon after the departure of Pierre I for northern Europe; thus they began their journey early in June.[57]

The ambassadors first visited Milan to confer with Bernabo Visconti. They were received honorably at his court and given an opportunity to present their plea for peace, but they accomplished nothing. Bernabo was bitter because of his defeat at Solara and desired no peace with the church or her allies. He would make no concessions. They then went to see Cardinal

---

[54] LMLU, no. 387, p. 53.

[55] LMLU, nos. 388–95, pp. 53–54. See also Wurm, *Cardinal Albornoz*, p. 184; Filippini, *Il Cardinale Albornoz*, p. 322.

[56] Mézières, *Life*, ed. Smet, p. 107 and n. 14; AASS, Jan. 29, III, 624 (sec. 66); Sorbelli, *Corpus chronicorum Bononiensium*, III, 162–64; letter of Urban V to John II dated August 5, 1363, in LMLU, no. 557, p. 75; Jorga, *Mézières*, p. 214 and n. 2.

[57] Mézières, *loc. cit.* I see no reason to accept the view expressed in Jorga, *Mézières*, p. 214 and n. 2, that the ambassadors really left Avignon on or shortly after May 1, the date of the papal letters to Albornoz. Even if the papal representative Niccolo Spinelli left then, there is no reason to question Mézières' statement that the other ambassadors left after Pierre I's departure.

Albornoz in Cesena.[58] On their way, they visited Bologna from Tuesday, June 13, to Thursday, June 15, 1363.[59] Here they must have met Gomez Garcia, a nephew of Albornoz, who was governor of the city.[60] At Cesena, they discussed the possibilities of peace with Albornoz. They found that he was also hard and embittered and desired to continue the war against Bernabo, whom he hated. He had no faith in treaties made with Visconti. After they had concluded their conference with Albornoz, the ambassadors returned to Milan, where they made no further progress.[61]

The difficulty of these negotiations was undoubtedly increased by the haughty and overconfident bearing of the French ambassadors. They were proud of their position as representatives of one of the greatest princes of Christendom and thought that they could easily make peace between the Visconti and the church. They took a contemptuous attitude toward Pierre de Thomas and Philippe de Mézières as representatives of a lesser prince. They hoped that all the credit for making peace could be gained for themselves and their king. However, they were totally unsuccessful. They soon became discouraged and returned to France. The negotiations broke down about the end of July.[62]

Meanwhile, Urban V also despaired of peace and therefore prepared to prosecute the war in Italy. In July, he informed Albornoz that he was going to preach the crusade against Bernabo Visconti in Germany and elsewhere. Not until the lord of Milan was defeated or accepted the papal terms did the

[58] Mézières, *Life,* ed. Smet, pp. 107–08; AASS, Jan. 29, III, 624 (sec. 66–67); Jorga, *Mézières,* p. 215.

[59] Sorbelli, *Corpus chronicorum Bononiensium,* III, 162–64.

[60] TCDD, II, 410; Jorga, *Mézières,* p. 215, n. 4.

[61] Mézières, *Life,* ed. Smet, pp. 108–09; AASS, Jan. 29, III, 624 (secs. 66–67).

[62] Mézières, *Life,* ed. Smet, pp. 108–09; AASS, Jan. 29, III, 624 (sec. 67). Mézières emphasizes the slights received by his friend Pierre de Thomas, but from his narrative it is apparent that he too felt the sting of the French ambassadors' scorn.

Pope intend to permit further preaching of the crusade to recover the Holy Land.[63] On August 5, the count of Milet and Philippe de Moulins arrived in Avignon on their way back to the French court from their unsuccessful mission to Italy. The third French ambassador, the bishop of Nevers, had already returned home. The two ambassadors reported that Albornoz had been willing to accept their suggestions, but Bernabo Visconti had remained obdurate and would not hear of a settlement. Thus, Urban V reminded the king of France in a letter, the suggestions of the Milanese ambassadors to the king during his recent visit to Avignon were full of the usual Visconti lies and deceptions. The Pope asked John to support the interests of the church against Bernabo, though he admitted that continued war in Italy would impede the projected expedition to the East.[64]

Pierre de Thomas and Philippe de Mézières remained at Milan. They still hoped to be able to make peace. Pierre prayed earnestly that God would assuage the wrath of Bernabo Visconti. His hopes and prayers were not in vain. Within two days after the departure of the French ambassadors, Visconti summoned Pierre de Thomas and Philippe de Mézières into his presence. Seated between them in a private conference, he said to them. "Now speak boldly to me about peace and say whatever seems best to you." Pierre reviewed the advantages that would come to Visconti as a result of making peace and the dangers of war. He reminded Bernabo that the war was hindering the crusade, which was so important to the welfare of Christendom. No doubt he pointed out that Urban V was prepared to fight to the finish if Bernabo refused the papal terms concerning Bologna and the fortress of Lugo, and the papal forces would continue to be led by the able warrior

[63] Letter of Urban V to Albornoz, July 11, 1363, LMLU, no. 535. p. 71, cf. Smet's appendix VI in his edition of Mézières, *Life,* p. 214.
[64] LMLU, no. 557, p. 75; Raynaldus, *Annales ecclesiastici, ad ann.* 1363, chap. 5.

Albornoz. After Pierre had delivered his speech, Bernabo thought for a while. Then with a great sigh, he said, "I have heard you freely, and I wholly desire peace with the church and henceforth to be a subject and faithful member of it. You may go to the cardinal at once and discuss peace terms with him, and I will place the issue of war and peace in your hands." [65]

It is probable that Visconti had begun to consider the advantages of making peace before he admitted it. Already on July 14, he had appointed Gualdisio de Lovexelli, doctor of laws and citizen of Cremona, and Francesco Caimbasilica as his envoys in any peace negotiations which should be undertaken. This was probably before the departure of the French ambassadors.[66] After Visconti had expressed willingness to make peace, these Milanese ambassadors went to the headquarters of Albornoz, together with Pierre de Thomas and Philippe de Mézières. Visconti had already agreed to an armistice on the basis of the Pope's terms, so Albornoz gave his consent. He appointed ambassadors to accompany those of the king of Cyprus and of Bernabo Visconti to Avignon for the peace negotiations. From Albornoz' headquarters, they proceeded to Bologna, where the truce was proclaimed on September 3. On the following day, they left for Milan.[67] There they conferred again with Bernabo, who added another ambassador, Bruno de Gluxiano. From Milan, the entire group went to Avignon to obtain Urban V's consent to the truce terms.[68]

[65] Mézières, Life, ed. Smet, pp. 109–10; AASS, Jan. 29, III, 624–25 (sec. 68–69).

[66] Filippini, Il Cardinale Albornoz, p. 323.

[67] Sorbelli, Corpus chronicorum Bononiensium, III, 168–69 (Cronaca A); 169–70 (Cronaca Villola).

[68] Mézières, Life, ed. Smet, p. 110; AASS, Jan. 29, III, 625 (sec. 69). The ambassadors are named in the treaty of peace between Bernabo Visconti and the church, March 13, 1364, TCDD, II, 412. See also Jorga, Mézières, pp. 218–19.

In the truce agreement, which was ratified by Urban V, Bernabo Visconti offered his submission to the church. In return for 32,000 florins he promised to surrender the castle of Lugo to the church, together with all fortified places which he held in the district of Bologna. He also agreed to destroy his fortifications in the Modenese territory. He insisted, however, that he be permitted to make his surrender not to his inveterate enemy Albornoz but to another legate whom the Pope should appoint. Albornoz himself requested to be relieved of further responsibility in this affair, either because he was opposed to the peace negotiations or because he recognized that his presence at the council table would hinder the success of the negotiations. As his successor, Urban chose Androin de la Roche, now known as the cardinal of Cluny, who several years earlier, before his elevation to the cardinalate, had served as papal legate in north Italy and had always been on good terms with the Visconti, partly because, with lesser diplomatic and military ability than Albornoz, he had never been so great a threat to them. On November 24, Androin was appointed as legate in Lombardy and on December 1, as vicar of Bologna.[69] Albornoz was left with the legation in central Italy.[70] The new legate received express instructions not to make any peace with Bernado in which the allies of the church in Italy were not included, nor should he enter into any new treaty until Bernabo should carry out the terms of his truce agreement. Urban urged Albornoz to confer with Androin and to aid him if necessary in either war or peace. The welfare of the church in Italy demanded that they work together. The Pope made it clear that Albornoz' prestige was not diminished

[69] Oreste Vancini, "Bologna della chiesa (1360–1376)," *Atti e memorie della R. Deputazione di storia patria per le provincie di Romagna,* series 3, XXIV (1906), 314; Filippini, *Il Cardinale Albornoz,* p. 327; Jorga, *Mézières,* p. 219 and n. 4.

[70] LMLU, no. 681, pp. 90–91.

because the territorial extent of his legation was decreased. Rather his prestige was increased, since he had suggested the change and had consistently acted in the interests of God and the church rather than in his own interest.[71]

In this period, Urban V attempted to lay the groundwork for a definitive peace with Bernabo Visconti, but he did not neglect to prepare for further warfare in case the lord of Milan should fail to fulfill his agreements. In December, 1363, he gave the cardinal of Cluny full power to release Visconti and his followers and supporters, lay and clerical, from all ecclesiastical censures and to receive them back into good standing in the Roman Catholic Church. He was also authorized to restore status and benefices to any cleric who had lost them through supporting Bernabo in spite of these censures.[72] Urban wrote to Albornoz ordering him to transfer to the cardinal of Cluny all prisoners of war taken in the struggle with Bernabo.[73] Nevertheless, in the same period, the Pope wrote to Albornoz and the allies of the church in Italy urging them to re-establish their league against the Visconti. He still hoped for peace, but he knew the perversity and inconsistancy of that old enemy of the church Bernabo, and certain news from Italy made him less hopeful than he had been before.[74]

Urban V likewise took steps to see that Bernabo Visconti did not receive 31,250 florins due to him under the truce terms without fulfilling his part of the agreement. This money was first disbursed from the papal treasury into the hands of the cardinal of Boulogne on December 5, 1363, in the presence of Androin de la Roche, Pierre de Thomas, and Philippe

[71] LMLU, no. 724, pp. 100–01.
[72] LMLU, nos. 734–35, pp. 102–03. Filippini, *Il Cardinale Albornoz*, p. 327, mentions a letter of November 23 giving Androin the power to absolve Bernabò.
[73] LMLU, no. 736, pp. 103–04.
[74] LMLU, nos. 725–30, p. 101; no. 733, p. 102.

de Mézières. He was to see that the money was spent in accordance with the terms of the agreement.[75] Later it was deposited at Genoa under the care of Stephen, abbot of the monastery of St. Allyre of Clermont, and of certain other men.[76] On January 28, 1364, the Pope warned Androin not to pay any of this money to Bernabo until he had surrendered the castle of Lugo and the castles of the church in the district of Bologna.[77]

The cardinal of Cluny was not able to go to Italy at once to assume the government of Bologna. Therefore on December 6, 1363, he commissioned Pierre de Thomas and Philippe de Mézières to go there and act as his vicegerents until he himself could make the journey.[78] At the same time, both men were commissioned by the Pope to represent him as well as Pierre I of Cyprus in the preparations for the crusade at Venice, and Pierre de Thomas was appointed as papal mediator between the Venetian republic and her rebellious colony of Crete.[79]

Thus the two men left Avignon en route for Bologna in December, 1363, intending to go later to Venice. On their way they first visited Amadeo VI, the "Green Count" of Savoy, who was planning to go on the crusade.[80] They continued their journey through Milan [81] and arrived at Cremona by January

[75] Karl Heinrich Schaefer, *Die Ausgaben der apostolischen Kammer unter den Päpsten Urban V und Gregor XI (1362–1378) nebst Nachträgen und einem Glossar für alle drei Ausgabebände* (Vatikanische Quellen, vol. VI; Paderborn, 1937), p. 56.

[76] Letter of February 12, 1364, LMLU, no. 815, p. 118; TCDD, II, 411; cf. Jorga, *Mézières,* p. 220, n. 7.

[77] LMLU, no. 782, pp. 113–14.

[78] Vancini, "Bologna della chiesa," *Atti e memorie,* XXIV, 315; Filippini, *Il Cardinale Albornoz,* p. 337.

[79] See below, pp. 237–38.

[80] Letter of Doge Lorenzo Celsi of Venice to Pierre I of Cyprus, January 29, 1364, *Liber secretorum collegii,* fol. 60v, published in Mas Latrie, *Histoire de Chypre,* III, 744.

[81] Sorbelli, *Corpus chronicorum Bononiensium,* III, 179–80.

6, 1364.[82] When they arrived in the territory of Modena, they took possession of the two castles constructed there by Bernabo Visconti, and on each of them they raised the banners of the church and the king of Cyprus. The captains and soldiers swore fealty to the new government.[83]

On Monday, January 15, the two friends arrived at Bologna. Four days later, they were joined by a third vicar of the cardinal of Cluny, Aimerico Catti, bishop of Bologna and papal treasurer in Italy. The three vicars visited the castles of Crevalcore, Castelfranco, Piumazzo, Crespellana, Serravalle, Rosselino, Aiano, and Samodia, which Bernabo had held in the district of Bologna. They also visited the places he had held in the lands of the church's allies. In each of them they had the soldiery swear fealty to them and raised the standards of the church and the king of Cyprus. They did likewise at the castle of Lugo, which had been mentioned so prominently in all the negotiations.[84] On Saturday, January 20, peace was proclaimed between Bernabo Visconti and the church and her ally the commune of Bologna. Two days later, the Hospitaller Fra Daniele de'Carretti, who had succeeded Gomez Garcia as rector of Bologna under Albornoz, turned the government of the city over to Aimerico Catti, Pierre de Thomas, and Philippe de Mézières. They in turn confirmed him in the rectorship, but he departed from the city on January 27, leaving the government in their hands.[85]

On Sunday, January 28, 1364, Pierre de Thomas and Aimer-

[82] In the letter cited in note 80 the doge mentions a letter which they had sent to him from Cremona on January 6.

[83] Sorbelli, *op. cit.,* III, 179–81. According to the peace treaty of March 13, 1364, TCDD, II, 414, these two castles were Castro Formiginio and Galoni di Cesio.

[84] Sorbelli *op. cit.,* III, 179–82; Mattheus de Griffonibus, *Memoriale historicum de rebus Bononiensium,* ed. L. Frati and A. Sorbelli (Muratori, *Rerum italicarum scriptores,* new edition, tome XVIII, part 2; Città di Castello, 1902), p. 66.

[85] Sorbelli, *op. cit.,* III, 181–83; Mézières, *Life,* ed. Smet, p. 111; AASS, Jan. 29, III, 625 (sec. 71).

ico Catti, and perhaps Philippe de Mézières as well, again visited the fortress of Lugo and the castles which Bernabo had held in Bolognese territory. Formerly they had merely obtained oaths of allegiance to the new government from the mercenaries who had held these places for the Visconti. Now they paid the Milanese troops the wages due to them, dismissed them, and replaced them with new garrisons loyal to the church. Thus they consolidated the church's control of Bologna.[86]

During this period, Pierre de Thomas and Philippe de Mézières faced many dangers in the cause of peace. As Pierre had learned on earlier peace missions, there were many petty tyrants, commanders of castles, and mercenary soldiers who did not want peace because they made their living by war. On one occasion, as Pierre and Philippe were making their rounds of the fortresses and came peaceably before a certain castle, they were suddenly confronted by a group of thirty Hungarians and other mercenaries, spurring on their horses and brandishing their swords as if they had come upon some enemies. Mézières expected sudden death, but Pierre de Thomas faced the angry soldiers and said to them firmly, "What do you want?" When they heard his voice, they replaced their swords in their scabbards and beat a hasty retreat. While the two emissaries of peace were riding unarmed among these fortresses, men were constantly being despoiled and killed on the roads all around them, but Pierre and Philippe escaped all dangers. Mézières attributes their good fortune to the virtues of Pierre de Thomas, but certainly they were also protected by their position as representatives of the Pope.[87]

[86] Sorbelli, *op. cit.*, III, 182–83; Mattheus de Griffonibus. *Memoriale historicum*, p. 66. Mattheus de Griffonibus states that Aimerico Catti paid off and dismissed the Milanese mercenaries, while the other chroniclers say that Pierre de Thomas did so. Probably both men were associated in this task and perhaps Mézières as well, although he is not mentioned in the sources as having been present on that occasion.
[87] Mézières, *Life,* ed. Smet, pp. 110–11; AASS, Jan. 29, III, 625 (sec. 70).

The two friends were also threatened in the city of Bologna. Among the nobles and citizens of Bologna, Cardinal Albornoz had some strong partisans, especially among those who had received subsidies from him during the war. One day, when Pierre de Thomas and Philippe de Mézières were out of the city to pacify a certain castle which was still making war against Bologna, they saw their opportunity to strike against the new leadership. The dissidents went from one section of the city to the other insinuating that the archbishop and the chancellor treacherously planned to deliver Bologna to Bernabo Visconti. The people began to murmur against Pierre and Philippe. Someone rang the city bell, and the people angrily congregated. The majority said, "Put the traitors to death!" but the cooler heads among the people opposed such a move.[88]

Pierre de Thomas and Philippe de Mézières did not return to Bologna until the next morning. As they approached the city, they recognized at once that something was wrong. Usually when they approached Bologna, a large number of nobles and citizens met them outside the city to receive them, but on that day no one was to be seen. When they came nearer to the city, they were met by some of their friends, who informed them of what had happened and advised them not to enter the city. The two men conferred briefly and then Pierre said, "As God is our witness, we are innocent of all treachery. The devil is trying to disturb the peace again by striking fear into us, but, God helping us, he shall not prevail. In the name of God let us be on our way." Thus they entered the city and went to their residence amid the murmurings of their enemies. There they continued to receive bad news. The hatred of the citizens was growing. Pierre de Thomas sought help through prayer. Mézières expected any moment

[88] Mézières, *Life*, ed. Smet, pp. 111–12; AASS, Jan. 29, III, 625 (sec. 71); Jorga, *Mézières*, pp. 224–25.

to hear a mob coming toward their residence shouting "Kill them!" [89]

After he had devoutly said mass, Pierre de Thomas called Mézières into his chamber and unfolded his plan to him. He sent to the Palazzo [90] and had the bell rung to call the people to meet there, for he desired to address them. Still grumbling and murmuring against them, the people came to the Palazzo in such crowds that Pierre and Philippe could scarcely make their way through them to take their places before the assembly. As they sat down, they saw the nobles who had stirred up the trouble seated on either side. Full of guile, the agitators looked now at them, now at the people. Pierre de Thomas obtained silence and began to speak. First he told some wonderful stories of miracles, frequently citing the Holy Scriptures, so that the ears of the people rang. When he had put them into a better mood, he began to discuss the immediate problem. He made it clear that they had really committed an offense not against him and Mézières but against the Pope and the king of Cyprus, whom they represented. He reprimanded the people for the disturbance but afterward excused and lauded them, probably placing the blame upon those who had incited them. He denounced those sowers of dissension but also called them to penitence and to the obedience of the church. He showed that the whole affair had been the work of the devil. He explained that he and Mézières were wholly innocent of the charges that had been made against them. He induced everyone to work for peace and to obey the church. Thus he

[89] Mézières, *Life*, ed. Smet, pp. 112–13; AASS, Jan. 29, III, 625 (sec. 72).

[90] According to the chronicles published in Sorbelli, *op. cit.*, III, 182–83, Pierre de Thomas and Philippe de Mézières were living in the Palazzo, the official residence of the governors of Bologna. However, since Mézières indicates that Pierre sent to the Palazzo to have the great bell rung, it would appear that they did not live there, though they conducted their business from that place.

turned the hearts of his hearers to true contrition and charity, and those who had recently been his enemies became his friends.[91]

Then a certain doctor of laws, one of the chief citizens of Bologna, arose in the midst of the people.[92] He replied graciously to the words of Pierre de Thomas and commended him for his fidelity and devotion to duty. On behalf of the people, he sought pardon from Pierre de Thomas and Philippe de Mézières, making excuses for them, glorifying Pierre, and demonstrating his genuine obedience to the church. From that time, peace reigned within the city, and the people cordially obeyed the representatives of the Pope. On that day Philippe de Mézières reports that he held the keys of the city, of its fort, and of 120 castles on behalf of Pierre de Thomas.[93]

Pierre de Thomas and Philippe de Mézières continued to govern Bologna until the arrival of Cardinal Androin de la Roche, papal vicar of Bologna, on Ash Wednesday, February 7, 1364. He was welcomed to Bologna by a great number of citizens, and on orders of Pierre de Thomas, Mézières surrendered the keys of the city to him.[94]

[91] Mézières, *Life,* ed. Smet, p. 113; AASS, Jan. 29, III, 626 (sec. 73). If Mézières' account is correct, Pierre de Thomas must have spoken to the people in Italian. Since it is certain that he knew French and Latin, it is probable that he had acquired a knowledge of Italian in the many months which he had spent in Italy on various missions.

[92] Jorga, *Mézières,* pp. 222, 225, suggests that this may be Francesco di Ramponi, a doctor of laws of whom the Bolognese chroniclers speak with high esteem.

[93] Mézières, *Life,* ed. Smet, p. 114; AASS, Jan. 29, III, 626 (sec. 74).

[94] Mézières, *Life,* ed. Smet, p. 114; AASS, Jan. 29, III, 626 (sec. 75); Sorbelli, *op. cit.,* III, 183–85; Mattheus de Griffonibus, *Memoriale historicum,* pp. 66–67. Mattheus de Griffonibus states that Androin arrived in Bologna on February 5, 1364, which was also the first day of Lent. This is impossible, for as the other chroniclers correctly state, Ash Wednesday fell on February 7, 1364. Mattheus also says that the keys of the city were given to the cardinal of Cluny by the *anziani* of the city. This contradicts the eyewitness testimony of

After the arrival of the cardinal of Cluny in Bologna to take charge of the city, Pierre de Thomas and Philippe de Mézières left it almost immediately and went to Venice to negotiate concerning the Cretan revolt and preparations for the crusade.[95] They stayed there for the remainder of the month of February and returned to Bologna about the beginning of March to take part in the ceremonies which attended the signing of the definitive peace between Bernabo Visconti and the church.[96] This treaty was signed on March 13, 1364, by Cardinal Androin de la Roche and the plenipotentiaries of Bernabo Visconti. In it, Bernabo surrendered all claims to the castles which he had held in the lands of Bologna, Modena, and Romagna. In return, he was to receive from the church 500,000 florins within eight years, payable in annual installments of 62,500 florins. If he should fail to receive one of these payments within a month after it was due, he was entitled to reoccupy the fortresses. The definitive possession of the castle of Lugo was left to the arbitration of Cardinal Androin.[97]

Though others worked out the terms of the definitive treaty, there can be no doubt that much of the success of the peace negotiations was due to Pierre de Thomas. It was he who, with the aid of Philippe de Mézières, convinced Bernabo Visconti to agree to an armistice which ended the fighting and opened the way for serious peace discussions. Their work in the armistice negotiations and in the government of Bologna

---

Philippe de Mézières that he himself gave the keys of Bologna to the cardinal. Perhaps the *anziani* had some part in the ceremony, which Mattheus says took place at a bridge outside the city.

[95] See below, pp. 242–46.

[96] According to Sorbelli, *op. cit.*, III, 187, Pierre de Thomas arrived in Bologna before the archbishop of Saragossa, who came on Saturday, March 2.

[97] The treaty of March 13, 1364, is published in TCDD, II, 411–15. See also Filippini, *Il Cardinale Albornoz*, pp. 340–42; Wurm, *Cardinal Albornoz*, pp. 188–89.

during the transition period was appreciated by Androin de la Roche and Bernabo Visconti, both of whom wrote letters to Pierre I of Cyprus commending them for their achievements.[98]

As Pierre de Thomas and Philippe de Mézières saw it, these negotiations were very much in the church's interest, for they succeeded in removing one of the principal impediments to the crusade. Wurm and Filippini, two modern biographers of Cardinal Albornoz, take a different viewpoint. They consider that this peace treaty was not at all advantageous to the church. Wurm believes that a moderate expenditure of force on the part of Albornoz at this time would have completely destroyed the power of the Visconti, who perennially threatened the papal states.[99] Filippini accepts this view and sees the peace as a betrayal of Italy. He believes that a glorious period of national unity and international influence would have come to Italy under the leadership of the church if the Visconti had been completely crushed. He asserts that Visconti greatly desired the peace, especially since his favorite son was captured at the battle of Solara, and that it was Albornoz who really opposed it. To Filippini the crusade appears as an excuse rather than a legitimate reason for the negotiations, since nothing had occurred in the East to demand immediate attention. He believes that King John II of France promoted the peace in Italy because of his well-known sympathy with the

[98] Letter of Cardinal Androin de la Roche to Pierre I, March 9, 1364, Paris, Bibliothèque de l'Arsenal, ms. 499, fol. 146r; letter of Bernabò Visconti to Pierre I, March 28, 1364, *ibid.*, fol. 146v. On March 9 Cardinal Androin wrote a letter of recommendation for Mézières to the Holy Roman Emperor Charles IV (*ibid.*, fols. 146r–146v), perhaps because Mézières planned to visit northern Europe. In a later undated letter Mézières thanked the cardinal for his letters (*ibid.*, fols. 145r–145v). On these letters see Neculai Jorga, "Collection de lettres de Philippe de Maizières [sic]," *Revue historique*, XLIX (1892), 308–09. I obtained a microfilm of these folios and examined the letters.

[99] Wurm, *Cardinal Albornoz*, pp. 189–90.

Visconti and that it was he who convinced Urban V to act against the true interests of Italy.[100]

These contentions are questionable from many viewpoints. It was by no means certain to contemporaries that the victory of Albornoz was assured. The long-range effects of such a victory are even more dubious. That Albornoz was more opposed to peace than Visconti was not the viewpoint of Urban V and other contemporaries. Pierre de Thomas and Philippe de Mézières concentrated their peace-making efforts in Milan precisely because it was there that they found real resistance. The contention that the French king was acting in the Visconti interest is refuted by the fact that his ambassadors could accomplish nothing in their court. Most absurd is the assertion that Urban V had no real interest in the crusade. When two kings were willing to take the cross, an occurrence by no means common in the fourteenth century, the Pope seized the opportunity to promote a crusade which seemed to have real possibility of success. Their willingness to go, rather than any unusual conditions in the East, formed the true background of the proposed expedition. To Urban V and other promoters of the crusade, including Pierre de Thomas, this was an object of great importance to all Christendom, which clearly called for the sacrifice of other interests. Nevertheless, the papacy did not make peace with Bernabo Visconti until he accepted the terms laid down in Avignon.[101]

[100] Filippini, *Il Cardinale Albornoz,* pp. 321–22, 324–26; 332–34.
[101] For this criticism of Filippini's viewpoint I am indebted to Joachim Smet's remarks in his edition of Mézières, *Life,* pp. 214–15. I fully agree with them.

# 10

# Preparations for the Crusade of 1365

WHEN THE PEACE TREATY WAS SIGNED AT BOLOGNA, PIERRE de Thomas could rejoice at the removal of one of the major obstacles to the crusade. Yet much remained to be done to make the expedition a reality. Already for three months, he had been concerned with two other pertinent problems. The more important of these was the preparation of a fleet to convey the host of God to the East. Closely related was the task of seeking to reconcile the rebellious colony of Crete with its home government, Venice. Since it was to Venice that the papacy looked to furnish ships for the crusade, there was no hope of organizing an expedition as long as that government was preoccupied with seeking to overcome the Cretan rebellion.

The revolt in Crete had broken out in the previous summer (1363), when some of the Venetian colonists became aroused against the home government because of a tax levied in Crete for repairs to the port of Candia. These colonists made an alliance with the leaders of the Greeks on the island to resist the Venetian authorities. When the duke of Crete, Leonardo Dandolo, refused to postpone collection of the tax, he was deposed, and all Venetian officers, merchants, and seamen were imprisoned. The revolutionaries chose a duke, Marco Gradenigo the Elder, to govern the island with the aid of a council of four colonists, to which some Greeks were soon added. The standard of St. Titus, patron of Crete, replaced that of St. Mark. The Greeks were given permission to ordain their priests freely,[1] and there was talk of introducing the Greek rite into the cathedral church, of which Pierre de Thomas, as archbishop of Crete, was pastor. The Venetians sent three representatives to win back the island by persuasion, but the rebels would not hear them.[2] In October, the Venetian government therefore called upon the governments of the Mediterranean world to break off all relations with the island of Crete.[3]

[1] By an act adopted by Duke Marino Grimani and his council on October 23, 1360, published in Ernst Gerland, *Das Archiv des Herzogs von Kandia im königlichen Staatsarchiv zu Venedig* (Strassburg, 1899), pp. 61–62 (cf. pp. 32–33 for the name of the duke), Greek ordinations were closely supervised by the government and the representative of the Roman Catholic archbishop of Crete.

[2] Neculai Jorga, *Philippe de Mézières et la croisade au XIV^e siècle* (Paris, 1896), pp. 229–31; Samuele Romanin, *Storia documentata di Venezia*, 10 vols. (Venice, 1853–61), III, 217–20; J. Jegerlehner, "Der Aufstand der kandiotischen Ritterschaft gegen das Mutterland Venedig (1363–65)," *Byzantinische Zeitschrift*, XII (1903), 78–88. A series of documents illustrating the background of this revolt is published in Gerland, *Das Archiv des Herzogs von Kandia*, pp. 43–59. A recent study of this background is Freddy Thiriet, "Sui dissidi sorti tra il Comune di Venezia e i suoi feudatari di Creta nel Trecento," *Archivio Storico Italiano*, CXIV (1956), 699–712.

[3] *Liber secretorum collegii*, fols. 31v, 32v, 33r. Letters were sent to the grand master of the Hospitallers, the king, queen, and regent of Cyprus, the emperor of Constantinople, the king of Hungary, the queen of Naples, Prince Robert of Taranto and Achaia, and the government of Ragusa. The letter to the king of Hungary is in MHSM, IV, 58, and *Monumenta Hungariae historica, Acta externa*, II, 624 (erroneously dated 1364).

Among the letters sent by Doge Lorenzo Celsi at this time was one dated October 11, 1363, to King Pierre of Cyprus. The doge informed him of the revolt and the Venetian blockade of the island of Crete and asked the king to forbid his subjects to go there or to aid the rebels. He pointed out that this revolt could greatly delay the crusade.[4] King Pierre replied from London, England, on November 24. He expressed his grief at the news of the revolt and his continued friendship for the republic of Venice. He sent the doge a copy of a letter which he was sending to his wife and to his brother the prince-regent of Cyprus, absolutely forbidding his subjects to trade in Crete or to receive ships from Crete and ordering Cretans who might appear in Cyprus to be treated in the same way as rebels against the king's own authority. Furthermore, although he was confident that the Venetians had sufficient power to crush the rebellion, he offered to come to Venice as soon as he was able with the warriors whom he expected to collect for the crusade and to sail to Crete to help quell the rebellion.[5] The governments of Hungary, Genoa, Naples, and Taranto likewise promised to cooperate with the Venetians in enforcing the blockade against Crete.[6]

Meanwhile, before he had learned of the revolt, King Pierre I had written to the doge from Calais on October 20. He announced that he had induced many knights from France, Germany, and elsewhere to take the cross. He planned to sail

[4] *Liber secretorum collegii*, fols. 32v–33r; Louis de Mas Latrie, *Histoire de l'île de Chypre sous le règne des princes de la maison de Lusignan*, 3 vols. (Paris, 1852–61), III, 742.

[5] LC, III, 23; Mas Latrie, *Histoire de Chypre*, II, 250–52. This letter reached Venice on January 17, 1364, according to a letter from the doge of Venice to Pierre I written on January 29. This is recorded in *Liber secretorum collegii*, fol. 60v (unpublished part), which I discovered in the microfilm at the Lea Library, University of Pennsylvania, which is the source of citations from this manuscript.

[6] LC, III, 21–22; MHSM, IV, 58; Jegerlehner, "Der Aufstand," *Byzantinische Zeitschrift*, XII, 88.

from Venice the following March and called upon the doge to fulfill his promises of aid in transporting the crusaders. The doge replied to this letter on November 29. He pointed out that while Venice had lost none of her interest in the crusade, she would be unable to give any material aid to it until after the suppression of the Cretan rebellion, since all her ships, armed and unarmed, would be needed for this purpose.[7]

Pope Urban V was disturbed about the Cretan rebellion because of its effect on the crusade. On October 15, he wrote to the people of Candia and urged them to submit to the Venetian authority not only because their actions were impeding the crusade but also because the protecting power of Venice was their only shield against attacks of Greeks and infidels.[8] At the same time, he wrote to Venice and urged the doge and his government to forgive the people of Crete and not to deal harshly with them.[9]

When the discord between Venice and her colony continued, on December 6, 1363, Urban commissioned Pierre de Thomas, archbishop of Crete, to mediate between the rebellious members of his diocese and their mother country. Pierre received full power to nullify agreements made by the rebels and to use ecclesiastical censures to enforce his efforts to make peace.[10] The Pontiff wrote to the doge of Venice and the people of Candia notifying them of this appointment. He declared that Pierre was well qualified for this work because of his industry and foresight, his gift of knowledge and devotion to duty and also because of his genuine concern for peace, for the welfare

---

[7] *Liber secretorum collegii,* fol. 42r, in Mas Latrie, *Histoire de Chypre,* III, 743. This letter was sent in duplicate to the Venetian consul in Flanders, who was to send the copies to Pierre I by two different messengers.

[8] LMLU, no. 663, p. 86.

[9] LMLU, no. 664, p. 86.

[10] *Reg. Vat.* 246, fols. 46v–48v. This and other letters of the period have been consulted in the microfilm mentioned in the Bibliography.

of both parties, and for the crusade.[11] On the same date, the Pope also wrote a letter to the doge about the crusade. He reminded him that the king of Cyprus had gathered a group of magnates with whom he hoped to sail to the East the next spring. He urged the Venetian government to provide galleys and other ships for their voyage. He announced that Pierre de Thomas and Philippe de Mézières, who were to deliver this letter to Venice, would act as the king's representatives in this business. He asked the doge to favor them and give them counsel.[12] Thus Pierre was commissioned to seek a solution for both problems which were vitally related to the cause of the crusade.

Although Pierre and Philippe did not reach Venice for a few months, the republic soon became aware of the Pope's desires. On December 17, Lorenzo Celsi wrote to Urban V, as he had written to Pierre I a few weeks earlier, expressing his regrets that Venice could not immediately aid the crusaders because of the Cretan rebellion.[13] Urban replied to this letter in January and expressed his disappointment. He reminded the doge of Pierre de Thomas' mission as papal mediator between Venice and Crete and hoped that the trouble would soon be settled. He suggested that after the conclusion of the rebellion, the republic would be able to assist the crusade more than she had previously anticipated by contributing the troops raised for the subjugation of Crete.[14]

On December 6, 1363, Pierre de Thomas and Philippe de

[11] *Reg. Vat.* 246, fols. 34v–35v. The letter to the doge is published in Georg Martin Thomas and Riccardo Predelli, *Diplomatarium Veneto-Levantinum,* II (Venice, 1899), 98, and summarized in LC, III, 23.

[12] *Reg. Vat.* 246, fols. 34r–34v.

[13] *Liber secretorum collegii,* fol. 46r.

[14] *Reg. Vat.* 246, fols. 68r–68v, published from the Venetian copy in Thomas and Predelli, *Diplomatarium Veneto-Levantinum,* II, 99, and in LC, III, 25–26. The letter is dated January 19, 1364.

Mézières had also been appointed to govern Bologna for a time as vicegerents of Androin de la Roche. As is discussed in the preceding chapter, they spent the next few months fulfilling this responsibility, before going to Venice. Nevertheless, they did not neglect the business of the crusade. They left Avignon for Bologna late in December, and on their way visited Count Amadeo VI of Savoy, who was preparing to go on the crusade. They talked with him about the situation in the East. He expressed his willingness to go to Crete and aid the Venetians in subduing the revolt before proceeding to the Orient.[15] He gave them an oral message to the Venetian government, and they also probably carried letters to the doge from Amadeo.[16] On January 6, 1364, they wrote to Lorenzo Celsi from Cremona and notified him of the count's suggestion. They urged the doge to provide for Pierre I's expedition with the understanding that it also would aid in the suppression of the Cretan rebellion before going farther eastward to fight the infidel. The letter arrived at Venice a week later, on January 13.[17] Three days later, the doge replied that he was sending the Venetian notary Desiderio Lucio, who was fully informed of the Venetian position and would negotiate with them about the crusade.[18]

By this time, Pierre de Thomas and Mézières were supervising the government of Bologna. Desiderio Lucio went to negotiate with them there. They indicated that they expected a

[15] Known from a letter of the doge to Pierre I of Cyprus, January 29, 1364, *Liber secretorum collegii*, fol. 60v, in Mas Latrie, *Histoire de Chypre*, III, 744.

[16] Mentioned in doge's letter to Amadeo of Savoy, February 24, 1364, *Liber secretorum collegii*, fol. 72v.

[17] Known from the doge's letter cited in note 15.

[18] *Liber secretorum collegii*, fol. 59r. At this time, Desiderio was also commissioned to go to Avignon and seek to obtain the Pope's brother, Ange Grimouard, bishop of Avignon, as protector of Venice (*ibid.*, fols. 59r–59v).

thousand knights to be in Venice for the crusade by the middle of March. Desiderio gave them reason to believe that the Venetian government was prepared to transport that many men to the East if they would go first to Crete to aid her in suppressing the rebellion. Desiderio submitted these suggestions to his home government by letter on January 24. On the same day, Pierre and Philippe also wrote to Venice, sending their letter by Carlo Geno, canon of Patras.[19]

Four days later, these letters were received by the Collegio at Venice. Its members decided to accept the terms suggested by the negotiators in Bologna and to invite Pierre de Thomas and Philippe de Mézières to come to Venice for further discussions. They were not pleased with the conduct of their envoy Desiderio, however. In a letter, they reprimanded him for talking too much and for revealing too completely the intentions and resources of the republic. If Pierre and Philippe should decide to come to Venice, Desiderio was ordered to accompany them as far as Chioggia and there to await further instructions from the government. If one or both of them should remain in Bologna to continue the discussions, he also should remain there but was warned to avoid going beyond the grant of authority which he had received.[20]

The proposals and attitudes of the Venetian leaders are most fully discussed in a letter of January 29 from the doge

[19] These letters are known from the doge's letter to Desiderio, January 28, 1364, *Liber secretorum collegii,* fol. 64r, and from his letters to Pierre de Thomas and Philippe de Mézières dated January 28, *ibid.,* and January 30, *ibid.,* fol. 63v. The earlier of the doge's letters to the two envoys of Pierre I is partially published in Mas Latrie, *Histoire de Chypre,* III, 745, n. 1.

[20] Action of Collegio, January 28, 1364, *Secreta collegii,* II, fols. 129r/131r–129v/131v. (In this part of volume II of the *Secreta collegii* there are two sets of page numbers, and it is impossible from the microfilm in the Lea Library, University of Pennsylvania, to determine which set is correct. Therefore I have used both.) See also the letters mentioned in the previous note.

to King Pierre I of Cyprus. They accepted the plan proposed by Pierre de Thomas and Mézières with some reluctance. They had already prepared an army of one thousand knights and two thousand infantry and the ships to transport them to Crete. The island was one of their chief bases in the East and they therefore considered its recovery essential not only to their own prestige but also to the crusade. Hence they desired to send their army there without delay. Nevertheless, because of their love for the king of Cyprus and their respect for his pious work, they were willing to wait until the middle of March. If by that time there were enough soldiers of the count of Savoy or other crusaders who were willing to aid Venice to suppress the Cretan rebellion before going to the Holy Land, the Venetians would transport them to Crete on the ships prepared for their own army. After the suppression of the revolt, the republic would convey them to Cyprus or wherever they desired to go. On this expedition the Venetians had provision for only one thousand knights, but after the pacification of Crete they would furnish passage for Pierre I and any other nobles who should come to Venice on their way to the East.[21]

It was probably shortly after obtaining these terms that Philippe de Mézières, who with Pierre de Thomas was still at Bologna, received a disturbing letter from King Pierre I written in his own hand. In it, the king announced that he expected to have two thousand crusaders at Venice by March, whereas the Venetians had provision for only half as many. Furthermore, he was no longer willing to stop at Crete to help

[21] *Liber secretorum collegii,* fol. 6ov, partially published in Mas Latrie, *Histoire de Chypre,* III, 744–45, and in Jegerlehner, "Der Auf-stand," *Byzantinische Zeitschrift,* XII, 119. In the manuscript, the date of this letter is clearly January 29 in Arabic numerals. Perhaps the Venetians were encouraged to make an extra effort by their recent receipt of Pierre I's letter of November 24 expressing willingness to aid them in Crete.

suppress the rebellion. He charged Mézières to go to Venice and seek to arrange for passage of his army on this basis. Thus the king nullified all the previous negotiations of his representatives and gave them less than two months to win acceptance of his difficult terms from the Venetian government. On good grounds, Mézières feared that he would be unable to carry out the king's command, and this greatly disturbed him. He referred the problem to Pierre de Thomas, who gave him great comfort and encouragement.[22]

As soon as the arrival of Cardinal Androin de la Roche on February. 7 freed them from their responsibilities in Bologna,[23] Pierre de Thomas and Philippe de Mézières went to Venice to present the king's newest plans. They were accompanied by the Venetian envoy Desiderio.[24] They arrived at Venice about the tenth of February.[25] Without delay, they

[22] Mézières, *Life,* ed. Smet, pp. 114–15; AASS, Jan. 29, III, 626 (sec. 76); letter of Doge Lorenzo Celsi to Pierre I, February 22, 1364, *Liber secretorum collegii,* fol. 71v, in Mas Latrie, *Histoire de Chypre,* III, 745. Mézières' account is vague. He mentions his distress at reading the king's letter but gives no account of the issues, which are known from the Venetian documents. Mézières gives two false impressions: (1) that this letter marked the beginning of the negotiations, and (2) that Pierre de Thomas entered them only as a personal favor to Mézières. It is possible that this particular letter of the king was addressed to Mézières alone, but Pierre de Thomas was already associated with him in this business by commission of Urban V as well as Pierre I.

[23] See above, pp. 230–31.

[24] In a letter of February 9 (*Liber secretorum collegii,* fol. 70v), the Collegio gave Desiderio permission to accompany them to Venice. He had previously been instructed to go only as far as Chioggia. Perhaps they reached there by February 9.

[25] That they arrived in February is stated in the doge's letter to Urban V, February 26, 1364, *Liber secretorum collegii,* fol. 72r, in Mas Latrie, *Histoire de Chypre,* III, 746–47. Mézières, *Life,* ed. Smet, p. 116, states that Pierre de Thomas argued with four Venetian sages for ten days before they agreed to the king's terms. This agreement was reached by February 22, the date of the doge's letter to Pierre I, *Liber secretorum collegii,* fol. 71v; in Mas Latrie, *Histoire de Chypre,* III, 745. Hence the arrival of the two envoys of Pierre I was no later than February 12 and could have been a few days earlier. See also Jorga, *Mézières,* p. 236.

presented the king's request to the doge of Venice and his council. The Venetians gave several reasons why they could not provide passage to the East by March for two thousand knights, especially if they were unwilling to go first to Crete. There was not sufficient time to equip so many ships. They feared for their commerce if they provoked a war with the sultan of Egypt by allying with the crusaders. They doubted the success of the crusade, since they saw no evidence that any of the Western powers were planning to join it; at least none of them had sent agents to Venice to make preparations. Most of all they cited the Cretan rebellion as an obstacle to their providing for the crusade. They were determined to put aside all other business until the island was reduced to subjection. Therefore they refused to lend or rent any ships for the crusade.[26]

Then, according to Philippe de Mézières, Pierre de Thomas with clear reasoning refuted the arguments of the doge, the nobles, and the merchants one by one. The Venetian leaders answered him as well as they could, but they were unable to prevail against him. Then they agreed to appoint four men, the wisest in all the city, two scholars and two others,[27] to refute his arguments. For ten days, these men met once or twice a day with Pierre de Thomas and Mézières to discuss the crusade. The moral and theological arguments on both sides were so subtle and complicated that Mézières could not hope to remember them. We can be certain that practical considerations were not neglected. At length, the Venetians were con-

---

[26] Mézières, *Life,* ed. Smet, pp. 115–16; AASS, Jan. 29, III, 626 (sec. 77). Mézières adds the death of King John of France, the captain general of the crusade, as another reason given for the despair of the Venetians concerning the success of the crusade. Here Mézières' memory played a trick on him, for John II did not die until April 8, almost two months after this meeting.

[27] Mézières, *Life,* ed. Smet, p. 116, line 16; AASS, Jan. 29, III, 626 (sec. 78): "duo littarati et duo laici."

vinced that, despite the Cretan revolt and their other objections, they should give their aid to the crusade.[28]

The new Venetian agreement was announced to Pierre I in
a letter written by the doge on February 22, 1364. The Venetians agreed to transport two thousand knights, the number
specified by the king, with their horses, armaments, retinues,
and victuals for three months into the territory of the sultan
or any other infidel land where the king desired to go. They
agreed to bear the expense of half these ships. These were to
wait at Brindisi or Otranto from the beginning until the
middle of June for the arrival of the crusaders. This was three
months later than the king had specified. The other half of
the ships were to be chartered at Venice by the king of
Cyprus and other crusaders. The Venetian government would
help them secure favorable terms from the shipowners. As they
had requested, the king and those barons who would travel
with him were also permitted to arm three or four galleys for
their journey to the East in spite of the Cretan rebellion.[29]
Four days later, the doge wrote to Pope Urban V. He reviewed
the history of the negotiations and the visit of Pierre de Thomas
and Philippe de Mézières to Venice in February. These two
men had reminded the Venetians of the strong love of the
Pope for them and of his keen interest in the crusade. Thus

[28] Mézières, Life, ed. Smet, p. 116; AASS, Jan. 29, III, 626 (sec.
78). The AASS gives forty days as the length of these discussions, where
Smet's edition gives ten. The validity of Smet's reading is demonstrated
by the fact that these negotiations took place entirely within the month
of February. The doge's letter of February 22 mentions the many discussions which the Venetians had had with Pierre de Thomas and Philippe
de Mézières before reaching a decision.

[29] Liber secretorum collegii, fol. 71v, in Mas Latrie, Histoire de
Chypre, III, 745–46. These terms are also discussed by Mézières, Life,
ed. Smet, p. 117; AASS, Jan. 29, III, 626–27 (sec. 78), and also in
a letter of Mézières to Count Amadeo VI of Savoy, March 26, 1364,
in Paris, Bibliothèque de l'Arsenal, ms. 499, fols. 145v–146r. This
letter is discussed in Neculai Jorga, "Collection de lettres de Philippe
de Maizières [sic]," Revue historique, XLIX (1892), 309–10.

they had induced them to put aside their own necessities and give greater aid to the crusade than had been requested. Pierre had asked merely for permission to hire ships at Venice. They not only granted this request but agreed to provide half the ships at their own expense.[30] The Venetian letters make it clear that Pierre de Thomas and Mézières acted as joint negotiators, although Pierre was apparently the spokesman and leader, as Mézières indicates in his account.

With great joy, Philippe de Mézières wrote to King Pierre I to inform him of the favorable agreement with Venice and to praise the works of Pierre de Thomas.[31] By the time he received this letter, the king had again changed his mind and rendered useless the skillful negotiations of his envoys. By February 17, before the conclusion of their discussions at Venice, Pierre I had decided to postpone the crusade again and to linger in northern Europe to seek recruits. He made this decision because some of his fellow crusaders, notably Count Amadeo VI of Savoy, would not be ready by March and because he despaired of receiving any aid from Venice before the suppression of the Cretan rebellion. He therefore wrote to the doge and announced that he would not be able to sail from Venice until August. He hoped that the revolt in Crete would be suppressed by that time.[32]

At Venice, Pierre de Thomas did not neglect his papal commission to mediate between her government and the island of Crete. He discussed the rebellion with the Venetian govern-

[30] *Liber secretorum collegii,* fol. 72r, in Mas Latrie, *Histoire de Chypre,* III, 746–47.

[31] Mézières, *Life,* ed. Smet, p. 117; AASS, Jan. 29, III, 627 (sec. 79).

[32] Letter of Pierre I to Lorenzo Celsi, February 17, 1364, summarized in LC, III, 27, and under date of February 27 in Mas Latrie, *Histoire de Chypre,* II, 252, n. 1. Jorga, *Mézières,* p. 240, dates it February 16. He believes it was written from Paris rather than Padua, as suggested in LC, *loc. cit.*

ment, which did not welcome his or the Pope's intervention. On February 23, 1364, the Collegio voted to give him permission to go to Crete if he desired to do so but requested him not to travel on a Venetian ship. Its members had already given their instructions and their terms to their ambassadors in Crete and did not think it wise to send any other message to them.[33] Three days later, they asked Pierre de Thomas and Mézières to present certain Venetian requests to the Pope and the king of Cyprus, who might use his influence in Avignon on their behalf. They desired Urban V to grant crusaders' indulgences to those serving in the Venetian forces against the Cretan rebels, since the island was populated chiefly by Greeks and schismatics. They also wished for Urban's intervention in a quarrel with Aragon and his permission to send two ships to trade with the Saracens in goods not ordinarily forbidden in commerce with them.[34]

About the first of March, Pierre de Thomas and Philippe de Mézières returned to Bologna from Venice. They stayed there until after the signing of the peace treaty on March 13.[35] On March 5, shortly after they had left Venice, the Venetian government sent the notary Andrea de Oltedo to them to suggest that they write to the king of Hungary to inform him of the plans for the crusade and to ask him to permit the crusaders to buy foodstuffs in his Adriatic lands if they should need to stop there on the way to the East. It is not known whether Pierre de Thomas and Philippe de Mézières ever sent such a letter.[36] Shortly after the signing of the treaty at Bologna

[33] *Secreta collegii*, II, fol. 137r/139r.

[34] Action of February 26, 1364, recorded in *Secreta collegii*, II, fol. 138r/140r. The last request was granted by the Pope on April 8, as recorded in LC, III, 128.

[35] See above, p. 231.

[36] *Liber secretorum collegii*, fol. 74v. The text of the Collegio's action is published in MHSM, IV, 64 (partially), and that of the proposed letter in *Monumenta Hungariae historica, Acta externa*, II, 608–09

the two friends separated for several months.

Philippe de Mézières went first to Milan. From here he wrote a letter to Count Amadeo of Savoy to inform him of the proposals for the crusade which the Venetians had made in February. He and Pierre de Thomas had represented the interests of Amadeo as well as those of Pierre I at Venice, and the Venetian government had left it to them or one of them to inform Amadeo of the arrangements.[37] Philippe also informed him that many nobles from England and Germany had already come to Venice for the crusade and others were continually coming. He expressed his disappointment at the reports which he had heard that Amadeo had decided to delay his sailing on the crusade until September. Evidently, he had not yet received the news that his royal master Pierre I had decided to postpone the start of the expedition for almost as long. In this letter to Amadeo, Mézières noted that he planned to return to Venice on business of Pierre I.[38] For the remainder of 1364 he passes out of sight. Jorga, his biographer, suggests that he traveled in northern Europe in this period.[39]

From Bologna, Pierre de Thomas went to Avignon, where he conferred with Urban V concerning the next steps to be taken in reference to the Cretan rebellion.[40] After a few months of

---

(with incorrect date March 2). This text was written before Pierre I's new delay until August was known. Interestingly, the time of the king's expected arrival in Venice is given as April instead of March, as it is given elsewhere. Apparently the Venetians no longer expected him by March.

[37] Letter of the doge to Amadeo, February 24, 1364, *Liber secretorum collegii,* fol. 72v.

[38] Paris, Bibliothèque de l'Arsenal, ms. 499, fols. 145v–146r; Jorga, "Collection de lettres," *Revue historique,* XLIX, 309–10.

[39] Jorga, *Mézières,* pp. 244–51, 261.

[40] In his letter of March 26 to Count Amadeo, cited in note 38, fol. 145v, Mézières excused Pierre de Thomas for not calling on Amadeo 'quia dictus archiepiscopus habuit ire ad curiam recta via pro aliquibus negociis arduis tangentibus passagium domini mei regis." See Jorga, *Mézières,* p. 242 and n. 2.

discussions in the Roman Curia, it was finally decided that, despite the objections of Venice, Pierre should go to Crete and try to pacify the island.[41] It was not necessary for him to make this voyage. When the Venetian fleet arrived in Crete in April, it had little difficulty in putting an end to the revolt, partly because a division had by now arisen between the native Greeks and the Venetian colonists. The rebellion was ended in May, and the joyous news reached Venice on June 4, two days after it was decided that Pierre should go to Crete but before he had left Avignon.[42]

Shortly after the conclusion of the trouble in Crete, on July 5, 1364, Urban V rewarded Pierre de Thomas for his faithful and self-effacing labors for the papacy by translating him from the archbishopric of Crete to the position of Latin patriarch of Constantinople. Though this was merely a titular dignity, it was one of great prestige. Included in its duties was the administration of the bishopric of Negroponte, which was canonically united to it.[43] Pierre succeeded Guglielmo Pustrella, who had

---

[41] Papal letter to Doge Gabriel Adorno and to the council and commune of Genoa, urging them not to assist the Cretan rebels, *Reg. Vat.* 246, fols. 206r–206v. There is a summary in LMLU, no. 979, p. 151, where, however, the statement about Pierre de Thomas is omitted.

[42] Jorga, *Mézières*, pp. 251–53; Romanin, *Storia di Venezia*, III, 219–24; Jegerlehner, "Der Aufstand," *Byzantinische Zeitschrift*, XII, 89–96, cf. documents on pp. 101–25.

[43] Mézières, *Life*, ed. Smet, p. 118; AASS, Jan. 29, III, 627 (sec. 80). Letter of appointment, *Reg. Vat.* 156, fol. 120r, see also Raynaldus, *Annales ecclesiastici, ad ann.* 1364, chap. 24, and Paul Edouard Didier Riant, "Dépouillement des tomes XXI–XXII de l'*Orbis christianus* de Henri de Suarez—Patriarcats de Constantinople et de Jerusalem," *Archives de l'Orient latin,* I (1883), 284. Riant dates this letter incorrectly July 6. Letters of notification to those in Pierre's new jurisdiction are recorded in *Reg. Aven.* 156, fols. 120r–120v. According to Hermann Hoberg, *Taxae pro communibus servitiis* (Vatican City, 1949), p. 41, Pierre de Thomas paid the *servitia communia* for the patriarchate of Constantinople, amounting to 1,150 florins, on July 13, 1364.

been patriarch of Constantinople from December, 1346, until his appointment as archbishop of Milan in August, 1361, and had been permitted to retain the administration of the patriarchate until the time of Pierre's appointment.[44] On the date of his elevation to the patriarchate, Pierre de Thomas also received his former bishopric of Coron *in commendam* for life; it was vacant through the death of his successor, George, a doctor of laws, who had been a canon of the church of Coron at his appointment to the bishopric.[45]

Five days after his appointment to the patriarchate, Pierre de Thomas' great interest in the crusade was recognized in his appointment as papal legate for the crusade. Though this was made effective on July 10, it was being considered seriously in the middle of May.[46] The office had been vacant since Janu-

---

[44] Conrad Eubel, *Hierarchia catholica medii aevi,* I (Münster, 1913), 206; D. Rattinger, S.J., "Der liber provisionum praelatorum Urbani V," *Historisches Jahrbuch der Goerres-Gesellschaft,* XV (1894), 66–67; Louis de Mas Latrie, "Les patriarches latins de Constantinople," *Revue de l'Orient latin,* III (1895), 439.

[45] Letter of Urban V to Pierre de Thomas, July 5, 1364, *Reg, Aven.* 156, fols. 103r–103v; letters of same date to the cathedral chapter and vassals of the church of Coron, to the clergy and people of the city and diocese of Coron, and to the archbishop of Patras, *ibid.,* fol. 103v; Rattinger, *op. cit.,* p. 64; Eubel, *Hierarchia catholica,* I, 212; Mézières, *Life,* ed. Smet, p. 118; AASS, Jan. 29, III, 627 (sec. 80).

[46] The record of his appointment in *Reg. Aven.* 156, fols. 45r–46r originally bore the date May 17, 1364, and was addressed to Pierre, archbishop of Crete. Its date was later altered to July 10 and the address changed to Pierre, patriarch of Constantinople, in view of his appointment to that office on July 5. The copies of this bull in *Reg. Vat.* 246, fols. 271r–273r, and *Reg. Vat.* 253, fols. 27r–27v, show only the altered form. It is thus published in Wadding, *Vita,* pp. 164–71, in LMLU, no. 1080, pp. 169–70, and in Raynaldus, *Annales ecclesiastici, ad ann.* 1364, chap. 24. It is possibly a confusion of the two dates which causes *Bull. carm.,* I, 116–18, to date the letter June 8. The bulls granting faculties to Pierre de Thomas in connection with his legation show similar alterations. Those recorded in *Reg. Aven.* 156, fols. 46r–56r, and *Reg. Aven.* 157, fols. 111r–112r, with a few exceptions were originally dated from May 17 to 21 and later altered to July 10. The form of address was altered in them as in

ary 17, when the former legate, Pierre's friend the Cardinal Talleyrand de Périgord, had died.[47] In his letter appointing Pierre de Thomas as legate, Urban V described him as a man after his own heart, outstanding in virtue, proved in the religious life, remarkable for his knowledge, sublime in his humility, magnanimous in his clemency, endowed with great foresight, and thoroughly instructed in the law of the Lord and the Catholic faith, who at other times had laudably exercised the office of legate in the East. As in the earlier period, he was given legatine authority throughout all the East, for the crusade was designed to help the Christians of that area. There he was authorized to build and plant, to root out and destroy for the good of the cause. He was given full power to reform churches and ecclesiastical persons, to make leagues and to ratify treaties in his jurisdiction. He was charged especially to aid the king of Cyprus and all who sought to go with him on the crusade. Already on June 30, the Pope had announced his appointment to King Pierre I of Cyprus, to the doges of Genoa and Venice, to Count Amadeo of Savoy, to Earl William of Warwick, to the Hospitallers, and to the Genoese podestà of Pera, all of whom had an interest in the crusade.[48]

---

the bull of appointment. The copies in *Reg. Vat.* 246, fols. 273r–276r, *Reg. Vat.* 253, fols. 27v–34r, and *Reg. Vat.* 261, fols. 87r–87v, give only the corrected date and address. Presumably these alterations were made so that Pierre's title on the bulls pertaining to his legation would correspond with his new title as patriarch. It appears that the Pope planned to make Pierre de Thomas legate of the crusade before he decided to grant him the patriarchate of Constantinople. The documents were altered to fit the later decision. The alterations on these bulls are discussed by Joachim Smet in his edition of Mézières, *Life*, p. 118, n. 32. I have examined them in the microfilm mentioned in the Bibliography.

[47] S. Baluze, *Vitae paparum Avenionensium,* ed. G. Mollat, I (Paris, 1914), 385, 396, 400.

[48] *Reg. Vat.* 246, fols. 241v–242v. The letter to King Pierre I is published in Wadding, *Vita,* pp. 172–73, and in *Bull. carm.,* I, 119. Summaries of this and other letters are in LMLU, nos. 1051–53, pp. 163–64, and Raynaldus, *Annales ecclesiastici, ad ann.* 1364, chap. 25.

As legate of the crusade, Pierre de Thomas received many faculties and privileges, mostly identical with those received for his earlier legation.[49] As befitted his higher rank in the hierarchy, he was authorized to procure ten florins a day from ecclesiastics through whose territory he might pass in the course of his travels as legate, as compared with six florins on his earlier legation.[50] He was commissioned to preach the crusade over a wide area, including the lands of Austria, Hungary, Venetia, Istria, the eastern shore of the Adriatic, the island of Sicily, and all the lands of the East.[51] He was given the power to release one hundred holders of benefices from the statutes which would otherwise prevent their going to the Holy Land without loss of their benefices.[52] He was charged to see that bishops should be appointed over cathedral churches in the East which should be occupied by faithful Christians after having been vacant or held by infidels.[53] Pierre de Thomas

---

[49] These faculties of 1364 are recorded in *Reg. Aven.* 156, fols. 46r–56r; *Reg. Aven.* 157, fols. 111r–113r, 116r–116v; *Reg. Vat.* 246, fols. 273r–276r; *Reg. Vat.* 253, fols. 27v–34r; *Reg. Vat.* 261, fols. 86v–88r. There are many duplications.

[50] *Reg. Aven.* 156, fols. 50r–50v; *Reg. Vat.* 246, fols. 273v–275v; *Reg. Vat.* 253, fols. 29v–30v. In the original letter of May 17 Pierre de Thomas, then archbishop of Crete, was authorized to procure eight florins a day. In the altered form issued on July 10, after he became patriarch of Constantinople, the sum was raised to ten florins. The alterations can be seen on the copy in *Reg. Aven.* 156. The grant of ten florins a day is mentioned in Mézières, *Life,* ed. Smet, p. 118; AASS, Jan. 29, III, 627 (sec. 80).

[51] *Reg. Aven.* 156, fols. 51r–55r; *Reg. Vat.* 253, fols. 31r–33v; summarized in Riant, "Dépouillement de Suarez," *Archives de l'Orient latin,* I, 284–85. On the basis of Riant's edition Kenneth M. Setton, *Catalan Domination of Athens, 1311–1388* (Cambridge, Mass., 1948), p. 60, indicates that this crusade was preached against the enemies of the faith in Athens, Thebes, and Neopatras, that is the Turks and their Catalan allies. However, as is made clear in the full text of the papal letter, the crusade was to be preached *in* these dioceses (among others) not against them. It was directed primarily against the Moslems in the Holy Land. The full text is in the microfilm mentioned in the Bibliography.

[52] *Reg. Aven.* 156, fol. 49v; *Reg. Vat.* 253, fol. 29v.

[53] *Reg. Aven.* 157, fols. 112v–113r; *Reg. Vat.* 261, fol. 88r.

had complained to the Pope about the failure of some ecclesiastics to pay the procurations due to him from his earlier
legation in the East. He was granted authority to proceed
against them with ecclesiastical censures.[54]

Pierre de Thomas probably left Avignon for Venice in July,
1364, not long after his appointment as legate of the crusade.[55]
On the way, he stopped at Milan to visit Bernabo Visconti on
behalf of Urban V. He discussed some intimate affairs of the
Visconti family which Bernabo had referred to the Holy See.[56]
He also brought the Pope's request that Bernabo seek to induce
Anechin Baumgarten, the leader of a notorious company of
mercenaries, to go on the crusade. Urban suggested that the
people of Italy would do well to pay the expenses of these
bands on the crusade if they could thus free their homeland
of such destructive marauders.[57]

At this time, Pierre de Thomas apparently paid another visit
to Bologna. where he conferred the degree of master of
theology upon the Carmelite Bernard of Bologna, who had
studied for many years at the University of Paris and was a
lecturer at the Carmelite school at Bologna. He had applied
to the Holy See to grant him a master's degree, since he was
not at a university which could grant degrees in theology. On
July 14, 1364, Urban V directed Pierre de Thomas to examine
him with the aid of four other masters of theology at Bologna
and if he was found worthy, to grant him a master's degree
in theology which would entitle him to the same standing as
a member of his order who graduated at the University of

[54] *Reg. Vat.* 251, fols. 315r–315v (July 10, 1364). ,
[55] Mézières, *Life,* ed. Smet, p. 119; AASS, Jan. 29, III, 627 (sec.
81). See also Smet's note 34, on p. 119.
[56] Letter of Urban V to Bernabò Visconti, July 9, 1364, *Reg. Vat.*
246, fol. 251r, in LMLU, no. 1069, p. 167.
[57] *Reg. Vat.* 246, fols. 239v–240r (June 25, 1364), in LMLU,
no. 1037, p. 161.

Paris.[58] On two other occasions in the past few years, Pierre had taken a similar part in granting master's degrees in theology by papal commission. On March 15, 1363, he had been authorized to grant such a degree in Venice to the Franciscan Ludovico di Santo Martino of that city, who had read the *Sentences* in most of the outstanding schools of his order and was then the principal lector in its school at Pisa.[59] In October, 1363, he was authorized, with four other masters of theology in Bologna, to examine Niccolo of Venice, prior general of the Friars Servants of Mary of the Order of St. Augustine, and to confer the degree upon him.[60]

It was probably during the summer of 1364 that Pierre de Thomas took part in the exercises which marked the founding of the theological faculty at the University of Bologna. This university, although noted for its work in civil and canon law, had hitherto possessed no theological faculty. Theological instruction was left to the schools established by the mendicant orders in the thirteenth century. After a university with a school of theology had been established in Florence in 1349, the Bolognese began to desire a theological faculty at their university. In response to their petitions, Innocent VI had authorized the founding of such a faculty in 1360, but political conditions delayed it for four years.[61]

[58] *Reg. Aven.* 156, fols. 568r–568v; *Reg. Vat.* 253, fol. 78v; *Bull. carm.*, I, 119–20. According to Smet's note 34 in his edition of Mézières, *Life*, p. 119, the original of this letter is in the Carmelite archive in Rome.

[59] *Reg. Aven.* 154, fols. 506r–506v; *Reg. Aven.* 155, fol. 372r; *Reg. Vat.* 252, fols. 47v–48r; see *Chartularium universitatis Parisiensis*, ed. H. Denifle and E. Chatelain, 4 vols. (Paris, 1889–1907), II, 536; III, 97.

[60] *Reg. Vat.* 154, fols. 631v–632r; *Reg. Vat.* 252, fols. 48r–48v.

[61] Albano Sorbelli and Luigi Simeoni, *Storia della Università di Bologna*, vol. I by Sorbelli on the Middle Ages (Bologna, 1944), pp. 129–36. The bull of founding, *Quasi lignum vitae* (June 30, 1360), is published in Franz Ehrle, *I più antichi statuti della Facoltà di Teo-*

In the statutes of the theological faculty of the University of Bologna, Pierre de Thomas is listed as the first among nine masters of theology who were its founders.[62] The foundation date is usually given as June 2, 1364,[63] but that is impossible, because Pierre de Thomas is known to have been in Avignon on that date.[64] It is more probable that this event occurred in July or August, when Pierre visited Bologna on his way from Avignon to Venice. Though he has sometimes received high praise for his work in founding the theological faculty at Bologna,[65] his participation was probably limited to formal ceremonies. He did not stay in Bologna long enough to take a significant part in the instruction or government at this school. The real architect of the theological faculty at Bologna was the Augustinian friar Ugolino Malabranca, who appears second on the list of founders. He taught there until 1367.[66]

It may be assumed that Pierre de Thomas arrived in Venice about the beginning of August, the month in which Pierre I of Cyprus was scheduled to arrive there to begin his expedition to the East. As usual, the legate was received with great honor. At Venice, many princes and nobles had already gathered for

logia dell'Università di Bologna, Contributo alla storia della scolastica medievale (Universitatis Bononiensis Monumenta, vol. I; Bologna, 1932), pp. 1–5.

[62] Ehrle, I più antichi statuti, pp. 5–6; Wadding, Vita, pp. 74–76. See also Sorbelli and Simeoni, Storia della Università di Bologna, I, 140.

[63] Ehrle, I più antichi statuti, p. cxlii; Sorbelli and Simeoni, Storia della Università di Bologna, I, 135–36.

[64] Papal letter of June 2, 1364, Reg. Vat. 246, fols. 206r–206v. Summary in LMLU, no. 979, p. 151, without mention of Pierre de Thomas, whose name is in full letter.

[65] As in the speech of Pope Benedict XIV before the Chapter General of the Carmelite Order on May 23, 1744, published in Bull. carm., IV, 326, in which he hailed Pierre as the real founder of this faculty.

[66] Sorbelli and Simeoni, Storia della Università di Bologna, I, 141. In 1367, Ugolino became prior general of his order. He served later (1371–74) as Latin patriarch of Constantinople.

the crusade, and they were glad to see him. The Venetians were prepared to fulfill the promises which they had made to Pierre de Thomas and Mézières earlier in the year.[67] The hopes of the crusaders were high but were soon deceived when Pierre I failed to appear as he had promised. The nobles who had assembled for the crusade were bitterly disappointed. Some of them doubted that the expedition would ever get started and sadly withdrew from the venture. The king's failure to keep his promises released the Venetians from theirs. The merchants who traded with the Moslems rejoiced and made fun of the crusade. Pierre de Thomas considered these setbacks as the work of the devil and gave himself to prayers and tears, trusting to God and to the Virgin Mary to make all things right.[68]

By October 29, Urban V recognized with displeasure that King Pierre I had extended his journey into northern Europe so long that it would be impossible for his expedition to sail until after the coming winter. He therefore advised Pierre de Thomas to cease collecting his procuration of ten florins daily from the clergy of Venice, so as not to be unduly onerous to them. Instead, until the day on which he went to sea, he was to live on the income from his own churches.[69] About a month earlier, the Pope had granted the concession that any clergyman in Pierre's company might receive the income from his benefices for two years without fulfilling the duties connected with them. Thus the legate's associates could go on the crusade without

[67] They were probably unwilling to give Pierre I the troops which they had hired for the reconquest of Crete, as Urban V had urged them to do in a letter of June 27, in *Reg. Vat.* 246, fol. 230v; LMLU, no. 1045, p. 163; Raynaldus, *Annales ecclesiastici, ad ann.* 1364, chap. 9.

[68] Mézières, *Life,* ed. Smet, pp. 119–20; AASS, Jan. 29, III, 627 (secs. 81–82).

[69] *Reg. Vat.* 246, fols. 358r–358v (October 29, 1364), cited by Smet in his edition of Mézières, *Life,* p. 121, n. 35.

fear of losing their benefices in Urban's drive against absenteeism.[70]

In this period, Urban V received a letter from the Byzantine Emperor John V through Michael Malaspina, a citizen of Genoa. In it, John expressed his interest in the crusade and offered to aid the expedition. In his reply, the Pope requested that the Byzantines give liberal aid if the crusaders should come to their land. He also urged the emperor and his people to abjure the schism and be reunited to the Roman Church. He announced that he would order the legate of the crusade and the captain whom he would later appoint to treat him and his subjects as friends, while abstaining from their errors.[71]

Early in November, Pierre de Thomas was called upon to act on a minor problem in Venice. Cardinal Androin de la Roche wrote to him from Bologna[72] and commissioned him to visit and reform the Augustinian convent of S. Georgio in Alga and to proceed against the prior, Friar Bertrando, who had already been canonically removed from office by the vicar of the bishop of Castello. This action was initiated because of accusations made against Bertrando by two friars of the Augustinian Order, Pasquale and Jacopo.

On November 11, 1364, King Pierre I at last returned to Venice from his long journey in northern Europe. The Venetian government provided a magnificent reception for him. The podestàs of the towns on the way were authorized to spend as much as 300 pounds each on his reception. The doge himself went out to meet him on the *Bucentaur*.[73]

[70] Letter of Urban V to Pierre de Thomas, September 23, 1364, *Reg. Aven.* 157, fol. 116r.

[71] Letter of Urban V to John V, October 16, 1364, *Reg. Vat.* 246, fols. 348v–349r; LMLU, no. 1305, p. 211; Raynaldus, *Annales ecclesiastici, ad ann.* 1364, chap. 27.

[72] LC, III, 36 (November 2, 1364).

[73] Guillaume de Machaut, *La Prise d'Alexandrie ou chronique du roi Pierre de Lusignan,* ed. Louis de Mas Latrie (Geneva, 1877), pp.

These festivities brought little joy to the king of Cyprus, for he was a discouraged man. For a year and a half, he had sought to obtain recruits from northern Europe for his crusade. He had found little interest in the cause among the great princes. Of these, only King John II of France, the captain of the crusade, had been interested in the holy war, and he had died on April 8, 1364, making the task of Pierre I even harder. Some of the lesser nobility had agreed to go on the crusade, but not as many as he had expected. Several times he had prolonged his travels in the hope of ultimate success, but at length he admitted his failure and returned to Venice. When Pierre de Thomas visited the king, he found him brooding over his disappointment. The legate comforted him and encouraged him to continue his good work, pointing out that in a holy war even a small number of men could win the victory with the help of God. Thus the king was encouraged and did not abandon the crusade. Instead, he continued to gather those of the faithful who were willing to go.[74]

The king opened new discussions with Venice concerning the ships required for the crusade. The republic no longer felt bound by the offers made in February, since the king had not appeared at the appointed time. After a few days, the Venetians agreed to provide ships at a just hire for all who desired to sail.[75] Three other ships were to accompany the fleet at the

---

47–48; Jorga, *Mézières*, pp. 199–200, 259. The instructions of the Collegio on October 26 for the entertainment of the king are published in Louis de Mas Latrie, "Nouvelles preuves de l'histoire de Chypre," *Bibliothèque de l'École des chartes*, XXIV (1873), 73–74. Sir George Francis Hill, *A History of Cyprus*, 4 vols. (Cambridge, 1940–52), III, 328, n. 1, and Mas Latrie, *Histoire de Chypre*, III, 815, note that Pierre I stayed in the palace of Federico Cornaro of Episkopi at this time.

[74] Mézières, *Life*, ed. Smet. pp. 120–21; AASS, Jan. 29, III, 627 (sec. 83).

[75] Machaut, *Prise d'Alexandrie*, pp. 48–49.

expense of the republic. They were to be commanded by Andrea
Gritti, Marino Zeno, and Andrea Paradisi.[76]

At the close of 1364, every serious obstacle to the crusade was
removed except one. This was a quarrel which had broken out
between Genoa and Cyprus earlier in the year and threatened
to lead to war. It had begun among seamen of the two nations at
Famagusta in Cyprus. Two Genoese seamen who had deserted
from Cypriote ships were apprehended and punished in the
usual way by cutting off their right ears to the sound of trumpets. Some Genoese sailors, infuriated by the treatment of their
countrymen, then murdered some Cypriotes on a galley which
they boarded. In reprisal, some Genoese sailors were killed by
Sicilian mercenaries serving in the fleet of Cyprus. The Genoese
podestà, Guglielmo Ermirio, seized a Pisan in the service of
the king of Cyprus and claimed that he was a Genoese. When
the man denied this, his tongue was cut out. The king's bailie,
Jean de Soissons, reported this outrage to the Admiral Jean
de Sur, who demanded that the podestà order the Genoese to
go to their homes and disarm, or he would have them cut down.
The podestà reminded him that in such a case he would have
the Genoese government to reckon with. Other quarrels ensued. Although when the regent, Jean de Lusignan, the king's
brother, heard of the trouble, he sought to make peace, the
Genoese podestà finally threw down his wand of office and
ordered all Genoese to leave the island, an action which was
confirmed by a Genoese ambassador who came in September.[77]

When news of this quarrel reached Avignon in June, 1364,
Urban V acted quickly. On June 19, he wrote to Doge Gabriel
Adorno of Genoa and expressed his sadness at hearing of the

---

[76] Jorga, *Mézières*, p. 260. Jorga's source is the unpublished chronicle of the Venetian Caroldo.

[77] Hill, *History of Cyprus*, II, 312–13; Leontios Makhairas, *Recital
concerning the Sweet Land of Cyprus entitled "Chronicle,"* ed. and
trans. R. M. Dawkins, 2 vols. (Oxford, 1932), I, 127–31; Jorga,
*Mézières*, pp. 255–57.

threatened war between Genoa and Cyprus. He praised King Pierre I for his rare qualities of prudence and justice. He urged Genoa not to withhold the aid which she had promised for the crusade nor to impede the holy war in any way.[78] On the same day, Urban wrote to Pierre I and urged him to redress any grievances that had been committed against the Genoese in Cyprus and to punish the guilty.[79] A week later, he learned that the Genoese were arming a number of galleys to convey their ambassadors to Cyprus. He urged them to desist from this course, which could lead to war. In case the Cypriotes should refuse satisfaction, Urban offered to reimburse the Genoese for damages suffered in Cyprus, if they would only refrain from taking drastic measures.[80] At this time, the Pope entrusted an oral message to the Genoese envoy Filippo de Varesio, who was about to return to his home city after doing business in Avignon.[81] Though the doge of Genoa did not answer his letters, Urban continued to work for peace. On July 2, the doge's brother, Gianotto Adorno, stopped at Avignon on his way home from France. Urban found him well disposed toward the king of Cyprus and asked him to work for peace at Genoa. He also appointed him as his spokesman in an embroilment of the doge with the archbishop of Genoa and in a quarrel between Florence and Pisa.[82]

By July 17, Urban V received the Genoese terms for peace with Cyprus. They required the king to punish both the Cyp-

---

[78] Reg. Vat. 246, fols. 220r–220v. In his edition of Mézières, Life, p. 222, n. 3, Smet dates this letter June 17. In the manuscript the date is June 19, as appears in the microfilm mentioned in the Bibliography.

[79] Reg. Vat. 246, fol. 219r; LMLU, no. 1027, p. 159.

[80] Papal letter to the Genoese government, June 25, 1364, Reg. Vat. 246, fols. 219r–220r; LMLU, no. 1034, p. 161.

[81] Reg Vat. 246, fols. 228r–228v; LMLU, no. 1035, p. 161.

[82] Reg. Vat. 246, fols. 244v–245r, cited by Jorga, Mézières, p. 259 and n. 2. In his edition of Mézières, Life, p. 223, n. 6, Smet cites this letter as appearing on fols. 224v–225r, but it does not appear on these folios in the microfilm cited in the Bibliography.

riotes who had injured Genoese citizens and the officers who
had neglected to see that justice was done. The Pope informed
Pierre I of these conditions and urged him to accept them and
to grant justice.[83] At the same time, he wrote to Adorno and
his council, thanked them for their willingness to seek peace,
and urged them to persist in this spirit.[84]

Unhappily these encouraging signs of Genoese good will
did not lead to an immediate peace, and preparations for war
continued. No further negotiations are recorded before Pierre I
returned to Venice from northern Europe. Late in 1364, the
Venetians sought to act as mediators. On December 24, they
sent two ambassadors, Francesco Bembi and Zacharia Contareni, to Genoa to discuss some injuries done to Venetian citizens
and subjects by the Genoese podestà of Pera. They were authorized also to discuss the quarrel between Cyprus and Genoa.
They were fully informed of Pierre I's rights and intentions.[85]
The Genoese were still inclined toward war against Cyprus,
so the Venetian ambassadors could not settle this issue.[86]

On January 28, 1365, the king of Cyprus chose his own
ambassadors to make peace with Genoa, namely, Pierre de
Thomas and Guido da Bagnolo, his royal physician. Their
appointment was made at the king's lodgings in Venice in the
presence of several witnesses, among whom were the king's
nephew Hugues of Galilee and Philippe de Mézières,[87] who

[83] *Reg. Vat.* 246, fol. 255r; LMLU, no. 1102, p. 174.

[84] *Reg. Vat.* 246, fol. 255v, cited by Jorga, *Mézières,* p. 259, n. 6,
and Smet in his edition of Mézières, *Life,* p. 223, n. 7.

[85] *Liber secretorum collegii,* fol. 133r; Mas Latrie, *Histoire de
Chypre,* III, 747–49.

[86] The result of the Venetian negotiations is mentioned in a papal
letter to Genoa, February 20, 1365, *Reg. Vat.* 247, fols. 51r–52v;
Wadding, *Vita,* pp. 175–81; *Bull. carm.,* I, 122–23.

[87] Letter of appointment contained in the treaty of peace of April
18, 1365, published in Mas Latrie, *Histoire de Chypre,* II, 253–54,
and in *Liber iurium Reipublicae Genuensis,* ed. Ercola Riccoti, II
(Historiae patriae monumenta, vol. IX; Turin, 1857), 734–35.

now reappears in the sources for the first time since the preceding March.[88] A month later, on February 20, Pierre de Thomas also received a commission from Urban V to work on this problem. In his letter of appointment, the Pope urged him to go to Genoa without delay to labor for peace according to the prudence which God had given to him. If he was unable to persuade the Genoese to make peace, he was instructed to constrain them under threat of ecclesiastical censures to accept a truce with Cyprus for a long period and to send ambassadors to Avignon to discuss the controversy.[89] At the same time, the Pope wrote to Pierre I of Cyprus[90] and to the government of Genoa,[91] informing them of the mission of Pierre de Thomas and urging them to settle their quarrel. The tone of his letter to Genoa is decidedly sharper, indicating that he considered her the real trouble-maker. By this dual commission, Pierre de Thomas was authorized to use his talents to help solve a problem which must have long concerned him because of his interest in the crusade and his friendship for Pierre I.

About the beginning of March,[92] Pierre de Thomas went to Genoa. He was accompanied by the physician Guido da Bagnolo, who shared his commission as envoy of Pierre I to

---

[88] Jorga, *Mézières*, pp. 244, 261.

[89] *Reg. Vat.* 247, fols. 50v–51r; Wadding, *Vita*, pp. 173–75; *Bull. carm.*, I, 121.

[90] *Reg Vat.* 247, fol. 50v; LMLU, no. 1602, p. 268.

[91] *Reg. Vat.* 247, fols. 51r–52v; Wadding, *Vita*, pp. 175–81; *Bull. carm.*, I, 122–23.

[92] Though it would normally be assumed that Pierre de Thomas went to Genoa shortly after his appointment as ambassador of Pierre I on January 28, the Pope's letter of appointment issued on February 20 indicates that he had not gone to Genoa by that date. It is possible, as Jorga, *Mézières*, p. 262, suggests, that the legate made a visit to Genoa after he received the king's commission and returned to Venice by February 20. Mézières, *Life*, ed. Smet, pp. 122–23; AASS, Jan. 29, III, 628 (secs. 84–85), is of no help, since he makes it appear that Pierre de Thomas visited Genoa only once at this time, whereas at least two visits are known from the papal records. Hence a third visit is quite possible.

the Genoese government, and probably by Philippe de Mézières and another knight Simon Thenouri.[93] In the city, Pierre stayed in a church of the Hospitallers. The ambassadors received a cool reception in Genoa, though it is difficult to believe the report of Mézières that all Genoese had been ordered to snub them completely and to refuse them hospitality, so that Pierre found lodgings only with difficulty and by virtue of his position as a papal legate.[94]

In this period, Pierre I complained to the Pope that he had heard rumors that the Hospitallers at Rhodes were considering an alliance with the Genoese against the kingdom of Cyprus. Urban thanked the king for the information and urged him to notify the Holy See of any others who might seek to inflame this quarrel, which the papacy was seeking to extinguish.[95] The Pontiff at once wrote to the grand master and convent of the Hospitallers. He reminded them that the quarrel between Genoa and Cyprus was a great obstacle to the crusade. He forbade them to join one side or the other.[96]

At the doge's palace in Genoa, Pierre de Thomas entered into negotiations with the government. He explained his cause with humility. The response of the Genoese leaders showed

---

[93] These names are all reported by Makhairas, *Chronicle*, I, 135, where the name of Pierre de Thomas is omitted, perhaps because of Makhairas' anti-Catholic bias. Jorga, *Mézières*, p. 261, believes that there is a good probability that Mézières was a member of the embassy to Genoa, although Mézières does not say that he was with Pierre in his account of the legate's difficulties in Genoa.

[94] Mézières, *Life*, ed. Smet, pp. 122–23; AASS, Jan. 29, III, 628 (sec. 84). Mézières also says that the retinue of Pierre de Thomas were stoned by the people, who were crying out for war against the king of Cyprus. He says that Pierre, as usual, remained calm while his associates feared for their lives.

[95] Papal letter to Pierre I, March 4, 1365; *Reg. Vat.* 247, fols. 57r–57v; Wadding, *Vita*, pp. 181–82; *Bull. carm.*, I, 123; LMLU, no. 1619, pp. 273–74.

[96] Letter of February 27, 1365, in *Reg. Vat.* 247, fol. 54v; LMLU, no. 1609, p. 270.

the bitterness of their hearts. They were not influenced by the pious admonitions of the Pope nor by the good offices of other princes and communes, who had urged them to make peace with Pierre I. They answered the legate proudly and uttered threats against the king of Cyprus. The legate sought to persuade them to peace as well as he knew how, sometimes with threats and sometimes with logical arguments or honeyed words.[97] Still they showed no interest in making peace. After some weeks, Pierre de Thomas felt it wise to return to Venice to confer with the king. When Urban V heard of this trip, he was displeased, although he knew that the legate intended to return to Genoa.[98] He urged him to return at once, for further delay in the peace negotiations would be detrimental to the cause of the crusade.[99]

On March 26, 1365, the Pope again wrote to the rulers of Genoa and Cyprus. He acknowledged the reception of an embassy from the doge of Genoa concerning some overseas interests of the republic and insisted that no satisfactory settlement of this business could be made until the trouble between Genoa and Cyprus should be settled. He urged the doge to cooperate in the peace negotiations which Pierre de Thomas would continue on behalf of the Holy See. If the quarrel could not be settled through the legate's mediation, he required Genoa to send ambassadors to Avignon for this purpose.[100] At this time, he likewise urged Pierre I to send an embassy to Avignon if peace could not otherwise be concluded.[101] He informed

[97] Mézières, *Life*, ed. Smet, p. 123; AASS, Jan. 29, III, 628 (sec. 85).

[98] Letter of Urban V to Genoese authorities, March 22, 1365, *Reg. Vat.* 247, fol. 66r; LMLU, no. 1649, p. 281.

[99] *Reg. Vat.* 247, fols. 66r–66v (March 22), published under incorrect dates in Wadding, *Vita*, pp. 183–84, and *Bull. carm.*, I, 124.

[100] *Reg. Vat.* 247, fols. 67v–68r, cited by Smet in his edition of Mézières, *Life*, p. 224, n. 13.

[101] *Reg. Vat.* 247, fol. 67v, cited by Smet in his edition of Mézières, *Life*, p. 224, n. 15.

Pierre de Thomas of this correspondence and instructed him
to come to Avignon to aid in the negotiations if the two powers
should decide to send their envoys there. The Pope also noted
that he had sent some letters to the legate through the archbishop of Genoa, who would deliver them to him on his return
to that city.[102]

There was no need to transfer the negotiations from Genoa
to Avignon, for upon their return to Genoa, Pierre de Thomas
and Guido da Bagnolo succeeded in making peace between the
two governments.[103] The peace treaty was signed at the hour
of vespers on April 18, 1365. It was secured only at the cost
of abject surrender by the king of Cyprus to the Genoese demands. In it, the king reaffirmed the grant of privileges given
to the Genoese by his predecessor King Henri I in 1232. He
agreed that its terms had been frequently broken by Cyprus
but promised that they would henceforth be faithfully observed. In addition, these privileges were so extended that the
royal government lost almost all authority over Genoese in Cyprus, even those in the royal service. Only cases involving
property held by a Genoese as a fief were exempt from the
jurisdiction of the podestà. Genoese trade with Cyprus was to
be absolutely unrestricted, except for a few minor provisions.
At the insistence of the Genoese, the Admiral Jean de Sur and
Jean de Soissons, the bailie of Famagusta, were to be exiled for
life to the island of Rhodes or farther west, because they were
blamed for the early disturbances at Famagusta, which had

[102] *Reg. Vat.* 247, fols. 67r–67v (March 26); LMLU, no. 1650,
p. 281; Wadding, *Vita,* pp. 184–85; *Bull. carm.,* I, 125.
[103] A papal letter of April 17 (LMLU, no. 1700, p. 291) reveals
that the king's chamberlain, Pietro Marozelli, had gone to Avignon on
royal business and received an oral message from Urban V to the
king. Jorga, *Mézières,* p. 264, n. 4, suggests that Marozelli was sent
to Avignon to discuss the quarrel between Genoa and Cyprus in response to the Pope's letter of March 26. This is not necessarily so,
since that letter contemplated the transference of negotiations from
Genoa to Avignon only if they became utterly hopeless at Genoa, which
never became the case.

started the quarrel. Others who had acted against the Genoese were to be punished. This treaty was ratified in the name of the king by Pierre de Thomas, who swore his oath in the manner of prelates by putting his hand on his breast,[104] and by Guido da Bagnolo, who took his oath upon the gospels. They promised that the king would observe this treaty under pain of a fine of 100,000 florins.[105]

When this treaty was presented to Pierre I in a French translation, he refused to confirm the banishment of the bailie and the admiral but accepted the rest of the treaty. Genoa gave him a safe-conduct for his return to the East from Venice.[106] The fact that Pierre I and his representatives accepted this humiliating treaty shows how desperately they desired a settlement with the Genoese so that they would be free to carry out their plans for the crusade.[107] The king was not able to receive reports from both his principal envoys until about a month after the treaty was signed. Guido da Bagnolo fell ill on the journey and was not able to return to Venice until May 13. Pierre de Thomas returned there somewhat earlier.[108]

---

[104] Mas Latrie, *Histoire de Chypre*, II, 265, n. 1.

[105] Hill, *History of Cyprus*, II, 314–16; Jorga, *Mézières*, pp. 264–65. The text of the treaty is published in *Liber iurium Genuensis*, II, 732–43, in Mas Latrie, *Histoire de Chypre*, II, 254–66, and in Carlo Pagano, *Delle imprese e del dominio dei Genovesi nella Grecia; libri quattro* (2nd. ed., Genoa, 1852), pp. 294–307.

[106] Makhairas, *Chronicle*, I, 139; Hill, *History of Cyprus*, II, 316.

[107] *Ibid.*

[108] In a letter to Doge Gabriel Adorno of Genoa, dated May 16, 1365, published in *Liber iurium Genuensis*, II, 744, in Mas Latrie, *Histoire de Chypre*, II, 266–67, and in Pagano, *Delle imprese e del dominio dei Genovesi nella Grecia*, pp. 293–94, Pierre I excused himself for not writing to Genoa earlier by explaining that he had not been informed of the terms of the treaty "usque ad quartam diem ante datam presentium" (May 13) because his envoy Guido da Bagnolo had been unable to return to Venice until that date and Pierre de Thomas had not wanted to discuss the treaty with the king before the arrival of his colleague. While it is undoubtedly true that Pierre I wanted to hear personally from both of his envoys before writing to Genoa, it is difficult to believe that the king learned nothing of the terms of the

After the conclusion of this treaty, the Genoese attempted to show a spirit of friendship toward Pierre I. They offered three galleys to accompany him to Cyprus and aid in the crusade. Since he planned to sail to the East before they could be ready, he requested that they sail first to Rhodes to find out where he was. Then if he was in Adalia or that region, they could come to him, or if he was in his own kingdom, they could come to Famagusta. The Genoese had also offered, according to information brought by Pierre de Thomas and Guido da Bagnolo, to urge the Pope to appoint Pierre I to the office of captain of the crusade, which was vacant since the death of King John II of France. King Pierre had also sent his own representatives to Avignon especially for this purpose.[109]

Every obstacle to the crusade of Pierre I was now removed. Pope Urban V learned of the peace between Genoa and Cyprus through letters sent to him by Pierre de Thomas, who also informed him that a great multitude of nobles and other armed men were continually coming from Germany and other regions to Venice to sail against the enemies of the Christian faith. The Pope wrote to Pierre I on April 26, 1365, and urged him to begin the expedition with all reasonable dispatch, lest some of the crusaders become discouraged and withdraw from the venture. He reminded the king that in such affairs loss results from delay, a lesson which King Pierre should already have learned from experience.[110]

---

treaty from Pierre de Thomas before Guido's arrival. Smet in his edition of Mézières, *Life,* p. 224, mentions this letter, giving May 4 rather than May 13 as the date on which the king was first informed of the treaty.

[109] Known from Pierre I's letter of May 16, cited in the previous note.

[110] *Reg. Vat.* 247, fols. 87r–87v; LMLU, no. 1724, p. 297; Wadding, *Vita,* pp. 186–87; *Bull. carm.,* I, 126; Raynaldus, *Annales ecclesiastici, ad ann.* 1365, chap. 18. Raynaldus dates this letter incorrectly April 30.

# 11

# The Expedition Against Alexandria

IN THE SPRING OF 1365, THE HEARTS OF PIERRE DE THOMAS, Philippe de Mézières, and King Pierre I of Cyprus were filled with joy. After many delays, the crusade for which they had so long planned and labored was about to become a reality. Crusaders from many nations had come to Venice to join the expedition. Most numerous were the Frenchmen, led by a goodly number of noble leaders.[1] The Englishmen were well represented. Among them were Richard, Lord Grey, who was one of the first to enter Alexandria with the banner of the cross, and Miles Stapleton, who was especially attached to the person of the legate. Pierre de Thomas considered them the

---

[1] Neculai Jorga, *Philippe de Mézières et la croisade au XIV<sup>e</sup> siècle* (Paris, 1896), pp. 278–79; *Chronique des quatre premiers Valois (1327–1393),* ed. Siméon Luce (Paris, 1862), p. 164; Guillaume de Machaut, *La Prise d'Alexandrie ou chronique du roi Pierre de Lusignan,* ed. Louis de Mas Latrie (Geneva, 1877), p. 74.

most courageous of the crusaders.[2] Some Germans had also joined the expedition. They were the most pious and best disciplined. They may have been members of the Teutonic Order. A few Italians took part in the crusade. We know the names of Pietro and Giacomo de'Rossi.[3] There were even two Byzantine nobles, John Lascaris Calopherus and Demetrius Angelus, who had both been converted to Catholicism by Pierre de Thomas.[4]

When the crusaders were ready to sail, Pierre de Thomas gave them all the sign of the cross and absolved them. King Pierre I took a vow before all the company that he would not again enter his kingdom until he had gone with the armies of the faithful into the lands of the enemies of the faith, even if it should mean his death. He sent many ships ahead to Rhodes laden with fighting men and about four hundred horses. Finally, on the morning of June 27, 1365, he and his company, including Pierre de Thomas and Philippe de Mézières, sailed from Venice to Rhodes in two galleys.[5] The wind was favorable, and they arrived at their destination quickly. They

[2] Carmesson, in *Vita, Spec. carm.*, II, 184–85; Mézières, *Life*, ed. Smet, p. 126; AASS, Jan. 29, III, 628 (sec. 88); Jorga, *Mézières*, p. 279. The judgment of Pierre de Thomas about the courage of the Englishmen is in his letter to the Pope and emperor after the crusade in Mézières, *Life*, ed. Smet, p. 138; AASS, Jan. 29, III, 632 (sec. 103).

[3] Jorga, *Mézières*, pp. 279–80.

[4] Leontios Makhairas, *Recital concerning the Sweet Land of Cyprus entitled "Chronicle,"* ed. and trans. R. M. Dawkins, 2 vols. (Oxford, 1932), I, 151; II, 115.

[5] Mézières, *Life*, ed. Smet, pp. 124–5; AASS, Jan. 29, III, 628 (secs. 86–87). The date of their sailing is known from a letter of the Venetian Collegio to the captain of the Gulf, June 27, 1365, *Liber secretorum collegii*, fol. 159v, in Louis de Mas Latrie, *Histoire de l'île de Chypre sous le règne des princes de la maison de Lusignan*, 3 vols. (Paris, 1852–61), III, 752. As noted *ibid.*, II, 272, and in LC, III, 41, Mézières was admitted to Venetian citizenship on June 22. Machaut, *Prise d'Alexandrie*, p. 53, reports that the king's oath was taken at Rhodes rather than at Venice, as Mézières says.

were welcomed magnificently by the new grand master of the Hospitallers, Raymond Bérenger, who had been elected after the death of Roger de Pins (May 28).[6] All the ships for his army of about six hundred men and the mariners and horses were at the king's own expense, except for one galley lent by the Venetians.[7]

At Rhodes, the king was met by other contingents. The largest came from his own kingdom. Before he had left Venice, he had sent word to his brother, Jean de Lusignan, regent of Cyprus, to prepare an army to join the crusade at Rhodes. His orders were received with enthusiasm. On June 25, Prince Jean appointed Jacques de Nores as vice-regent of Cyprus, so that he himself would be free to go on the crusade. After a few months of preparation, a fleet of about sixty ships[8] left Cyprus bearing a large company of armed knights, archers, and artillerymen. Many Cypriote nobles were in the fleet, as well as the archbishop of Nicosia, the bishop of Limassol, and the commander of the Hospitallers in Cyprus. They arrived in Rhodes on August 25, and the king received them with great joy, which was shared by Pierre de Thomas. The legate blessed the army and glorified God, so that all who heard him were aroused to the destruction of the enemies of the faith. The

[6] Delaville le Roulx, *Les Hospitaliers à Rhodes jusqu'à la mort de Philibert de Naillac* (Paris, 1913), pp. 146–52.

[7] Mézières, *Life*, ed. Smet, p. 125; AASS, Jan. 29, III, 628 (sec. 87). Jorga, *Mézières*, p. 278, says that thirty ships were in this fleet. Machaut, *Prise d'Alexandrie*, p. 49, says that Pierre I stopped at Candia, while on p. 52 he says that no stops were made. Mézières mentions none. Machaut, *op. cit.*, pp. 50–51, says that the king became very seasick at this time.

[8] This is the figure given by Mézières, *loc. cit.* A total of 108 ships is given in Makhairas, *Chronicle*, I, 147. The number is given as ninety-two by Francesco Amadi in *Chroniques d'Amadi et de Strambaldi,* ed. René de Mas Latrie, I, (Paris, 1891), 414, and by Florio Bustron, *Chronique de l'île de Chypre,* ed. René de Mas Latrie (Paris, 1886), p. 262.

regent of Cyprus was unable to join the army at Rhodes until later because at the last minute he became ill.[9]

The crusading fleet was also augmented by ships from the knights of Rhodes and from the Genoese. The Hospitallers provided four ships and one hundred men for the expedition.[10] The Genoese sent three galleys. Before the king left Venice, he had sent a galley with Henri Giblet to Genoa to announce that he had accepted the peace treaty. Upon receiving this news, the Genoese sent Giacomo Salvago to Cyprus as their podestà. With him, they sent three galleys which they had promised for the crusade. Giblet accompanied these galleys on their voyage to the East. They met the king at Rhodes. He sent them to Cyprus to announce the peace treaty there. Then the Genoese galleys returned to Rhodes to join the crusading fleet.[11]

During the time when the crusaders were idle at Rhodes, quarrels naturally broke out among the men. On one occasion, many Cypriotes and Rhodians on the ships were killed in a fight among drunken sailors. The king and the grand master acted quickly to prevent any further trouble. They decreed the death penalty for brawling, and the quarreling was thus brought to an end.[12]

[9] Mézières, *Life,* ed. Smet, p. 125; AASS, Jan. 29, III, 628 (sec. 87); Makhairas, *Chronicle,* I, 147–49; Jorga, *Mézières,* pp. 281–82; Sir George Francis Hill, *A History of Cyprus,* 4 vols. (Cambridge, 1940–52), II, 329; Aziz Suryal Atiya, *The Crusade in the Later Middle Ages* (London, 1938), p. 342.

[10] Makhairas, *Chronicle,* I, 149; Mézières, *Life,* ed. Smet, pp. 125, 127; AASS, Jan. 29, III, 628–29 (secs. 87, 91). Makhairas calls the ships of the Hospitallers galleys, while Mézières calls them *huisserii,* horse transport ships. On this type of ship see Charles de la Roncière, *Histoire de la marine française,* I (Paris, 1899), 251.

[11] Makhairas, *Chronicle,* I, 149. Makhairas makes little mention of these Genoese galleys in his account of the crusade, probably because of an anti-Genoese bias. On this point, see Dawkins' note, *ibid.,* II, 4–5. It should also be noted that Genoa's participation in the crusade was half-hearted at best, and her ships probably did not distinguish themselves.

[12] Makhairas, *Chronicle,* I, 149.

When the Turkish rulers of Asia Minor learned of the preparations on Rhodes for the crusade, they became fearful. The emirs of Ephesus and Miletus sent ambassadors to the king of Cyprus and offered to serve him and pay him tribute if he would refrain from attacking their territories. They also appealed to the grand master to intercede with the king on their behalf. Pierre I agreed to make treaties of peace with them, since his crusade was directed not against them but against the sultan of Egypt.[13]

While the crusaders were waiting at Rhodes, Pierre de Thomas was busy ministering to their spiritual needs. He preached to them, conferred crusaders' crosses upon men of all nationalities, including members of the Orthodox faith, heard confessions, absolved sinners, and visited the sick. He worked among all classes, from the king's council to the seamen and the poor. He was so greatly respected by the men that anyone who had kissed his hand or had received his benediction considered himself safe from all dangers that day. He led devout processions and celebrated solemn masses for the success of the crusade. In his preaching, he was so effective that he moved his hearers to tears, elevated their thoughts, and prepared them to undergo death if necessary for the cause of Christ. He ministered so diligently that he scarcely took time to eat or sleep.[14]

While the crusading host was at Rhodes, Pierre I received a welcome letter from Pope Urban V. In it, the Pontiff expressed his joy that the king had been able to sail from Venice with a large company of warriors for the service of Christ. He gave

---

[13] Makhairas, *Chronicle,* I, 149; Mézières, *Life,* ed. Smet, p. 127; AASS, Jan. 29, III, 629 (sec. 90). Hill, *History of Cyprus,* II, 329–30, errs in saying that the emirs appealed to Roger de Pins, who died on May 28.

[14] Mézières, *Life,* ed. Smet, p. 126; AASS, Jan. 29, III, 628–29 (sec. 88).

his blessing upon the expedition and urged the crusaders to wage the war of God with all their might.[15]

As the time for sailing approached, Pierre I informed his council that he intended to attack the sultan of Egypt at Alexandria. Apparently he had decided upon this plan sometime before this but had hitherto kept it a secret. Even now, it was revealed only to the inner circle of trusted leaders.[16] Rumors about it were rife, and neither the king nor the legate discouraged them. The common viewpoint was that Syria was their destination. The king encouraged this idea by sending a ship to Cyprus to forbid further trade between Cyprus and Syria and by urging all Cypriotes in Syria to leave that country. According to Makhairas, Pierre de Thomas talked of an expedition to Syria. It should be noted, however, that Syria was the ultimate goal of the crusaders, who expected to invade that land after the subjugation of Egypt. Thus they would free Jerusalem from Moslem control.[17]

Pierre I kept his plans secret chiefly because he feared the treachery of the Italian maritime republics. They had great commercial interests in Egypt and could be easily tempted to betray the crusaders by informing the sultan of their plans in return for mercantile concessions. His apprehensions were not wholly unfounded. Although she had given much assistance to the crusaders, the republic of Venice was half-hearted in her devotion to the cause and more than a little concerned lest her

[15] Letter of July 19, 1365, *Reg. Vat.* 247, fol. 131v; *Reg. Vat.* 244E, fol. 70r, no. 156; LMLU, no. 1887, p. 329.

[16] Mézières, *Life,* ed. Smet, pp. 127–28; AASS, Jan. 29, III, 629 (secs. 91, 93). Machaut, *Prise d'Alexandrie,* pp. 60–64, tells how the king made the decision to go to Alexandria at Rhodes on the advice of his chamberlain, Percival of Cologne, who had once been to Alexandria and believed that it could be taken with little difficulty. It is probable, however, that the king had decided upon the destination much earlier, although he had not announced it until this time.

[17] Makhairas, *Chronicle,* I, 151; Hill, *History of Cyprus,* II, 329, 331; Atiya, *Later Crusade,* p. 347.

commerce suffer through it. The Venetians had exacted a promise from the king of Cyprus that if he went to Alexandria he would not go before the end of October, 1365.[18] At the time of Pierre's departure, the Venetian Collegio instructed the captain of the Gulf to follow him with three galleys and to keep them informed of his destination and plans. This body ordered the Venetian officials in Crete to send a ship to follow these galleys and directed those in Modon and Coron to send a second ship on a like mission. When the king's destination was known, the ship from Crete was to go to Venice at once to inform the home government, while the ship from Modon and Coron was to remain with the crusading fleet to see how the king's business would prosper, and afterward go to Venice to give a full report.[19] On July 3, the Venetians wrote to their *provveditori* in Crete and advised them that in the event of an attack by Pierre I against any place or places in Turkey with which the Venetians had treaties for the welfare of their island of Crete, they should send ambassadors to the rulers of those places immediately to excuse the Venetians as best they could and to assure them that the attack was being made without their knowledge. This report should also be spread among the Turks in the Venetian service in Crete.[20]

Meanwhile, Venetian trade with the Egyptians continued as usual while Pierre I was organizing his crusade. On August

[18] This promise, which was not kept, was mentioned in the deliberations of the Senate on September 29, 1370, recorded in Senato, *Misti,* XXXIII, fol. 77, published in Louis de Mas Latrie, "Nouvelles preuves de l'histoire de Chypre," *Bibliothèque de l'École des chartes,* XXIV (1873), p. 79, n. 1. In 1370, the Venetians decided to demand an indemnity because the Venetian consul and other Venetians had been maltreated and despoiled while the crusaders held Alexandria in October, 1365.

[19] *Liber secretorum collegii,* fols. 154r, 155r, 159v, in Mas Latrie, *Histoire de Chypre,* III, 751–52.

[20] *Liber secretorum collegii,* fol. 159v, in Mas Latrie, *Histoire de Chypre,* III, 752–53.

25, 1365, Pope Urban V gave the Venetians license to send six
galleys to trade with Alexandria and other places in the sultan's
dominions, and on September 23, he granted a similar license
for eight ships.[21] On September 4, the Venetian government
gave instructions to their galleys, which were to sail the next
day under terms of the license granted in August. Because of
the uncertainty of the plans of the king of Cyprus, they were
instructed to confer with the Venetian authorities in Crete or
with their consuls and merchants in Alexandria in case any
evident danger should develop. In any quarrels between the
Venetians and residents of Alexandria, the merchants were
authorized to deal with the local kadi or judge. If they gained
any information about the movements of the king of Cyprus
and could find a *galedolum* or other ship to send to Venice
with the news, they were instructed to do so.[22]

Several reasons have been suggested for Pierre I's choice of
Alexandria as the primary objective of his crusade. Most significant was its economic importance to the Mameluke state. Alexandria was the chief port of the sultan's dominions. Its capture
could cut off the trade which furnished most of the revenue
of his government. When the sultan was thus weakened, an
army could advance to Cairo and destroy the Moslem power
which was holding the Holy Land in subjection. Thus Jerusalem could be liberated.[23] This strategy had been suggested
earlier in the fourteenth century by King Henri II of Cyprus[24]

[21] LC, III, 42–43.
[22] Senato, *Misti,* XXXI, fols. 111v–112v (September 4, 1365);
Jorga, *Mézières,* p. 278.
[23] Mézières, *Life,* ed. Smet, p. 127; AASS, Jan. 29, III, 629 (sec. 91)
says that Pierre I planned to attack the sultan of Babylon, who was
occupying the holy city of Jerusalem and his heritage, not at the
tail but at the head.
[24] Atiya, *Later Crusade,* pp. 58–60; Delaville le Roulx, *La France
en Orient au XIV^e siècle; expéditions du Maréchal Boucicaut,* I (Paris,
1886), 61–62.

and by the Venetian writer Marino Sanudo.[25] The leaders of the crusade also apparently recognized that, although the walls of Alexandria were very strong, the harbor was ill defended, and it was therefore not impossible to take the city. Then too it is possible that King Pierre was anxious to annex so desirable a commercial center to his territories. Although his crusaders were attracted by the rich booty of the city, this does not appear to have been a factor in the king's thinking, especially in view of his later actions. The persecution of Christians in the sultan's domains, cited by some as a cause for the crusade,[26] probably had little influence on the king's plans except as it represented one of the evils of Moslem rule, which he was seeking to destroy in this expedition.[27]

At the end of September, 1365, the fleet was ready at last to sail from Rhodes. According to Mézières, it contained about a hundred ships of all types. All of these the king had hired at his own expense, except for four horse transport ships and a few other ships of the Hospitallers. In this fleet were about ten thousand warriors, one thousand of whom were nobles. They had about 1,400 horses.[28]

A few days before the crusaders left Rhodes, the king and

[25] Atiya, Later Crusade, pp. 114–27; Delaville le Roulx, France en Orient, I, 32–39.

[26] Makhairas, Chronicle, I, 143–45; Arab chronicler al-Nuwairī, cited by Atiya, Later Crusade, pp. 349–50.

[27] Ibid., pp. 349–51; Hill, History of Cyprus, II, 330.

[28] Mézières, Life, ed. Smet, p. 127; AASS, Jan. 29, III, 629 (sec. 91). Makhairas, Chronicle, I, 151, states that there were 165 ships in the fleet, but Mézières' account is more contemporary, and Makhairas probably exaggerates. Makhairas is followed by Chroniques d'Amadi et de Strambaldi, I, 414; II, 67, and by Bustron, Chronique, p. 262. On the number of warriors Machaut, Prise d'Alexandrie, p. 74, gives a slightly smaller number, eight thousand. Mézières does not mention either Venetian or Genoese ships in the crusading fleet, although in the Life, ed. Smet, p. 125; AASS, Jan. 29, III, 628 (sec. 87), he had spoken of a Venetian ship which accompanied Pierre I to Rhodes, and Makhairas, Chronicle, I, 149, mentions three Genoese galleys that came to Rhodes for the crusade.

all the nobles and barons devoutly received the eucharist from Pierre de Thomas. In all the fleet, there was not a Catholic who had not made his confession and taken communion, although some of them had not confessed for ten or twenty years. Mézières reports that most of them had come on this expedition not because of devotion to the crusade but because of avarice, vanity, and the urging of the king. The ministrations of Pierre de Thomas are said to have been so effective that even Moslems who were servants of Christians on the expedition were converted and did penance.[29]

Just before the fleet sailed from Rhodes, Pierre de Thomas boarded the king's galley to pronounce a general benediction upon the crusaders. He went to the highest place on the royal galley, from which he could be seen by all the host. The king stood beside him. All the standards on the galleys were lowered. The legate began a long and very beautiful prayer, in which he made many allusions to the Old and New Testaments. He blessed the ships, the weapons, the individual crusaders, the sea, and the army as a whole, thanking God for the coming destruction of the enemies of the faith. With bowed heads, the king and all the army responded to the benedictions of the legate, and a deep spirit of devotion reigned among them. At the conclusion of the benediction, the royal standard, a red lion on a golden field,[30] was lifted high. All the trumpets in the army sounded, and the soldiers raised their standards and shouted, "Long live Pierre of Jerusalem and Cyprus, our king, against the Saracen infidels!" Pierre de Thomas then took leave of the king after pronouncing a special blessing upon

---

[29] Mézières, *Life,* ed. Smet, p. 126; AASS, Jan. 29, III, 629 (sec. 89).
[30] Hill, *History of Cyprus,* II, 71. Mézières, *Life,* ed. Smet, p. 128; AASS, Jan. 29, III, 629 (sec. 92) mentions a large red lion in the standard.

him and with Philippe de Mézières went to his own galley.[31]

The fleet sailed from Rhodes on Saturday, October 4, 1365.[32] Most of the crusaders still did not know their destination. The king led the fleet toward the coast of Asia Minor. The crusaders landed on the island of Crambusa near Cape Chelidonea at the western edge of the Gulf of Adalia, where they took on a good quantity of fresh water. After an overnight stay, they left the island on the following morning after the king had heard mass, probably celebrated by Pierre de Thomas.[33]

Only when they were on the high seas after leaving Crambusa, did Pierre I at last inform the army of its destination. The king ordered the galleys to draw together in the midst of the sea. A trumpet was sounded, and the king publicly announced that they were sailing against Alexandria. At first

[31] Mézières, loc. cit. Makhairas, Chronicle, I, 149, also notes that Pierre de Thomas had a galley of his own. Jorga, Mézières, p. 285, gives an account of the benediction.

[32] This is the date accepted by Jorga, Mézières, p. 284, Hill, History of Cyprus, II, 331, and Atiya, Later Crusade, p. 347. Machaut, Prise d'Alexandrie, p. 64, says that the crusaders sailed from Rhodes on Monday, September 28, 1365. This statement is questionable not only because September 28 fell on a Sunday in 1365 but also because, according to it, the fleet took five days to sail the relatively short distance from Rhodes to Crambusa. It is virtually certain that the fleet sailed from Crambusa on Sunday, October 5. Machaut says that they sailed from there on a Sunday morning after mass, and according to Mézières, Life, ed. Smet, p. 129; AASS, Jan. 29, III, 629 (sec. 92), the arrival of the crusaders at Alexandria, known to have occurred on Thursday, October 9, took place "in quarto die a recessu terrae," that is, on the fourth day from Crambusa (not from Rhodes, as some have supposed). Since Mézières intimates that the fleet sailed directly from Rhodes to Turchia, it is logical to date their sailing from Rhodes about a day before they left Crambusa. Machaut speaks of their sailing de place en place, but this is not probable. Both Machaut and Mézières intimate that the stay at Crambusa was brief.

[33] Mézières, Life, ed. Smet, pp. 128–29; AASS, Jan. 29, III, 629 (sec. 93); Makhairas, Chronicle, I, 151; Machaut, Prise d'Alexandrie, p. 64. Modern accounts are Jorga, Mézières, pp. 285–86; Atiya, Later Crusade, p. 347; Hill, History of Cyprus, II, 331.

there was a murmur among the soldiers. They protested that Alexandria was too great a city for them to overcome. It was rumored that it was absolutely invincible, that its emir could put 500,000 men into the field in an hour. The king reminded them that God was with them on this crusade and with His help one man could chase a thousand; and two men, ten thousand.[34] The men took courage and vowed to follow Pierre I. They shouted, "On to Alexandria!" as though it were but a small castle or a town already captured.[35] The fleet sailed directly across the Mediterranean, aided by a favorable wind. They became separated on the high seas, but all ships arrived at the Old Harbor of Alexandria early on the morning of Thursday, October 9, 1365, after four days at sea.[36]

The general state of Alexandria and Egypt favored the designs of the crusaders. The governor of Alexandria was absent on a pilgrimage to Mecca. Lulled to complacency by a long period of peace, the sultan's government had allowed the garrison to become depleted. The crusaders arrived at the season of the Nile inundation, when it was impossible to send prompt reinforcements from Cairo. The government of Egypt was in a sorry state. The sultan was a mere boy, placed on the throne by Yalbogha, the most powerful of the Mameluke emirs, a selfish and unscrupulous man, widely detested for his exactions

[34] Deuteronomy 32:30.

[35] Mézières, *Life,* ed. Smet, p. 129; AASS, Jan. 29, III, 629 (sec. 93); Machaut, *Prise d'Alexandrie,* pp. 64–67. Atiya, *loc. cit.,* and Hill, *loc. cit.,* state erroneously that the destination was announced at Crambusa.

[36] Makhairas, *Chronicle,* I, 151; Machaut, *Prise d'Alexandrie,* p. 67, and Mézières, *Life,* ed. Smet, pp. 129–30, 132, all agree on this date, as do the best Arabic sources, discussed by Atiya, *Later Crusade,* p. 348, n. 2. The edition of Mézières, *Life,* in AASS, Jan. 29, III, 629–30 (secs. 93, 97), through a copyist's error gives the arrival date as October 3. The early morning hour is given by Mézières. Machaut has "l'heure de nonne." The voyage to Alexandria is also discussed in the letter of Pierre de Thomas in Mézières, *Life,* ed. Smet, p. 135; AASS, Jan. 29, III, 631 (secs. 100–01).

and cruelties. It is not known to what degree the leaders of the crusade were aware of these conditions, but they were probably at least partially informed by the Latin merchants who traded in Egypt. On the other hand, the ease with which Alexandria could be taken should not be exaggerated. Its fortifications were famous throughout the West. Its walls were thick, its towers high and solid, its many entrances furnished with gates of strong timber reinforced with steel.[37]

Pierre I was fully aware of the difficulties he faced and therefore proceeded with great caution and patience. He could have landed on the day of his arrival at Alexandria, but instead, after taking counsel, he decided to rest on Thursday and to attack the city on the folowing day.[38] He sent out a reconnaissance boat, which returned at full speed under volleys of Saracen arrows. The galleys were brought together in one solid block in the middle of the harbor.[39]

When news of the arrival of the crusaders' fleet spread through Alexandria, large numbers of people began to pour out of the city and to congregate along the shore. From Arabic sources, it appears that they were largely curiosity seekers, but to the crusaders they appeared as a multitude of defenders, preparing to ward off the invasion. After nightfall, a series of lanterns was lighted on the walls to make it impossible for the attackers to infiltrate the city in the darkness. Nevertheless, Christian spies in native garb were able to land that night to examine the state of the defenses.[40]

Pierre de Thomas was unhappy about the king's decision to rest for a day before attacking Alexandria. He was eager to

[37] Atiya, *Later Crusdae*, pp. 351–52; Jorga, *Mézières*, pp. 286–91.
[38] Mézières, *Life*, ed. Smet, p. 130; AASS, Jan. 29, III, 629 (sec. 94).
[39] Arab chronicler al Nuwairī, cited by Atiya, *Later Crusade*, p. 353.
[40] Atiya, *Later Crusade*, p. 353; Mézières, *Life*, ed. Smet, pp. 130–31; AASS, Jan. 29, III, 629–30 (secs. 93–94); Machaut, *Prise d'Alexandrie*, p. 67. Throughout this account I am indebted to Atiya for presentation of the Arabic viewpoint of this crusade.

get into the fight against the enemies of the faith, for which he had so long prepared. He also had a great desire for martyrdom. It appears that he was not present in the council of war, which had been held about noon on Thursday, as the Saracens were gathering on the shore. He therefore did not know the reason for the delay. When he saw the Saracens gathering on the shore and shouting, the legate came to Philippe de Mézières weeping because of his great desire to strike against the infidel hordes and cried out to him, "O my brother, most excellent chancellor, in memory of the passion of our Lord let us go with our galley; let us go to the shore! I cannot stand so great a reproach to the cross." Mézières understood and admired Pierre's spirit, but he was also a practical soldier. Laughingly he responded, "My father, the hour of your death is not yet come. This is not the time to disembark. I respectfully decline to do this." The legate was greatly disappointed. Even had he been inclined to do so, Mézières could not have granted Pierre's request, for he had been placed in command of the forces in the legate's galley and was subject to the orders of the king.[41]

On Friday morning, the Christian forces prepared for the attack. It was a beautiful day, and the shields, the arms, and the galleys of the crusaders glittered in the morning sunlight. The king and his council of war decided to go ashore at about nine o'clock in the morning to begin their holy war.[42] As the host prepared to go to battle, Pierre de Thomas stood on the most prominent place in his galley, armed nobly and holding aloft in his hands his jeweled cross, which was believed to contain a relic of the true cross. He blessed the army on his right and on his left, calling to all in a loud voice, "O chosen soldiers of God, let us be greatly strengthened in the Lord and

[41] Mézières, *Life,* ed. Smet, p. 130; AASS, Jan. 29, III, 629-30 (secs. 93-94); Jorga, *Mézières,* p. 291.

[42] Mézières, *Life,* ed. Smet, p. 131; AASS, Jan. 29, III, 630 (sec. 95): "hora tertiarum."

in His holy cross. Fearing not the enemy and hoping for victory from God, wage manfully the war of God, because today the gates of paradise are open." Thus he prepared the hearts of his listeners for the struggles that lay ahead.[43]

At the appointed hour the king's trumpet sounded, and the ships moved toward the land. The Saracens were ill-prepared for this attack. They were confident that so great a city could not be seriously threatened by so small a force. Since daybreak, a large number of people had left the protection of the massive walls of Alexandria and collected upon the shore. Some were sightseers, and some were merchants who took the opportunity to sell their wares. The defense forces were small and poorly armed. The acting governor, Janghara, a man of weak and indecisive character, unwisely agreed to make a stand outside the walls at the instigation of those who had property there. As the ships of the crusaders approached the shore, they were showered with arrows, and a small band of volunteers tried to prevent their landing by wading into the water. They soon found themselves in deep water, where they were easily overcome by the invaders, who then leaped ashore. As they began to land in large numbers, the Saracens, including most of the defense forces, fled into the city in wild confusion. A Bedouin corps alone offered resistance, which was unsuccessful. At length, the gates were shut, and those who did not reach them in time were left to be slaughtered by the crusaders.[44]

[43] Mézières, *loc. cit.;* Atiya, *Later Crusade,* p. 355. Mézières mentions that Pierre de Thomas on this occasion had a cross "cum ligno Domini." This is undoubtedly the alleged piece of the true cross in crystal trimmed with silver and gold which Pierre left to Mézières, as noted in Neculai Jorga, "Le Testament de Philippe de Mézières," *Bulletin de l'Institut pour l'Étude de l'Europe sud-orientale,* VIII (1921), 120, 132; Jorga, *Mézières,* pp. 402–03.

[44] Atiya, *Later Crusade,* pp. 353–56; Machaut, *Prise d'Alexandrie,* pp. 68–77; Mézières, *Life,* ed. Smet, pp. 131–32; AASS, Jan. 29, III, 630 (secs. 95–96); Makhairas, *Chronicle,* I, 151.

Pierre de Thomas was in the thick of the battle, blessing and encouraging the crusaders. When the arrows began to fall around him, he did not turn his back or show any sign of fear, either on the sea or after they had landed. He was so anxious to reach the shore that he refused to protect himself with a shield, even though innumerable arrows were falling around him, and Mézières repeatedly warned him to be more careful.[45] He seems, nevertheless, to have escaped unscathed, though a legend grew up after his death that he was wounded at Alexandria and died of those wounds.[46]

After the enemy had retreated into the city, King Pierre halted all offensive operations temporarily so that his men could rest and the horses be disembarked from the ships. In this period, the leaders held another council of war. A group of discontented barons tried to dissuade the king from attempting to capture Alexandria, which they said was too strong. Pierre I overcame their opposition by appealing to their sense of

[45] Mézières, *Life,* ed. Smet, p. 131; AASS, Jan. 29, III, 630 (sec. 95).

[46] The best manuscripts of Mézières, *Life,* published in Smet's edition, at no place say that Pierre de Thomas was wounded at Alexandria. The first writer to say that he was wounded in the crusade was his contemporary, Johann of Hildesheim, in his *Defensorium Ordinis Fratrum gloriosissimae Dei Genetricis Mariae de Monte Carmelo,* published in *Spec. carm.,* I, 149. A slightly different version of this passage is found in Oxford, Bodleian Library, ms. Selden 41 supra, fol. 95v, quoted in Mézières, *Life,* ed. Smet, p. 159, n. 18. At a later date, a gloss was added to Mézières, *Life,* stating that Pierre de Thomas was wounded by the darts of the enemy at Alexandria and died of those wounds. This gloss is printed in the critical apparatus of Smet's edition, p. 159, and is included in the text in AASS, Jan. 29, III, 637 (sec. 133). Wadding, *Vita,* pp. 66–67, noted that many writers considered Pierre de Thomas a martyr on the basis of this story, but Wadding himself did not accept it, for he had seen a French manuscript of Mézières' biography in which this story was added in a marginal note. The length to which a legend can grow appears in the Gallican martyrology of André de Saussay mentioned by A. Dujarric-Descombes, "Recherches sur les historiens du Périgord au XVIIe siècle," *Bulletin de la Société historique et archéologique de Périgord,* IX (1882), 484, in which it is said that Pierre was captured by infidels and ended his days in the midst of tortures.

loyalty. He announced that he planned to take the city by storm. Meanwhile, the acting governor organized the defense of the city, sent all gold and silver from the state treasury to Cairo for safekeeping, and arrested about fifty European consuls and merchants. After a while, the crusaders stormed the city and were able to enter it at a weak spot by the Customs Gate. The banners of the cross were planted on the walls and towers of Alexandria.[47] The city was captured in the middle of the afternoon on Friday, October 10, 1365.[48]

The entrance of the crusaders into Alexandria did not solve all their problems. Armed bands of Saracens still controlled the countryside, and in time the sultan's army was certain to arrive from Cairo. Unfortunately, in the early stages of the conquest, some of the crusaders had unwisely burned the land gates, which were essential to their own defense. The crusaders, led by Pierre I himself, sought to repair this damage by destroying the bridge which alone gave access to the ruined gates from Cairo, but they were driven back into the city by the Saracens. On the night after the conquest, a large body of Saracens forced their way inside the walls through one of the land gates, and it was only with difficulty that the crusaders drove them all from the city by the next morning.[49]

[47] Atiya, *Later Crusade,* pp. 356–62; Machaut, *Prise d'Alexandrie,* pp. 77–91. Mézières, *Life,* ed. Smet, pp. 132–33; AASS, Jan. 29, III, 630 (secs. 96–97), gives a vague account of the attack.

[48] Mézières, *Life,* ed. Smet, p. 132; AASS, Jan. 29, III, 630 (sec. 97) says that the city was captured at the ninth hour, about three o'clock in the afternoon. Smet's edition gives the date correctly as October 10, whereas the AASS edition, based on a poorer manuscript, gives it as October 4. The date of the capture is also given as October 10 by Machaut, *Prise d'Alexandrie,* pp. 95–96, by Carmesson, *Vita,* in *Spec. carm.,* II, 184, and by the best Arabic sources as noted in Atiya, *Later Crusade,* p. 348, n. 2. Strambaldi in *Chroniques d'Amadi et de Strambaldi,* II, 68, gives the incorrect date October 5, while the second life of Urban V in Baluze-Mollat, *Vitae paparum Avenionensium,* I, 386, gives it as October 11.

[49] Atiya, Later Crusade, pp. 362–64; Machaut, *Prise d'Alexandrie,* pp. 91–100.

After these Saracens were driven from the city, King Pierre I called a council of war on the peninsula between the city and the sea. Pierre de Thomas and Philippe de Mézières were present. The king announced that the enemy was put to flight and urged the leaders of his forces to defend the city against all comers.[50] Most of the barons were not of this opinion. The opposition was led by Guillaume Roger, viscount of Turenne, who said that the Christian garrison could not hold and defend Alexandria against "five hundred times five hundred" Saracens, who would seize them as in a trap.[51] The English contingents supported him in this contention, as they had apparently agreed to do beforehand.[52] At first, some of the French crusaders, very many of the Germans, and all the Italians cursed them for their suggestion,[53] but in the end they offered no effective resistance to the withdrawal. Many of the crusaders supported the viscount of Turenne and the English, including the admiral of Rhodes, some of the French, and even some of Pierre I's own Cypriote contingents. The king's two brothers and Jean de Sur, admiral of Cyprus, belonged to this group.[54] In vain, the king appealed to the leaders not to desert the cause. He reminded them that they had been able to capture the city, which was surely more difficult than to defend it. The walls of Alexandria were strong enough to withstand a large army. They had provisions for ten months, and by that time he expected aid to come from Rhodes, Constantinople, and the West,

[50] Machaut, *Prise d'Alexandrie,* pp. 100–01.

[51] *Ibid.,* pp. 101–02; letter of Pierre de Thomas after the crusade in Mézières, *Life,* ed. Smet, p. 138; AASS, Jan. 29, III, 632 (sec. 103); Jorga, *Mézières,* p. 298. Because of his relationship to Pope Clement VI and to the cardinal of Beaufort, later Pope Gregory XI, Pierre de Thomas suppressed the name of Guillaume Roger.

[52] Letter of Pierre de Thomas in Mézières, *loc. cit.; Chronicon Moguntinum* in *Die Chroniken der deutschen Städte vom 14 bis 16 Jahrhundert,* XVIII, part I, ed. C. Hegel (Leipzig, 1882), 170.

[53] Letter of Pierre de Thomas in Mézières, *loc. cit.*

[54] Machaut, *Prise d'Alexandrie,* pp. 102–03; Jorga, *Mézières,* pp. 301–02; Atiya, *Later Crusade,* pp. 364–65.

when men should learn that the crusaders had been able to capture the greatest city in Egypt. He declared that the crusaders would be more wicked than Herod if they gave up Alexandria, since it was the key to the liberation of the holy city, Jerusalem, so long desired by many faithful Christians everywhere.[55]

Pierre de Thomas also made a speech in which he urged the crusaders not to abandon the city. He reminded them of St. Thomas, who went to India Major for the love of our Saviour, where he died piteously simply because he sought to do what was right. He urged them to follow this example, as he reminded them, "Also you have come hither, saying that you are bound to do His easy service, from which it would be a great sin for you to leave, for it seems to me that good and evil cannot go together. Likewise, it is said that he who serves does not receive his reward unless he perseveres."[56] He lamented, wept, and cried out to heaven in an effort to persuade the soldiers not to abandon the city. He showed them how it would redound to the honor of God, the ultimate conquest of Jerusalem, and the welfare of all Christendom if they should hold the city of Alexandria. He reminded them that their leaving the city to fall again into Moslem hands would be a reproach to the Christian faith.[57] He showed them many things from the sacred page, but all his words were in vain, for they answered him shortly, "Let us go away from here. Life is short, and we do not want to die, cut off by hunger without striking a blow. To tell the truth, our power is nothing against theirs."[58]

---

[55] Machaut, *Prise d'Alexandrie,* pp. 103–06; Mézières, *Life,* ed. Smet, pp. 133–34; AASS, Jan. 29, III, 630 (sec. 98); Jorga, *Mézières,* pp. 299–301.

[56] This speech, reported by Machaut, *Prise d'Alexandrie,* pp. 106–07, may be imaginary, but it is faithful to the known style of Pierre de Thomas.

[57] Mézières, *Life,* ed. Smet, p. 134; AASS, Jan. 29, III, 630 (sec. 98).

[58] Machaut, *Prise d'Alexandrie,* p. 107. Makhairas, *Chronicle,* I, 153, says that the king took counsel with the legate and the knights and

Philippe de Mézières likewise opposed retreat. His hopes for the success of the crusading movement were never higher than just after the capture of Alexandria. The king had called him to his quarters by the Customs Gate to announce that he would give him the third part of Alexandria for the formation of the new crusading order of which he had long dreamed. This part of the city would be administered by Mézières himself, with the advice and counsel of Pierre de Thomas, who perhaps would have been named as Catholic patriarch of Alexandria.[59] Therefore in the council of war, Mézières begged the nobles not to abandon the city. He offered to guard the tower where the greatest danger was with forty companions and fifty seamen.[60] His words had no more effect than those of the king and the legate.

After the council of war, it became apparent to most members of the expedition that they could not hold the city, because so few were willing to attempt to do so. During the next several days, the majority of the crusaders devoted themselves to plundering the city, which was their chief interest in the crusade. The destruction of property, atrocities against the people, and loss of life in Alexandria were terrible. The crusaders made no distinction between Moslem and Christian, and even the property of Europeans was not spared. When the invaders left the city, it was a ruin, and the streets were covered with the corpses of murdered and mutilated men, women, and children. About five thousand were carried into captivity, including Jews and Eastern Christians.[61] The king abstained

---

they all said to him, "We are there too long; this is no advantage to us at all: rather let us go back home (to Cyprus)." Nowhere does Makhairas err more than here, where he lists Pierre de Thomas among those who desired to abandon Alexandria.

[59] Jorga, *Mézières,* pp. 299–300.

[60] *Ibid.,* p. 301; letter of Pierre de Thomas in Mézières, *Life,* ed. Smet, p. 138; AASS, Jan. 29, III, 632 (sec. 104).

[61] Atiya, *Later Crusade,* pp. 365–67; Jorga, *Mézières,* pp. 97–98.

from this pillage, as did Mézières. We can be sure that Pierre de Thomas and many other decent people likewise refrained from it.[62]

When they gathered all the plunder they could carry, most of the crusaders returned to the ships. Thus within a few days, most of the army was simply waiting to sail. King Pierre I remained in Alexandria and sought to arouse the rank and file to remain with him and hold the city. At first, some of them were willing to stay, but the majority induced them not to do so.[63] In the end, the king found few who would remain with him. Machaut says that there were but 120 of them. In discouragement, King Pierre went to the legate. "Sire," advised Pierre de Thomas, "go from galley to galley and entreat them, to see if we can in some way induce them to stay." The king followed this suggestion and went from one ship to another, but none of the men would disembark again.[64]

Meanwhile, a few days after the crusaders took the city, the advance guard of the Saracen relief army from Cairo had reached Alexandria under the command of the regular governor of the city, who had just returned from his pilgrimage to Mecca. It is reported that he was able to supplant the banners of the crusaders by those of the sultan by Monday, October 13. On Tuesday, he sent a Jew named Jacob to Pierre I to negotiate an exchange of Moslem prisoners for Europeans taken as hostages just before the Christian attack on the city proper. To reach the king, Jacob crossed forty ships loaded with the fruits of plunder and crowded with captives. He found Pierre I on one of the galleys in a tent with openings overlooking the sea. The king was dressed in a robe embroidered with gold

[62] Makhairas, *Chronicle*, I, 153; Hill, *History of Cyprus*, II, 333, n. 2.

[63] Mézières, *Life*, ed. Smet, p. 134; AASS, Jan. 29, III, 630 (sec. 98).

[64] Machaut, *Prise d'Alexandrie*, pp. 108–09.

and studded with pearls. On his head was a golden crown surmounted by a glittering jewel. One monk was on his right and another on his left. One of these was probably Pierre de Thomas.[65] The negotiations amounted to nothing, for the king demanded written messages from the prisoners to prove that they were still alive, and these could not be procured before the crusaders' fleet found it advisable to sail.[66]

In a few days, the main relief army from Cairo entered some parts of Alexandria. With most of his army already in the ships, Pierre I had no choice but to withdraw from the city with his faithful band.[67] On Thursday, October 16, 1365, one week after their arrival in the harbor, the Christian fleet left Alexandria to return to Cyprus.[68] The fleet had a difficult

[65] Philippe de Mézières could not have been the other monk, as suggested by Atiya, *Later Crusade*, p. 369, for he was a knight and not a member of a religious order. Perhaps it was the archbishop of Nicosia or the bishop of Limassol, whose companies are mentioned among the crusaders in Makhairas, *Chronicle*, I, 147.

[66] Atiya, *Later Crusade*, pp. 368–69.

[67] In his letter to the Pope and emperor after the crusade in Mézières, *Life*, ed. Smet, p. 139; AASS, Jan. 29, III, 632 (sec. 104), Pierre de Thomas declared that, although the admiral of the Hospitallers warned of the imminent approach of the sultan's army, no Saracens could be seen coming toward the city nor did they dare enter its walls, so greatly did they fear the crusaders. Apparently his enthusiasm for the cause and his desire to hold the city blinded him to the true facts of the case, which are known from Arabic writers cited by Atiya, *Later Crusade*, pp. 367–68.

[68] This date for the withdrawal is clearly given in the best Arabic sources, as noted in Atiya, *Later Crusade*, p. 367, n. 6. In his letter to the Pope and emperor in Mézières, *loc. cit.*, Pierre de Thomas wrote that the crusaders left Alexandria on the sixth day. If this is calculated from the day when the city was completely subjugated by the crusaders, October 11, it agrees with the Arabic sources. Machaut, *Prise d'Alexandrie*, p. 109, says only that the withdrawal occurred two days after the king went from galley to galley making a final plea to the crusaders not to desert the city, but he does not tell exactly on what day the king made this plea. Jorga, *Mézières*, p. 302, n. 4, and Atiya, *loc. cit.*, confuse this final plea in Machaut's account with the council of war in which the barons first decided on withdrawal, which Machaut, *op. cit.*, p. 100, seems to date October 11.

passage on the return voyage. A violent storm arose, and the ships were scattered. The men in the army feared greatly. Pierre de Thomas declared that the tempest was a judgment of God upon them for abandoning Alexandria. Every day he said to Mézières, "This adversity is the wrath of God because Alexandria is abandoned, and in time you will see even greater things. Doubt it not." Nevertheless, at length the fleet arrived safely at Limassol and Famagusta in Cyprus.[69]

When the army was safe in Cyprus, Pierre I thanked the foreign troops for their services and paid them well, and they departed for their homes.[70] The king returned to his capital, Nicosia, and Pierre de Thomas went with him. At the legate's prompting, a great victory procession was held. Pierre de Thomas preached about the victory at Alexandria, thanked God for it, and encouraged the king of Cyprus to continue the crusade which he had begun against the sultan. Pierre I responded by appointing the legate as his ambassador to the Roman Curia to report on the capture of Alexandria and to appeal to the Pope and the Western princes for further aid against the Saracens. Pierre de Thomas accepted this assignment, and taking leave of the king, went to Famagusta to prepare for the voyage to Avignon.[71] The admiral of Cyprus, Jean de Sur, was directed to convoy him to the West. The admiral proceeded to Rhodes with the understanding that Pierre de Thomas would meet him there. In March, 1366, after the legate's death, Jean de Sur himself would go to Avignon to deliver the royal letters.[72]

---

[69] Mézières, *Life*, ed. Smet, pp. 134–35, 140; AASS, Jan. 29, III, 631–32 (secs. 99, 107); Machaut, *Prise d'Alexandrie*, pp. 109–10; Makhairas, *Chronicle*, I, 155; Atiya, *Later Crusade*, p. 369.

[70] Machaut, *Prise d'Alexandrie*, pp. 110–11.

[71] Mézières, *Life*, ed. Smet, pp. 140–41; AASS, Jan. 29, III, 632 (sec. 107).

[72] Makhairas, *Chronicle*, I, 155–57; *Chroniques d'Amadi et de Strambaldi*, I, 415; II, 69; Bustron, *Chronique*, p. 263.

After the retreat from Alexandria, Pierre de Thomas in his own handwriting wrote a letter to Pope Urban V and the Holy Roman Emperor Charles IV about the crusade. It is a long letter written in a highly literary style, replete with scriptural quotations and allusions. In it, Pierre presents the viewpoint that the crusaders totally lacked the strength to capture Alexandria and that their victory was purely a miracle of God, who would have enabled them to hold the city if only they had had the faith and courage to remain there. Pierre also gives some interesting details of the crusade, to which reference has been made at appropriate places in the foregoing narrative.[73]

Much of the letter is devoted to lamentations over the failure of the Christian host to make the most of their victory at Alexandria, such as the following passage, "O wounds inflicted, a wound and a bruise and a swollen sore, a wound in the face, a bruise of infamy, a sore swollen with insanity! [74] O wound in the face! For the leaders were wounded, all agreeing in the same counsel, the knights who seemed to be the strongest, the most illustrious, and the bravest, as the face in the body, who like Peter said to Christ the King, 'If we must die with thee, yet will we not leave thee,' but struck with fear, not at the voice of a handmaiden,[75] because none was near, nor at the power of the adversary, because none could be discerned, they left Alexandria,[76] not trusting in God, without foresight, totally cleft asunder, as if God, who had introduced them into the city, were not strong enough for its custody, not waiting for Him to establish His guard upon the walls. O bruise of infamy! Will not the heathen say, 'Where is their God?' who

[73] The letter of Pierre de Thomas is included in Mézières, *Life,* ed. Smet, pp. 135–40; AASS, Jan. 29, III, 631–32 (secs. 100–06).

[74] Here Pierre alludes to Isaiah 1: 5, 6.

[75] Cf. Matthew 26: 35, 69–72.

[76] Feminine accusative pronoun *eam,* apparently referring to the city of Alexandria.

before said, as I have actually heard related, 'God is fighting for them. Our Mohammed is defeated. The God of the Christians is great and strong.' Then thou wilt be derided who appearest glorious in thy hosts, and those who have not known thee will repeat it in their testimonies and will not inquire after thy name. Our glory is turned into shame; our feast day is converted into weeping, our sabbaths into reproach, His honors to naught." [77]

In his letter, the legate called upon the Pope to exhort the people to take the cross and to encourage them by granting indulgences and by offering the treasury of the church for the crusade. To the emperor, he addressed the following plea and solemn warning: "And thou, O invincible emperor, upon whom the eyes of all Israel rest, that thou mayest begin the good work, king of kings and lord of lords; thou, to whom God has given wisdom greater than Solomon's and power greater than Pharaoh's and, as report has it, sufficient money; to whom kings will offer help, the Venetians and Genoese and other maritime powers sufficient ships, the lord Pope the assistance of indulgences, and the people, touched with devotion, will offer themselves, and the clergy their fastings and prayers, the whole world in one accord, show, O lord, thy power, and come and deliver us. Free that holy city, Jerusalem, who for so long a time has been a handmaiden. To thee she cries out, she cries out, she cries out, and her cry reaches even to the ears of the Lord of Sabaoth, which if thou wilt not hear and heed, I fear—and not I alone, but many with me— that God will pour out his anger against thee and thou wilt perish before thy time." [78]

[77] Mézières, *Life,* ed. Smet, p. 137; AASS, Jan. 29, III, 631 (sec. 102).

[78] Mézières, *Life,* ed. Smet, pp. 139–40; AASS, Jan. 29, III, 632 (secs. 105–06). There is no evidence that this letter was actually delivered to the Pope and the emperor. Pierre de Thomas himself probably planned to take it to Europe on his journey to Avignon which was prevented by his death.

In Europe, the news of the victory of the crusaders at Alexandria was received by many with rejoicing. The Pope and his court were very much pleased. Several nobles offered their aid to Pierre I to complete the good work which he had begun. Chief among them was Count Amadeo VI of Savoy, who was still preparing to go to the East to fulfill a vow made in 1363. On the other hand, the Venetians were displeased with the results of the crusade. They feared for their trade with the sultan's dominions. They at once sought to make a treaty with the sultan for the resumption of the trade which had been disrupted by the war. The sultan refused to come to terms with any Christian state while he was still at war with Cyprus. The Venetians therefore induced the king of Cyprus to open peace negotiations with the Egyptian government. Meanwhile, they reported in Europe that peace was already concluded between Cyprus and Egypt, thus discouraging any further help to Pierre I. Count Amadeo of Savoy diverted his crusade to the Byzantine Empire, to aid it against the Turks.[79]

While the Venetians were trying to make a separate peace with the sultan, Pierre de Thomas forbade all Catholics to go to Egypt under pain of excommunication.[80] Mézières reports that many ships sailed to Alexandria in spite of this decree, but most of them suffered some mishap, and some had been wrecked or captured by the Saracens. He also tells a tale about a group of crusaders who were trying to return to the West from Cyprus and were driven back before Alexandria three or four times as a punishment for their unwillingness to hold the city during the crusade, although in one case they had traveled

[79] Makhairas, *Chronicle,* I, 155–63; Atiya, *Later Crusade,* p. 371.

[80] According to *Reg. Aven.* 156, fols. 48v, 50v–51r, and *Reg. Vat.* 253, fols. 29r–29v, 30v–31r, the legate received power on July 10, 1364, to excommunicate persons who traded with Moslems and to annul all leagues made with Moslems.

a thousand miles westward before being driven back toward Alexandria.[81]

The peace negotiations between Cyprus and the sultan were lengthy and complicated. Not until the latter half of 1370, after the death of Pierre I, was peace finally made between the two governments.[82] Even then the Egyptians did not forget the damage done to Alexandria by the expedition led by the king of Cyprus. They took their revenge in 1426, when King Janus of Cyprus was carried into captivity in Cairo and regained his throne only by becoming tributary to Egypt. At that time, Cyprus lost its independence for five centuries. This was the most enduring result of the crusade of 1365. Its short-range results were no less undesirable. The Mameluke power was not weakened as much as was hoped, and the Christians acquired no land base for a reconquest of the Holy Land. The plunder taken by the Latin adventurers was gained at the expense of the Eastern Christians, whose property in the lands of the sultan was confiscated to pay for the damage at Alexandria. Trade between Europe and Alexandria was temporarily disrupted, and all types of spices were rarer and more expensive than before. Thus in spite of the spectacular capture of Alexandria, the crusade was a failure.[83]

His participation in the crusade of 1365 is the most famous event in the life of Pierre de Thomas. His actions on that occasion did him credit. He conducted himself with great bravery and showed an admirable devotion to duty. His spiritual ministrations were a source of strength to the soldiers in the attack

[81] Mézières, Life, ed. Smet, p. 141; AASS, Jan. 29, III, 632–33 (secs. 108–09).

[82] Atiya, Later Crusade, pp. 371–76; Hill, History of Cyprus, II, 335–47, 351–60, 372–76.

[83] Atiya, Later Crusade, pp. 376–78. On the rarity of spices, see Thomas Walsingham, Historia Anglicana, ed. Henry Thomas Riley, 2 vols. (Rerum Brittanicarum medii aevi scriptores, vol. 28, part 1, London, 1863), I, 302.

on Alexandria. Throughout the campaign, he was the principal supporter of Pierre I in his efforts to keep the crusaders true to their noblest ideals. Yet this was not necessarily his finest hour. His bravery at Alexandria was no greater than at the time when he traveled through the battle lines from Venice to Hungary on a peace-making mission or faced the angry mob at Bologna or publicly proclaimed the gospel of Christ in Moslem-ruled Jerusalem. While his encouragement, advice, and counsel were of inestimable value to Pierre I of Cyprus at Alexandria, he was not a warrior but a diplomat, and he accomplished his greatest work for the church and for the cause of the crusade in his efforts to make peace between Christian nations and to bring about the union of the churches.

The failure of the crusade at Alexandria was a great disappointment to Pierre de Thomas, especially because he felt it was so unnecessary. As has been noted above, he believed that the crusaders could have held the city against the sultan's armies from Cairo if they had only chosen to do so; then further conquests could have been won in Egypt, and the way could have been opened for the reconquest of the Holy Land by Christian forces. Although this belief was shared by King Pierre I and by Philippe de Mézières, both of whom were soldiers, it is difficult to believe that it was correct. The crusading force was small and operating far from its base, while the Saracens had superior numerical strength and all Egypt at hand to support them. Perhaps if the crusaders had not destroyed the land gates, they could have defended the city until reinforcements could have come from Europe. Lacking such defenses, they probably would have been overwhelmed before long, and the advice of the barons who desired to abandon the city, although distasteful to the enthusiasts in the company, was wise.

# 12
# Last Illness, Death, Funeral, and Cult

PIERRE DE THOMAS DID NOT LIVE LONG AFTER THE CRUSADE of 1365. The last few months of his life were spent in Famagusta, where he had gone to prepare for his new mission to Avignon for King Pierre I. These were sad days for him. His disappointment at the abandonment of Alexandria by the crusaders weighed heavily on his spirit. Never again did Mézières see him as happy as he had ordinarily been before the crusade. He was now about sixty years old and was ready for death, if it was the will of God. Yet it would be a mistake to believe that he had lost all hope. As he planned for his journey to the West, on which Philippe de Mézières was to accompany him, he still believed it possible to arouse enthusiasm in Avignon for a new crusade.[1] His letter to the Pope and the Holy Roman emperor, which was written in this

---

[1] Mézières, *Life,* ed. Smet, p. 142; AASS, Jan. 29, III, 633 (sec. 110).

period, still shows much hope and enthusiasm for the cause.[2]

His last illness came upon him suddenly during the Christmas season of 1365. On Christmas Eve, he went from the Carmelite church in Famagusta, where he was staying, to the cathedral of St. Nicholas to celebrate matins. Robed in the vestments of his office with the miter on his head, he celebrated matins and three solemn Christmas masses. While going to the cathedral, returning from there, and celebrating mass, he was exposed to the cold. The ground was covered with deep mud. Pierre was weakened by the many fasts and vigils which he kept, and he refused to wear any heavier clothing in the cold weather than he was accustomed to wear in the summer. He recognized that he had caught cold, but he paid no attention to it. Throughout the remainder of the Christmas season, he celebrated many masses and was so ardent in the divine worship that he did not spare himself, though he was not feeling altogether well. On Saturday, December 27, 1365, he went from the Carmelite church in his bare feet through deep mud to the church of St. Mary of Cana outside the city, and there he celebrated a solemn mass on the cold stone floor, still barefooted. When his friends reprimanded him for not taking better care of his health, he replied by citing the example of the ancient hermits in the deserts, who constantly went barefooted.[3]

On Sunday and Monday, although his illness grew worse, he continued to celebrate masses, as if trying to conceal his condition. On Tuesday, December 30, a high fever seized him, and his household began to fear for his life. At once, they sent for Philippe de Mézières, who had remained at Nicosia when Pierre went to Famagusta. Mézières came to Famagusta

[2] Mézières, *Life,* ed. Smet, pp. 135–40; AASS, Jan. 29, III, 631–32 (secs. 100–06).

[3] Mézières, *Life,* ed. Smet, pp. 142–43; AASS, Jan. 29, III, 633 (sec. 111).

as quickly as he could and arrived on the following day. With him he brought the king's physician.[4] Mézières found his friend better than he expected from the reports which he had received. He stayed with him until Saturday, January 3, 1366, and placed him under the care of the royal physician. On that Saturday, Pierre assured him that he would be all right and constrained him to return to Nicosia to expedite the preparations for their journey to the West. Mézières left him only with reluctance. Before he left, Pierre called for him and talked to him as friend to friend. With great contrition, he discussed his life and his sins, although to Mézières his greatest sins scarcely seemed to be sins at all. Mézières consoled him as best he could. Then Pierre said, "My brother, I am a great sinner, but I have a good judge, an upright and merciful God, to whom I am returning, and I do not despair of pardon." These words struck fear into Mézières' heart concerning Pierre's physical condition, but since he said he was getting better, he did not presume to ask him about the disposition of his property. Then the legate said to him, "Go now, that you may return quickly, because I intend to leave here in the coming week." Mézières interprets these words as a prophecy of his death, but it appears that Pierre actually expected to be well enough to travel the next week.[5]

[4] This was probably Guido da Bagnolo from Reggio, who was the king's physician as early as May 7, 1360, when he received a grant of citizenship at Venice, recorded in LC, II, 312. He accompanied Pierre I on his trip to the West in 1362. He served as Pierre de Thomas' fellow ambassador to Genoa in the early months of 1365 (See above, pp. 260–65). See Jorga, *Mézières,* p. 103, n. 4; p. 144, n. 1; p. 145; p. 152, n. 2; p. 261 and n. 2, 4; p. 265 and n. 3; pp. 310, 312, 314; p. 324, n. 5; p. 375, n. 6. However, the Venetian records also mention another physician to the king of Cyprus in this period, Biagio Gori of Florence, who was granted Venetian citizenship on August 6, 1365 (LC, III, 42).

[5] Mézières, *Life,* ed. Smet, pp. 143–44; AASS, Jan. 29, III, 633 (secs. 111–12).

That day, after Mézières had left him, Pierre de Thomas began to get worse and perhaps began to recognize that he might be near death. Yet no fear of death could be detected in his words, and he showed wisdom, discretion, and a feeling of security more than at any time in his life. On that day, the magnates of the city visited him, among whom was Pietro Marozelli, chamberlain of the kingdom of Cyprus.[6] The legate ordered him to have his galley ready by Tuesday, for he expected to leave Famagusta that day. He still expected to sail toward Avignon.[7]

On Sunday, January 4, at the hour of terce, Pierre called his confessor, Friar Arnaldus de Solino, O. Carm.,[8] and with great diligence, marvelous contrition, and the shedding of many tears, he made a long general and particular confession. Then with great devotion, he heard mass celebrated by his confessor. After mass, he put on a mean leather garment over his tunic and scapular and called his household before him. He preached to them admirably, always maintaining that he was right with God. When this discourse was completed, he ordered a cheap and abominable sack to be brought to him and said, "This is the white and pleasant raiment in which Christians ought to be buried." Placing the sack on his head, as if it had been a jewel, he said such words of devotion that all were moved to tears, and he himself wept, moved by love for his friends. Then he asked for a rope and put it around his neck, binding and tying it through his mouth. With great contrition he said,

[6] Jorga, Mézières, p. 103 and n. 3; p. 151 and n. 3; p. 264, n. 4; pp. 285, 313, 354, 371, 373, n. 9; p. 375, n. 6; p. 376 and n. 7; p. 398. Pietro Marozelli, alias Malosel, Malocello, or Malosello, chamberlain of the kingdom of Cyprus, figures prominently in the affairs of the realm. He served as a royal envoy to the Roman Curia in 1365. He took part in the crusade at Alexandria.

[7] Mézières, Life, ed. Smet, p. 144; AASS, Jan. 29, III, 633 (sec. 113). Mézières takes Pierre's statement as a prophecy of his death, which came on that Tuesday.

[8] As noted by Smet in his edition of Mézières, Life, p. 144, n. 3, this man is not known from other sources.

"This rope is not sufficient to punish a sinner such as I. How many, many times have I offended my God with my false tongue." Then he ordered himself to be put on the ground and from there gave another excellent spiritual discourse to his household, again asserting that he was right with God and promising them that God would provide for them after his death. Then he turned toward his processional cross, which was believed to contain a relic of the true cross. He worshiped it, kissed it, and said many marvelous things. Then with folded hands, he implored pardon of his household. "O my friends and brothers," he said, "how many labors and dangers you have sustained in my service—hunger, thirst, cold, storms, and tribulations. I have not treated you nor honored you nor taken care of you as I ought to have done, and you have borne me and all my ways kindly. How many times have I placed you in danger of death! How can I repay you? Forgive me, forgive." [9] His household could not answer, for they were too overcome by emotion.[10]

Next he requested his confessor to bring him the consecrated host which was over the altar before him. With hands folded before the sacrament, with great devotion he uttered the prayer, "God be propitious to me, a sinner." Afterward he confessed the articles of the faith one by one perfectly and with great reverence. With deep contrition and tears, he declared that, if in his disputations, preaching, conversations, or otherwise he had ever said anything contrary to the faith and

[9] As recorded in Alphonse Fierens, *Suppliques d'Urbain V* (Analecta Vaticano-Belgica, vol. VII; Rome, Brussels, Paris, 1914), pp. 664–65, a group of *familiares* of Pierre de Thomas on June 16, 1366, petitioned Pope Urban V for a special indulgence because they had undergone not a few dangers and hazards both on land and on the sea in going with him to the lands beyond the sea. Among them was Johannes Rete of the diocese of Tournai. Urban granted him full remission of his sins at the hour of his death. Presumably a similar grant was made to others of Pierre's household.
[10] Mézières, *Life*, ed. Smet, pp. 144–46; AASS, Jan. 29, III, 633–34 (secs. 113–14).

precepts of the Roman Catholic Church, he retracted it before God with all his heart. He then prayed two ritual prayers of his order and received communion with unfeigned faith and devotion. Afterward, he rested again, seated on his bed. His confessor and the master of his lodgings, the noble Huguettus de Maymon,[11] asked him if he did not want the rope removed from his neck. Pierre said, "Stop! Stop! Do not take it away. This is not sufficient punishment for my sins. If I did not fear my Saviour, I would do much more to my body, which has sinned so greatly against its God." He requested them to leave him for a while so that he could rest, and they did so.[12]

From that time, he constantly fixed his eyes above in contemplation, and he said, "Oh why did my son the chancellor leave?" Two priests came to visit him, Lord Bernard, papal engrosser, and his companion, Lord Peter.[13] At that time, Pierre de Thomas said that he saw demons in the air around the foot of his bed. When his visitors asked him how he was, he said, "I am doing well, but pray to God for me, that it may please Him to liberate me from these demons." Later he said, "The Blessed Virgin Mary is holding them back; pray for me." He ordered them to take his cross from the head of his bed and to place it by the wall at the foot of the bed, where he saw the demons. When they did so, the demons vanished from his sight.[14]

Then he called his household together and publicly, in the

[11] Huguettus de Maymon is not otherwise known, as is noted by Smet in his edition of Mézières, *Life,* p. 146, n. 7,

[12] Mézières, *Life,* ed. Smet, p. 146; AASS, Jan. 29, III, 634 (sec. 115).

[13] Smet in his edition of Mézières, *Life,* p. 147, n. 8, suggests that this *Petrus eius socius* is probably Pierre Roquette who shared the perils of Pierre de Thomas' voyage to Serbia.

[14] Mézières, *Life,* ed. Smet, pp. 146–47; AASS, Jan. 29, III, 634 (sec. 116). In this passage the AASS edition has the difficult reading concerning the demons, "Beata Virgo Maria ipsos timuit," to which is added the gloss "id est, timore percussit." The true reading is "Beata Virgo Maria ipsos tenuit."

presence of them all, he made his last will and testament, which was recorded by an authorized notary. He made his will completely, distinctly, and very wisely, so that the archbishop of Nicosia avowed that he could not have disposed of his goods any more completely had he been in perfect health. When his confessor asked him whom he desired to appoint as his executors, he said, "Previously I have appointed and established the chancellor as my champion, and to him I have committed my body and soul and goods, and again I desire him." [15] In addition to Mézières, he named Raymond de la Pradèle, archbishop of Nicosia,[16] and Bérenger Grégoire, dean of Nicosia and papal collector, as his executors. When his friends inquired about his burial, he said, "Bury me at the entrance to the choir, so that all men can and ought to walk over my body and also, if it is possible, even the goats and dogs." [17]

Although the last will and testament of Pierre de Thomas is no longer extant, some of its provisions are known from the writings of Mézières, especially from his own will drawn up in Venice, January 20, 1369. Pierre de Thomas directed that

---

[15] Mézières alludes to this in his testament of January 20, 1369, published in Neculai Jorga, "Le Testament de Philippe de Mézières," *Bulletin de l'Institut pour l'étude de l'Europe sud-orientale,* VIII (1921), 128.

[16] Louis de Mas Latrie, "Histoire des archevêques latins de l'île de Chypre," *Archives de l'Orient latin,* II (1884), 272–77. The references to the presence of Raymond de la Pradèle at the death and funeral of Pierre de Thomas in January, 1366, are the first clear references to him as archbishop of Nicosia, although his predecessor, Philippe de Chambarlhac, had died in June, 1361. He may have been on the crusade of 1365, for Leontios Makhairas, *Recital concerning the Sweet Land of Cyprus entitled "Chronicle,"* ed. and trans. R. M. Dawkins, 2 vols. (Oxford, 1932), I, 147, says that the company of the archbishop of Nicosia was on the crusade.

[17] Mézières, *Life,* ed. Smet, pp. 147–48; AASS, Jan. 29, III, 634 (secs. 117–18). In his own will of 1369 Mézières followed his master's example. In a passage published in Jorga, "Le Testament," p. 127, he ordered that his body be buried in flat ground over which faithful Christians and even sinners and dogs would walk, for, said he, it is more fitting that dust should keep company with dust than with stones.

after his death his body should be garbed in the habit of a simple Carmelite friar.[18] He desired that it should finally be interred at the Carmelite house of Bergerac, where he had first entered the order.[19] To Philippe de Mézières, he left a slave named Benedictus,[20] a chalice, and the ornamental robes in which he had celebrated mass and the other offices of the church for about twelve years.[21] He also left Mézières his precious jeweled cross, said to contain a relic of the true cross. This had been given to him in 1360 by the Christians of Syria. With it, he is reported to have stilled the angry sea,[22] and he carried it before him during the attack on Alexandria.[23] He had it with him at the time of his last illness, as has been noted above. In his will of 1369, Mézières directed that it should be given to the church in which he should be buried.[24] Shortly afterward, on December 23, 1370, he gave it to the Scuola di S. Giovanni Evangelista in Venice, where he had spent a considerable period of time. There it remains to the present time.[25]

[18] Mézières, *Life,* ed. Smet, p. 154.

[19] Mézières, *Life,* ed. Smet, p. 187; Jorga, "Le Testament," pp. 128–29.

[20] Jorga, "Le Testament," p. 131. Mézières directed in his will that after his death the slave Benedictus should serve his friend Johannes Bette or someone else, as seemed best to his executors, not as a slave but as a free Christian for the good of his body and soul. He directed his executors to pay 300 ducats to Benedictus.

[21] Jorga, "Le Testament," p. 133. Apparently Pierre de Thomas had used these robes ever since his appointment as bishop of Patti and Lipari in 1354. Mézières left the chalice and robes to one of his executors, Niccolò Morosini.

[22] See above, p. 174.

[23] See above, p. 280.

[24] Jorga, "Le Testament," p. 132. In this will Mézières speaks of this cross as "the most venerable wood of the holy cross in crystal, decorated with silver and gold, which I received from my blessed father, the lord legate."

[25] Jorga, *Mézières,* pp. 394, 402–03; Smet's note 4 in his edition of Mézières, *Life,* p. 145. Smet notes that further information on the Scuola di S. Giovanni Evangelista may be found in Giuseppe Marino

On Sunday night, Pierre de Thomas and his household rested. The next morning, Huguettus, the master of his lodgings, came into the room. Pierre held him by the hand and said, "It is done according to the will of my God. We shall not again go together. Please send for my brother the chancellor." All that day, he grew worse with the double tertian fever. He was visited by many people, and his condition was aggravated because he spoke to all of them. To those who came to console him, he often said, "Life or death is all the same to me, for if I am necessary for the crusade, so that I ought to labor, I am willing to do so, and if I am not necessary, I am content with death; that is, may the will of my God, Jesus Christ, be done." That day, he tried three times to say the canonical hours, but because of bodily weakness he was unable to do so, although his mind remained clear. He asked his confessor to say his hours for him and in his presence, which he did. With sadness, Pierre revealed to them that from the day of his profession into the Carmelite Order he had never until this day missed saying his hours on the land or on the sea, even in times of sickness and evident danger.[26]

At about an hour before midnight on Monday, he had two consecrated white candles brought before him. At midnight, before the sounding of the bell for matins, he sent his confessor to request Bishop Simon of Laodicea, O.P., vicar of Famagusta,[27] to come vested in his ceremonial robes and ac-

---

Urbani de Gheltof, *Guida storico-artistica della Scuola di S. Giovanni Evangelista in Venezia* (Venice, 1895), and in *Vita del glorioso S. Giovanni apostolo ed evangelista con alcuni miracoli della santissima croce che conservasi nella scuola grande di detto santo, avuto in dono fino dall'anno 1370* (Venice, 1752).

[26] Mézières, *Life,* ed. Smet, pp. 148–49; AASS, Jan. 29, III, 634 (secs. 118–19).

[27] Eubel, *Hierarchia catholica,* I, 292, 367; Jorga, *Mézières,* p. 62, n. 2; pp. 314, 316. Simon was consecrated as bishop of Laodicea on July 4, 1345. He served as one of the envoys of the king of Cyprus

companied by the cathedral chapter of Famagusta to give him
extreme unction. Meanwhile he called all his household before
him and ordered the doors of the room and of the house to
be opened. Before the arrival of the bishop, he asked for the
service book. In it he found the office of extreme unction and
read it aloud. Then he had himself placed on the floor on a
sack full of chaff. He was dressed from head to toe in a dirty
old sack over an old scapular and tunic of his order. He also
put sackcloth on his head. Thus Bishop Simon of Laodicea
found him on his arrival. The bishop saluted Pierre, who responded by beginning the penitential psalms. Without any
help, he got halfway through them; then his strength failed,
and he asked Simon to join him. Thus he completed all seven
psalms with the litany. Afterward, the bishop of Laodicea
solemnly anointed him, and Pierre responded to the words of
the ceremony. During the anointing, Pierre tried to hide the
vile and unclean tunic and scapular which he wore next to his
skin. At the completion of the office of extreme unction, he
devoutly said the *Confiteor Deo,* and Simon granted him absolution. Later Simon testified that at this time he sensed a
fragrance coming from the body of Pierre de Thomas such as
he had never known before. It seemed not to be of this world
but of paradise.[28]

Again Pierre asked pardon from the bishop, the clergy, his
own household, and all who were gathered there if he had
displeased any of them or had made their way harder in the
exercise of his office. He also asked them to seek pardon for

to Avignon in 1350 at the negotiation of a league against the Turks,
as recorded in LC, II, 184, and Mas Latrie, *Histoire de Chypre,* II,
217–18.

[28] Mézières, *Life,* ed. Smet, pp. 149–50; AASS, Jan. 29, III, 634–35
(sec. 120). Testimony of Simon of Laodicea, probably given on April
14, 1366, in Mézières, *Life,* ed. Smet, pp. 175–77, and Carmesson,
*Vita,* in *Spec. carm.,* II, 191–92.

him from any whom he might have offended in Cyprus or elsewhere. Then his confessor and others standing about him begged him, "Father, Father, give us your blessing." While the bishop of Laodicea and all present knelt on the floor, he gave them his benediction: "May the blessing of God the Father Almighty and of the Son and of the Holy Spirit descend upon you and remain forever," and with his own hands sprinkled them with holy water. With tears, the bishop besought him to order himself placed upon his bed, but Pierre replied, "It is not fitting for a Christian to die save in dust and ashes." Then he said to the bishop, "You may go now, for I am consoled and am doing well." Pierre also raised his eyes, made the sign of the cross, and said, "O you other accursed ones, now you have no power with me, for I am right with my Creator, Jesus Christ." The bishop of Laodicea and his clergy retired. The legate had the passions of Christ read to him. Afterward, his household left him, and he rested.[29]

On Monday evening, Pierre had called his whole household before him. He had had a chest brought in containing almost a thousand florins. This money he divided with his own hand to the members of his household according to the division established in his will. This he did with such discretion, devotion, and maturity that everyone marveled. They were amazed that a dying man could possess such wisdom and discretion and that his soul could remain for so long in a body devoid of human strength. He was nothing but skin, nerves, and bones.[30]

On Tuesday, January 6, the royal physicians came to comfort him, but Pierre de Thomas said, "I have no need of earthly physicians, for I have my spiritual physician, Jesus Christ, who

[29] Mézières, *Life,* ed. Smet, pp. 150–51; AASS, Jan. 29, III, 635 (secs. 121–22).

[30] Mézières, *Life,* ed. Smet, p. 151; AASS, Jan. 29, III, 635 (sec. 122).

already has healed me." The physicians left him, seeing that they could do nothing for him. All day, the magnates of the city came to visit him, and to each of them he replied by name, "May it be well with you; I am well, very well." Toward the hour of vespers, when Huguettus, the master of his lodgings, entered his room, he asked for Philippe de Mézières. Huguettus assured him that Mézières would soon come. Giacomo de' Rossi, a friend of Pierre who had fought at Alexandria, entered the room and looked at him sadly. Pierre said to him, "O my son, I am well, do not grieve. Many are called; few are chosen, but I am called and chosen. Christ calls me; I go to Christ. Do not grieve, my son, do not grieve." That evening, the king's bailie entered his room with a great company of magnates and asked whether he would take any food. Pierre replied by placing his hand on the cross and saying, "I have indeed received of this fruit of life, who rules and sustains me, in whom I trust. I want Him and nothing else." Then he drew the cross before his face and embraced it as best he could, but he could no longer guide it without help. His condition became worse, and he lost the power of speech.[31]

About half an hour before sunset that evening, Philippe de Mézières arrived in Famagusta and went to the lodgings of his dying friend. When he arrived, the household of the legate said to him, "Hurry, hurry, our father is dying. He is expecting you. He has lost his speech, but he cannot die." Already Pierre de Thomas' hands, arms, and legs were cold. When he saw Mézières, his voice and strength returned. He raised his right hand from the bed and took Mézières by the hands. He spoke to his friend for some length of time. Briefly

[31] Mézières, *Life,* ed. Smet, pp. 151–53; AASS, Jan. 29, III, 635 (secs. 123–25). On Giacomo de' Rossi, see Jorga, *Mézières,* p. 280 and notes 4, 5, pp. 314, 317, 320 and note 2.

he outlined the arrangements which he had made for his funeral and the disposition of his property, just as if he had not been sick. Mézières, fearing that it would hurt him to talk for so long, said as well as he knew how, "My father, now is the time when you will contemplate that excellent Divinity whom you have preached so much in your life." Pierre answered, "Brother, so I do. You may go; you may go. Provide for my affairs and my household and do not return again to me," for he saw how much it grieved Mézières to see him on his deathbed. Nevertheless, Mézières was glad that he was able to talk to his friend once more before he passed away.[32]

Mézières then left his friend for a time. He called all the legate's household together and a notary, probably the one who had recorded Pierre's will two days before. He made certain that all the requests of the dying man were written down. Afterward he returned quickly to the bedside of Pierre de Thomas and assured him that provision had been made for the fulfillment of all his requests. Then he consoled him spiritually as well as he could, because he was almost completely cold. To his admonitions, Pierre quietly replied, "Very well, very well." While Mézières was with him in the room, which was also full of men and women weeping and wailing, at the second hour of the night, about eight in the evening by modern reckoning, on January 6, 1366, Pierre de Thomas died quietly. His body did not move, nor was there any sign of death, so that he was gone for some time before anyone presumed to close his eyes. When his death was announced, there was much crying and lamentation in the house, so greatly was he loved by his friends.[33]

As he had ordered, the body of Pierre de Thomas was

[32] Mézières, *Life,* ed. Smet, p. 153; AASS, Jan. 29, III, 635–36 (sec. 126).

[33] Mézières, *Life,* ed. Smet, pp. 153–54; AASS, Jan. 29, III, 636 (secs. 126–27).

dressed in the habit of the Carmelite Order, as if he had been but a simple friar. His episcopal gloves were placed on his hands and sandals on his feet. His miter was placed at his feet. Thus he was laid in state in the Carmelite church of Famagusta. When his friends returned to their homes, many devout women remained around his bier to keep vigil. At the fourth watch of the night, it is reported that a certain nun who had been prostrate in prayer rose up and by chance turned her face toward the body of Pierre de Thomas. Suddenly she saw a bright and splendid ray of light which shone down from the highest point in the church upon the body of the legate. She was amazed at the sight and aroused the other women, many of whom had fallen asleep. While she told them about it, suddenly that heavenly light disappeared. When the women went over to the body, they found a clear and unmistakable sign of the light, for the face and the whole body were moist and fresh, like those of a man coming from the baths. The prudent women among them secured a good quantity of cotton, with which they wiped off the face and breast of Pierre de Thomas. Many miracles were later reported from the use of this cotton.[34]

The death of Pierre de Thomas did not become generally known in Famagusta until the next morning. The news spread rapidly, and with one accord the people began to congregate at the Carmelite church to pay their last respects to his remains. The church was soon full of men and women, including not only Catholics but also Eastern Christians of various communions, and Moslems. Among them were some Greek monks who in his lifetime had hated Pierre because of his efforts to convert them. Now they kissed his hands and feet. Anyone who could have the slightest particle of his garment as a relic con-

[34] Mézières, *Life,* ed. Smet, pp. 154–55; AASS, Jan. 29, III, 636 (secs. 127–28).

sidered himself blessed. At this time, a wondrous thing was noted. A pleasant odor came from the legate's body, which was all the more remarkable because in his lifetime, as his friend Mézières testifies, it commonly gave off an unpleasant odor on account of the severe penances to which he subjected himself and the vile rags which he wore next to his skin. His complexion was clearer than it had been when he was alive, and his limbs remained supple, with no trace of stiffening.[35]

After about five days,[36] Archbishop Raymond of Nicosia came with other prelates and celebrated the solemn office of the dead over the body of Pierre de Thomas. So great a crowd was coming and pressing into the church that they could hardly finish the funeral service. According to Mézières, Pierre's body was venerated even by those Catholics, not a few and not without power, who in his lifetime had considered him a sinner.[37]

As was the custom in that day, the archbishop of Nicosia made arrangements for a funeral sermon to be preached over the body of Pierre de Thomas on the night before the funeral exercises. To preach this sermon, he chose Juan Carmesson, doctor of theology, the Franciscan provincial of the Holy

[35] Mézières, *Life,* ed. Smet, pp. 155–56; AASS, Jan. 29, III, 636 (sec. 129).

[36] The date of the funeral of Pierre de Thomas is not clearly stated by Mézières. However, it is noted in the official account of the opening of Pierre's tomb on May 8, 1366, recorded in Mézières, *Life,* ed. Smet, p. 182, and in Carmesson, *Vita,* in *Spec. carm.,* II, 194, that his body lay in the Carmelite church of Famagusta for eleven days before burial. In Mézières, *Life,* ed. Smet, p. 157; AASS, Jan. 29, III, 637 (sec. 132) after the account of his funeral it is said that his body remained in the church six days before burial. If Mézières means, as is probable, that these six days should be reckoned from the funeral, a comparison with the other record would indicate that Pierre's funeral was held about five days after his death, January 11 or 12, 1366.

[37] Mézières, *Life,* ed. Smet, p. 156; AASS, Jan. 29, III, 636 (sec. 130).

Land.[38] Although Carmesson had little time to prepare for this occasion, he preached an excellent sermon, demonstrating the sanctity of the patriarch and legate by many clear and reasonable arguments. Those present noted with surprise that in the sermon Carmesson frequently referred to Pierre de Thomas as a saint. While it is permissible for a Catholic personally to regard a person as a saint even though that person has not been canonized by the church, it is improper to designate such a person as a saint in a public utterance. Afterward Carmesson was questioned on this point by the archbishop of Nicosia. He replied that in his preparation for the sermon he had not planned to speak of Pierre as a saint, but while he was preaching, he felt constrained, as he believed, by the Holy Spirit and the merits of the man to call him a saint, so that he could not do otherwise. Now he really believed him to be a saint.[39] This Juan Carmesson later wrote a biography of Pierre de Thomas, which seems to be largely a condensation and rearrangement of the one written by Philippe de Mézières. Carmesson probably wrote it to promote the legate's canonization, for it is arranged topically to present his virtues, and not chronologically, like Mézières' work.[40]

---

[38] Girolamo Golubovich, O. F. M., *Biblioteca bio-bibliografica della Terra Santa e dell'Oriente Francescano*, series I, vol. V (Quaracchi, 1927), 95–96. Little is known about Carmesson. He was originally from the kingdom of Aragon. He received the doctorate of theology by a grant of Urban V dated April 22, 1363. By that time, he was already the Franciscan provincial of the Holy Land but had not yet left for the East.

[39] Mézières, *Life,* ed. Smet, pp. 156–57; AASS, Jan. 29, III, 636–37 (sec. 131).

[40] Juan Carmesson, *Vita sancti Petri Thomae patriarchae Constantinopolitani, legati apostolici* (Antwerp, 1666), also published in Daniel a Virgine Maria (ed.), *Speculum carmelitanum,* II (Antwerp, 1680), 171–95. The latter edition has been used in the present study. In his edition of Mézières, *Life,* pp. 37, 42–47, Joachim Smet suggests that Carmesson's biography was written in the latter part of 1366. Carmesson's material is generally a mere summary of events related by

The body of Pierre de Thomas lay in state at the Carmelite church at Famagusta for six days after his funeral,[41] always remaining supple, as in life. People flocked around his bier night and day and venerated him as a saint. Everyone desired to have some of his relics, and when they could have none, they ran cotton over his body and preserved it. Later many sick persons are said to have received health through it.[42] Eleven days after his death, his body was laid to rest in a sepulcher, over which was placed a large marble slab cemented into place at the level of the ground [43] and surmounted by his sculptured effigy.[44]

The death of Pierre de Thomas was a severe personal blow to Philippe de Mézières, who loved him dearly and had come to depend upon him for spiritual help and guidance. His grief is clearly manifested in the biography of the legate which he began to write shortly after his death. He was writing it in the Lenten season of 1366 [45] and probably concluded it before he left Cyprus about the end of June.[46] At the close of the biography, there is an elaborate lamentation, extolling Pierre de Thomas' virtues, expressing his friends' sorrow at his passing, and witnessing Mézières' joy that his friend had now left the cares of earth to receive a well-earned reward from the

---

Mézières, usually with less detail and color. Therefore it is of limited value and has been used sparingly. However, as noted above, pp. 146–47, Carmesson relates an incident from Pierre's mission to Constantinople in 1357 which is not in Mézières and must therefore be based on some other contemporary testimony. It is found in *Spec. carm.*, II, 180.

[41] See above, note 36.

[42] Mézières, *Life,* ed. Smet, pp. 157–58; AASS, Jan. 29, III, 637 (sec. 132).

[43] Mézières, *Life,* ed. Smet, p. 182; Carmesson, *Vita,* in *Spec. carm.*, II, 194.

[44] Mézières, *Life,* ed. Smet, p. 183; Carmesson, *loc. cit.*

[45] Mézières, *Life,* ed. Smet, p. 185.

[46] Smet's opinion expressed in his edition of Mézières, *Life,* p. 37; Jorga, *Mézières,* p. 324.

Heavenly Father.[47] Mézières also wrote a separate lamentation on the death of Pierre de Thomas which later became incorporated into the biography.[48] On Passion Sunday, March 22, 1366, he was somewhat consoled by a dream in which Pierre appeared to him and comforted him.[49]

The death of Pierre de Thomas was not only a great personal loss to Philippe de Mézières but also a severe blow to the cause of the crusade in which they were both so much interested, together with King Pierre I of Cyprus. Of the three enthusiasts for the crusade, Pierre de Thomas had the greatest influence in Avignon. The king's recognition of this fact is shown by his insistence that the legate serve as his envoy to the court of Pope Urban V to explain the failure of the crusaders to

[47] Mérières, Life, ed. Smet, pp. 159–62; AASS, Jan. 29, III, 637–38 (secs. 133–36).

[48] Mézières, Life, ed. Smet, pp. 163–68, cf. p. 37.

[49] The account of this dream is in Mézières, Life, ed. Smet, pp. 184–85. Mézières relates that he was writing his friend's biography and grieving greatly over his death in the Lenten season of 1366. At about the eighth hour of the night on Passion Sunday, he dreamed that he was in a church with some men who were planning to go on a crusade. Suddenly, while standing by a certain seat in the church, he saw Pierre de Thomas surrounded by his retinue, saying his hours, and preparing and vesting himself to celebrate mass. Pierre then went to the altar and began the service. Mézières went part way to the altar and was kneeling in prayer. Suddenly, Pierre, as though caring nothing for the introit and the other mysteries of the mass and violating them, elevated the sacred host, while everyone adored it from the church. When this was done, he stepped a little toward the altar, still surrounded by his accustomed retinue. Then, leaving the altar, he quickly came toward Mézières, as he was accustomed to do in his lifetime. Mézières became afraid and tried to get away, but soon he found himself face to face with his friend. All fear then departed from him. Pierre de Thomas led him to a certain seat in the church. Seated there, still holding his hand, he began to talk to him. Mézières was convicted of sin and began to weep, but Pierre comforted him, as he had always done in life. He talked to him for quite a while. Pierre's hands were neither cold nor hot but were as those of a healthy person, and he was dressed in a white hood. When Mézières was comforted, his friend vanished from his sight.

hold Alexandria and to appeal for further assistance. It is possible that Pierre de Thomas could have secured some further support for the crusade from the West if he had lived to make the journey to Avignon, although it is doubtful that there would have been enough response from Europe to secure the conquest of Egypt. As it was, while the Pope admired the personal heroism of the king of Cyprus, he no longer depended upon him as the champion of Christianity against the Moslems. No further efforts were made at this time to aid the kingdom of Cyprus, to break the power of the Mameluke state, or to recover the Holy Land for Christendom.[50]

While the body of Pierre de Thomas lay in state in the Carmelite church of Famagusta, miracles began to be reported at his bier. For example, the Franciscan Friar Giovanni da Faenza, guardian of the convent of Paphos,[51] reported that some days before the octave of Epiphany he had been afflicted with a severe inflammation of the throat. His throat was so sore for nine days that he was unable to eat or sleep because of the pain. He heard of the fame and holiness of Pierre de Thomas and of the devotion which the people had toward him and commended himself to God and to the sanctity of the lord patriarch. On the Saturday in Epiphany, January 10, 1366, he went to the Carmelite church at Famagusta with the brother who was appointed to minister to him. He found the body of Pierre de Thomas still lying in state and placed the right hand of the deceased on his sore throat. At once he sensed that he was better, and soon he was completely healed.[52]

A Greek slave girl named Costa belonging to Dame Sibilia, widow of one Niccolo of Ancona, shortly after the death of the legate suffered from a painful ailment of the bowels with

[50] Halecki, *Un Empereur,* pp. 102–03.
[51] Golubovich, *Biblioteca bio-bibliografica,* V, 117.
[52] Mézières, *Life,* ed. Smet, pp. 170–71; AASS, Jan. 29, III, 638 (appendix, sec. 1); Carmesson, *Vita,* in *Spec. carm.,* II, 189–90.

continual high fever which lasted for five days. Her mistress went to the church where Pierre's body lay. She took a piece of cotton cloth and wrapped it around his head, then took it home and placed it over the head and side of the slave girl. As soon as the cotton touched her head, her health began to return.[53] A woman named Maria had a severe headache. At the advice of a friend named Elisa [54] she took some cotton cloth and made a fillet around the head of Pierre de Thomas, then touched it to her own head and was quickly cured. Later that same piece of cotton cured Elisa of a pain in her side and helped her friend Sibilia to bear a healthy baby boy after three days of prolonged and dangerous labor. The boy was christened Petrus Thomae in honor of this miracle.[55]

After the entombment of Pierre de Thomas, similar miracles continued to be reported. Some of these were performed with bits of cotton that had touched the body of the legate while he lay in state.[56] In other cases, water which had been poured over his tomb was collected and used as an ointment or given to the sick to drink, and they were healed.[57] Earth from the vicinity of the tomb was also used to touch afflicted parts of the body, and cures were reported.[58] A monk of Episkopi in Cyprus, Nicholas by name, had an arm that had been withered for five

[53] Mézières, Life, ed. Smet, pp. 173–74; Carmesson, Vita, in Spec. carm., II, 190–91.

[54] This name is variously spelled Elisa, Alisa, and Allisa in the same passage. She was apparently of German nationality, for she is called the daughter of the late Nicolaus Cassel.

[55] Mézières, Life, ed. Smet, p. 175; Carmesson, Vita, in Spec. carm., II, 191.

[56] Mézières, Life, ed. Smet, pp. 174, 181–82; Carmesson, Vita, in Spec. carm. II, 191, 193–94.

[57] Mézières, Life, ed. Smet, pp. 173, 181, 184; Carmesson, Vita, in Spec. carm., II, 190, 193, 195.

[58] Mézières, Life, ed. Smet, pp. 183–84; Carmesson, Vita, in Spec. carm., II, 194–95.

years. After devoutly offering one lighted candle and a hand
made of wax at the tomb of Pierre de Thomas, he was healed.
Within a year, he had the same trouble with the other arm
and was healed after vowing to offer a wax hand at Pierre's
tomb.[59] Some persons were healed simply by praying to Pierre
de Thomas to intercede for them.[60] Every type of sickness and
disability was reported cured through his merits, including
blindness.[61]

As the reports of these miracles began to be circulated, the
friends of Pierre de Thomas decided to take steps to authenti-
cate them with a view to his canonization. On April 14, 1366,
Simon, bishop of Laodicea and vicar of the diocese of Famagusta, instituted an inquiry into these miracles at the request
of King Pierre I of Cyprus, which was formally presented by
Philippe de Mézières. A large number of ecclesiastics and magnates were present, including Dominicus Stephani or Losteph,[62]
the Carmelite provincial of the Holy Land, Juan Carmesson,
who held a similar position in the Franciscan order, and several Carmelite friars. They heard a number of witnesses who

[59] Mézières, Life, ed. Smet, pp. 183–84; Carmesson, Vita, in Spec.
carm., II, 194.
[60] Mézières, Life, ed. Smet, pp. 179–80; Carmesson, Vita, in Spec.
carm., II, 192–93.
[61] For further details see the ecclesiastical process into these miracles
published in Mézières, Life, ed. Smet, pp. 168–84, and in Carmesson,
Vita, in Spec. carm., II, 189–95. This material is not found in AASS,
since it was not in the manuscript of Mézières' biography used to prepare that edition. On the manuscripts see Smet's edition of the Life,
pp. 34–47.
[62] Mézières, Life, ed. Smet, pp. 169–70; Carmesson, Vita, in Spec.
carm., II, 189. The surname of the Carmelite provincial of the Holy
Land is usually given in the ecclesiastical process as Stephani, though
in one place (Mézières, op. cit., p. 179; Carmesson, op. cit., p. 193) it
appears as Lestese. In the minutes of the Carmelite Chapters General
of 1369 and 1372, published in ACG, I, 65, 68, he is called Losteph
and Lostoph. In his edition of Mézières, Life p. 170, n. 6, Smet suggests that his name may have been Lo Stefano.

claimed to have been healed of sicknesses and disabilities through the merits of the late patriarch of Constantinople.[63] Some accounts of healing were presented by members of the commission itself. The Carmelite provincial prior of the Holy Land claimed to have been healed of an itching skin disease of twenty-five years duration when he placed his hand on the ground where Pierre de Thomas was buried and afterward touched the afflicted part.[64] Bishop Simon of Laodicea reported that in March, 1366, he was cured from a sudden attack of a serious illness only when he was able to touch his body with a riding cap which had belonged to the legate.[65]

On May 8, 1366, at about noon, Philippe de Mézières opened the tomb of Pierre de Thomas in the presence of Juan Carmesson, Dominicus Stephani, and other discreet persons, to examine his body for evidences of sanctity. They found his corpse in essentially the same condition in which it had been while lying in state in January. There was some evidence of blackening but still no noticeable stiffening. In the tomb there was a musty odor, such as one would find in a prison or a subterranean house, but no odor of decay. Before the tomb was closed again, the body was examined by Bishop Simon of

[63] Mézières, op. cit., pp. 170–78; Carmesson, op. cit., pp. 189–92. It is not clear just how far in the ecclesiastical process the testimony of the inquiry of April 14 runs. Apparently it extends as far as is indicated above and closes with the testimony of the presiding officer, Bishop Simon of Laodicea. The only difficulty in this viewpoint is the account of a miracle of April 17 in the middle of this passage (Mézières, op. cit., p. 174; Carmesson, op. cit., p. 191). Perhaps this date is incorrect. One manuscript has it April 7, as noted in Smet's critical apparatus. Also the process may have begun on April 14 and continued on later days.

[64] Mézières, Life, ed. Smet, pp. 171–72; Carmesson, Vita, in Spec. carm., II, 190.

[65] Mézières, Life, ed. Smet, pp. 177–78; Carmesson, Vita, in Spec. carm., II, 192.

Laodicea, Bérenger Grégoire, dean of Nicosia, and by other persons, both clerics and laymen.[66]

Two years later, in May, 1368, when King Pierre I of Cyprus made a visit to the papal court, then in Italy, he informed Urban V of the miracles of Pierre de Thomas in the presence of Cardinals Guillaume d'Aigrefeuille [67] and Pierre de Monteruc.[68] Mézières was also present. Pierre I requested the Pope to proceed at once to the canonization of "the blessed legate." Urban agreed to the request and ordered that the miracles already reported and all future miracles attributed to Pierre de Thomas should be written down in official documents which would furnish all the faithful with clear proof of his sanctity. Letters to this effect were sent to the archbishop of Nicosia.[69]

At the same time, the king of Cyprus petitioned the papacy concerning the body of Pierre de Thomas. In his will, the legate had requested that his remains should be sent for final interment to the Carmelite convent of Bergerac, where he had entered the order. At the request of the people of Cyprus,

[66] Mézières, *Life,* ed. Smet, p. 182; Carmesson, *Vita,* in *Spec. carm.,* II, 194.

[67] Eubel, *Hierarchia catholica,* I, 1, 19, 153; Baluze-Mollat, *Vitae paparum Avenionensium,* II, 413–15. Guillaume d'Aigrefeuille became archbishop of Saragossa in 1347 and hence is commonly called the cardinal of Saragossa. In 1350 he was elevated to the cardinalate by Clement VI with the title of S. Maria in Trastevere. In 1367 he succeeded Albornoz as bishop of Sabina. He died at Viterbo on October 4, 1369.

[68] Eubel, *Hierarchia catholica,* I, 1, 39, 387; Baluze-Mollat, *Vitae paparum Avenionensium,* II, 449–55; Ursmer Berlière, O. S. B., "Les Archdiacres de Liége au XIV⁰ siècle," *Bulletin de la commission royale d'histoire* (of Belgium), LXXV (1906), 202–05. Pierre de Monteruc became bishop of Pamplona in 1355. The next year Innocent VI appointed him as a cardinal with the title of St. Anastasia. He was a nephew of Innocent VI and was vice-chancellor under Popes Urban V, Gregory XI, and Clement VII. He died in Avignon in May, 1385.

[69] Mézières, *Life,* ed. Smet, pp. 186–87.

Pierre I asked that those remains, which had been responsible for so many miracles of healing on the island, should not be removed thence immediately. Urban V responded by issuing a decree that the body of Pierre de Thomas should not be translated from Cyprus within the next decade. He ordered Cardinal Pierre de Monteruc, his vice-chancellor, to send a letter to that effect to Archbishop Raymond of Nicosia.[70] In his will made in January, 1369, Philippe de Mézières left a legacy of 200 ducats for the translation of Pierre's body to Bergerac. He provided, however, that if the will of God was shown by some sign or miracle that the relics of the legate ought to remain under the protection of the kingdom of Cyprus and the Catholics of the East, this money should be used for other pious uses in the name of Pierre de Thomas.[71] It appears that Pierre's remains were never removed to Bergerac but remained permanently at the Carmelite convent in Famagusta. The exact location of his tomb is not now known.[72]

In 1375, there was some interest in the Carmelite order to seek the canonization of Pierre de Thomas. In that year, the Chapter General, meeting at Puy-en-Velay, authorized the prior general to tax the order for the canonization of the holy legate, as well as for some other special objects.[73] This is the last such effort recorded in the fourteenth century.

In the Carmelite missal printed in 1509, under date of January 7, Pierre de Thomas is honored as *"Sanctus Petrus Thomae, Episcopus et Confessor,"* as he is also in the missal of 1551. In the breviary printed in Venice in 1573, he is honored as bishop

[70] *Ibid.,* pp. 187–88. The letter, dated Montefiascone, May 21, 1368, is published on p. 188.

[71] Jorga, "Le Testament," pp. 128–30.

[72] Camille Enlart, "Fouilles dans les églises de Famagouste de Chypre," *The Archeological Journal,* LXII (1905), 196. Enlart searched for the tomb of Pierre de Thomas among the ruins of the Carmelite church at Famagusta, but he could not find it.

[73] ACG, I, 76.

and martyr, because of the legend that he died of wounds received at the attack on Alexandria.[74] In 1628, the Sacred Congregation of Rites approved the Carmelite office and mass of *"Sanctus Petrus Thomae, Episcopus et Martyr,"* to be celebrated on January 29. Since the canonization of St. François de Sales, whose feast is observed by the Roman Catholic Church on that date, the feast of St. Pierre de Thomas has been transferred by the Carmelite Order to the fifteenth of February.[75] Thus Pierre is venerated as a saint in his order, although he has not been canonized by the Roman Catholic Church.

Pierre de Thomas is also the object of special veneration at certain places associated with his life. On December 20, 1614, the Sacred Congregation of Rites gave permission to the Carmelite friars of the convent of St. Martin in Bologna to celebrate the feast of "St. Thomas the Martyr, of the Carmelite Order" on the first Sunday after the octave of Epiphany, because he was regarded as the founder and institutor of the theological college in that convent.[76] Pierre is also venerated in the country of his birth, though not as a saint. On April 5, 1663, François de Salignac, bishop of Sarlat, received permission to celebrate the feast of the Blessed Pierre de Thomas in his diocese on the last day of January. This is the only instance of official veneration of Pierre de Thomas outside the Carmelite Order.[77]

[74] *Spec. carm.,* I, 785–86; II, 170, 197.

[75] *Spec. carm.,* I, 995; II, 170; Patrick Romaeus McCaffrey, O. Carm., *The White Friars, an Outline Carmelite History with Special Reference to the English-Speaking Provinces* (Dublin, 1926), p. 83.

[76] *Bull. carm.,* III, 438. However, Pierre de Thomas was not a founder of the theological school at the Carmelite convent of Bologna, where, according to MHC, p. 53, there was a *studium generale* as early as 1324, long before he visited that city. As noted above, pp. 253–54, he was a founder of the theological faculty of the University of Bologna, which enabled students at the schools of religious orders in that city to receive degrees in theology more easily.

[77] *Spec. carm.,* II, 225.

# 13

# Personality and
# Place in History

OUR KNOWLEDGE OF THE PERSONALITY OF PIERRE DE THOMAS
is limited. The formal style of his own two letters that remain
and of the archival materials prevent them from giving much
insight into the man Pierre. The writings of his friend Philippe
de Mézières are of greater help for this purpose, but the at-
mosphere of hero worship which pervades them partially ob-
scures Pierre's true nature. The available data has been discussed above in the chronological framework of his life, as it
appears in the sources. At the risk of some repetition, this
material will now be presented topically, together with some
generalizations about the man which have become evident in
this study of his life.

We know little about his personal appearance except that
he was small and undistinguished in appearance.[1] In her recent

[1] Mézières, *Life,* ed. Smet, p. 58; AASS, Jan. 29, III, 612 (sec. 7).
Mézières describes Pierre as "parvus corpore et modicae apparentiae."

biography, Daphne Pochin-Mould suggests that his growth may have been stunted by the severe privations of his youth in a poor family.[2] He probably showed evidence of his peasant origin throughout his life. His friend Mézières lets it be known that, at least in his later life, the severe penances to which he subjected himself and the dirty clothes which he always wore next to his skin as a penitential practice caused his body to have an unpleasant odor.[3]

Pierre was a deeply religious man, whose life was characterized by deep faith and saintly living. He was sincerely devoted to the ideals and practices of the Carmelite Order and especially venerated the Virgin Mary, patron saint of his order.[4] He was concerned about the welfare of the whole Catholic Church of his day and was unfailingly loyal to it and its leaders, even though he recognized their weaknesses and sometimes preached against them. He was a man of deep humility, who did not seek or desire glory for himself, although he insisted upon receiving the highest degree of respect when he was serving as a representative of the Pope and the church, so that the honor of the church and thereby her power to do good might not be diminished.[5]

Pierre de Thomas was not a joyless fanatic. He had a winsome personality and was at ease in any company .His general observance of the Carmelite rules, especially with regard to eating, did not prevent him from enjoying festive occasions and contributing to them by his presence. At such times, he

[2] Daphne Pochin-Mould, *The Life of Saint Peter Thomas* (New York, 1961), p. 19.
[3] Mézières, *Life,* ed. Smet, p. 156; AASS, Jan. 29, III, 636 (sec. 129).
[4] Mézières, *Life, ed. Smet,* pp. 54–56, 60–62; AASS, Jan. 29, III, 611–13 (secs. 3, 4, 10–14).
[5] Compare his attitude as a pilgrim in Cyprus in Mézières, *Life,* ed. Smet, p. 80; AASS, Jan. 29, III, 617 (sec. 34), with his actions at the court of Stephen Dushan, *ibid.,* ed. Smet, p. 67; AASS, Jan. 29, III, 614 (sec. 20).

probably had to take advantage of dispensations from the rules of his order, but he recognized that the ascetic life was only one phase of the church's plan for realizing Christian ideals on the earth, and through active participation in the affairs of the larger world he was able to work more effectively to promote the ideals of his order and of the church at large. In Avignon, he associated with the cardinals and frequently attended their banquets. On the island of Cyprus, he was closely associated with the king and other knights. His friendship with Philippe de Mézières shows that he was capable of forming warm human relationships. His pleasing personality no doubt led to his being called into the papal diplomatic service and helped him to achieve a large measure of success in that field.

His devotion to the Latin church tended to make Pierre rigid and legalistic in his thinking. In his dealings with the Orthodox communions of the East, there is no evidence that he ever came to a real understanding of their viewpoints. He knew only one right way, and he came to persuade them to accept it. The most revealing evidence of this attitude is his edict forbidding Latin clergymen in the East to grow beards, a practice which was in accordance with the customs of the Greek East but contrary to the canons of the Western church. That this rigidity was not shared by all churchmen of the West was proved when Urban V annulled the edict.[6] Pierre's one-sided approach was a real handicap at times and caused him trouble in Serbia and Cyprus, but there is no evidence that it was generally considered a vice. The papacy valued him as a diplomat precisely because he could be trusted to support papal policy vigorously and without deviation. His adversaries were

----

[6] Letter of Urban V to the regular and secular clergy in the Genoese colony of Pera, in Caffa, and in other Orthodox and Moslem lands, June 12, 1365, published in *Bullarium franciscanum*, VI, ed. Conrad Eubel (Rome, 1902), 392.

generally no less convinced of the rectitude of their own positions.

One episode in his life shows that he could be objective in evaluating the claims of two opposing sides when no religious issue was involved. Throughout the peace negotiations between Venice and Hungary, discussed in chapter 5, he enjoyed the confidence of both sides, although they could not come to an agreement and toward the close of the negotiations increasingly distrusted each other.

The life of Pierre de Thomas was characterized by hard work and determination combined with optimism and enthusiasm. When he undertook a task, he pursued it diligently until he had succeeded or had clearly failed in spite of his best efforts. These qualities can be seen in his early education, in his rise within the Carmelite Order, and in his various diplomatic activities and other missions for the papacy. In all his efforts, a spirit of boundless enthusiasm and joy can be seen, especially when he was convinced that he was working in the cause of God. In the discouragements which often attended the preparations for the crusade of 1365, his optimism and faith served to overcome the fears and feelings of depression which threatened to overwhelm Philippe de Mézières and King Pierre I of Cyprus.[7] Only after the failure of the crusade at Alexandria did the characteristic spirit of joy leave Pierre de Thomas never to return.[8]

On many occasions, Pierre showed great courage and bravery, based upon his strong faith in God and hope of eternal life. There can be no doubt that he had a willingness, if not a desire, to be a martyr for his faith. Perhaps Mézières at some points exaggerates this characteristic of the man, but he was

---

[7] Mézières, *Life,* ed. Smet, pp. 115, 121; AASS, Jan. 29, III, 626–27 (secs. 76, 83).

[8] Mézières, *Life,* ed. Smet, p. 142; AASS, Jan. 29, III, 633 (sec. 110).

an eyewitness of Pierre's willingness to advance in the attack on Alexandria for the glory of God without any thought of personal danger.[9]

Pierre excelled as a public speaker. In preaching, he knew how to win an audience by telling jokes or interesting stories. Then he could present his message to them with great effectiveness and even more them to tears. This ability has been noted on several occasions in his life. In Bologna, it once saved him from a dangerous situation.[10] It stood him in good stead in his diplomatic missions. His ability as a lecturer was probably the chief factor in his success in the academic world. He was also esteemed as a theologian, but he apparently was not in the first rank in this field, for his works have not survived, as many have. His talents lay more in the practical field.

Pierre de Thomas must have had some administrative ability. As he rose to a high rank in the papal service, he traveled with a large retinue and was responsible for large sums of money to provide for them. For this purpose, as has been noted above in connection with his various missions, he received both lump sums from the papacy and the authority to procure stated sums per day while serving as papal nuncio or legate. He also must have received considerable revenues from his dioceses. A few glimpses of this phase of his work appear in the papal records. In 1364, when he was appointed as legate of the crusade, he complained to Urban V that some of the procurations due him from his earlier legation in the East remained unpaid. Perhaps he was in debt. The Pope authorized him to employ ecclesiastical censures to collect this money.[11] Later in the year, when it became evident that it would be necessary for Pierre to spend the winter in Venice, where he had already been staying for a

[9] Mézières, *Life,* ed. Smet, pp. 130–31; AASS, Jan. 29, III, 630 (secs. 94–95).
[10] See above, pp. 52–53, 64–65, 71–72, 199–201, 229–30.
[11] *Reg. Vat.* 251, fols. 315r–315v (July 10, 1364).

considerable period, Urban directed him to cease collecting his daily procuration of ten florins a day from the clergy of Venice, so that he would not become unduly burdensome to them. Until the day he sailed on the crusade, he was to live from the income of his dioceses as if he were not a papal legate.[12]

The place of Pierre de Thomas in history is largely based upon his participation in three important movements of his day, the crusade to recapture the Holy Land, the defense of Europe against the Turks, and the efforts to achieve church union. The background and details of his participation in these concerns of the papacy have already been discussed. It now remains to make some general observations about their relation to the onward march of history.

The idea of a crusade to free the Holy Land from the Moslem yoke, the burning passion of Pierre de Thomas' later years continued to be promoted for a time by Philippe de Mézières and others, but it proved to be a dying cause, which belonged more truly to the eleventh and twelfth centuries than to the fourteenth. However, the related question of the defense of Europe against the Turks, which had been the primary concern of Pierre's first legation to the East, was just beginning to be an important issue in his day, as the Ottomans swept from Asia into Europe. It continued to be an important concern of West European leaders for several centuries, until the Ottoman strength declined to the point where the Turks were no longer a menace.

Pierre de Thomas' work on the union of the Greek and Latin churches came at the beginning of a century of intensified activity in that area which preceded the fall of Constantinople in 1453. Interest in church union has never died. In fact, it

[12] *Reg. Vat.* 246, fols. 358r–358v (October 29, 1364), cited by Smet in his edition of Mézières, *Life,* p. 121, n. 35. At this time, Pierre was administrator of the bishoprics of Negroponte and Coron.

has appeared with renewed strength in the twentieth century, as is witnessed by the prominent place of this issue on the agenda of the ecumenical council under Popes John XXIII and Paul VI.

A study of the life of Pierre de Thomas is also valuable for the light which it can throw upon the period in which he lived, the period of the Avignonese papacy. At its worst, this has been assailed as a time when the Roman Catholic Church and its leaders were completely corrupt and dominated by selfish interests and political considerations. At its best, it has been recognized as a time when there was much luxury and worldliness in the church, when the church was more interested in developing a complex and efficient organization than in emphasizing great spiritual truths or fighting the evils of society, when the church was dominated by practical men rather than by heroes of the faith.

Pierre certainly was not typical of the age in which he lived. In a time of luxurious living among churchmen, he gloried in the simplicity of the apostolic age and lived by a strict monastic discipline which grew out of the reforming spirit of the earlier Middle Ages. In a practical-minded age, he frequently sought to do what seemed impossible, trusting that God would bring it to pass, by a miracle if necessary. In an age when most men were dominated by selfish interests, he dedicated his life wholly to the service of God. In an age of nominal Christianity, he had a deep faith and lived a saintly life. In an age when most men had lost interest in crusades, he accepted the liberation of Jerusalem as his chief goal. In an unheroic age, he frequently showed a willingness to die as a martyr for the Catholic faith.

Yet he was highly honored in Avignon and had much influence there. He was a friend of Popes Innocent VI and Urban V and of the powerful Cardinal Talleyrand de Périgord. He rose to a high position in the hierarchy. He was entrusted with a number of important diplomatic missions for the papacy. For several years, he was the chief papal representative in the East and the principal adviser to the papacy on Eastern affairs. At the preaching of the crusade in 1365, he seems to have had a very definite influence in papal policy. Even if this influence resulted more from acceptance of the ideals which he represented than from his personal prestige, it was nevertheless significant.

The relationship of Pierre de Thomas to the leaders at Avignon reveals something very significant about them. The men who led the Roman Curia in the pontificates of Innocent VI and Urban V had not totally forgotten the more spiritual, idealistic, and heroic goals of the church, or they would have had nothing in common with Pierre de Thomas, nor he with them. He knew them well, and yet he honored them and worked with them. Thus he showed that he believed they were in essence upholding the true principles of Christianity. While the spirit of Pierre de Thomas was certainly not its dominant spirit, the Avignonese papacy cannot be fully understood without recognition of the fact that a heroic, dedicated, and saintly soul like him could and did have real influence within it. Although in general it is a waste of time to seek at Avignon for the stuff of which martyrs are made,[13] it is nevertheless instructive to note that at least one man made of that stuff was not a stranger there.

[13] As is noted by Norman P. Zacour, *Talleyrand, the Cardinal of Périgord (1301–1364)* (Transactions of the American Philosophical Society, new series, volume 50, part 7; Philadelphia, 1960), p. 73.

# Bibliography

## I. REFERENCE WORKS

Brom, G., *Guide aux Archives du Vatican*. 2nd edition. Rome, 1911.

Chanlaire, Pierre Grégoire, *Atlas national de France*. Paris, 1814.

Chevalier, Ulysse, *Répertoire des sources historiques du moyen âge; bio-bibliographique*. New edition. Paris, 1905–07. 2 vols.

Da Mosto, Andrea, *L'Archivio di Stato di Venezia, indice generale, storico, descrittivo ed analitico*. Bibliothèque des "Annales Institutorum," vol. V. Rome, 1937–40. 2 tomes.

Eubel, Conrad, *Hierarchia catholica medii aevi*. 2nd edition. Münster, 1913. Volume I.

Fink, Karl August, *Das vatikanische Archiv; Einführung in die Bestände und ihre Erforschung*. Rome, 1951.

Gams, Pius Bonifacius, *Series episcoporum ecclesiae catholicae.* Ratisbon, 1873.

Graesse, J. G. T., *Orbis Latinus: oder Verzeichnis der wichtigsten lateinischen Orts- und Ländernamen.* 2nd edition by F. Benedict. Berlin, 1909.

Potthast, A., *Wegweiser durch die Geschichtsbewerke des europäischen Mittelalters bis 1500.* Berlin, 1896. 2 vols.

Roumejoux, Anatole de, *Essai de bibliographie périgourdine.* Société historique et archéologique du Périgord, publications. Sauveterre, 1882.

Spruner, K. von, and Menke, Th., *Handatlas für die Geschichte des Mittelalters und der neueren Zeit.* Dritte Auflage. Gotha, 1880.

## II. SOURCES

*a. Documentary*

### I. MANUSCRIPTS

Paris, Bibliothèque de l'Arsenal.

Mézières, Philippe de, Letters and Papers. Ms. 499, fols. 134r–163r.

Rome, Archivio Segreto Vaticano.

Innocent VI, Litterae secretae, *Reg. Vat.* 235–38.

———, Litterae communes, *Reg. Aven.* 126, copied in *Reg. Vat.* 225; *Reg. Aven.* 127, copied in *Reg. Vat.* 227; *Reg. Aven.* 132–34; *Reg. Aven.* 140, copied in *Reg. Vat.* 234; *Reg. Aven.* 141, 144, 148; *Reg. Vat.* 241, 244.

Urban V, Litterae secretae, *Reg. Vat.* 245–47.

———, Litterae communes, *Reg. Aven.* 154, copied in *Reg. Vat.* 252; *Reg. Aven.* 155; *Reg. Aven.* 156, copied in *Reg. Vat.* 253; *Reg. Aven.* 157, copied in *Reg. Vat.* 261; *Reg. Vat.* 251.

Note: A microfilm containing most of the letters concerning

Pierre de Thomas in the above registers is in the library at Whitefriars Hall, Washington, D.C. This microfilm was prepared at the Vatican Library from a list of letters furnished by Joachim Smet, O. Carm., who had gone through the registers looking for materials about Pierre de Thomas. Fr. Smet kindly had this microfilm sent to me for use in my research. Most of the archival references in this study are based upon this microfilm. With the permission of Fr. Smet and his order a positive copy of it has been placed in the Henry Charles Lea Library at the University of Pennsylvania in Philadelphia.

Venice, Archivio di Stato.

*Liber secretorum collegii* (1363–66). Formerly in the Biblioteca Capponi, Florence.

*Secreta collegii,* vol. II (1354–63).

Senato, *Misti,* vols. XXVII–XXXI (1354–66).

Note: Microfilms of the above volumes are in the Henry Charles Lea Library at the University of Pennsylvania.

## 2. PUBLISHED

Bliss, W. H., and Tremlow, J. A., *Calendar of Entries in the Papal Registers relating to Great Britain and Ireland. Papal Letters, A.D. 1362–1404.* London, 1902. Volume IV.

Böhmer, J. F., *Regesta imperii, VIII. Die Regesten des Kaiserreichs unter Kaiser Karl IV (1346–1378),* ed. Alfons Huber. Innsbruck, 1877.

Cerasoli, Francesco, "Innocenzo VI e Giovanna I di Napoli; documenti inediti dell'Archivio Vaticano," *Archivio storico per le province napoletane,* XXII (1897), 183–203, 351–70, 507–28; XXIII (1898), 3–21, 275–304.

———, and Cipolla Carlo, "Innocenzo VI e casa Savoia, documenti dell'Archivio Vaticano," *Miscellanea di storia italiana,* XXXVIII (1902), 141–215.

Cornaro, Flaminio, *Ecclesiae venetae antiquis monumentis, nunc etiam primum editis, illustratae ac in decades distributae.* Venice, 1749. 12 vols.

Cydones, Demetrius, *La Correspondance de Démétrius Cydonès,* ed. Giuseppe Cammelli. Société d'Edition "Les Belles Lettres." Paris, 1930.

———, *Correspondance,* ed. R. J. Loenertz, O. P. Vol. I. Studi e testi, vol. 186. Vatican City, 1956.

Denifle, H., and Chatelain, E., *Chartularium universitatis Parisiensis.* Paris, 1889–97. 4 vols.

Déprez, Eugène, *Innocent VI (1352–1362). Lettres closes, patentes et curiales se rapportant à la France.* Bibliothèque des écoles françaises d'Athènes et de Rome. 3rd series, vol. IV, fasc. 1. Paris, 1909.

Dubrulle, M., *Les Registres d'Urbain V. Recueil des bulles de ce pape.* Bibliothèque des écoles françaises d'Athènes et de Rome, 3rd series, vol. XVII, fasc. 1. Paris, 1926.

Ehrle, Franz, *I piu antichi statuti della Facoltà di Teologia dell'Università di Bologna, contributo alla storia della scolastica medievale.* Universitatis Bononiensis Monumenta, vol. I. Bologna, 1932.

Fejer György, *Codex diplomaticus Hungariae ecclesiasticus et civilis.* Buda, 1829–44. 11 tomes, each with more than one volume.

Fierens, Alphonse, *Lettres d'Urbain V (1362–1370): vol. I (1362–1366).* Analecta Vaticano-Belgica, vol. IX. Rome, Brussels, Paris, 1928.

———, *Suppliques d'Urbain V (1362–1370).* Analecta Vaticano-Belgica, vol. VII. Rome, Brussels, Paris, 1914.

Gasnault, Pierre, and Laurent, M.-H., *Innocent VI (1352–1362). Lettres secrètes et curiales.* Bibliothèque des écoles françaises d'Athènes et de Rome. 3rd series, vol. IV, tome I. Paris, 1959–60. This is evidently a revised and enlarged second edition of the colection by Déprez.

Gelnhausen, Johann von, *Collectarius perpetuarum formarum Johannis de Geylnhausen,* ed. Hans Kaiser. Innsbruck, 1900.

Gerland, Ernst, *Das Archiv des Herzogs von Kandia im königlichen Staatsarchiv zu Venedig.* Strassburg, 1899.

Hoberg, Hermann, *Taxae pro communibus servitiis ex libris obligationum ab anno 1295 usque ad annum 1455 confectis.* Studi e testi, vol. 144. Vatican City, 1949.

Hoffmann, J. W., *Sammlung ungedruckter Nachrichten, Documenten und Urkunden.* Halle, 1736–37. 2 vols.

Huber, Alfons, *Addimentum primum ad Regesta imperii VIII (1346–1378).* Innsbruck, 1889.

Jorga, Neculai, "L'Épître de Philippe de Mézières à son neveu," *Bulletin de l'Institut pour l'étude de l'Europe sud-orientale,* VIII (1921), 27–40.

———, "Le Testament de Philippe de Mézières," *Bulletin de l'Institut pour l'étude de l'Europe sud-orientale,* VIII (1921), 119–40.

Jourdain, Charles Marie Gabriel Brechillet, *Index chronologicus chartarum pertinentium ad historiam universitatis Parisiensis ab ejus originibus ad finem decimi sexti saeculi.* Paris, 1862.

Lecacheux, P., and Mollat, G., *Urbain V (1362–1370). Lettres secrètes et curiales se rapportant à la France.* Bibliothèque des écoles françaises d'Athènes et de Rome. 3rd series, vol. V. Paris, 1902–54.

Ljubic, Sime, *Listine o odnosajih izmedju juznoga slavenstva i mletacke republike. Monumenta spectantia historiam Slavorum meridionalium,* vols. I–V, IX, XII, XVII, XXI–XXII. Zagreb, 1868–91.

Monsignanus, Eliseus, O. Carm., and Ximenez, Joseph A., O. Carm. (eds.), *Bullarium carmelitanum.* Rome, 1715–68. 4 vols.

*Monumenta Hungariae historica, Acta externa.* See Wenzel, Gusztav.

Paoli, Sebastiano, *Codice diplomatico del sacro militare Ordine Gerosolimitano, oggi di Malta.* Lucca, 1733–37. 2 vols.

Predelli, Riccardo (ed.), *I libri commemoriali della Republica di Venezia, regesti.* Monumenti storici pubblicati dalla R. Deputazione Veneta di storia patria, sèrie prima, documenti, I, III, VII–VIII, X–XI, XIII, XVII. Venice, 1876–1914.

Prochno, J., *Acta Urbani V (1362–70).* Monumenta Vaticana res gestas Bohemicas illustrantia, III. Prague, 1944.

Rattinger, D., S. J., "Der liber provisionum praelatorum Urbani V," *Historisches Jahrbuch der Goerres Gesellschaft,* XV (1894), 51–95.

*Repertorio diplomatico visconteo.* Raccolti e pubblicati in forma di registro dalla Società storica lombarda. Milan, 1911–18. 2 vols.

Riccoti, Ercola (ed.), *Liber iurium reipublicae Genuensis.* Historiae patriae monumenta, vols. VII and IX. Turin, 1854–57.

Sbaraglia, Giovanni Giacinto, *et. al.* (eds.), *Bullarium franciscanum.* Rome, 1759–1904. 7 vols.

Schaefer, Karl Heinrich, *Die Ausgaben der apostolischen Kammer unter Benedikt XII, Klemens VI und Innocenz VI (1335–1362).* Vatikanische Quellen zur Geschichte der päpstlichen Hof-und Finanzverwaltung, 1316–1378, vol. III. Paderborn, 1914.

———, *Die Ausgaben der apostolischen Kammer unter Johann XXII nebst den Jahresbilanzen von 1316–1335.* Vatikanische Quellen, vol. II, Paderborn, 1911.

———, *Die Ausgaben der apostolischen Kammer unter den Päpsten Urban V und Gregor XI (1362–1378) nebst Nachträgen und einem Glossar für alle drei Ausgabebände.* Vatikanische Quellen, vol. VI. Paderborn, 1937.

Schafarik, Joannes, *Acta archivi veneti spectantia ad historiam Serborum et reliquorum Slavorum meridionalium.* Belgrade, 1860–62. 2 vols.

Smićiklas,Tade, *et al.*, *Codex diplomaticus regni Croatiae, Dalmatiae et Slavoniae.* Zagreb, 1874–1934. 15 vols.

Theiner, Augustin, *Codex diplomaticus dominii temporalis S. Sedis.* Rome, 1861–62. 3 vols.

———, *Vetera monumenta historica Hungariam sacram illustrantia.* Rome, 1859–60. 2 vols.

———, *Vetera monumenta Slavorum meridionalium historiam illustrantia.* Rome, 1863–75. 2 vols.

———, and Miklosich, Franz, *Monumenta spectantia ad unionem ecclesiarum Graecae et Romanae.* Vienna, 1872.

Thomas, Georg Martin, and Predelli, Riccardo, *Diplomatarium Veneto-Levantinum.* Monumenti storici pubblicati dalla R. Deputazione Veneta di storia patria. sèrie prima, documenti, vols. V and IX. Venice, 1880–99.

Wenzel, Gusztav, *Magyar Diplomacziai Emlékek az Anjou Koraból. Monumenta Hungariae historica, Acta externa,* 4 osztály, part A. Budapest, 1874–76. 3 vols.

Werunsky, Emil, *Excerpta ex registris Clementis VI et Innocentii VI summorum pontificum historiam s. r. imperii sub regimine Karoli IV illustrantia.* Innsbruck, 1885.

Wessels, Gabriel, O. Carm. (ed.), *Acta capitulorum generalium Ordinis Fratrum B. V. Mariae de Monte Carmelo.* Rome, 1912–34. 2 vols.

Zimmerman, Benedict, O.C.D., *Monumenta historica carmelitana.* Lerins, 1907.

*b. Literary*

Amadi, Francesco, *Chroniques d'Amadi et de Strambaldi,* ed. René de Mas Latrie. Collection des documents inédits sur l'histoire de France, première série, histoire politique, vol. VII. Paris, 1891–93. 2 vols. (Vol. I contains the chronicle of Amadi and vol. II that of Strambaldi.)

Baluze, S., *Vitae paparum Avenionensium, hoc est historia pontificum Romanorum qui in Gallia sederunt ab anno*

*Christi MCCCV usque ad annum MCCCXCIV.* New edition, ed. G. Mollat. Paris, 1914–27. 4 vols.

Bustron, Florio, *Chronique de l'île de Chypre.* Collection des documents inédits sur l'histoire de France; mélanges historiques, vol. 100. Paris, 1886.

Capgrave, John, *The Chronicle of England,* ed. Francis Charles Hingeston. Rerum Brittanicarum medii aevi scriptores, no. 1. London, 1858.

Carmesson, Juan, *Vita sancti Petri Thomae patriarchae Constantinopolitani, legati apostolici,* ed. Daniel a Virgine Maria, O. Carm. Antwerp, 1666. Also published in *Spec. carm.,* II, 171–95. The latter edition is used in this work.

*Chronicon Moguntinum,* in *Die Chroniken der deutschen Städte,* vol. XVIII, part I, ed. C. Hegel. Leipzig, 1882.

*Chronique des quatre premiers Valois.* See Luce, Siméon.

Delachenal, Jean Pierre François Roland, *Chroniques des règnes de Jean II et Charles V.* Société de l'Histoire de France. Paris, 1910–20. 3 vols.

Denifle, Heinrich, O. P., "Quellen zur Gelehrtengeschichte des Carmeliten Ordens im XIII und XIV Jahrhundert," *Archiv für Literatur-und Kirchengeschichte des Mittelalters,* V (1889), 365–84.

Froissart, Jean, *Oeuvres de Froissart.* Publiées avec les variantes des divers manuscrits par M. le baron Kervyn de Lettenhove. Brussels, 1867–74. 19 vols.

———, *Chroniques de J. Froissart,* ed. Siméon Luce. Société de l'Histoire de France. Paris, 1869–88. 8 vols.

Galbraith, V. H. (ed.), *The Anonimalle Chronicle, 1333 to 1381.* Publications of the University of Manchester, no. 175; Historical Series, no. 45. Manchester, 1927.

Hildesheim, Johann of, *Defensorium Ordinis Fratrum gloriosissimae Dei Genetricis Mariae de Monte Carmelo per modum dialogi,* in *Spec. carm.,* I, 145–59.

Knighton, Henry, *Chronicon Henrici Knighton: vel Cnitthon, monachi leycestrensis,* ed. Joseph Rawson Lumley. Rerum Brittanicarum medii aevi scriptores, no. 92. London, 1889–95. 2 vols.

Luce, Siméon, *Chronique des quatres premiers Valois (1327–1393).* Société de l'Histoire de France. Paris, 1862.

Machaut, Guillaume de, *La Prise d'Alexandrie ou chronique du roi Pierre de Lusignan,* ed. Louis de Mas Latrie. Publiée pour la Société de l'Orient latin. Geneva, 1877.

Makhairas, Leontios, *Recital concerning the Sweet Land of Cyprus, entitled "Chronicle,"* ed. and trans. R. M. Dawkins. Oxford, 1932. 2 vols.

Mattheus de Griffonibus, *Memoriale historicum de rebus Bononiensium,* eds. L. Frati and A. Sorbelli. RISS, new edition, tome XVIII, part 2. Città di Castello, 1902.

Mézières, Philippe de, *Vita Sancti Petri Thomasii,* in *Acta Sanctorum bollandiana.* New edition, ed. Jean Carnadet, vol. III. Paris, Rome, 1863. (Originally published in 1643 by Gottfried Henschen, S. J.)

————, *Vita Sancti Petri Thomasii ex ordine fratrum beatissimae Virginis Mariae de Monte Carmelo, episcopi Pactensis et Coronensis, archiepiscopi Cretensis et patriarchae Constantinopolitani ac legati apostolici,* ed. Gottfried Henschen, S. J. Antwerp, 1659.

————, *The Life of Saint Peter Thomas,* ed. Joachim Smet, O. Carm. Textus et studia carmelitana, vol. II. Rome, 1954.

Molinier, A., "Le *Miroir historial* de Jean de Noyal (1223–1380)," *Annuaire-Bulletin de la Société de l'Histoire de France,* XX (1883), 246–75.

Moranville, H., *Chronographia regum Francorum (1270–1380).* Société de l'Histoire de France. Paris, 1891–97. 3 vols.

Muratori, Ludovico Antonio, *Rerum italicarum scriptores ab anno aerae christianae quingentesimo ad millesimum quingentesimum.* Milan, 1723–51. 28 vols.

Nangis, Guillaume de, *Chronique latine de Guillaume de Nangis de 1113 à 1300 avec les continuations de cette chronique de 1300 à 1368,* ed. H. Géraud. Société de l'Histoire de France. Paris, 1843. 2 vols.

Pompei, Alphonsus, O. F. M. Conv., "Sermones duo parisiensis saeculi XIV de conceptione Beatae Virginis Mariae et Scoti influxus in evolutionem sententiae immaculistae Parisiis, *Miscelianea francescana,* LV (1955), 480–507.

Smet, Joseph Jean de, *Corpus chronicorum Flandriae.* Brussels, 1837–65. 4 vols.

Sorbelli, Albano (ed.), *Corpus chronicorum Bononiensium.* RISS, new edition, tome XVIII, part 1. Città di Castello, 1905–39. 4 vols.

Strambaldi, Diomede. See Amadi, Francesco.

Thompson, Edward Maude, *Chronicon Angliae ab anno 1328 ad annum 1388, auctore monacho quondam Sancti Albani.* Rerum Brittanicarum medii aevi scriptores, no. 64. London, 1874.

Trissa, Jean, *De magistris parisiensibus,* in MHC, pp. 376–93, and in Denifle, "Quellen zur Gelehrtengeschichte des Carmeliten Ordens im XIII und XIV Jahrhundert," *Archiv für Literatur- und Kirchengeschichte des Mittelalters,* V, 365–84, and in Xiberta, *De scriptoribus scholasticis seculi XIV ex ordine Carmelitarum,* pp. 23–39.

————, *De prioribus generalibus,* in Xiberta, *op. cit.,* pp. 39–42.

Villani, Matteo, *Cronica di Matteo Villani a miglior lezione ridotta,* ed. Ignazio Moutier. Florence, 1825–26. 6 vols.

Walsingham, Thomas, *Historica Anglicana,* ed. Henry Thomas Riley. Rerum Brittanicarum medii aevi scriptores, no. 28, part I. London, 1863. 2 vols.

# III. SECONDARY LITERATURE

*a. Manuscripts*

Besançon, Bibliothèque de,

Gallien, Louis, O. Carm., "De historia priorum et procuratorum generalium et priorum provincialium," Mss. 784–90. Paper, seventeenth century. 7 vols.

Brussels, Koninklijke Bibliotheek,

Armand Gerard, canon of Sarlat, letter to Gottfried Henschen, S. J., April 29, 1662. Ms. 8495, fols. 132r–135v.

*b. Earlier Printed Works*

Bale, John, *Scriptorum illustrium Maioris Brittaniae . . . catalogus*. Basel, 1557–59. 2 parts.

Bosio, Jacomo, *Dell'Istoria della sacra religione et illustrissima militia di San Giovanni Gierosolimitano*. Rome, 1594–1621. 3 vols.

Bostius, Arnoldus, O. Carm., *De illustris viris Ordinis beatissimae Dei Genetricis Virginis Mariae de Monte Carmelo,* in *Spec. carm.,* II, 886–96, in Carmesson, *Vita,* pp. 107–12, and in Daniel a Virgine Maria, *Epitomè,* pp. 3–9.

————, *De patronatu et patrocinio beatissimae Virginis Mariae in dicatum sibi Carmeli Ordinem,* in *Spec. carm.,* I, 375–431.

Bullaeus, C. E., See Du Boulay, César Égasse.

Bzovius, Abraham, *Annalium ecclesiasticorum post Caesarem Baronium continuatio*. Cologne, 1616–30. 9 vols., numbered XIII–XXI.

Ciaconius, Alphonsus, O. P., *Vitae et res gestae pontificum Romanorum et S. R. E. cardinalium ab initio nascentis ecclesiae usque ad Clementem IX p. o. m.* Rome, 1677. 4 vols.

Cornaro, Flaminio, *Creta sacra sive de episcopis utriusque ritus graeci et latini in insula Cretae*. Venice, 1755. 2 vols.

Daniel a Virgine Maria, O. Carm., *Dissertatio apologetica pro revelatione ac sponsione SS. Virg. Deiparae Mariae, facta S. Petro Thomasio, Patriarchae Constantinop. de patrocinio et perpetua duratione Ordinis Fratrum eiusdem Beatissimae Virginis Dei Genetricis Mariae de Monte Carmelo.* Antwerp, 1659. Bound with the 1659 edition of Mézières, *Vita Sancti Petri Thomasii.*

————, *Epitome vitae S. Petri Thomasii et scala virtutum quibus tamquam gradibus ad supremum perfectionis fastigium conscendit.* Antwerp, 1659. Bound with the 1659 edition of Mézières, *Vita Sancti Petri Thomasii.*

————, *Speculum carmelitanum.* Antwerp, 1680. 2 vols. in 4.

————, *Vinea Carmeli seu Historia Eliani Ordinis Beatissimae Virginis Mariae de Monte Carmelo, contracta in variis opusculis, regulam, originem, propaginem, eventus varios, patrocinium multiplex, viros illustres, et provincias omnes delineantibus.* Antwerp, 1662.

Du Boulay, César Égasse, *Historia universitatis parisiensis, ipsius fundationem, nationes, facultates, magistratus, decreta, censuras & iudicia in negotiis fidei, privilegia, comitia, legationes, reformationes; item antiquissimas Gallorum academias, aliarum quoque universitatum & religiosorum ordinum, qui ex eadem communi matre exierunt, institutiones & fundationes, aliaque id genus cum instrumentis publicis & authenticis a Carlo M. ad nostra tempora ordine chronologico complectens.* Paris, 1665–73. 6 vols.

Fabricius, Johann Christian, *Bibliotheca Latina mediae et infimae aetatis.* Hamburg, 1734–46. 6 vols.

Faleoni, Celso, *Memorie historiche della chiesa Bolognese e suoi pastori.* Bologna, 1649.

Felibien, Michel, *Histoire de la ville de Paris.* Paris, 1725. 5 vols.

Finetti, Francesco, S. J., *Panegirico in lode di S. Pietro Tommasi, fundatore del Collegio de' Teologi di Bologna.* Bologna, 1797.

Gonzalez Davila, Gil, *Teatro ecclesiastico de las ciudades e iglesias catedrales de España.* Salamanca, 1618. Vol. I in 5 parts.

Grossi, Joannes, O. Carm., *Viridiarum Ordinis B. Virginis Mariae de Monte Carmelo,* in *Spec. carm.,* I, 131–44.

Joseph de Santa Teresa, O. Carm., *Flores del Carmelo; Vidas de los santos de nuestra señora del Carmen; que reza su Religion, assi en comun, como en particulares conventos.* Madrid, 1678.

Lezana, Joannes Baptista de, O. Carm., *Annales sacri, prophetici, et eliani Ordinis Beatae Virginis Mariae de Monte Carmeli.* Rome, 1645–56. 4 vols.

Loredano, Giovanni Francesco, *Histoire des rois de Chypre de la maison de Lusignan.* Paris, 1732. 2 vols.

Michel du Saint-Esprit, O. Carm., *La Vie admirable de S. Pierre Thomas.* Paris, 1652.

Palaeonydorus, Joannes, O. Carm., *Fasciculus tripartitus historiarum prophetici et eliani Ordinis Beatissimae Virginis Mariae de Monte Carmeli,* in *Spec. carm.,* I, 220–73.

Paulo di S. Ignatio, O. Carm., *Anno memorabile de' Carmelitani.* Milan, 1688. Vol. I. Contains Italian translation of the biographies of Pierre de Thomas by Juan Carmesson and Luke Wadding.

Pedro de la Epifania, O. C. D., *Vida y milagros de S. Pedro Thomas, carmelita, patriarcha de Constantinople, martyr illustrimo y abogado contra la mortal peste y epidemia.* Seville, 1655.

Philippe de la Très Sainte Trinité, O. C. D., *Decor Carmeli religiosi in splendoribus sanctorum ac illustrium religiosorum et monalium.* Lyons, 1665. 3 parts.

Pirri, Rocco, *Sicilia sacra disquisitionibus et notitiis illustrata.*

3rd edition, ed. Antonio Mongitore. Venice, 1733. 2 vols.

Quillicus, Giuseppe Maria, O. Carm., *Il legato apostolico espresso mirabilmente nella vita prodigiosissima dell'invitissimo martire S. Pietro Tomaso Carmelitano, discritta e divisa in tre parti.* Lucca, 1674.

Raynaldus, Odoricus, *Annales ecclesiastici ab anno quo desinit Caesarius Cardinalis Baronius MCXCVIII usque ad annum MDXXXIV continuati.* Cologne, 1690–94. 9 vols., numbered XIII–XXI.

Saracenus, Petrus Thomas, O. Carm., *Menologium Carmelitarum in duas distributum partes:* . . . Bologna, 1627.

Tracagnus, Marcus, O. Carm., *Oratio de laudibus S. Petri Thomae martyris, habita Bononiae.* Venice, 1581.

Trithemius, Johannes, *De scriptoribus ecclesiasticis,* published in Johann Albert Fabricius, *Bibliotheca ecclesiastica.* Hamburg, 1718.

Ughelli, Ferdinando, *Italia sacra.* 2nd ed., Niccolo Coleti. Venice, 1717–22. 10 vols. in 9.

Verci, Giovanni Battista, *Storia della marca trivigiana e veronese.* Venice, 1786–91. 20 vols.

Villers, Cosma de, *Bibliotheca carmelitana.* Arles, 1752. 2 vols. Facsimile edition, ed. Gabriel Wessels, O. Carm., Rome, 1927.

*Vita del glorioso S. Giovanni apostolo ed evangelista con alcuni miracoli della santissima croce che conservasi nella scuola grande di detto santo, avuto in dono fino dall' anno 1370.* Venice, 1752.

Wadding, Luke, *Annales Minorum seu trium Ordinum a S. Francisco institutorum.* 3rd edition. Quaracchi, Italy, 1931–35. 25 vols. Originally published in the seventeenth century.

————, *Scriptores Ordinis Minorum, quibus accessit syllabus illorum qui ex eodem Ordine pro fide Christi fortiter occubuerunt.* Rome, 1650. Editio novissima, Rome, 1906.

————, *Vita et res gestae B. Petri Thomae Aquitani, ex*

*Ordine B. Mariae Virginis a Monte Carmelo, Patriarchae
Constantinopolitani et Sedis Apostolicae legati.* Lyons, 1637.


c. *Modern Works*

Adeney, Walter F., *The Greek and Eastern Churches.* Edin-
burgh, 1908.

Albasini, Costanzo, O. F. M., *San Domenico e i suoi a Venezia.*
Venice, 1922.

Ambrosius a St. Theresa, O. C. D., "Monasticon carmelitanum,
seu lexicon geographicum omnium fundationum universi
Ordinis Carmelitarum ab initio eiusdem Ordinis usque ad
nostra tempora." *Analecta Ordinis Carmelitarum Discalceatorum,"* XXII (1950), 45–144, 201–96, 381–480, 569–
616.

Andrew of St. Mary, O. C. D., *The Order of Our Lady of
Mount Carmel; an Historical Notice.* Bruges, 1913.

Antoine-Marie de la Présentation, O. C. D., *Le Carmel en
France; étude historique.* Toulouse, 1936–39. 7 vols.

Atiya, Aziz Suryal, *The Crusade in the Later Middle Ages.*
London, 1938.

Biscaro, Gerolamo, "Le relazioni dei Visconti di Milano con
la Chiesa. L'arcivescovo Giovanni, Clemente VI e Innocenzo
VI," *Archivio storico lombardo,* series 6, vol. V (1928),
pp. 1–96.

Bloch, Marc, *Les Caractères originaux de l'histoire rurale française.* Instituttet for Sammenlignende Kulturforskning, serie
B, skrifter, XIX. Oslo, 1931.

Boislisle, A., "Projet de croisade du premier Duc de Bourbon,"
*Annuaire-Bulletin de la Société de l'Histoire de France,* IX
(1872), 230–36, 246–56.

Boissonade, Jean François, *Anecdota nova.* Paris, 1844.

Bollandists, Society of the, *Bibliotheca hagiographica latina
antiquae et mediae aetatis.* Brussels, 1898–1901. 2 vols.

————, *Catalogus codicum hagiographicorum latinorum saeculo XVI qui asservantur in Bibliotheca Nationali parisiensi.* Brussels, 1889–93. 3 vols.

Brehier, Louis, "Attempts at Reunion of the Greek and Latin Churches," *Cambridge Medieval History,* IV (New York, Cambridge, 1923), 594–617.

————, *L'Église et l'orient au moyen-âge—les croisades.* 4th edition. Paris, 1921.

Brown, Horatio F., *Studies in the History of Venice.* New York, 1907. 2 vols.

Brun, Robert, *Avignon au temps des papes.* Paris, 1928.

Burke, Peter Thomas, O. C. D., *A Medieval Hero of Carmel.* Dublin, 1901.

Caioli, Paulo, O. Carm., *S. Andrea Corsini, Carmelitano, vescovo di Fiesole, 1301–1374.* Florence, 1929.

Camera, Matteo, *Elucubrazioni storico-diplomatiche su Giovanna I, regina di Napoli, e Carlo III di Durazzo.* Salerno, 1889.

Cammelli, Giuseppe, "Demetrio Cidonio," *Studi italiani di filologia classica,* new series, vol. I (1920), 140–61.

————, "Personnagi bizantini dei secoli XIV–XV attraverso le epistole di Demetrio Cidonio," *Bessarione, pubblicazione periodica di studi orientali,* XXIV (1920), 77–108.

Campbell, Anna Montgomery, *The Black Death and Men of Learning.* New York, 1931.

Claretta, Gaudenzio, "Roberto di Durazzo dei reali di Napoli e la famiglia di Jacopo di Savoia, principe d'Acaja," *Atti della Reale Accademia delle Scienze di Torino,* XV (1879), 743–70.

Couture, Leonce, "Le Bienheureux Pierre de Thomas, est-il né a Condom?" *Revue de Gascogne,* XXXVIII (1897), 88.

Delahaye, Hippolyte, S. J., "Saints de Chypre," *Analecta bollandiana,* XXVI (1927), 161–301.

Delaville le Roulx, Joseph Marie Antoine, *La France en Orient au XIV^e siècle; expéditions du Maréchal Boucicaut.* Paris, 1886. 2 vols.

————, *Les Hospitaliers à Rhodes jusqu'à la mort de Philibert de Naillac (1310–1421).* Paris, 1913.

Denifle, Heinrich, O. P., *Die Entstehung der Universitäten des Mittelalters bis 1400.* Berlin, 1885. Vol. I of a projected work, *Die Universitäten des Mittelalters.* No more was published.

Déprez, Eugène, "Les Funerailles de Clément VI et d'Innocent VI d'après les comptes de la cour pontificale," *Melanges d'archéologie et d'histoire de l'École française de Rome,* XX (1900), 235–50.

Discalced Carmelites of Boston and Santa Clara, *Carmel, its History, Spirit, and Saints.* Compiled from approved sources by the Discalced Carmelites of Boston and Santa Clara. New York, 1927.

Donaver, Federico, *La storia della repubblica di Genova.* Genoa, 1913. 2 vols.

Dräseke, J., "Der Übergang der Osmanen nach Europa im XIV Jahrhundert," *Neues Jahrbuch für das klassische Altertum, Geschichte und deutsche Literatur,* XXXI (1913), 476–504.

Du Cange, Charles du Fresne, *Histoire de l'empire de Constantinople sous les empereurs français jusqu'à la conquête des turcs.* New edition, Paris, 1826. 2 vols.

Dujarric-Descombes, "Recherches sur les historiens du Périgord au XVIIᵉ siècle," *Bulletin de la Société historique et archéologique de Périgord,* IX (1882), 67–76, 162–88, 257–93, 371–412, 464–86.

Duvergé, Suzanne, "La Rôle de la papauté dans la guerre de l'Aragon contre Gênes (1351–1356)," *Mélanges d'archéologie et d'histoire de l'École française de Rome,* L (1933), 221–49.

Eckhart, Ferenc, *A Short History of the Hungarian People.* London, 1931.

Enlart, Camille, "Fouilles dans les églises de Famagouste de Chypre," *The Archeological Journal*, LXII (1905), 195–217.

Escande, Jean Joseph, *Histoire du Périgord*. Cahors, 1934. 2 vols.

Feret, Pierre, *La Faculté de théologie de Paris et ses docteurs les plus célèbrés—moyen âge*. Paris, 1894–97. 4 vols.

Fessler, Ignaz, *Geschichte von Ungarn*. Leipzig, 1815–25. 10 vols.

Filippini, Francesco, *Il Cardinale Egidio Albornoz*. Bologna, 1933.

————, "La seconda legazione del Card. Albornoz in Italia (1358–1367)," *Studi storici*, XII (1903), 263–337; XIII (1904), 3–52; XIV (1905), 29–68.

Fournier, Marcel, *Les Statuts et privilèges des universités françaises depius leur fondation jusqu'en 1789*. Paris, 1890–94. 4 vols.

Fraknoi, Vilmos, *Magyarország egyházi és politikai összeköltetései a római Szent-székkel* (*Les relations ecclesiastiques et politiques de la Hongrie avec le Saint-Siège*). Budapest, 1901–03. 3 vols.

Franklin, Alfred Louis Auguste, *Les Anciennes bibliothèques de Paris, églises, monastères, collèges, etc.* Paris, 1867–73. 3 vols.

Gasquet, Francis Aidan, *The Great Pestilence* (*A.D. 1348–9*), *Now Commonly Known as the Black Death*. London, 1893.

Gay, Jules, *Le Pape Clément VI et les affaires d'Orient* (*1342–1352*). Paris, 1904.

Gibbons, Herbert Adams, *The Foundation of the Ottoman Empire, a History of the Osmanlis up to the Death of Bayezid I* (*1300–1403*). New York, 1916.

Giustiniani, Agostino, *Annali della Repubblica di Genova*. 3rd edition. Genoa, 1854. 2 vols.

Göller, E., "Aus der Kanzlei der Päpste und ihrer Legaten,"

*Quellen und Forschungen aus italienischen Archiven und Bibliotheken,* X (1907), 319–24.

Golubovich, Girolamo, O. F. M., *Biblioteca bio-bibliographica della Terra Santa e dell'Oriente Francescano.* Quaracchi, Italy, 1906–48. 21 vols. in 3 series.

Gourges, Alexis J. D. de, *Dictionnaire topographique du département de la Dordogne, comprenant les noms de lieu anciens et modernes.* Paris, 1873.

Hackett, John, *A History of the Orthodox Church of Cyprus.* London, 1901.

Halecki, Oskar, *Un Empereur de Byzance à Rome, vingt ans de travail pour l'union des églises et pour la défense de l'Empire d'Orient, 1355–1375.* Travaux historiques de la Société des Sciences et des Lettres de Varsovie, vol. VIII. Warsaw, 1930.

Hecker, I. F. C., *The Epidemics of the Middle Ages. No. I, The Black Death in the Fourteenth Century,* trans. B. G. Babington. Philadelphia, 1837.

Hill, Sir George Francis, *A History of Cyprus.* Cambridge, 1940–52. 4 vols.

Hodgson, F. C., *Venice in the Thirteenth and Fourteenth Centuries.* London, 1910.

Homan, Bálint, *Gli Angioini di Napoli in Ungheria, 1290–1403,* trans. Luigi Zambra and Rodolfo Mosca. Reale Accademia d'Italia, Studi e documenti, VIII. Rome, 1938.

Jegerlehner, J., "Der Aufstand der kandiotischen Ritterschaft gegen das Mutterland Venedig," *Byzantinische Zeitschrift,* XII (1903), 78–125.

Jireček, Joseph Konstantin, *Geschichte der Serben.* Gotha, 1911–18. 2 vols.

Jorga, Neculai, "Collection de lettres de Philippe de Maizières [sic] (notice sur le ms 499 de la Bibl. de l'Arsenal)," *Revue historique,* XLIX (1892), 39–57, 306–22.

———, "Latins et Grecs d'Orient et l'établissement des Turcs

en Europe, 1342–1362," *Byzantinische Zeitschrift,* XV (1906), 179–222.

————, *Philippe de Mézières (1327–1405) et la croisade au XIV^e siècle.* Bibliothèque de l'École des Hautes Études, sciences philologiques et historiques, vol. 110. Paris, 1896.

Kaeppeli, Thomas, O. P., "Deux nouveaux ouvrages de Fr. Philippe Incontri de Péra, O. P.," *Archivum Fratrum Praedicatorum,* XXIII (1953), 161–83.

Kidd, Beresford James, *The Churches of Eastern Christendom from A.D. 451 to the Present Time.* London, 1927.

Koch, Heinrich Hubert, *Die Karmelitenklöster der niederdeutschen Provinz 13. bis 16. Jahrhundert.* Freiburg im Breisgau, 1889.

Kretschmayr, Heinrich, *Geschichte von Venedig.* Gotha, 1905–34. 4 vols.

Léonard, Émile G., *Histoire de Jeanne I^re, reine de Naples, comtesse de Provence (1343–1382).* Monaco and Paris, 1932–37. 3 vols.

Loenertz, Raymond J., O. P., "Fr. Philippe de Bindo Incontri, O. P., du couvent de Péra, inquisiteur en Orient," *Archivum Fratrum Praedicatorum,* XVIII (1948), 265–80.

————, *Les Recueils de lettres de Démétrius Cydonès.* Studi e testi, vol. 131. Vatican City, 1947.

Luchaire, Achille, *Manuel des institutions françaises, période des Capétiens directs.* Paris, 1892.

Magnan, Jean Baptiste, *Histoire du B. Urbain V et de son siècle d'après les manuscrits du Vatican.* 2nd edition. Paris, 1863.

Marti de Barcelona, O. F. M. Cap., "Fra Pere Tomàs," *Estudis franciscans,* XXXIX (1927), 90–103.

Mas Latrie, Louis de, *Commerce et expéditions militaires de la France et de Venise au moyen-âge.* Paris, 1879.

————, "Histoire des archevêques latins de l'île de Chypre," *Archives de l'Orient latin,* II (1884), 207–328.

————, *Histoire de l'île de Chypre sous le règne des princes de la maison de Lusignan.* Paris, 1852–61. 3 vols.

————, "Nouvelles preuves de l'histoire de Chypre," *Bibliothèque de l'École des chartes,* XXIV (1873), 47–87.

————, "Les Patriarches latins de Constantinople," *Revue de l'Orient latin,* III (1895), 433–56.

Mazzetti, Serafino, *Repertorio di tutti i professori, antichi e moderni, della famosa Università e del celebre Istituto delle Scienze di Bologna.* Bologna, 1848.

McCaffrey, Patrick Romaeus, O. Carm., *The White Friars, an Outline Carmelite History, with Special Reference to the English-Speaking Provinces.* Dublin, 1926.

Melchior de Ste. Marie, "Carmel (Ordre de Notre-Dame du Mont-Carmel)," *Dictionnaire d'histoire et de géographie ecclésiastique,* ed. Alfred Baudrillart, *et. al.,* XI (Paris, 1939), cols. 1070–1104.

Mercati, Giovanni, *Notizie di Procoro e Demetrio Cidone.* Studi e testi, vol. 56. Vatican City, 1931.

Miller, William, *Essays on the Latin Orient.* Cambridge, 1921.

————, "The Gattilusj of Lesbos, 1355–1462," *Byzantinische Zeitschrift,* XXII (1913) 406–47. Also published in *Essays on the Latin Orient,* pp. 313–53.

————, *The Latins in the Levant, a History of the Frankish Empire (1204–1566).* London, 1908.

Mollat, G., "La Diplomatie pontificale au XIV$^e$ siècle," in *Mélanges d'histoire du moyen-âge dediés à la mémoire de Louis Halphen* (Paris, 1951), pp. 507–12.

————, *Les Papes d'Avignon, 1305–1378.* 9th edition. Paris, 1949.

Mould, Daphne Desiree Charlotte Pochin. See Pochin-Mould, Daphne.

Müntz, E., "L'Argent et le luxe à la cour pontificale d'Avignon," *Revue des questions historiques,* LXVI (1899), 5–44, 378–406.

Muratore, Dino, *Una principessa sabauda sul trono di Byzantio—Giovanna di Savoia, imperatrice Anna Paleologina.* Chambéry, 1906.

Nohl, Johannes, *The Black Death, a Chronicle of the Plague,* trans. C. H. Clarke. London, 1926.

Norden, Walter, *Das Papsttum und Byzanz, die Trennung der beiden Mächte und das Problem ihrer Wiedervereinigung bis zum Untergange des byzantinischen Reichs.* Berlin, 1903.

Novak, Gregorio, "L'alleanza veneto-serba nel secolo XIV," *Archivio veneto-tridentino,* VIII (1925), 1–39.

Pagano, Carlo, *Delle imprese e del dominio dei Genovesi nella Grecia; libri quattro.* 2nd edition. Genoa, 1852.

Pall, Francisc, "Les Croisades en Orient au bas moyen-âge; observations critiques sur l'ouvrage de M. Atiya," *Revue d'histoire du Sud-Est européen,* XIX (1942), 563–83.

Parraud, A., *Vie de Saint Pierre Thomas de l'ordre des Carmes, fervent serviteur de Marie, patriarche titulaire de Constantinople, légat de la croisade de 1365.* Avignon, 1895.

Plieux, A., "Les Deux derniers abbés de Condom," *Revue de Gascogne,* XXII (1881), 32–35.

Pochin-Mould, Daphne, *The Life of Saint Peter Thomas.* New York, 1961.

Prou, Maurice, *Étude sur les relations politiques du pape Urbain V avec les rois de France Jean II et Charles V (1362–1370).* Bibliothèque de l'École des Hautes Études, sciences philologiques et historiques, vol. 76. Paris, 1888.

Purković, Miodrag Al., *Avinjonske pape i srpske zemlje.* Pozarevac, 1934.

Rashdall, Hastings, *The Universities of Europe in the Middle Ages,* ed. F. M. Powicke and A. B. Emden. Oxford, 1936. 3 vols.

Riant, Paul Edouard Didier, "Dépouillement des tomes XXI–

XXII de l'*Orbis christianus* de Henri de Suarez (Paris, Bibl. Nat. lat. 8983–8985)—patriarcats de Constantinople et de Jerusalem," *Archives de l'Orient latin*, I (1883), 257–87.

Rodd, Sir Rennell, *The Princes of Achaia and the Chronicles of Morea, a Study of Greece in the Middle Ages*. London, 1907.

Romanin, Samuele, *Storia documentata di Venezia*. Venice. 1853–61. 10 vols.

Rosier, Irenaeus, O. Carm., *Biographisch en bibliographisch overzicht van de vroomheid in de nederlandse Carmel van 1235 tot het midden der achttiende eeuw*. Studien en tekstuitgaven van *Ons Geestelyk Erf*, 10. Tielt, 1950.

Sbaraglia, Giovanni Giacinto, *Supplementum et castigatio ad scriptores trium Ordinum S. Francisci a Waddingo aliisve descriptos*. Editio nova. Rome, 1908–36. 3 parts.

Schaefer, Karl Heinrich, *Deutsche Ritter und Edelknechte in Italien während des 14 Jahrhunderts*. Quellen und Forschungen aus dem Gebiete der Geschichte, herausgegeben von der Goerres-Gesellschaft, vols. XV, XVI, XXV. Paderborn, 1911–40.

Scheepstra, Trijntje Jantine Annette, *Van den heilighen drien Coninghen. Middelnederlandse Teksten*. Groningen, 1914.

See, Henri, *Les Classes rurales et le régime domanial en France au moyen-âge*. Paris, 1901.

Setton, Kenneth M., "Archbishop Pierre d'Ameil in Naples and the Affair of Aimon III of Geneva (1363–1364)," *Speculum*, XXVIII (1953), 643–91.

———, "The Byzantine Background to the Italian Renaissance," *Proceedings of the American Philosophical Society*, C (1956), 1–76.

———, *Catalan Domination of Athens, 1311–1388*. Cambridge, Mass., 1948.

Sorbelli, Albano, "La lotta tra Genova e Venezia per il predominio del Mediterraneo; I. 1350–1355," *Memorie della R. Accademia delle Scienze dell'Istituto di Bologna, Classe di Scienze morali,* series I, vol. V (1910–11), 87–157. Also published separately, Bologna, 1921.

———, *La signoria di Giovanni Visconti a Bologna e le sue relazione con la Toscania.* Bologna, 1901.

———, and Simeoni, Luigi, *Storia della Università di Bologna.* Bologna, 1944–47. 2 vols.

Souchon, Martin, *Die Papstwahlen von Bonifaz VIII bis Urban VI und die Entstehung des Schismas 1378.* Brunswick, 1888.

Spinka, Matthew, *A History of Christianity in the Balkans, a Study in the Spread of Byzantine Culture among the Slavs.* Studies in Church History of the American Society of Church History, vol. I. Chicago, 1933.

Tamizey de Larroque, Philippe, "Le Bienheureux Pierre Thomas, est-il né à Condom?" *Revue de Gascogne,* XXXVII (1896), 534–36.

Teetaert, Am., "Pierre Thomas," *Dictionnaire de théologie catholique,* ed. A. Vacant, E. Mangenot, and E. Amann, vol. XII, part 2 (Paris, 1935), 2046–48.

Temperly, Harold V. W., *History of Serbia.* London, 1917.

Thorndike, Lynn, *University Records and Life in the Middle Ages.* Columbia University Records of Civilization, no. 38. New York, 1944.

Urbani de Gheltof, Giuseppe Marino, *Guida storico-artistica della Scuola di S. Giovanni Evangelista in Venezia.* Venice, 1895.

Vancini, Oreste, "Bologna della chiesa (1360–1376)," *Atti e memorie della R. Deputazione di storia patria per le provincie di Romagna,* series 3, vols. XXIV (1906), 239–320, 508–52; XXV (1907), 16–108.

Ventimiglia, Mariano, O. Carm., *Historia chronologia priorum generalium latinorum Ordinis beatissimae Virginis Mariae de Monte Carmelo*. Naples, 1773, and facsimile reprint, Rome, 1929.

Villier, M., "La Question de l'union des églises entre Grecs et Latins depuis le concile de Lyon jusqu'à celui de Florence, 1274–1438," *Revue d'histoire ecclésiastique,* XVII (1921), 260–305, 515–32; XVIII (1922), 20–60.

Voinovitch, Louis de, *Histoire de Dalmatie.* 2nd edition. Paris, 1934. 2 vols.

Werunsky, Emil, *Der erste Römerzug Kaisers Karls IV (1354–1355).* Innsbruck, 1878.

————, *Geschichte Karls IV und seiner Zeit.* Innsbruck, 1890–92. 3 vols.

Wurm, Hermann Joseph, *Cardinal Albornoz, der zweite Begründer des Kirchenstaates; ein Lebensbild.* Paderborn, 1892.

Xiberta y Roqueta, Bartholomé María, O. Carm., *De scriptoribus scholasticis saeculi XIV ex Ordine Carmelitarum.* Bibliothèque de la Revue d'histoire ecclésiastique, fasc. VI. Louvain, 1931.

Zacour, Norman P., *Talleyrand: the Cardinal of Périgord (1301–1364).* Transactions of the American Philosophical Society, new series, volume 50, part 7. Philadelphia, 1960.

Zarek, Otto, *The History of Hungary,* trans. Peter P. Wolkonsky. London, 1939.

Zimmerman, Benedict, O. C. D., *The Carmelite Order.* London, 1913.

————, "The Carmelite Order," *The Catholic Encyclopedia,* ed. Charles G. Herbermann, et al., III (New York, 1908), 354–70.

————, "Les Carmes aux universités du moyen âge," *Études carmelitaines mystiques et missionaires,* year XVII (1932), vol. I, 82–112.

# Index